NEW CLASSICS
from The Guthrie Theater

❧

NEW CLASSICS
from The Guthrie Theater

Classical Adaptations
for the American Stage
by Barbara Field

CONTEMPORARY PLAYWRIGHTS SERIES

A Smith and Kraus Book

A Smith and Kraus Book
Published by Smith and Kraus, Inc.
177 Lyme Road, Hanover, NH 03755
www.smithkraus.com

First Edition: May 2003
10 9 8 7 6 5 4 3 2 1
Manufactured in the United States of America

Cover and Text Design by Julia Hill Gignoux, Freedom Hill Design
Cover photo by Joe Giannetti. Adam, the Creature played by John Carroll Lynch, and Victor, performed by Curzon Dobell, in the 1988 Guthrie Theater production of *Playing with Fire* by Barbara Field, adapted from the Mary Shelley novel, directed by Michael Maggio. Set design by John Arnone and costumes by Jack Edwards.

The Library of Congress Cataloging-In-Publication Data
Field, Barbara, 1935–
New classics from the Guthrie Theater : classical adaptations for the American Stage / by Barbara Field. — 1st ed.
p. cm. — (Contemporary playwrights series)
Contents: A Christmas carol — Pantagleize — Marriage — Monsieur de Molière — Camille — Great expectations — Playing with fire.
ISBN 1-57525-369-0
I. Guthrie Theater. II. Title. III. Series.
PS3556.I3665N49 2003
812'.54—dc21
2003042786

To my beloved mentor, Michael Langham,
the "founder of the feast,"
and to my children, Maria and Jim,
who bring joy to my life.

The author would like to acknowledge
Dennis Behl and Michael Dixon for their valuable assistance.

Contents

Foreword

I warmly welcome this anthology of Barbara Field's adaptations of great classic novels for the stage. There is a very special talent to translating the narrative and the scope of a great novel to the stage. Each character and situation from the book must be given new theatrical life, while the spirit of the original is retained. This demands sensitivity to the intention of the author, together with an insight into the possibilities that live theater provides. In these adaptations, Ms. Field displays her unique ability to create individual works of theater without losing the very ingredients that made them great works of literature. As numerous productions throughout the world have attested, these plays work brilliantly for audiences who know the source material as well as for those whose introduction to the original works comes through her skillful treatment for the stage.

All these works were presented by The Guthrie Theater in Minneapolis. As a theater founded by the Irish director Sir Tyrone Guthrie with the intention of presenting the great works of classical drama for an audience of the upper Midwest, it is entirely appropriate that its repertoire should include the great literature included in this volume. The most successful production in the history of this great theater has been Ms. Field's adaptation of Charles Dickens's *A Christmas Carol*. It has been presented annually since its first production in 1975, and it has been enjoyed by millions of Minnesotans since then. Many different actors and directors have created their own visions of this work, and it is now a cherished part of Minnesota's cultural life. For many people, this adaptation of the great Victorian story is their first experience of the theater as an art form. There is nothing more beautiful to observe than the face of a child who, simultaneously, discovers the magic of live performance and the pleasures and terrors of Dickens's masterpiece.

I hope that the publication of this volume will encourage directors, actors, and teachers to stage productions of these wonderful works. They will find great challenges and exciting rewards, and their audiences will have the chance to hear these classical stories told in a wonderfully theatrical way.

Joe Dowling
Artistic Director, The Guthrie Theater

Introduction

For a playwright, there can be no better way to hone one's craft than to adapt from another medium, another author.

You learn about structure, how to translate a novel's plot into a workable arc of action for the stage. You inherit a set of characters and must show the individual traits and behaviors of each — *show,* not talk about. Most important, you are forced to ask yourself "What is this novel about?" If you are to serve that book faithfully, you must make that writer's intention *your* intention. And that raises the interesting question of how far an adaptor can move from the source work, and still honor the intention of its author. The introduction to *Playing with Fire* (after *Frankenstein*) will address that question.

Finally, you learn volumes about style. How does a character's speech in 1840s England differ from a character speaking in the France of 1840? How must contemporary actors live convincingly in these diverse cultures? How must they breathe and move? How can the playwright help them to achieve the specifics of their play's era and place in performance?

In addition to the pleasure of living within the skin (albeit temporarily) of great authors, mastering this craft has had a profound effect on my original works, giving me greater flexibility and control. As a musician would say, it "got my chops up" as a writer.

My first adaptation for the Guthrie was *A Christmas Carol* in 1975, one of the very first *Carols* done in regional theaters. The Muse was kind in making this my first venture, for Dickens was the consummate man of theater. He made the task easy. If as a novice I had had to tackle Flaubert, for example, I might still be writing my first draft. We only intended to run the play for one season — at most two. Twenty-seven years later it's still going strong.

Since then, I've had the honor of collaborating with Ghelderode, Dumas *fils*, Gogol, Bulgakov, and Mary Shelley as their translator to the stage. And my relationship with the Guthrie has continued during the tenures of five artistic directors: Michael Langham, Alvin Epstein, Liviu Ciulei, Garland Wright, and Joe Dowling. The Guthrie, known worldwide as a classical repertory theater, has been a hospitable and welcoming home for me.

Barbara Field

A Christmas Carol

ADAPTED FROM THE NOVEL
A CHRISTMAS CAROL BY CHARLES DICKENS

To Stephen Kanee, friend and fellow conspirator, with love

I

Charles Dickens's *A Christmas Carol* adapted by Barbara Field, 1975 set model by designer Jack Barkla. Courtesy of The Guthrie Theater.

CONTEXTUAL MATERIAL ON *A CHRISTMAS CAROL*

Late in 1974, when I took up my post as literary manager at the Guthrie, Artistic Director Michael Langham asked me to write an adaptation of the Dickens novella for the 1975 holiday season, "as a gift to the community." To my delight it was to be staged by resident director Stephen Kanee. Stephen and I had been fellow students in the graduate theater program at the University of Minnesota, and we were dear friends. It was a welcome collaboration.

We quickly determined that we did not want a Freudian *Carol,* an outerspace *Carol,* or a deconstructed *Carol.* We wanted to take the source material seriously and play it straight. A design team of good friends was assembled. As soon as I learned that Jack Barkla, of the Children's Theatre, was to be the scenic designer, I knew I could write a fluid script without fear of being trapped in deadly scene changes. His set rested on the asymmetrical Guthrie stage like a dark, beautiful piece of sculpture, yet it was totally utilitarian. Duane Schuler, a gifted sculptor of light and shadow, did the lighting design; Jack Edwards created handsome period costumes; and Hiram Titus supported it all with a rich musical score, which was, in the good old days, played by live musicians.

The actual work of adaptation was almost too easy. Dickens had wrought a tale that fit easily onto the stage. His dialogue needed very little adjustment. The shape of the story had a perfect dramatic arc.

Only one scene was completely invented for the play: the first meeting of young Ebenezer Scrooge and his beloved Belle. I felt we needed to see that moment to grasp how much he would lose as he grew into the cynical figure we meet at the top of the play.

The Fezziwig party scene has metamorphosed over the years into its present form: a kaleidoscope of *three* Christmas Eve parties, in which we can chart the deterioration of the Ebenezer-Belle relationship, and his gradual descent into venality.

During the first few years of production, I used "bookend" scenes of the Charles Dickens family, and the author himself strolled among the players, talking to us, the audience. My dramaturgical reason for putting Dickens in the play sprang from my need for a strong narrative voice. How can you do *Carol* without starting with "Marley was dead to begin with"? Dickens wrote the book because he was pressed for money, but in the course of writing it, he underwent a conversion worthy of Scrooge. Creating the novella ended up giving him boundless joy, and it was fun for the audience to share this double reformation. Some years later, I employed a more direct way of dealing with the narrative, by assigning it to various actors *à la* "Nicholas Nickleby." The change helped to streamline and focus the action, and it is this later version that appears in this book.

A CHRISTMAS CAROL
Adapted for The Guthrie Theater by Barbara Field

Director . . . . Gary Gisselman
Set Designer . . . . Neil Patel
Costume Designer . . . . Jess Goldstein
Lighting Designer . . . . Marcus Dilliard
Composer . . . . Victor Zupanic
Musical Director . . . . Anita Ruth
Sound Designer . . . . Scott W. Edwards
Dramaturgy . . . . Michael Lupu
Vocal Coach . . . . Mira Kehoe
Associate Director/Movement Coach . . . . Myron Johnson
Stage Manager . . . . Martha Kulig
Assistant Stage Manager . . . . Chris A. Code

CAST (IN ALPHABETICAL ORDER)
BELLE, ELLA . . . . Erin Anderson
JOE . . . . Michael Booth
MRS. FEZZIWIG, MRS. GRIGSBY . . . . Barbara Byrne
BOB CRATCHIT . . . . Gerald Drake
MR. GRUB, THE UNDERTAKER . . . . Nathaniel Fuller
EBENEZER SCROOGE . . . . Peter Michael Goetz
MRS. FRED . . . . Kathleen Humphrey
MR. FEZZIWIG, SNARKERS . . . . Richard S. Iglewski
FIDDLER, KROOKINGS . . . . Michael Kissin
GHOST OF CHRISTMAS PAST, MRS. DILBER, DOROTHEA . Wendy Lehr
MARIGOLD FEZZIWIG, JANE . . . . Angela Mannella
YOUNG JACOB MARLEY, GRASPER, CECIL . . . . Bill McCallum
GHOST OF CHRISTMAS PRESENT . . . . Isabell Monk
YOUNG SCROOGE, EDWARDS . . . . Kris L. Nelson
DICK WILKINS, ELLIOTT . . . . Togba Norris
JACOB MARLEY, GHOST OF CHRISTMAS YET TO COME, MR. QUEEZE,
THE SCHOOLMASTER, BLACKINGS FOREMAN . . . . Richard Ooms
FORREST, TOPPER . . . . Benjamin Stewart
FRED . . . . Baton Tinapp
BLAKELY, SOPHIA . . . . Suzanne Warmanen
PETUNIA FEZZIWIG . . . . Maya Washington

SQUEEZE . . . . Jon Whittier

MRS. CRATCHIT . . . . Sally Wingert

NARRATION . . . . Narration is shared among the cast

Members of the acting ensemble also appear as Street People, Storybook Characters, Londoners, Vendors, members of Fezziwig's Staff and Guests, and "the surplus population."

A CHRISTMAS CAROL

ACT I

STAVE ONE: MARLEY'S GHOST

A quartet sings, a funeral procession with a coffin enters, crosses the stage, as:

NARRATION: Marley was dead to begin with. There is no doubt whatever about that. Seven long years dead.

The death certificate was signed by the clergyman, the clerk, the undertaker, and the chief mourner. Scrooge signed it. And Scrooge's signature was as good as gold, for he was an excellent man of *business*.

Old Marley was as dead as a doornail.

Mind! We don't mean to say we know of our own knowledge what there is particularly dead about a doornail. I might have been inclined to regard a coffin nail as the deadest piece of ironmongery in the trade. But the wisdom of our ancestors is in the simile and I shall not disturb it.

Permit me to repeat emphatically that Marley was dead as a doornail.

Scrooge knew he was dead? Of course he did. How could it be otherwise? Scrooge and Marley were partners for I don't know how many years. Scrooge was his sole executor, his sole administrator, his sole friend, his sole mourner, and his sole heir.

But even Scrooge was not so dreadfully cut up by the sad event, for he proved to be an excellent man of business on the very day of the funeral, for he solemnized it with a fine bargain.

(Scrooge takes a paper from Mr. Snarkers, then exits.)

GRASPER: Wait — didn't he bury Mr. Marley today?

SNARKERS: Yes indeed, old Marley's gone to the devil at last.

GRASPER: And he's holding the wake at the stock exchange? The nerve!

(They go. Afternoon crossover. A throng of people in the street.)

NARRATION: There is no doubt Marley was dead — you must understand this or nothing wonderful can come of our story. And yet his name still stood painted on the warehouse door. Scrooge had never bothered to paint it out. "Scrooge and Marley."

Oh! But he was a tightfisted hand at the grindstone, was Scrooge! A squeezing, wrenching, grasping, scraping, clutching, covetous old sinner!

Hard and sharp as flint, from which no steel had ever struck out generous fire; secret, and self-contained, and solitary as an oyster.

To edge his way along the crowded paths of life, warning all human sympathy to keep its distance, was the very thing he liked.

(A quartet sings a carol as Scrooge's office comes on.)

Once upon a time — of all good days in the year, on Christmas Eve — old Scrooge was busy in his countinghouse.

It was cold, bleak, biting weather — foggy withal; but Scrooge carried his own low temperature always about with him. He iced his office in the dog days and didn't thaw it one degree at Christmas. External heat and cold had little influence on him.

(Clock strikes three.)

Three o'clock, but it was quite dark already. It had not been light all day. *(Scrooge is at his desk. Cratchit is at his own counter, scribbling away. His fingers are nearly frozen. Cratchit sneezes, Scrooge glares.)*

Scrooge kept the coal box in his own room and so surely as the clerk, Bob Cratchit, came in with the shovel, the master predicted that it would be necessary for them to part.

Wherefore the clerk tried to warm himself at his candle, but not being a man of strong imagination, he failed.

(Laughter off. Fred enters.)

FRED: A merry Christmas, Uncle. God save you!

SCROOGE: *(Paying no attention.)* Bah! Humbug!

FRED: Christmas a humbug, Uncle? You don't mean that, I'm sure.

SCROOGE: I mean it. I mean it! Look at you — what right have you to be merry? You're poor enough.

FRED: What right have you to be dismal? You're rich enough.

SCROOGE: Bah! Humbug.

FRED: Don't be cross, Uncle.

SCROOGE: But I live in a world of fools. Merry Christmas? Out upon "Merry Christmas!" What's Christmas to you but a time for paying bills without money; a time for finding yourself a year older, and not an hour richer?

FRED: Yes, but —

SCROOGE: If I had my way, every idiot who goes about with a "Merry Christmas" on his lips should be boiled in his own pudding, and buried with a stake of holly in his heart —

FRED: Uncle!

SCROOGE: Nephew! You keep Christmas in your own way, and let me keep it in mine.

FRED: But you don't keep it.

SCROOGE: Let me leave it alone, then. What profit has it ever brought you?

FRED: It is true, I not have profited from Christmas, but I've always thought it a good time, a kind, forgiving, charitable, pleasant time. The only time in the long calendar of the year, in fact, when men and women open their shut-up hearts freely, and think of people below them as if they really were fellow passengers to the grave, and not another race of creatures bound on other journeys. And so, Uncle, though it has never put a scrap of gold or silver in my pocket, I believe that it has done me good, and will do me good; and I say, God bless it!

(Bob Cratchit applauds.)

SCROOGE: *(To Bob.)* Let me hear another sound from you, and you'll spend your Christmas looking for a new situation. *(To Fred.)* Stop distracting my clerk, Nephew, or I'll bill you for his time!

FRED: Uncle —

SCROOGE: You're such a powerful speaker, Nephew, I wonder you don't go into Parliament.

FRED: Come to dinner tomorrow, Uncle.

SCROOGE: I'll see you in Hell, first —

NARRATION: He said it — yes indeed he did. He went the whole length of the expression, and said he would see him in that extremity first.

FRED: But why? Why? You have yet to meet my wife. Please, Uncle, come and dine with us —

SCROOGE: "Us." I see you're still a prisoner of marital bliss. Why did you get married?

FRED: Because I fell in love.

SCROOGE: Because you fell in love?! Good afternoon!

FRED: I want nothing from you; why cannot we be friends? I've never asked you for a penny, sir, and never shall.

SCROOGE: Ha!

FRED: Why are we enemies? We're family.

SCROOGE: Good afternoon.

FRED: I'm sorry to find you so resolute against me. But I came here in homage to Christmas, and I *will* keep my Christmas humor to the last. And so . . . a merry Christmas, Uncle —

SCROOGE: Good afternoon.

FRED: And a happy New Year — !

(Scrooge hurls his paperweight at Fred, who catches it.)

SCROOGE: Good afternoon!

FRED: Why, thank you, Uncle, I shall treasure this fine paperweight. *(Going, stops at Cratchit's desk.)* Greetings of the season, Bob. And to your good wife.

CRATCHIT: And the same to you, Mr. Fred, the same to you!

(Fred exits.)

SCROOGE: There's another fellow — my clerk with fifteen shillings a week, and five mouths to feed —

CRATCHIT: Six —

SCROOGE: Even worse — talking about a merry Christmas. Next year I'll seek refuge in a madhouse.

CRATCHIT: Yes, sir.

SCROOGE: What's that?

CRATCHIT: Nothing, sir.

(Two charitable citizens of beatific countenance enter. Blakely is round, Mr. Forrest is lean and deaf as a post.)

CRATCHIT: Two visitors, sir.

BLAKELY: Scrooge and Marley's, I believe? Have I the pleasure of addressing Mr. Scrooge or Mr. Marley?

SCROOGE: Addressing Mr. Marley would be no pleasure. Mr. Marley has been dead these seven years. *(Struck by a thought.)* Seven years ago, this very night.

BLAKELY: We have no doubt his generosity has survived in his partner.

SCROOGE: Oh? Why?

(Scrooge resumes scribbling away at work. Mr. Forrest, who hasn't heard a word, of course, goes on enthusiastically.)

FORREST: Mr. Scrooge, Mr. Marley: At this festive time of year it is with urgency that we provide for the poor and destitute. Many thousands are in want of the basic necessities. Hundreds of thousands are in want of common comforts, sir —

SCROOGE: Are there no prisons?

BLAKELY: Plenty of prisons.

SCROOGE: And the workhouses? They still exist?

BLAKELY: I wish I could say they did not.

SCROOGE: And the treadmill? The poorhouse? They're still in full vigor?

BLAKELY: Both very busy, sir.

SCROOGE: Thank heavens — I was afraid they had been stopped in their useful course.

FORREST: We are raising a fund to buy the poor some food and means of warmth, Mr. Marley —

BLAKELY: Mr. Scrooge.

SCROOGE: It doesn't matter.

BLAKELY: At this time of year, want is felt keenly, and abundance rejoices. What shall I put you down for?

SCROOGE: Nothing.

BLAKELY: Ah, you wish to remain anonymous?

SCROOGE: I wish to be left alone. Since you ask me what I wish, gentlemen, that is my answer. I cannot afford the luxury of making idle people merry. I am taxed — outrageously taxed — to support those fine old institutions: the workhouse, the treadmill —

BLAKELY: Many can't go there, sir, and many would rather die —

SCROOGE: If they had rather die, they had better do so, and decrease the surplus population.

(Blakely drops his papers in horror.)

SCROOGE: Besides, I don't know that to be true.

BLAKELY: But you should know it, sir.

SCROOGE: It's none of my business, and as mine occupies me profitably enough . . . good afternoon.

(Blakely pulls Forrest out the door. Scrooge and Cratchit resume work. A boy stands in the doorway and starts to sing a carol. Scrooge chases him out with a ruler. The city clocks strike seven. Cratchit prepares to leave.)

SCROOGE: *(Mutters.)* Yes, I know it's time to close up.

NARRATION: In the street the fog and darkness thickened, and at length the hour of shutting up the countinghouse arrived. Most shops and businesses had shut up early, and lords and laborers alike commenced their celebrations.

SCROOGE: You'll want all day tomorrow, I suppose?

CRATCHIT: If quite convenient, sir.

SCROOGE: It's not convenient — and it's not fair. If I was to deduct half a crown for your holiday, you'd think yourself ill-used.

CRATCHIT: It's only once a year, sir.

SCROOGE: A poor excuse for picking my pockets every December 25th. I am a victim — a victim of humbug! Cratchit, take your Christmas, but be here all the earlier next morning.

(Scrooge storms out.)

CRATCHIT: I shall, sir. Thank you, Mr. Scrooge, and a merry —

(Cratchit wraps his muffler round his neck and races out of the office like a boy released from school. Street activity. Carol quartet.)

NARRATION: Scrooge took his melancholy dinner in his usual melancholy tavern; and having read all the newspapers, he beguiled the rest of the dinner hour with his favorite volume, his banking book.

He lived in a gloomy set of rooms that had once belonged to his deceased partner, Jacob Marley. No one lived there now but Scrooge.

The fog and frost so hung about the house that it seemed the Genius of the Weather sat in mournful meditation on the threshold.

Now it was a fact that there was nothing peculiar about the knocker on the door, except that it was very large.

It was also a fact that Scrooge had seen it night and day during his whole residence in that place. It was also a fact that Scrooge was not a fanciful man.

And then let any man explain, if he can, how it happened that Scrooge saw in the knocker not a knocker, but —

(A face appears in the door knocker.)

SCROOGE: Jacob — Jacob Marley! No, it can't be you, you're dead.

NARRATION: As Scrooge stared at it . . . it was a knocker once more. Not being a man to be frightened by echoes, Scrooge entered through the door and slowly climbed the stairs.

(The door slams shut, echoing loudly.)

NARRATION: It was dark, but Scrooge cared not a button for that.

(Scrooge starts undressing for bed.)

SCROOGE: I like the dark. Darkness is cheap, and cheapness is tonic for the sensible man. I like the cold. It nips the bones and keeps the blood from overheating. I like solitude. It makes me independent. No one can make demands on me, no one can do me injury, there's nothing I need share. I deem solitude to be a state of bliss!

(He checks the room, locks the door.)

MARLEY'S VOICE: Ebenezer . . .

SCROOGE: No one behind the curtain, nothing under the bed . . . good.

NARRATION: Thus secured against surprise, he put on his dressing gown and slippers, and sat down to eat his gruel.

SCROOGE: Mrs. Grigsby — ?

(Mrs. Grigsby enters, bringing a bowl of gruel. She goes. Scrooge sits in his chair.)

NARRATION: But there, floating on the top of the bowl was the face of his old partner.

MARLEY'S VOICE: Ebenezer Scrooge . . .

(Scrooge starts, throws the bowl away.)

SCROOGE: Absurd! Humbug!

(An old bell begins to ring. He gets up to look at it. It stops ringing. He sits down. The bell starts to ring again, joined by a cacophony of bells.)

SCROOGE: Is a man not to have a decent night's sleep?!

(Suddenly, from the cellar comes a horrible clanking and rattling of chains. The cellar trap opens with a boom, and from below appears Jacob Marley.)

SCROOGE: How now, what do you want of me?

MARLEY: Much.

SCROOGE: Who are you?

MARLEY: Ask me who I was.

SCROOGE: You're mighty particular for a ghost. Well, who were you?

MARLEY: In life I was your partner, Jacob Marley.

SCROOGE: Jacob! You don't look at all well. Can you sit down?

MARLEY: I can.

SCROOGE: Then have a seat, and let me tell you all about our thriving business.

MARLEY: *Business!!!*

SCROOGE: I see, you haven't come to discuss business.

MARLEY: You don't believe in me.

SCROOGE: I don't.

MARLEY: What evidence would you have of my reality besides your senses?

SCROOGE: I don't know.

MARLEY: Then why do you doubt your senses?

SCROOGE: Because little things affect them. You might be the result of my dinner — an undigested bit of beef, a blot of mustard, an undercooked potato — there's more of the gravy than the grave about you, whatever you are!

(Marley raises a frightful cry and rattles his chains.)

SCROOGE: *(On his knees.)* Dreadful apparition, why do you trouble me?

MARLEY: Man of the worldly mind, do you believe in me?

SCROOGE: I do. I must. But why do spirits walk the earth, and why do they visit me?

MARLEY: It is required of every man that his spirit must walk among his fellow man, and if that spirit goes not forth in life, it is condemned to do so after death. It is doomed to wander through the world — oh woe is me! — and witness what it might have changed to happiness.

(Again, Marley cries out and rattles his chains.)

SCROOGE: But why are you fettered, Jacob?

MARLEY: I wear the chain I forged in life. I made it, link by link and yard by yard, and of my own free will I wore it. Is its pattern strange to you? You have your own chain, Ebenezer, and yours was as heavy as mine seven

Christmas Eves ago . . . and you have labored on yours since. It will be colder, heavier —

SCROOGE: No, no — Jacob — Jacob Marley, speak comfort to me.

MARLEY: I have none to give. Comfort is conveyed by other messengers, for other, better kinds of men. *(A bell strikes.)* Nor have I time. I cannot stay, I cannot rest, I cannot linger anywhere. Mark me — in life my spirit never roved beyond the narrow limits of our countinghouse. Now weary journeys lie before me.

SCROOGE: Seven years, and traveling all the time?

MARLEY: The whole time — no rest, no peace, incessant torture of remorse.

SCROOGE: You travel fast?

MARLEY: On the wings of the wind.

SCROOGE: You must have covered a lot of ground in seven years —

MARLEY: Oh fellow-captive, regret alone cannot make amends for opportunities misused! Yet such was I, such was I.

SCROOGE: You were always a good man of business, Jacob.

MARLEY: *Business!!* Mankind was my business. The common welfare was my business. Charity, mercy, forbearance, benevolence were all my business, but I did not heed them. The dealings of my trade were but a drop of water in the comprehensive ocean of my business. Why did I walk through crowds of fellow-beings with my eyes turned away — *(He holds up his chains.)* Hear me, Ebenezer, my time is nearly gone.

SCROOGE: I will. But don't be hard on me, Jacob, and don't be so flowery — *(A gong sounds.)*

MARLEY: My time is nearly gone. How it is that I appear before you in a shape that you can see, I may not tell. I have sat invisible beside you many and many a day.

(Scrooge shivers.)

MARLEY: I come tonight to warn you that you have yet a chance and hope of escaping my fate . . .

SCROOGE: You were always a good friend to me, Jacob. Thank'ee.

MARLEY: You will be haunted by three spirits.

(Scrooge's countenance falls.)

SCROOGE: Is that the chance and hope you mentioned, Jacob?

MARLEY: It is. Expect the first tomorrow night, when the bell tolls one.

SCROOGE: Couldn't I take 'em all at once and have it over with?

MARLEY: Expect the second on the next night at the same hour. The third on the third night, when the last stroke of twelve has ceased to vibrate.

SCROOGE: I . . . think I'd rather not.

MARLEY: Without their visits you cannot hope to shun the path I tread.

(Phantoms appear, confused sounds, voices, lights.)

MARLEY: See how the air is filled with phantoms? They wander restlessly as I do.

SCROOGE: I — I know some of these ghosts — *knew* them.

MARLEY: The misery with us all is that we seek to interfere for good in human matters, but have lost that power forever. Heed these spirits, Ebenezer Scrooge. Remember what has passed between us, and look to see me no more.

(Marley disappears down the trap. Scrooge turns back into the room, checks it out, looks under the bed.)

SCROOGE: H-humbug!

(He blows out his candle. It comes on again, etc. The bed curtains are closed.)

NARRATION: Being much in need of repose, Scrooge fell asleep upon the instant.

STAVE TWO:
THE FIRST OF THE THREE SPIRITS

The stage is dark. Slowly Scrooge's bed comes into relief, and the bells of a nearby church begin to chime. Scrooge peeks through his bed curtains.

SCROOGE: Ten . . . eleven . . . twelve — but it was past two when I went to bed — something's wrong with the clock — it's got an icicle in its works — It's not possible I've slept through a whole day-and-a-half. It's not possible that it's now twelve noon and something's happened to the sun?! It was a dream. Or was it? "Expect the first ghost when the bell tolls one." *(The church bell chimes the first quarter.)* A quarter past twelve. *(The bell chimes the half hour.)* Half past the hour. *(The bell chimes the third quarter.)* Quarter to it. *(The bell chimes the hour.)* The hour itself — *(A city clock strikes one. Triumphant.)* And nothing else!

(A light. The Ghost of Christmas Past opens the curtains.)

SCROOGE: Are you the spirit whose coming was foretold to me?

PAST: I am.

SCROOGE: Who and what are you?

PAST: I am the Ghost of Christmas Past.

SCROOGE: Long past?

PAST: No, your past. I am your memory, your transport, your history, your gadfly — come walk with me.

SCROOGE: Where are you going — what are you doing? What business brings you here?

PAST: *Business?* Your welfare, your education, your reclamation —

SCROOGE: This reclamation, how much will it cost me?

PAST: Take heed! Beware! Look sharp!

(The bed disappears.)

SCROOGE: A good night's sleep might have been more beneficial to my welfare. Why don't you run along . . . or float along —

PAST: Shut me out at your peril! I have come about the business of your reclamation. Come, and walk with me.

(Past clasps him by the arm.)

SCROOGE: The weather's not fit for walking. It's freezing outside. I've only my slippers on and I've a head cold. Spirit, I'm a mortal and liable to fall!

PAST: Bear but a touch of my hand there, on your heart, and you shall be upheld.

(Past leads Scrooge forward.)

PAST: Ah, here we are . . .

NARRATION: The city had vanished and Scrooge found himself in the country.

SCROOGE: Good heavens, I know this place.

PAST: Do you?

SCROOGE: Of course, it's my old school, I was a boy here. I would know it blindfolded.

PAST: Your lip is trembling . . . and what's that on your cheek?

SCROOGE: It is snow . . . snow.

SCHOOLMASTER'S VOICE: *(Off.)* Hurry, boys, the coach is waiting! Laggards, don't make me punish you for missing your coach!

(Sound of sleigh bells, off.)

SCHOOLMASTER: Hurry, you lazy brats!

(Boys with baggage exit.)

SCROOGE: Look, it's Billy, and Thomas, and Jeremiah —

(School boys exit with their valises.)

BOYS: Merry Christmas, Ebenezer! See you in the New Year. *(Etc.)*

(Scrooge draws back.)

PAST: Don't worry, these are but shadows of the things that have been — they have no consciousness of us. But the school is not quite deserted. A solitary boy is left there still.

SCROOGE: I know. *(He sobs.)* And look, my books, my dear, dear books. My *Robinson Crusoe* — such adventures we had together. *(He reads over the boy's shoulder.)* Ah, *The Arabian Nights* . . . *Ali Baba* . . . .

(A fantastical figure appears.)

SCROOGE: Look, it's Ali Baba! Dear old Ali Baba —

(Ali Baba brandishes his sword.)

SCROOGE: He was always my friend — came whenever I needed him —

YOUNG EBENEZER: Are your band of thieves prepared to rescue the princess?

(Another figure appears.)

YOUNG EBENEZER: Robinson Crusoe, and his parrot! The Sultan has locked the princess in the tower!

(A third figure appears.)

SCROOGE: And Puss in Boots — Halloo! *(Suddenly his mood changes.)* Poor boy . . . I wish . . .

PAST: What?

SCROOGE: Nothing. Nothing. There was a boy singing a Christmas carol at my door last night. I wish I had given him —

(Fan enters.)

SCROOGE: Never mind.

NARRATION: Suddenly the princess appeared.

SCROOGE: Look, Spirit, it's my sister, Fan!

(Scrooge comes close to her, studies her.)

SCROOGE: Fan! Isn't it odd? You're so young and I'm so old —

FAN: I have come to bring you home, little brother. Home, home, home!

EBENEZER: Home, dear Fan?

FAN: Yes, Father is so much kinder than he used to be, and when I asked him if you might come home, he said yes — we'll be together all Christmas long.

EBENEZER: Oh, Fan!

FAN: And you're to be a man! And never come back here. And look, Ebenezer, I've brought you a present.

EBENEZER: What is it, Fan?

(She hands him a box, inside is a round globe.)

EBENEZER: What's this?

FAN: A paperweight . . . you put it on top of papers, to keep them from blowing away.

EBENEZER: It's beautiful. Thank you, Fan.

FAN: And look what Father gave me.

(She opens a music box, which plays "The Holly and the Ivy.")

PAST: Your sister Fan. She was a delicate creature, was she not? But possessed of a generous heart.

SCROOGE: So she was, Spirit.

PAST: She died a young woman, and had, as I recall, children?

SCROOGE: One child.

PAST: Your nephew Fred.

SCROOGE: Yes. Yes.

SCHOOLMASTER: Here is your trunk, Master Scrooge. So . . . I hear you're leaving us? On to better things? Your father writes me that he has found you a situation.

EBENEZER: What's a situation?

SCHOOLMASTER: A job! Work! Immediately after Christmas you go to London.

EBENEZER: London? But where shall I live? I want to stay home. Fan — ?

FAN: *(She is fading.)* Ebenezer . . . dear brother . . .

SCHOOLMASTER/FOREMAN: Faster, boy, faster! Elbow grease! Nose to the grindstone! Earn your wages!

(He drags little Ebenezer off by the ear.)

PAST: Six shillings a week was not a bad wage for a ten-year-old boy.

SCROOGE: I was abandoned . . . but I learned.

PAST: You learned, yes. You learned to save your shillings and pence.

SCROOGE: I learned to be self-sufficient. The dark stain of poverty never stuck to me — let us go, Spirit, I have seen enough.

PAST: You don't know the meaning of the word *enough.*

NARRATION: The spirit gave Scrooge a wise little nod and drew him forward through his past. They left the country, and suddenly they were in the busy thoroughfares of London.

(A small ice pond. A bench. Belle sits watching her charges, William and Anna Rose, skating.)

BELLE: Come children, it's time to go home, we'll be late for tea.

SCROOGE: Belle — it's Belle!

BELLE: William, take off your skates. Anna Rose —

(Ebenezer, a young man of twenty, enters with a huge hamper of purchases. He can't see where he's going, and William crashes into him. They both fall on the ice. Packages fly.)

BELLE: Watch out, William — oh dear, look what you've done!

WILLIAM: Oops, sorry, sir.

EBENEZER: No harm done.

BELLE: Oh, please let me help you up, sir —

(She lends him a hand, he succeeds in pulling her down as well. They both look around, stunned, then laugh.)

EBENEZER: I'd ask you to have a seat, madam, but you already have —

(They laugh again.)

BELLE: William, lend a hand to Mr . . . ?

EBENEZER: Scrooge, Ebenezer Scrooge, madam.

(William manages to get him up.)

EBENEZER: Slowly does it, lad, let me find my footing . . . there.

BELLE: Heavens, your bundles are scattered everywhere. I hope nothing's broken.

EBENEZER: What's a biscuit or two? *(He helps her up off the ice.)* Here you go . . . I hope nothing's broken.

BELLE: What's a bone or two? I'm joking, Mr. Scrooge.

(He seats her on the bench.)

BELLE: William, since you knocked him down, it's only fair you help Mr. Scrooge collect his bundles.

(Both children do so.)

BELLE: It looks like you're planning quite a feast, sir.

EBENEZER: Me? Oh no, no indeed, I'm only the delivery boy. All this belongs to my employer, Mr. Fezziwig. His annual Christmas party is tonight. Old Fezziwig's very openhanded that way.

BELLE: Don't you love Christmas?

EBENEZER: I do. I mean, yes indeed.

BELLE: The warmth, the spirit, the good smells.

EBENEZER: As I said, Mr. Fezziwig's very kind — generous to a fault.

BELLE: Impossible!

EBENEZER: What? Oh, you're absolutely right! Which is why he'd be delighted if I offered you a peppermint. *(He opens a box, peers inside.)* No, they're chocolates, ordered specially for the occasion.

BELLE: Even better.

(They each take a piece.)

EBENEZER: May the children — ?

BELLE: Yes. *(The children come over to them.)* One piece each, then home!

CHILDREN: Thank you, sir.

(They go.)

EBENEZER: You have quite a handsome family, madam. They look like you —

BELLE: Oh! Oh dear! You're quite mistaken, sir, these are not my children —

EBENEZER: But —

BELLE: They are my charges. I am their governess. I work for my bread, Mr. Scrooge, just as you do.

EBENEZER: I'm glad — not that you must work, but — I mean that I'm glad to meet —

BELLE: My name is Belle Crawford. Miss Belle Crawford.

EBENEZER: Miss Belle . . . at the risk of appearing impertinent, may I venture to . . . that is, would you consider . . . May I invite you to Mr. Fezziwig's party? That is . . . he encourages us to bring our special friends, and since I have no friends —

BELLE: I'd like very much to come, Mr. Scrooge.

(He hands her another chocolate. The scene fades.)

SCROOGE: Belle, dear Belle —

NARRATION: The stars were particularly bright that night, and the laughter, unable to keep within the confines of the houses, crept beneath the doorjambs and echoed in the streets. And about everything there hung an air of expectation.

PAST: Do you know this place?

(Fezziwig's warehouse appears. Dick Wilkins is readying decorations for a party.)

SCROOGE: Know it? I was apprenticed here!

(Fezziwig enters.)

FEZZIWIG: Hilli ho, Dick! Ebenezer!

SCROOGE: Why, it's old Fezziwig, bless his heart! Old Fezziwig alive again!

(Ebenezer enters with bundles.)

EBENEZER: Here I am, sir, I've just had the most delightful accident —

FEZZIWIG: Ho, there! Dick! Ebenezer!

SCROOGE: Dick Wilkins . . . he was very much attached to me, was Dick!

FEZZIWIG: Ho, my boys. No more work tonight. It's Christmas Eve, Dick, Christmas Eve, Ebenezer! Finish up, and do it before a man can say Jack Robinson!

NARRATION: The floor was swept and watered. The lamps were trimmed. And fuel was heaped upon the fire.

(The guests begin to enter, bearing gifts.)

NARRATION: In came the fiddler with his fiddle — he tuned it like fifty stomachaches, and made a whole orchestra of it. In came Mrs. Fezziwig, one glorious, substantial smile. In came the two Misses Fezziwig, beaming and loveable. In came the two young fellows whose hearts they broke. In came what seemed like all of London . . . . And in came Belle . . .

(They sing "Deck the Halls.")

FEZZIWIG: My dear friends — my dear neighbors — my dear children —

CHILDREN: Mr. Fezziwig!

FEZZIWIG: Tonight we'll do it! We'll eat and drink and trip the light fantastic. And we'll have music, right, Sam?

(The fiddler plays a flourish on his fiddle. All cheer. The socializing is in full swing.)

NARRATION: And away they all went.

(Music. They dance.)

BELLE: Such a lovely party, Mr. Scrooge.

EBENEZER: Ebenezer. Isn't it grand? I wish my clothes were —

BELLE: Were what?

EBENEZER: A little less worn. And look at my boots — they're brown and clumsy, not black and elegant.

BELLE: Oh dear. Does that mean I must apologize for my shoes as well?

EBENEZER: Of course not. You're a princess in a fairy tale. I've never seen anyone as perfect as you, you're —

BELLE: Cinderella?

EBENEZER: Precisely! And at midnight, does your dress turn to rags?

BELLE: Close enough. I borrowed this gown from my employer. Tomorrow I shall be quite myself again, dressed in plain brown wool.

EBENEZER: It doesn't matter that there's no glass slipper. You'd be quite as splendid in brown wool —

BELLE: Or brown boots? You have a nice smile, Ebenezer.

EBENEZER: Me? Smile? I'm not exactly famous for my smile, Miss Belle. *Trés belle.*

SCROOGE: Love!

PAST: Love, indeed. Romance, hope — a healthy percentage of mortals' time is spent on love. You're a man who respects figures — why do you suppose they do it?

SCROOGE: Because they're fools. It's a useless commodity, love; it produces nothing but excess children . . . and pain. Love's a humbug.

PAST: Pain? Indeed.

FEZZIWIG: Now come, such a feast we'll have, my friends. A blazing haunch of good English beef, and savory meat pies. And pickles, of course! *(Cheers.)* And sweets and puddings! *(Cheers.)* Hot mulled wine and punch! *(The young men cheer.)* And Mrs. Fezziwig's rich mince pies — magnificent! *(Cheers. The cook enters with a huge goose, covered.)*

FEZZIWIG: And of course — the Goose!

(The goose escapes the carving knife. They all chase it, capture it at last.)

NARRATION: Scrooge and the Spirit quickly traveled through time to the next Christmas Eve. And Mr. Fezziwig's annual party.

(Dick and Ebenezer enter with a broom, hammer.)

EBENEZER: Tonight everything must be perfect — like clockwork! It must all be absolutely perfect.

DICK: I wonder who'll be here?

EBENEZER: Everyone.

DICK: Everyone? Even Belle?

EBENEZER: Of course Belle, you fool. Tonight, Dick, I plan to set the date for our wedding.

DICK: Congratulations, Ebenezer. By the way, have you mentioned it to the bride?

EBENEZER: No, it's a surprise. Why?

DICK: I just wondered. They're coming!

(The party enters.)

FEZZIWIG: Christmas Eve! Christmas Eve, dear friends, dear children — tonight we'll do it! We'll make merry, and dance away the night . . . a thorough celebration.

MRS. F: Mr. F. has such a way with words.

FEZZIWIG: My wife, my beautiful, bountiful wife — yes, I mean you, Mrs. F. — and I bid you welcome. Now don't be modest, Mrs. F., you're as handsome as the day I met you —

MRS. F: Get on with you!

FEZZIWIG: Come, give us a song!

MRS. F: Oh no, I couldn't, I couldn't. Oh, very well.

(Song.)

FEZZIWIG: *(In tears.)* Beautiful, my dear, simply beautiful. *(He kisses her.)* And my daughters. You all know my daughters . . . Petunia — she came first.

(Petunia enters.)

FEZZIWIG: And Marigold, the baby.

(Marigold enters.)

MRS. F: Don't they look a treat, Mr. F?

FEZZIWIG: Blooming, positively blooming!

MRS. F: I laced them in good and tight — they can scarce breathe, but they have shape! And I sprinkled them with violet water and I dusted them with rice powder — they near sneezed their heads off! Are they not works of art?

FEZZIWIG: Peerless. And last, but not least, our little surprises: Basil and sweet Marjoram.

(The little children join them. Ebenezer enters.)

FEZZIWIG: But none can compare with their dear old mum.

MRS. F: He's such a rake! Tonight, Mr. F., I hope our girls will find —

FEZZIWIG: What, Mrs. F?

(She giggles, points.)

FEZZIWIG: Ah, romance! Girls, your mum wishes you to look sharp tonight and find an eligible suitor each.

PETUNIA & MARIGOLD: Papa! Really, Papa!

MRS. F: *(To Ebenezer.)* Where is Miss Belle, tonight?

EBENEZER: Late, ma'am.

MRS. F: There, there . . . she'll be along at any time.

EBENEZER: She's careless about time. I'll have to speak to her about that.

MRS. F: But not on Christmas Eve.

FEZZIWIG: No, Ebenezer, on Christmas Eve time takes a holiday and dances in the streets. Which reminds me — Sam! Music! We must have music!

(They dance. Belle enters.)

FEZZIWIG: Belle, Belle, our Christmas bell.

SCROOGE: Such a splendid party, Spirit.

PAST: A small matter for Mr. Fezziwig, to make these silly folk full of gratitude.

SCROOGE: Small?

PAST: He spends but a few pounds of mortal money. For this does he deserve such praise?

SCROOGE: It's not that, Spirit. The happiness he gives is quite as great as if it cost a fortune . . . oh dear . . .

PAST: What's the matter?

SCROOGE: Nothing . . . in particular.

PAST: Something, I think.

SCROOGE: No. I only wish I could have a word or two with my clerk just now, that's all.

PAST: *(Indicating Belle and Ebenezer.)* Listen . . .

BELLE: Goodness, I'm out of breath.

EBENEZER: Dancing puts the roses in your cheeks.

BELLE: Flattery, Mr. Scrooge?

EBENEZER: No, truth. Belle, have you a father?

BELLE: Everyone has a father. Why?

EBENEZER: Because I'm getting on so well at Mr. Fezziwig's warehouse, that tomorrow night I shall go to your father and ask for your hand. *(They laugh.)* And when we are married, we'll be so rich —

BELLE: So happy —

EBENEZER: That you'll have a gown for every day of the week.

BELLE: No need.

EBENEZER: No need? But a rich gown would set you ablaze like a jewel. Clothes make a statement, Belle.

BELLE: I beg your pardon?

EBENEZER: Others judge us by our —

BELLE: Boots? Come, now, Ebenezer . . . .

(Young Mister Marley enters, spots Ebenezer.)

EBENEZER: I have great dreams for us, Belle. Ambitions. I don't intend to stay here much longer. I plan to set up my own business. I've been saving —

MARLEY: Ah! Mr. Scrooge, a word, please.

EBENEZER: Mr. Marley.

BELLE: Ebenezer, it's Christmas —

EBENEZER: Only a minute, Belle, it's business.

BELLE: Need we talk about business at a party?

MARLEY: Good evening, Miss Belle, are you enjoying yourself?

BELLE: I was —

EBENEZER: Belle! Belle, you've met Mr. Marley? A merry Christmas, Jacob.

MARLEY: For us, I think it will be.

EBENEZER: Do I catch your meaning, sir? You've obtained the mortgages?

MARLEY: At a price you'll like.

EBENEZER: All three buildings?

MARLEY: As of this evening, the properties are ours. There'll be great profit, if we don't let sentiment get in the way.

BELLE: You mean heart?

MARLEY: No, I mean good sense, Miss Belle. Common sense. Old Fezziwig thinks I have no heart at all.

(He starts to go.)

EBENEZER: Some feel that he has too much.

MARLEY: Just so.

(He exits.)

BELLE: Too much heart?

(She turns to go.)

EBENEZER: Belle —

SCROOGE: Belle, don't go —

EBENEZER: Come, my dear, you're quite right. We'll join the others.

(Everyone dances off the stage.)

NARRATION: Young Ebenezer Scrooge devoted himself to work. His business was lucrative, and that was all that mattered. His pence and shillings quickly grew into pounds and guineas.

And by the third Christmas party at the Fezziwigs', he was his own man.

SCROOGE: What's wrong with that?!

(The company enters, singing "Panpatapan." They cross over and out. Fezziwig spots Belle and Ebenezer.)

FEZZIWIG: Ebenezer, so glad you could join us this year.

EBENEZER: My pleasure, sir.

FEZZIWIG: You've been quite a stranger to us — I hope your business is prospering?

EBENEZER: Indeed. And your own business thrives?

FEZZIWIG: Middling . . . middling. Miss Belle, how lovely you look tonight. Come have a glass of punch.

(Fezziwig goes off. Belle holds Ebenezer back.)

BELLE: I must speak to you, Ebenezer —

EBENEZER: Later, my dear.

BELLE: I cannot wait.

SCROOGE: Spirit, no, take me home. I cannot bear to watch.

PAST: Just one more scene. Our time grows short.

EBENEZER: Your fingers are cold. You've scarcely smiled this evening. If something's wrong, tell me. I was never very good at guessing.

BELLE: I have been displaced in your heart.

EBENEZER: I don't know what you mean —

SCROOGE: *(To Ebenezer.)* Good grief, listen to the girl!

BELLE: Your new love cheers and comforts you better than I ever could —

EBENEZER: Are you jealous? Of whom? What love?

BELLE: A golden one. You want to be rich, so rich that no one in the world can hurt you. You fear the world too much.

EBENEZER: Here's irony indeed! There's nothing in the world so cruel as poverty; yet there's nothing the world professes to condemn so severely as the pursuit of wealth!

BELLE: That pursuit is the only passion you permit yourself —

EBENEZER: I've grown wiser, but I've not changed toward you. Have I?

BELLE: Our contract is an old one, made when we were both poor and content to be so. When it was made you were another man —

EBENEZER: I was a boy!

BELLE: Ebenezer, I release you —

SCROOGE: Do something — kiss her, win her back —

EBENEZER: Have I ever sought release?

BELLE: Tell me, if you were free today, would you seek a dowerless girl?

SCROOGE: Yes! Tell her yes, tell her you would!

EBENEZER: You think not?

BELLE: Be honest. Regret would follow and we would spend our lives in misery. And so I release you, with a heart full of love for the man you once were —

SCROOGE: Say something!

(The party dances in.)

FEZZIWIG: Ladies and gentlemen — no, my friends, my dear warm friends. The comfort, the cheer of Christmas, and of good friends. I have an announcement to make, a very important . . . *(He begins to weep.)* My daughters, the Misses Fezziwig: my sweet Petunia and my radiant Marigold are . . . are . . . *(Sobs.)*

MRS. F: Mr. F. is such a sentimentalist. Yes, our daughters are engaged to be married.

(Cheers; couples embrace.)

MRS. F: Wedding dates to be announced at the first opportunity. *(Cheers.)* Well done, girls. *(To Fezziwig.)* Pull yourself together.

FEZZIWIG: Yes, indeed, let us drink to the happy couples — and, yes, let us also drink to Belle and Ebenezer. *(Cheers.)* Where is Belle? Come, Ebenezer — smile . . .

ALL: Smile. Smile. Smile. Smile. Smile.

EBENEZER: Humbug!

ALL: Humbug?

(Mad dance: The music plays with more fire and energy. Ebenezer pulls Petunia wildly into the dance, then shoves her away. He grabs Marigold. His roughness is frightening, and finally the dancers flee. Ebenezer is alone on stage with Scrooge and Past. Ebenezer looks around wildly, almost seems to see Scrooge. They stare at each other for an instant, then.)

EBENEZER: It's all . . . humbug!

(He runs off.)

SCROOGE: Spirit, show me no more, I beg you. Leave me! Take me home! *(Scrooge runs at Past with a blanket to put out its light, and Past vanishes. Scrooge leaps into his bed. Blackout.)*

END ACT I

ACT II

STAVE THREE:
THE SECOND OF THE THREE SPIRITS

Scrooge peeks out from behind his bed curtains. The bell tolls one.

SCROOGE: I'm awake. I'm alert. And I'm ready for anything. Nothing scares me, nothing at all, short of a cross between a rhinoceros and a baby!

NARRATION: A blaze of ruddy light streamed upon him.

And being only light, it was more alarming than a dozen ghosts. *(The light pursues Scrooge.)*

And Scrooge was powerless to make out what it meant.

He was apprehensive that he might be at that very moment an interesting case of spontaneous combustion.

At last he thought — as you or I would have thought at first, for it is always the person not in the predicament who knows what ought to have been done —

I say, at last he began to think the source and secret of the ghostly light might be from above.

(The Ghost of Christmas Present enters on a huge throne, bedecked with fruits and vegetables and sweets.)

SCROOGE: Good grief!

PRESENT: Come forward, come and know me better. *(He laughs.)*

SCROOGE: Who are you?

PRESENT: I am the Ghost of Christmas Present. Look upon me, little man, you've never seen the like of me before. *(Laughs.)*

SCROOGE: I —

PRESENT: Speak up, don't quake — I shan't damage you. Have a peach? Are you ready to go? Last night my comrade took you traveling through time. I'll take you traveling through space.

SCROOGE: Have I a choice? *(Present shakes his head.)* I didn't think so. Likely I'll catch my death of cold, tempting providence in my slippers. Catarrh. Lumbago. Pneumonia . . . Oh, what's the use, Spirit, conduct me where you will. I was forced forth last night and I learnt a lesson which is working now. Tonight, if you have aught to teach me, let me profit from it.

PRESENT: Come, little man.

(Scrooge climbs up onto the throne, it travels. Snow crossover. Shoveling, snowballs, busy people.)

NARRATION: They looked upon the city streets on Christmas morning. Smooth white snow on the roofs, much dirtier snow on the ground.

Nothing very cheerful in the climate — and yet there was an air of joy abroad, for the people were jovial and full of glee.

Poor families emerged from scores of bystreets and lanes, carrying their dinners to the bakers' shops to cook in their giant ovens.

So intent in their progress were these humble merrymakers, that at times they tumbled up against each other.

FIRST MAN: Ow — hey, you've near broke my foot, you idiot! Crippled me for life, you have.

SECOND MAN: Then don't stick your bloomin' foot in the middle of the road, you sod.

(They start to argue. The Spirit sprinkles the contents of his torch on them.)

SECOND MAN: Sorry, mate, didn't mean to offend.

FIRST MAN: My fault entirely, I believe. Merry Christmas, mate.

(They go off.)

SCROOGE: Spirit, is there something special in your torch?

(Scrooge and Present descend from the throne, which magically leaves the stage.)

PRESENT: Flavor! Zest! My own blend of spices to remind you poor mortals that life is short and must be savored while it lasts. Deliciousness pours from my torch and lights on every table . . . the poor ones most of all.

SCROOGE: Why the poor?

PRESENT: They need it most of all.

(They are now in a small room in Camden Town. A mother and her children are preparing dinner.)

SCROOGE: Where are we? Who are these people?

PRESENT: The family of your "fifteen-shillings-a-week" clerk, Bob Cratchit. That's Mrs. Cratchit, with her daughter Belinda. They both wear threadbare gowns, made brave with ribbons. Ribbons make a good show for a mere sixpence.

(Peter runs in.)

PRESENT: And Master Peter Cratchit, who seems to be swallowed up in a castoff collar of his father's. And here comes Tom —

(Tom enters.)

TOM: Mother —

SCROOGE: Good heavens — too many children!

PETER: The potatoes are almost done, Mother.

TOM: And I smelled it — I stood outside the baker's shop and I smelled our goose!

MRS. CRATCHIT: Tom, how could you tell you were smelling our goose? And Peter . . . the potatoes can't be done, I'm not ready for them. You positively can't allow them to be done!

PETER: How can I stop them? Are you teasing me, Mum?

MRS. CRATCHIT: Of course I'm teasing you. But what's keeping your precious father, and Tim? And where on earth is Martha? She can't still be busy in that millinery shop —
(Martha enters.)

MARTHA: Here's Martha, Mum.

CHILDREN: Martha, Martha!

MRS. CRATCHIT: Bless your heart, how late you are. And your hands — they're like ice.

MARTHA: I got away as soon as I could, believe me. We had to work late last night — Peter! You're as tall as me! And we had to clear away the mess this morning. Tom! Belinda!

MRS. CRATCHIT: So long as you're here. Come, sit by the fire, girl, and have a good warm. Don't they feed you in that place?

MARTHA: They gave us all day tomorrow off.

MRS. CRATCHIT: I wish I could say the same for your father. That miserable job is wearing him out.

SCROOGE: These little ruffians are wearing him out!
(Peter looks out the door.)

PETER: Father's coming! He and Tim are coming — hide, Martha! Quick, we'll surprise him! Behind the table!
(Martha obliges.)

PETER: *(To Tom.)* One squeak from you, Tom, and I'll pound you —
(The room grows silent. Cratchit enters with Tim on his shoulders.)

CRATCHIT: Mrs. Cratchit, my love; children. *(He sets Tim down.)* It's cold out there. *(He kisses Mrs. C. on the cheek.)* Still the prettiest girl in Camden Town, I declare. Merry Christmas, my dears — *(He holds out his arms and they run to him. But something is missing. He looks around.)* Where's Martha? Mrs. Cratchit, where's our girl?

MRS. CRATCHIT: Not coming.

CRATCHIT: *(Crestfallen.)* Not coming, on Christmas Day?!

SCROOGE: She's under the table, Cratchit. Under the table. *(To Present.)* He never listens to a thing I tell him.

MRS. CRATCHIT: Isn't it a pity, Bob?

(Martha emerges from beneath the table, creeps up on her father.)

MARTHA: I can't bear teasing him. Surprise! Father, here I am!

CRATCHIT: Martha! Dear girl . . .

MARTHA: Father, you looked as if you might cry.

CRATCHIT: My clever family played a trick on me, eh, Mrs. Cratchit?
(The children climb all over him.)

CRATCHIT: I do believe I am what is called a "family man."

SCROOGE: Spirit, they're mauling him. Stop that! He'll have no strength for work tomorrow.

CRATCHIT: Children, do I smell something? Do I hear something bubbling in your mother's laundry boiler?

PETER: The pudding! It's steaming away in the washhouse — come, have a look, Tim.

SCROOGE: What's wrong with that little one?

CRATCHIT: Be careful, children.
(Peter and Tom gather up Tim; Belinda follows them off.)

MRS. CRATCHIT: Don't touch — only smell.

CRATCHIT: Ah, Martha, my love.

MRS. CRATCHIT: That's it, you two have a good stretch-out. Look at you . . . the idle rich. You shall be idle this day, that will be my Christmas pleasure. But as for rich —

CRATCHIT: We're rich.

SCROOGE: On fifteen bob a week?

CRATCHIT: We're rich.

MRS. CRATCHIT: How did little Tim behave in church?

CRATCHIT: As good as gold — better. But he gets so thoughtful sitting by himself so much. He says the strangest things. He told me, coming home, that he hoped people saw him in church, because he was a cripple —

MRS. CRATCHIT: Bob!

CRATCHIT: Because it might be pleasant for people to remember on Christmas Day, the miracles that made lame beggars walk and blind men see.
(Martha embraces him, but she shares a look with her mother.)

CRATCHIT: But he's growing stronger every day, don't you agree, Martha? Yes, I do believe he's growing hearty and strong.
(The children come back, singing. Tim uses his crutch to reach his father. The others applaud.)

TOM: The pudding will be gorgeous.

BELINDA: It smells heavenly.

SCROOGE: Spirit, that little boy —

PRESENT: Tim.

CRATCHIT: Martha, tell us about the milliner's shop.

MARTHA: Well, it's feathers and ribbons and bows and straw — hats and more
hats — *(Bitterly.)* Fourteen hours a day.

MRS. CRATCHIT: It's cruel.

PETER: It must go right to your head.

(All laugh: Cratchit regards Peter proudly.)

CRATCHIT: Incorrigible!

SCROOGE: "Go right to your head" . . . .dreadful boy.

MARTHA: You wouldn't believe the fine customers! In furs! I saw a Countess.
And a Lord, day before yesterday — he wasn't an inch bigger than our
Peter here.

(Peter straightens up, lords it.)

MARTHA: But it's strange . . . they can never seem to decide what they want.

CRATCHIT: We don't have that problem, do we?

MARTHA: "Do I want the gray velvet with red cherries, or the blue straw with
cornflowers?"

PETER: "Such a crisis, Countess. You mustn't be subjected to the stress. We'll
have them both!"

CRATCHIT: My lad's a positive wag.

MARTHA: He's a goose —

(Mrs. C. jumps up in shock.)

MRS. CRATCHIT: Good heavens, the goose! Peter, run to the baker's and fetch
the goose! Belinda, mash the potatoes. I'll tend to the gravy.

CRATCHIT: And I'll make the punch.

MRS. CRATCHIT: Bob, go easy on the gin in that punch of yours . . . remember last year.

(There is a flurry of activity. Perhaps a carol.)

MARTHA: I do confess, I'm starving.

(Peter and Tom come in with the goose.)

PETER: Here it is, it's ready!

CRATCHIT: Now children, settle down.

(They get seated, bow their heads.)

CRATCHIT: For that which we are about to receive, may the Lord make us truly
thankful.

MRS. CRATCHIT: Look at your father, children, he's beaming like the man in
the moon.

CRATCHIT: Because I'm a rich man.

SCROOGE: He keeps saying that. Not on 15 shillings a week, you're not!

CRATCHIT: *(Removing the platter cover.)* And now . . .

PETER: Our goose is cooked!

SCROOGE: Goose . . . cooked? Cheeky lad!

MARTHA: Such a handsome bird!

BELINDA: I can't wait.

CRATCHIT: It's a feast.

SCROOGE: You must be joking, Cratchit, that goose is a humbug!

MRS. CRATCHIT: Remarkably cheap for the size of it, very generous, isn't it?

SCROOGE: It's scrawny! *(To Present.)* So minute a bird for so many people . . . ?

NARRATION: There never was such a goose. Its tenderness and flavor, size and cheapness elicited universal admiration. And, eked out with applesauce and mashed potatoes, it was a sufficient dinner for the whole family.

TOM: I'm going to burst!

BELINDA: The best we've ever had.

NARRATION: For once everyone had enough. Wonderful word, *enough.* And the youngest Cratchits in particular were steeped in onion and sage to the eyebrows!

(Mrs. Cratchit rises nervously.)

NARRATION: But now a moment of high anxiety is at hand!

MRS. CRATCHIT: I'm so nervous . . . so nervous.

CRATCHIT: Children, it's the annual pudding crisis.

MRS. CRATCHIT: Don't tease me, Bob. What if it's not thoroughly cooked? What if it should break when I turn it out. *(Horror-struck.)* What if someone climbed over the wall and nicked it while we were busy eating goose?

CRATCHIT: Then I'd make a pudding of the thief! Face the challenge, my dear. Belinda will accompany you.

(Mrs. C. and Belinda go out to fetch the pudding.)

CRATCHIT: It happens every Christmas, eh? Oh, my dear family, such a day, such a day! Wait — I smell something.

(Mrs. C. and Belinda enter with a blazing pudding.)

CRATCHIT: Salute the pudding. Salute your mother! It's another triumph, my dear, the greatest triumph since you married me.

MRS. CRATCHIT: I confess I had my doubts about the quantity of flour.

CRATCHIT: But first, gather round the hearth. It's time for our punch, served in the family crystal.

SCROOGE: Such a small pudding for so large a family.

PRESENT: You think so? Any Cratchit would blush to hint at such a thought. They had enough . . . wonderful word, *enough.* It means something different to each man.

CRATCHIT: I believe I've outdone myself this year. *(He raises his cup.)* My lords and ladies, I give you Mr. Scrooge, the Founder of the Feast.

MRS. CRATCHIT: Founder of the Feast indeed! I wish I had him here, I'd give him a piece of my mind to feast upon, and I hope he'd have a good appetite for it.

CRATCHIT: My dear, it's Christmas day.

MRS. CRATCHIT: It should be Christmas day, I'm sure, on which one drinks the health of such a stingy, odious, hard, unfeeling man as Mr. Scrooge is —

CRATCHIT: My dear —

MRS. CRATCHIT: You know he is, Robert! But I'll drink his health for your sake, and the day's, not for his. Long life to him. A merry Christmas and a happy New Year — he'll be merry and happy, I've no doubt.

ALL: Mr. Scrooge.

CRATCHIT: And to us — a merry Christmas. God bless us!

(They drink.)

TIM: God bless us, every one.

PRESENT: Behold them, one of the most fortunate families I visit tonight —

SCROOGE: Fortunate? Their clothing is shabby, their shoes are far from waterproof, and that minuscule goose —

PRESENT: They are happy and grateful, and contented with the time.

SCROOGE: Spirit . . . tell me if Tiny Tim will live?

PRESENT: I see a vacant seat in the chimney corner, and a crutch without its owner —

SCROOGE: No, no, kind Spirit, say he will not die.

PRESENT: If he be like to die, he had better do it and decrease the surplus population.

(The Cratchits and their room disappear.)

SCROOGE: Spirit —

PRESENT: Man, if man you be at heart, forebear your wickedness. You must discover what the surplus is, and where it is. You would decide which men shall live, which men shall die? It may be that in the sight of heaven you are more worthless and less fit to live than millions like this poor man's crippled child. Oh God, to hear the insect on the leaf pronouncing on the too much life among his hungry brothers in the dust!

Come, the day is waning and you've more to learn.

(Carolers, singing in French, German, Italian . . .)

NARRATION: They sped through the lonely darkness, over land, over sea, over an unknown abyss whose depths were secrets as profound as death.

Scrooge suddenly saw the planet with great clarity. He grew to know the "surplus population."

He observed, tallied, totaled in his best countinghouse way.

He peeked into the soul of humanity, heard the carol on its lips, and understood the memory of bygone Christmases in its heart.

Being a man who respected numbers, the very quantity of human souls preoccupied with Christmas thoughts gave him pause.

He turned in mid-ocean to ask the Spirit to explain . . . and found himself in a bright, dry, warm parlor instead.

(The fog drifts away and the lights come up on Fred's house. A party is in progress. Fred enters with Cecil, laughing, in mid-conversation.)

SCROOGE: I recognize that laugh. It belongs to my nephew, Fred.

CECIL: Surely you exaggerate, Fred?

FRED: I swear it's true! He said that Christmas was a humbug —

MRS. FRED: More shame for him, Fred.

SCROOGE: *(To Present.)* Is that the wife? *(The Spirit nods.)* She's poor, you know. Not a ha'penny to her name. *(He moves closer to her, studies her.)* I confess she's what you'd call provoking. And satisfactory . . .

PRESENT: Oh, perfectly satisfactory.

CECIL: I hear he's rich, Fred.

SOPHIA: Oodles of money.

MRS. FRED: But you can't prove it by any largesse Fred's received.

FRED: *(Seating Mrs. Fred, who's quite pregnant.)* I don't desire anything — oh, but he has given me a gift — this old paperweight.

(He pulls it out of his pocket.)

CECIL: That's thoughtful.

FRED: He shied it at me yesterday. I quite treasure it.

(As he passes it around, Scrooge makes a grab for it.)

MRS. FRED: I've no patience with him.

DOROTHEA: Neither have I.

FRED: His offense carries its own punishment, my love. He takes it into his head to dislike us and he won't come to dine. The result? He cheats himself —

SCROOGE: What?! How?!

FRED: Well, in truth, I guess he doesn't lose much of a dinner —

MRS. FRED: He loses a very good dinner —

FRED: A repast faultlessly wrought by my wife and her two lovely sisters —

EDWARDS: A feast —

TOPPER: Fit for a king.

SOPHIA: That must be true, for there's not a single bite left.

MRS. FRED: Fred had three servings —

TOPPER: *(Eyeing Dorothea.)* Food, food, another benefit of marriage. A bachelor's a wretched outcast of society, underfed and unloved, dependent on others for scraps of affection and crumbs of comfort . . . oh, desolation!

MRS. FRED: Wipe your tears, Desolation, before they make the carpets mildew. I wish some nice young lady would take pity on Topper and end his misery. Any volunteers?

(The others look at Dorothea.)

FRED: My uncle has missed something far more important that our dinner.

TOPPER: Could anything be more important?

FRED: My wife herself.

MRS. FRED: Thank you, my dear.

FRED: He's lost much by not knowing her. She is so altogether . . . satisfactory. But I'll try again next year, for I pity him. If my good humor puts him in the mood to leave his poor clerk fifty pounds, I'll feel it's worth the effort —

SCROOGE: Fifty pounds — are you mad?

MRS. F: Enough about your uncle. Let's have a game! Blindman's Buff?

FRED: Yes! Topper, you must be the blindman.

(Applause. Fred binds Topper's eyes, Mrs. F. twirls him around.)

ALL: One . . . two . . . three!

(Mrs. Fred's sister, Dorothea, is the object of Topper's chase. She really wants to be caught, and he's cheating, in order to catch her, but other guests keep getting in the way. Shrieks and giggles.)

SCROOGE: Spirit, that man is cheating. I believe he can see perfectly well.

PRESENT: Yes, the game is fixed, I'm afraid.

(Finally Topper catches her and extracts a prize — a kiss, cheers. Then they sing "The Holly and the Ivy." Finally, Mrs. Fred's other sister, the quiet one, speaks up.)

SOPHIA: Let's play a quiet game now: Yes and No.

PRESENT: We must be going —

SCROOGE: No, wait, here's another game —

PRESENT: We cannot stay.

(Present leaves, unnoticed by Scrooge.)

SCROOGE: One half-hour, Spirit. It's so warm and cosy here, and I want to play —

MRS. FRED: Yes and No. Fred, you start it.

FRED: Well then . . . let me see . . . aha. It's an animal.

SOPHIA: A live animal?

FRED: Yes.

TOPPER: Wild or tame?

MRS. FRED: He can only answer yes or no.

TOPPER: Wild, then?

FRED: I'd say . . . yes.

EDWARDS: Is it a cat?

FRED: No.

CECIL: Does it growl?

FRED: Yes. Yes, indeed.

SOPHIA: Is it a tiger?

FRED: No.

DOROTHEA: An insect?

FRED: No.

CECIL: A wolf?

FRED: No.

TOPPER: A wildebeest?

FRED: A wildebeest does not growl.

TOPPER: How do you know?

SCROOGE: A lion?

MRS. FRED: Perhaps . . . a lion?

FRED: No.

TOPPER: Is it a bear?

EDWARDS: Does it live in a zoo?

MRS. FRED: In a menagerie?

CECIL: In the desert?

EDWARDS: Is the animal indigenous to Australia?

FRED: Good grief, no. No, no, no and no.

SCROOGE: Is it kept in England?

TOPPER: Can it be found in the streets?

FRED: Yes.

SCROOGE: London! London!

SOPHIA: Could it be . . . London?

FRED: Yes!

TOPPER: Is it lead around by a rope or chain?

FRED: No.

MRS. FRED: Is it a carnivore?

FRED: I suppose so, yes.

CECIL: Does it have spots?

FRED: No spots.

TOPPER AND DOROTHEA: Stripes?

FRED: No stripes.

DOROTHEA: I know what it is, Fred! I know!

FRED: Well?

DOROTHEA: It's your Uncle Scro-o-o-ge.

FRED: Aha! Yes!

(Cheers, laughter.)

TOPPER: You cheated, old man. When I asked, "Is it a bear," you ought to have answered yes.

(Laughter.)

FRED: Ah me, he's given us plenty of merriment this evening. It would be ungrateful not to drink his health.

(They raise their glasses.)

FRED: I give you Uncle Scrooge.

ALL: Uncle Scrooge.

(They drink.)

SCROOGE: Oh dear, I don't know what to say — (He glances off.) I don't deserve —

(The party dances off.)

SCROOGE: Spirit, wait — where did he go? Spirit, come back.

(The party at Fred's has disappeared and the Ghost of Christmas Present is revealed, looking thinner and smaller.)

SCROOGE: Spirit — you look quite worn. Are spirits' lives so short?

PRESENT: My life upon this globe is very brief. It ends tonight.

SCROOGE: Tonight!

PRESENT: At midnight. Hark, the time is drawing near.

(Chimes ring.)

SCROOGE: Spirit, I see something strange protruding from your skirt. A foot . . . or a claw . . .

PRESENT: It might be a claw, for all the flesh there is on it. Look here. Oh man, look down, behold these wretches . . .

(Present reveals two children, who crawl from beneath his robes. They are wretched, abject, miserable.)

SCROOGE: Are these your children?

PRESENT: They are man's. And yet they cling to me. This boy is Ignorance, this girl is Want. Beware them both and all their kind, but most of all beware this boy, for on his brow I see written Doom, unless the writing be erased.

SCROOGE: Have they no refuge? No resource?

PRESENT: Are there no prisons? No workhouses?

(The bells toll twelve and the world around Scrooge begins to spin. Present and the two children are superceded by the Phantom: the Ghost of Christmas Yet-to-Come.)

STAVE FOUR: THE LAST OF THE SPIRITS

SCROOGE: Am I in the presence of the Ghost of Christmas Yet-to-Come? Ghost of the Future, I fear you more than any specter I have seen, yet will I travel with you, and do it with a grateful heart. Will you speak to me? Lead on, Spirit. The night is waning fast, and it is precious time to me. Lead on. *(Scrooge observes a funeral procession, which is led by the undertaker and followed by four men of business.)*

GRASPER: Well, Mr. Snarkers, I see Old Scratch has claimed his own at last. The fellow's dead.

SNARKERS: Dead as a doornail. *(They laugh.)* What do you know about it?

GRASPER: Not much, either way. I only know he is dead.

SQUEEZE: When did he die?

GRASPER: Ah, Mr. Squeeze. Last night, I believe.

SNARKERS: I thought he'd never die.

SQUEEZE: What did he die of?

KROOKINGS: Hardening of the heart.

(They laugh.)

SQUEEZE: God knows, he was as tough as the devil himself.

SNARKERS: The devil will be an intimate of his now, eh?

GRASPER: What's he done with his money?

KROOKINGS: He hasn't left it to me, that's all I know.

SQUEEZE: Anyone planning to attend the funeral?

SNARKERS: I don't mind going if a lunch is provided. But I must be fed if I go.

GRASPER: I'll offer to go if everyone else will . . . .

KROOKINGS: You know, I'm what you'd call one of his particular friends, Yes, he said hello to me once in the street.

(They laugh, exit.)

SCROOGE: There's a trivial conversation, don't you think? Evidently someone's died. Jacob Marley? No, no, that happened long ago, and you're all about the future, aren't you? Well, I'll be guided by you entirely, Spirit. I'm sure it will all become clear in due course, won't it? Still you say nothing. Won't you answer?

NARRATION: Scrooge felt the phantom's eyes keenly upon him as they traveled to a part of town that Scrooge had never laid eyes on.

The whole place reeked of filth, misery, crime.

In a wretched alley there was a rag and bone shop, where iron, old rags, bottles and greasy offal were bought and sold. And amidst the merchandise was Joe, the proprietor, a grimy rascal.

(Joe is expecting customers. The Undertaker lurks in the shadows. Mrs. Grimsby enters with a bundle, followed by the laundress, Mrs. Dilber.)

GRIMSBY: Good day to ye, Joe.

JOE: If it isn't Mrs. Grimsby, lookin' lovely as ever.

SCROOGE: Spirit, that's my charwoman, Mrs. Grimsby. What's she doing in a sordid place like this?

GRIMSBY: 'Ave you met Mrs. Dilber, the laundress?

JOE: Enchanted.

LAUNDRESS: Likewise.

(She curtsies as if to royalty, Joe pinches her cheek, and she cringes.)

GRIMSBY: Now, Joe, it's her first time here and she's that scared!

(The Undertaker clears his throat, steps forward.)

JOE: Oh my soul, look who else is honoring us with a visit. Mr. Grubb, the undertaker!

(The others draw away from the Undertaker.)

JOE: Ill-met by moonlight, my old friends. What a strange coincidence . . . all of you coming here with merchandise at the same time. It's what I'd call an embarrassment of riches.

(They all laugh.)

JOE: Who's first?

GRIMSBY: I was —

UNDERTAKER: I beg to disagree.

GRIMSBY: You saw me, Joe. I'm to be first, then the laundress, let her to be second. And the undertaker last; the undertaker is always last, eh?

JOE: As you like. I'll buy it all, whatever you bring, be it linen or lead, candlesticks, nutpicks, old stones . . . or old bones. I do love my trade, don't you know. Happy in my work.

(No one moves for a moment.)

JOE: My, ain't we polite.

GRIMSBY: She's afraid. *(To Mrs. Dilber.)* You've a perfect right to look after yourself, love, the dead man always did.

DILBER: True, no man more so, and my little ones never get enough to eat.

GRIMSBY: Then don't stand there quaking. Who'll be the wiser?

UNDERTAKER: No one will be the wiser. If he'd been half human in life, he'd have someone to look after him in death, 'stead of gasping out his last breath all alone —

JOE: Enough pretty sentiment — let's do business.

(The Undertaker steps in front of the two women and thrusts a small package at Joe.)

JOE: What have we here? A pencil case, pair o' sleeve buttons, spectacles, a balance wheel . . . and an old paperweight.

SCROOGE: Oh, look —

JOE: Not worth much, any of it. There, ten shillings, and I wouldn't give you sixpence more if you pickled me for it —

UNDERTAKER: I will be pickling you, one day soon, in my workroom.

JOE: Very funny. Who's next?

(Mrs. Dilber moves forward cautiously.)

JOE: Towels . . . nice pair o' boots, a pair o' wool knickers, with holes in the seats, two pretty little silver teaspoons, sugar tongs . . . and an old copy of *Robinson Crusoe* — You'll do fine in this business. *(He calculates, hands her a coin, pinches her cheek.)* That's your account, my dear . . . and may I repent of my liberal nature.

(Mrs. Grigsby bustles forward.)

GRIGSBY: Now you'll see somethin' Joe, I'm quite the collector.

(She unfurls her bundle.)

JOE: A splendid bed-curtain —

GRIMSBY: With brass rings an' all, and tassels . . . .and fully lined!

DILBER: Cor!

JOE: What'd you do, love, pull them down right in front of the corpse?

GRIMSBY: He didn't object. Here's a woolen blanket —

JOE: With nary a moth hole in sight.

GRIMSBY: 'Course not — even the bedbugs couldn't bear to stay in his room, it were that cold!

JOE: Where he's going he won't be needing it to keep warm. And what's this? A fine linen shirt?

DILBER: You don't mean you stripped the shirt off his corpse?!

GRIGSBY: *(With a glare at the Undertaker.)* Some fool put it on him to be buried in, but I took it off. Waste not, want not —

(They roar with laughter. Joe counts out coins for her.)

JOE: This is the end of it, ya see. He frightened everyone away from him when he was alive, to profit us now he's dead.

(They laugh, the scene dissolves.)

SCROOGE: Oh horrible, horrible . . . jackals! Spirit, I see, I see. The case of this unhappy man might be my own. My life tends that way now. *(He almost bumps into a stripped bed with a sheet-covered corpse.)* Merciful heavens, what's this?

(Two pallbearers roll on the empty bed (no curtains). A body lies beneath a single sheet on the bed. The Phantom gestures to the head. Scrooge approaches, but cannot bring himself to lift the sheet.)

SCROOGE: No, Spirit, I cannot — I cannot lift that sheet. If this man could be raised up now, what would be his foremost thought? Avarice? Hard dealing? They have brought him to a fine end, truly. He is quite alone.

(The pallbearers leave with the bed, and there is a dreadful sound of rats scratching and the yowl of a cat.)

SCROOGE: What's that? A cat at the door?

(A child's coffin is brought on.)

SCROOGE: Rats gnawing through the baseboard? What do they want? Oh horrible, horrible. Spirit, I am desolate. Show me some kindness and mercy in death.

(The Phantom points again.)

SCROOGE: Oh no, no, Spirit — please, it cannot be —

(Mrs. Cratchit, Belinda, Martha, Tom, Peter. The ladies are sewing on a shroud, Peter is reading from the Bible.)

PETER: "And he called to him a little child and set him in the midst of them and said, verily I say unto you: except ye become as little children, ye shall in no wise enter the kingdom of heaven . . . "

(Mrs. Cratchit wipes her eyes.)

MRS. CRATCHIT: It's the color of the cloth — it's hard to see, and it hurts my eyes. There, all better. The candle light makes them weak, and I wouldn't want your father to see me with weak eyes, when he comes home . . . not for the world. Peter, isn't he late?

PETER: He walks a little slower than he used to . . . before Tim . . . .

MRS. CRATCHIT: I have known him to walk with Tim upon his shoulders very fast indeed.

BELINDA: And so have I.

MRS. CRATCHIT: But Tim was light to carry, and your father loved him so — they seemed to float along together.

(Bob enters.)

MRS. CRATCHIT: Ah, Bob, your tea is ready on the hob.

CRATCHIT: Isn't the sewing coming along nicely. Such nimble fingers. I've just been to the place where Tim will rest. I wish you all could have seen it, it would have done you good to see how green a place it is. But I'll take you there often — we'll visit every Sunday . . . my little child . . . my little, little child . . . I met Mr. Scrooge's nephew on my way home, Mr. Fred. When I told him our sad news, he said, "I'm heartily sorry for it, Mr. Cratchit — " (He knew my name, fancy!) "And heartily sorry for your good wife." Now how did he come to know that?

MRS. CRATCHIT: Know what, dear?

CRATCHIT: That you're a good wife.

(The children smile.)

CRATCHIT: And he handed me his card, and offered to be of any service . . . I shouldn't be surprised if he got our Peter a better situation.

MRS. CRATCHIT: Just think, children . . . .

MARTHA: And then Peter will be keeping company with some young lady and setting up for himself —

PETER: Get on with you — !

CRATCHIT: It's as likely as not, Peter. But children, however and whenever we part from one another, I'm sure we shall none of us forget poor Tim, shall we?

CHILDREN: Never, father, never.

(The lights fade on the Cratchits.)

SCROOGE: Spirit, tell me, are these the shadows of things that will be? Or are they the shadows of things that may be? Answer, Prince of Death, for I know you now and you are He. Death is the subject of your lesson, and that I must study . . .

(Gravestones appear. The Phantom gestures to one of them. Scrooge approaches it.)

SCROOGE: Here lies the wretched man whose name I now must learn. Before I draw near this stone, Spirit, hear me.

(The Spirit gestures to the stone.)

SCROOGE: No, Spirit, I am afraid to look — (The name on the stone is revealed.) No, Spirit, no, no, no — Spirit, hear me — I am not the man I was. Why show me this if I am past all hope?

(The Phantom starts away. Scrooge follows and falls.)

SCROOGE: Good Spirit, assure me that I may yet change these shadows you have shown me.

(He kneels.)

I will honor Christmas in my heart and try to keep it all the year. The spirits of the past, present, and future will strive within me. I shall not shut out the lessons I have learned.

Oh, tell me I may sponge away that name — !

(But by now we are back in his bedroom, with his bed, chair, etc. The bed is no longer bare, but fully dressed, curtains and all.)

STAVE FIVE: THE END OF IT

Scrooge is still on his knees before the bed.

SCROOGE: I will honor Christmas in . . . my own bed?! Yes! The bedpost's my own! The bed's my own! And Time — Time is my own to make amends in! Oh Jacob Marley, I say it on my knees, old Jacob, on my knees! I will honor Christmas in my heart and try to keep it all the year. You'll see, Jacob, my life shall be a celebration! *(He rises.)* Must get dressed. Where's my shoe? My shirt? Mrs Grigsby! I can't find a thing.

(Mrs. Grigsby enters.)

SCROOGE: Ah, Mrs. Grigsby, look, my bed curtains, you didn't tear them down rings and all. They're here — I'm here —

(She helps him dress. The bed goes off.)

SCROOGE: This miserable old sinner has come to his senses at last! And at long last, I understand my business here on Earth. Oh, I am as light as a feather. I'm as happy as an angel. I'm as merry as a schoolboy. I'm as giddy as a drunken man. I don't know what day it is! I don't know how long I've been among the Spirits. Mrs. Grigsby, old Jacob came up through there, and the Past opened the curtains on the bed, just opened them! And from above . . . *(He finds the peach that Christmas Present gave him.)* Oh my! *(He kisses Mrs. Grigsby on the cheek, laughs. She bolts.)* I don't know anything — I'm quite a baby, but I don't care, I'd rather be a baby!

(The bells begin to ring at nearby church. A ragged boy, Simon, appears below.)

SCROOGE: Bells! *(He spots Simon.)* Hallo — hallo, there, lad. What's today?

SIMON: Eh?

SCROOGE: What's today, my fine fellow?

SIMON: Today? Why, Christmas Day.

SCROOGE: Christmas Day? I haven't missed it? The Spirits have done it all in one night — they can do anything they like, of course they can!

SIMON: The what?

SCROOGE: The spirits.

SIMON: Spirits? Ha!

SCROOGE: Ha indeed. In fact, ha, ha. Laugh, my lad.

SIMON: I never laugh. As I see it, gov'ner, life is no laughing matter. *(He starts to leave.)*

SCROOGE: Oh dear, that will never do. Lad, wait — have a peach?

SIMON: What do I have to do for it?

SCROOGE: Nothing, but wait — *(He hands him a small coin. It's still hard for him to unglue the money from his hand, but he does. He smiles, the boy flashes a minute smile back, which fades.)* Lad, do you know the poulterer's on the next street?

SIMON: I should hope I did.

SCROOGE: An intelligent boy, a remarkable boy. Do you know if they've sold the prize turkey in the window? Not the little prize turkey, the big one.

SIMON: What the one as big as me?

SCROOGE: Delightful boy! Yes, my buck.

SIMON: It's hanging there now.

SCROOGE: Splendid — go and buy it.

SIMON: Go on!

SCROOGE: No, I'm in earnest. Go and buy it, and tell them to bring it here. Come back with the man and I'll give you a shilling. *(Simon starts off.)*

SCROOGE: Wait — come back with him in less than five minutes and I'll give you half a crown! *(Simon runs off like a shot.)*

SCROOGE: I'll send it to Bob Cratchit's! It's twice the size of Tiny Tim! Bob shan't know who sent it. I can imagine the look on his face. *(He laughs heartily.)*

NARRATION: Really, for a man who had been out of practice for so many years, it was a splendid laugh, a most illustrious laugh — the father of a long line of laughs. *(Simon returns with the poulterer, and a huge bird.)*

POULTERER: Here's your prize bird, gov'ner.

SCROOGE: Now that's a turkey — it could never have stood on its own two legs, they'd have snapped off. You can't carry that all the way to Camden Town, you must have a cab. *(He distributes coins.)* This is for the turkey. And this is for the cab.

POULTERER: Thank you, sir.

SCROOGE: Oh — the address — Number 7 Delancey Passage. Don't forget — Camden Town.

POULTERER: Right, gov'ner.

(He goes.)

SCROOGE: And a merry Christmas! *(To Simon.)* And as for you my boy . . .

(He hands him a coin.)

SIMON: Name's Simon.

(He smiles.)

SCROOGE: Merry Christmas, Simon.

(The boy runs off.)

SIMON: Merry Christmas, gov'nor.

SCROOGE: I'll visit the foundling homes, the workhouses . . . I shall endeavor to bring food to the hungry and ease to the sick. And I'll buy toys for all the children, and I'll play with them too! Such a turkey — I wish I could see Bob's face!

(Christmas morning crossover. Various people shout "Merry Christmas.")

NARRATION: Scrooge said afterward that of all the joyous sounds he had ever heard, those were the most joyful in his ears.

(Carolers surround Scrooge. They sing, he joins them.)

NARRATION: Scrooge had not gone far, however, when he saw two familiar figures.

(He approaches them.)

SCROOGE: Sir — madam — how do you do?

BLAKELY: Mr. Scrooge?

SCROOGE: Scrooge is my name, although I fear it may not be pleasant to either of you. Allow me to beg your pardon, and will you have the goodness to accept my pledge —

(Scrooge whispers in Blakely's ear.)

BLAKELY: Lord bless me! My dear Mr. Scrooge, are you serious?

SCROOGE: Not a farthing less. A great many back-payments are included, I assure you.

(Blakely speaks into Forrest's earphone.)

FORREST: My dear sir, I don't know what to say to such munificence —

SCROOGE: Don't say anything, but please come and see me. Will you come and see me?

BLAKELY: We will! Merry Christmas!

FORREST: A very merry Christmas, Mr. Marley!

NARRATION: He went to church, and walked about the streets, and watched the people hurrying to and fro, and patted children on the head, and ministered to beggars. Scrooge never dreamed that any walk — any thing — could give him so much happiness.

(Scrooge purchases a sprig of mistletoe from a vendor.)

NARRATION: In the afternoon, he turned his steps toward his nephew's house.

(Scrooge knocks on a door. A little maid appears.)

MAID: May I help you, sir?

SCROOGE: Is your master at home, my dear? Nice girl, very . . .

MAID: Yes, sir, in the dining room.

SCROOGE: Thank you, my dear.

(He enters.)

MAID: *(After him.)* I'll show you, if you please.

SCROOGE: Thank 'ee, but he knows me.

(The party appears. Scrooge enters from the center door, Maid following.)

MRS. FRED: Bless us, are you —

SCROOGE: Your Uncle Scrooge? Yes.

MRS. FRED: *(Yells.)* Fred!

SCROOGE: *(Yells.)* Nephew!

FRED: Who is it, dear? Why — Uncle!

SCROOGE: Nephew! I believe you've made off with my paperweight!

FRED: Yes, but I —

SCROOGE: Keep it, Nephew, as a memento. It was a gift from your mother. Only could you be so kind as to let me stay?

FRED: Of course.

SCROOGE: You see, I've come to dinner.

MRS. FRED: Yes, indeed, let me take your coat. Come in, come in.

SCROOGE: Young woman, you are provoking . . . bewitching . . . and altogether satisfactory.

(He steals a kiss.)

FRED: Uncle, I shan't be able to trust you alone with her.

SCROOGE: Will there be games tonight? Blindman's Buff, I hope. And perhaps Yes and No?

FRED: Of course, of course.

SCROOGE: You see, I know the answer to Yes and No.

NARRATION: He felt at home in five minutes. Wonderful party, wonderful games . . . wonderful unanimity. Wonderful happiness.

(The scene fades, Scrooge's office comes on.)

NARRATION: But the crowning delight of the very altered Mr. Ebenezer Scrooge came when he arrived at the office the next morning. *(The office clock ticks noisily.)* Oh, he was early there! He couldn't wait to catch Bob Cratchit come in late.

SCROOGE: I have my heart set on it!

NARRATION: The clock struck nine. No Bob. A quarter past.

NARRATION WITH SCROOGE: No Bob.

(The tardy Bob tries to sneak in unobserved.)

SCROOGE: Good afternoon, Cratchit.

CRATCHIT: I'm very sorry, sir, I am behind my time.

SCROOGE: A full eighteen-and-a-half-minutes past your time.

Step this way, if you please.

CRATCHIT: It's only once a year, sir. It shall not be repeated. I was making rather merry, yesterday. Such an unexpected feast we had —

SCROOGE: I cannot stand for this sort of thing any longer. And therefore . . .

(He pushes Bob.) Therefore . . . I am about to . . . raise your salary! *(He pushes Bob, who grabs his ruler.)* A merry Christmas, Bob, a merrier Christmas than I have given you for many a year. I shall raise your salary, and we'll discuss your affairs this very afternoon, over a bowl of smoking Bishop! Build up the fires, and buy another scuttle of coal before you dot another *i*, Bob Cratchit.

(He holds out his hand; Cratchit, still weak-in-the-knees, shakes it enthusiastically. Town crossover.)

SCROOGE (AS NARRATOR): Scrooge was even better than his word. He did it all, and infinitely more.

(Simon comes in, waves at Scrooge.)

SCROOGE (AS NARRATOR): He became as good a friend, as good a master, as good a man as the good old city knew. Some people laughed to see the alteration in him. But he let them laugh. His own heart laughed, and that was quite enough for him. He had no further commerce with spirits, but lived upon the Total Abstinence Principle ever afterward.

And to Tiny Tim, who did not die, he was a second father.

And it was always said of him, that he knew how to keep Christmas well, if any man alive possessed the knowledge.

May that be truly said of us, and all of us.

And so, as Tiny Tim observed . . . .

TINY TIM: God bless us, every one.

SCROOGE: Every one.

END OF PLAY

Pantagleize

Translated and Adapted from the Play by Michel de Ghelderode

To my collaborators
Stephen Kanee, Jack Barkla, Duane Schuler,
Jack Edwards, and Hiram Titus,
with loving thanks for the art and the camaraderie

The Guthrie Theater acting company in a scene from the 1977 Guthrie
Theater production of Ghelderode's *Pantagleize*, adapted by Barbara Field
and directed by Stephen Kanee, with set design by Jack Barkla and costumes by Jack Edwards. Photo credit: Robert Ashley Wilson.

CONTEXTUAL MATERIAL FOR *PANTAGLEIZE*

If I had never gotten out of bed this morning . . .

Pantagleize

Pantagleize remains an archetype, an exemplary man, and a fine example who has nothing to do with the dangerous thing, intelligence, and a great deal to do with that savior, instinct.

Michel de Ghelderode

Ghelderode's *Pantagleize,* the story of an innocent trapped in a world not of his own making, was a favorite play of mine and of Associate Artistic Director Stephen Kanee. Seldom seen on the American stage because of its unusually large cast size, the Guthrie, with its wonderful resources, seemed the perfect venue for it. And in our acting company was the perfect actor to embody the naïve hero, Richard Russell Ramos. We also had the creative support of our design team, Jack Barkla (set), Duane Schuler (lights), Jack Edwards (costumes), and Hiram Titus (music). By this time the team had developed a common vocabulary and aesthetic with which to proceed.

We had no intention of turning the play into a musical, and indeed it is not one. But as I wrote, I kept tossing words up into the air and they tumbled down onto the page in verse. So there are a couple of songs and anthems in the piece.

Who was this eccentric Belgian writer, Ghelderode? Like many of his other works, *Pantagleize* has a "public" aspect, with people (characters? audiences?) witnessing and participating in the action. Ghelderode's *bêtes* were militarism, religion, political corruption, and he mocked them unsparingly. His style was the *Grotesque*. He found his inspiration in the work of three Flemish painters: Bosch, Breughel, and his own contemporary, James Ensor. We tried to put that spirit on the stage in this adaptation.

PANTAGLEIZE

Adapted for The Guthrie Theater by Barbara Field
Music composed by Hiram Titus

Director . . . . Stephen Kanee
Scenic Designer . . . . .Jack Barkla
Costume Designer . . . . Jack Edwards
Lighting Designer . . . . Duane Schuler
Sound Designer . . . . Tom Voegli
Conductor . . . . Dick Whitbeck
Stage Manager . . . . Michael Facius

CAST (IN ORDER OF APPEARANCE)

PANTAGLEIZE . . . . Richard Russell Ramos
BAMBOOLA . . . . Arnold Wilkerson
FORTUNE-TELLER . . . . Fran Bennett
INNOCENTI . . . . Robert Breuler
BLANK . . . . Guy Paul
CREEP . . . . Peter Michael Goetz
BANGER . . . . Don R. Fallbeck
RACHEL SIBERCHATZ . . . . Sharon Ernster
BALLAD-MONGER . . . . Matthew Kwiat
GENERAL MACBOOM . . . . Oliver Cliff
CORPORAL . . . . Frank S. Scott
BANK MANAGER . . . . Don Amendolia
ASSISTANT BANK MANAGER . . . . James Sweeney
MACBOOM'S TROOPS . . . . Peter Aylward, James Hartman,
    Roger Kozol, Matthew Kwiat, Michael Laskin, James Noah
TRIBUNAL SOLDIER . . . . Don Amendolia
TRIBUNAL SOLDIER . . . . Roger Kozol
DISTINGUISHED COUNSEL . . . . Fran Bennett
GENERALISSIMO . . . . Michael Laskin
OFFICER . . . . .Peter Aylward
A SOLDIER . . . . .James Hartman
WAITERS, SOLDIERS, TRIBUNAL MEMBERS, REVOLUTIONARIES, ETC.:
Greg Barnell, Russell Curry, Jeffrey Davies, Maury Engler, Greg Irwin,
Jeffrey Jamison, David Kwiat, Jason Murray, Scott Murray, Tena Murray, Carlotta Schoch, Carol Vincent.

SETTING
The play takes place in a city of Europe, on the morrow of one war and the eve of another.

PANTAGLEIZE

SCENE ONE

Pantagleize's room. Dingy early morning light. A bed with an umbrella. An enormous calendar, reached by a ladder. Pantagleize is in the bed, only his feet are visible. An alarm goes off. Bamboola shuffles in carrying a lighted candle and a feather duster. He crosses to the bed.

BAMBOOLA: Pzzzzzzz. Ship Ahoy. Boss? Pzzzzzz. Boss? *(The feet tremble.)* He sleepin'!

(He sees audience.) I good nigger/work. He bourgeois/sleep. *(To Pantagleize.)* Boss? Five past six. I don't know what I'm gonna do to get him out of bed.

(The feet tremble again. Pantagleize makes an explosive snort, then a groan. Bamboola shrugs, turns away. He puts down the candle, reaches into his pocket, withdraws a revolver. He opens the barrel, patiently begins to load it with bullets from his other pocket as he talks.)

BAMBOOLA: Big night for niggers is a comin' . . . good nigger . . . bad nigger . . . eat civilized folks. *(He licks his lips.)* Honky stew, Bourgeois Bourguignon. Yassuh. Niggers gonna sleep twelve hours a day, drink pale ale. *(He closes the revolver barrel.)* All rotten. All blow up! *(He pockets the revolver, crosses to Pantagleize again.)* Hey, boss? Pantagleize sir? It's five past six. *(To audience.)* 'Scuse me. *(He gives the bed a vicious kick.)* Boss?

(The feet move, but the head is still asleep.)

PANTAGLEIZE: No no no no no no, I do not approve of violence. You wish to cross the Atlantic? Go then — go! We'll get a divorce. I'm frightened of water.

BAMBOOLA: Dreaming? *(Broad.)* Oh, boss! *(Soft.)* . . . in the profound ocean deep of your dreams, listen to Bamboola.

(He leaps up, singing falsetto, uses his feet as percussion by kicking the sides of the bed.)

BAMBOOLA: Patata golo bili patata
ZooZoo gili bobo pata

Booloo pata zizi pata
Pototo gili bobo pata

PANTAGLEIZE: *(Screams out.)* Shipwreck! *(He leaps out of bed, onto his feet, fully awake.)*

BAMBOOLA: Mornin' boss. Ten past six, no sign of rain.

PANTAGLEIZE: I've been dreaming, no question. *(Yawn.)* Now I must wake up . . . and live.

(He shivers in the morning chill.)

BAMBOOLA: *(Bows.)* Mornin' boss.

PANTAGLEIZE: What's that?

BAMBOOLA: In Africa, polite people say "good morning" . . . when they see the light.

PANTAGLEIZE: Of course. Good morning, Bamboola, sleep well?

BAMBOOLA: Lawsy, yes. Good nigger sleep well — he happy nigger.

PANTAGLEIZE: I've slept too much. I slept through the alarm.

BAMBOOLA: Not me. Bamboola waiting for signal. And when signal sounds —

PANTAGLEIZE: What signal?

BAMBOOLA: Big night comin' when all folks sleep the same . . .

PANTAGLEIZE: Bamboola, if your "big night" ever came to pass, you'd still be a bootblack, I'd still be a philosopher — take comfort in that. *(Bamboola rolls his eyes.)* We've pleasant enough professions. *(Defensively.)* Look, how many shoes do you have to shine a day? *(He indicates that you can count them on one hand.)* After which you play poker with the taxi drivers. After which you dance in the street for tips. After which — you sleep. Whereas I, Pantagleize, am engaged in mental toil. I read manifestoes on modern art which tell me nothing. I go for a walk. I write a column for a fashion magazine and sign myself with the name of "Ernestine" — Although I never look at women. My girlfriend is a monkey in the zoo. Her name is Cleopatra — she has fleas, eats half my lunch every day, then grimaces hideously at me. I love her. So you must understand, my dear Bamboola, whenever your big night comes to pass, we'll carry on with our habitual grace, even if it comes tomorrow or the day after.

BAMBOOLA: So soon?

PANTAGLEIZE: Or even today.

BAMBOOLA: Boss!?

(He blows out the candle — it is lighter outside.)

PANTAGLEIZE: You want to make a speech?

BAMBOOLA: Make a speech, I speak. "I will be heard. *(A "turn.")* The blacks will be made white. The whites will be made charitable. The poor pariahs of civilization will — " Still listening, boss? "The spark of freedom will ignite into a towering flame, the flame will consume the mad old world, and from the ashes of the flame will spring — "

PANTAGLEIZE: ". . . the reborn spirit of the exploited masses!" I know, I know. "Reaction will tremble before its own bank vaults, where flows the blood of the enslaved." I wrote that —

BAMBOOLA: You?

PANTAGLEIZE: Yes, they paid me a good money for composing that pamphlet.

BAMBOOLA: What?

PANTAGLEIZE: But it was signed by a Mr. Innocenti.

BAMBOOLA: Innocenti?

PANTAGLEIZE: I'll write anything. One must make ends meet, Bamboola, by ghostwriting polemic literature or by shining shoes — by the way, have you finished my shoes yet? We are judged by our feet, you know. Thank you.

(Bamboola tosses Pantagleize his shoes.)

PANTAGLEIZE: *(Bamboola shakes his head.)* Tell me, what century are we in?

BAMBOOLA: The twentieth.

PANTAGLEIZE: And the date?

BAMBOOLA: The date? The . . . The . . .

PANTAGLEIZE: A stammering bootblack — and you wish to save the world through your oratory? Look, I hired you to polish my shoes and wake me up each morning with the weather and the date, promptly at six. You wake me up late. You tell me its not raining — without ever checking out the window. And all you've done is spit on my shoes. Shame on you!

BAMBOOLA: Bamboola sorry, boss, Bamboola sorry.

PANTAGLEIZE: *(Guilt-stricken.)* You're not ill? *(Light dawns.)* Bamboola, you wouldn't perchance be in love? Look me in the eye! In love? *(Pantagleize adores the idea.)* Be certain you're not making a fatal mistake, Bamboola. He's so simple, so impressionable. Love your fellow man, love your country, love mankind . . . but beware of loving *one* woman! Never mind, I'll check the date myself.

(He crosses to the ladder, climbs, lifts the preceding page, reads aloud. Bamboola gazes from below with dawning amazement.)

PANTAGLEIZE: Today's patron saint is . . . *(He squints.)* Saint Babylus. Recipe of the day, a handy dessert: "Serve hot, swallow quick." And here, the joke of the day. "There was a young lady named Venus . . ." *(He reads to himself.)* Ho. Ho ho. Ha? Heh heh heh. A total eclipse of the sun today. *(Looks up, notices Bamboola.)* You ill, Bamboola? You're looking very pale for a black man. Aha, it's the date — May first. An unhappy memory, no doubt? A shattered romance?

BAMBOOLA: Not ill, Boss, never ill . . . (*His eyes remain riveted on the calendar.*) Oh, boss . . . today is . . . today is . . . today is . . .

(*The light slowly dawns upon Pantagleize.*)

PANTAGLEIZE: I see! Of course — I completely forgot — thank you for remembering. My birthday. Today, Bamboola, I'm forty years old. Forty. (*He turns on the ladder, begins a little oration.*) Forty years old. A sad day. I have reached the apex of my life. Why sad? Because I always dared to hope that I would have a destiny. But at forty, one is automatically enrolled on the list of failures. What have I done on this planet, except ponder what I ought to do? I — I who have dreamed of being a captain, an explorer, astronaut, champion cyclist, member of parliament, prophet, tenor, one-man-band, blazing meteor, actor — I'm forty, and my destiny has never begun. Or perhaps my destiny is to have no destiny? The older I grow, the less I understand. I possess nothing — Neither vanity nor pride, nor love nor self-respect. I possess nothing but my peculiar name, my crucial age, and a very shaky intellectual ballast — out of date, at that. If I were a fine young fellow like you —

BAMBOOLA: Boss not stay sad. Be happy. You may not be a fine young fellow but you is different. And besides — today is the day! Today — May first! Today he may come. Today he might walk upon the earth.

PANTAGLEIZE: Who?

BAMBOOLA: He. HE.

PANTAGLEIZE: He who?

BAMBOOLA: Who? He! The man of the hour. He who will give the signal. All can change, today, boss . . . even your destiny.

PANTAGLEIZE: You really think so? I must have my horoscope cast. Has anyone ever foretold your fate?

BAMBOOLA: Yassuh! Bamboola foretell his own fate. Bamboola look into the fire . . . Bamboola become prime minister!

PANTAGLEIZE: My congratulations. When you're prime minister, remember me. Meanwhile, we must await events, as always. Nothing is as harmonious, logical, or mathematically pleasing as events — after they've occurred. What events will they be? Who knows? Who cares? We do know that it's not raining, and that it's the first of May.

(*Bamboola gives an enormous whoop of joy.*)

PANTAGLEIZE: All of which inspires me to take a stroll — for after all, the day promises to be a lovely one.

(Bamboola freezes. Pantagleize looks at him.)

BAMBOOLA: *(Whispers.)* Boss?

PANTAGLEIZE: What?

BAMBOOLA: You said?

PANTAGLEIZE: Said what?

BAMBOOLA: What you said — about the weather? You said — the *day,* the *day!!*

PANTAGLEIZE: *(Shrugs.)* Oh. I said, "What a lovely day."

BAMBOOLA: *(Whispers, incredulous.)* What. A. Lovely.

BAMBOOLA AND PANTAGLEIZE: Day.

PANTAGLEIZE: I said that — a whim. We . . . I didn't think it was *that* good. "It's the first of May — Oh what a lovely day."

(Bamboola begins to leap about, off the wall.)

BAMBOOLA: Hey! Hey. Lovely day! Lovely day.

PANTAGLEIZE: You've gone mad.

BAMBOOLA: Mad? With joy! *(He lifts up Pantagleize, whirls him about.)* Bamboola happy!

PANTAGLEIZE: Unhand me, unhand me this instant!

BAMBOOLA: Oh boss, oh boss . . . *(He embraces him.)*

PANTAGLEIZE: Your manners are hardly those of a future prime minister. One trivial pronouncement on the weather sends you roaring about like . . . look, I said, "Oh what a lovely day." I could be wrong, right? But each morning, when I step outside, I say to all those innumerable ghosts who pass me by, some trite conventional catchphrase, a cliché to save me the trouble of saying anything intelligent. For example, I say: "Life is precious." Or, "The frost is on the pumpkin." Or "The daffodils are popping." They always nod, and answer, "How true." "Exactly." So, my over-excited friend, my daily task is to find the appropriate "Phrase of the Day." Today it's not raining, so I'll say that the day is fine — it's that simple. Yes, in an assured voice, with an inspired air, I'll utter that shred of a lyric, "Oh what a lovely day."

(Bamboola collapses, groaning.)

PANTAGLEIZE: Come on, pull yourself together.

BAMBOOLA: You're serious?

PANTAGLEIZE: Why not? It's within my legal rights — freedom of speech. I'll say it to all men, everywhere —

BAMBOOLA: Boss. Brother! Comrade!! Confrère!!! It's truly you!

PANTAGLEIZE: *(Inspects himself in mirror.)* Of course it's me.

BAMBOOLA: Then we need not put on acts! I know you know.

PANTAGLEIZE: *(Bewildered.)* You know that I know. I know that I know nothing. Socrates. Look, Bamboola, any imbecile can gaze at the sky and say, "Oh what a lovely day." It's not subtle, but it seems safe enough.

BAMBOOLA: *(Hilarious.)* Safe enough! Ha ha ha ha . . . wonderful joke! Oh aha ha ha. — And it's you, Pantagleize.

PANTAGLEIZE: Yes. I, Pantagleize.

BAMBOOLA: You're the one we've waited for so long.

(He dances about — a menacing war dance.)

PANTAGLEIZE: Yes, I, Pantagleize. Could this all have something to do with my destiny? I really must have my horoscope looked into.

BAMBOOLA: Too much to hope for . . . unbelievable . . . irresistible. *(He bursts into tears.)* Bamboola happy.

PANTAGLEIZE: *(Weeps sympathetically.)* I also happy. Dry your tears — we must try to understand.

BAMBOOLA: No time to understand — we must march. *(Pantagleize marches, puzzled.)* This is the day — *(Going.)* You've made it ours — blood brother, comrade at arms! *(Going.)* And long live . . . long live . . . the . . .

(He is off. Pantagleize looks after him, bewildered.)

PANTAGLEIZE: Long live what? All I said was "Oh what a lovely day." Any idiot could have told him that. I really should have my horoscope looked into. My glove, my hat. *(Off.)* Bamboola wait for me. My umbrella, who knows it might turn out bad after all.

(He strolls out of his house, moves jauntily down the street, turns a corner, and encounters his horoscope, a mechanical gypsy in a glass booth. He takes a coin from his pocket, slips it into the machine. The doll starts to move. Amplified voice.)

FORTUNE-TELLER: You, so far without a destiny,
Will commence yours unexpectedly
Upon your fortieth birthday.
Your destiny
Is with the eclipse linked
Suddenly aflame, and then as soon extinct
Begin it in the morning
End it in the evening
So the stars foretell
So the stars foretell —
(Pantagleize kicks the machine, which continues smoothly.)
Expect no further details
Of this historic destiny
A diplomatic silence prevails

From now until eternity.

(The machine gives a gurgle and a ping, and it shoots a little card out of a slot, then grinds to a halt. Pantagleize retrieves the card.)

PANTAGLEIZE: *(Reads.)* ". . . historic destiny . . . diplomatic silence . . . eternity." You see, it's no laughing matter.

(Full of dignity, he strolls off.)

SCENE TWO

A cafe. Innocenti, the waiter, is cleaning up, preparatory to opening the cafe for the day. He sets the tables, chairs, stools, some bottles, glasses.

INNOCENTI: *(Yawns.)* Not enough sleep. *(He makes a face.)* I live in a stench — pew! Some filthy job, serving. I'm a slave in a black coat, serving drinks to fools who argue, fart, sing off key, vomit into the toilet — and miss. In order that you should serve beer, your mother bore you, eh? *(Yawns again.)* And in this world, there are people sick because they sleep too much. Bloodsuckers — parasites! I'd like to serve them . . . a revolutionary cocktail. I'd . . .

(Pounding at the door.)

BLANK: *(Outside.)* Open up!

INNOCENTI: We're not open yet.

BLANK: *(Off.)* Open up, man, for the long tongue is hung and with the thirst of dragon the throat of morning swallows the trolleys and factories swagger the twilight time melts in my —

INNOCENTI: — I needed this? All right, I hear you. *(He opens door.)* Up so early — or haven't you been to bed?

BLANK: *(Enters.)* There's a mob who has awakened. Beware the sleeper.

INNOCENTI: You can stop with the immortal verse, poet. The last customer left long ago . . . not a soul here to buy you a drink in exchange for your drivel. So now you'll have to speak in "free verse."

BLANK: Wow, that's funny. I come, as I do always, to trample on my heart. *(He takes an imaginary step, crushes a heart.)* Like that. Look, man, look into the depths of my eyes — you'll see I come from the region of light.

INNOCENTI: Shove off. *(They clean up a moment.)*

BLANK: Waiter? *(Innocenti grunts.)* What if I were to tell you . . . the moment has come?

INNOCENTI: I'd say it's the moment for you to leave. Go. Good-bye. Sleep until noon, you bum. Don't come back till you're sober. Leave the Workers to their work.

BLANK: Hell, I'm a worker . . . in my fashion. I fashion chimeras. But tonight — I'll throw away the poet's mask and be a man among the others. What's the date today?

INNOCENTI: *(Shrugs.)* All days are the same, when the people are enslaved. All days are filled with disgust when the people —

BLANK: There's the calendar, take a look.

INNOCENTI: Humor the artist. *(He crosses to calendar, peers up at it.)* It's . . . oh . . . it's —

BLANK: The very day. Now he knows why I didn't sleep last night. *(Orates.)* O flaming red date! Figure of fire! Today, waiter.

INNOCENTI: *(Very still.)* So. It comes at last. I tremble with joy. Tell me the plan —

BLANK: A plan: massive yet delicate, like precision machinery. We are to obey mysterious forces. Our leaders are at the top of a lighthouse, and we're on the ocean floor, in the darkness, knowing nothing but the signal —

INNOCENTI: Tell me about the signal!

BLANK: Who'll give it? No one knows. All we can do is wait for the man of the hour, our messiah, to give the sign. We fight against the most relentless power there is: man himself. *(Matter-of-fact.)* That's it, that's all I know. Blood poetry, it is. Today I shall be pure and beautiful, a poet on the floor of the amphitheater. *(He is, for an instant, touched, and therefore real.)* Here, Innocenti, Comrade, give us a — a fraternal kiss!

INNOCENTI *(Moved in his turn.)* Comrade! *(They embrace.)*
(Terrible din. Bamboola enters wearing a gray bowler. And with a small arsenal of handguns in the lining of his vest. He is ecstatic.)

BAMBOOLA: Comrades! Bamboola happy!

BLANK: *(Terrified of him.)* Tarantula! Epileptic wildman!

BAMBOOLA: *(Smiling.)* Wildman scalp poet. *(He pushes a casual fist into Blank's face. Blank staggers.)* Laugh, boy! — laugh quick or —

BLANK: Hahaha.

INNOCENTI: Hahaha.

BAMBOOLA: And now — we dance. Bamboola's dance!
(He claps his hands, begins to dance. The others copy him, repeating after him "Aya. Aya." During the dance Creep, a plainclothesman, enters and observes the scene.)

CREEP: *Danse macabre!*
(Bamboola's sixth sense picks up the enemy.)

BAMBOOLA: Stop! *(The dance stops in mid step.)* Bamboola, child of the bush, smells wild beast loose. *(He listens for a sound.)* No matter. We'll dance later, when it's over.

BLANK: You must have information — you're excited.

BAMBOOLA: I, black man, know more than you, white boy.

(He motions them into a corner. Creep crosses to a high stool by the bar, unnoticed.)

INNOCENTI: Tell us all — first, what about the signal?

(Bamboola begins signing his information to them with his fingers; Creep cranes his neck, jots down the information.)

INNOCENTI: Where will the signal come from — and how — and when?

(His eyes sweep the room coolly, [missing Creep].)

BAMBOOLA: Hush — a slip of you' lip will sink the ship!

BLANK AND INNOCENTI: A slip of the lip will sink the ship.

INNOCENTI: And what about the sequence of events?

BAMBOOLA: The walls have ears. I use code.

(Bamboola looks at, discards the bar towels, regards his fingers for an instant.)

BLANK: *(Inspired whisper.)* Try modern verse.

BAMBOOLA: Modern verse? Very nice: you alabaster monkey.

Ici radio Roo-coo-coo
Miss Kakakarak number two
Hello, hello, Central telephoning
Thousand million stars crack zoning
Munition depot good evening sector
Tutut three-ministry eigenvector
Six ministry police eat chocolate
Sector four drink heavy nitrate
Massa come toy soldiers nursemaids
At midday left flank shows grenades
Long love proletata class soup
Suppressed flash columns four in group
Tonight . . . eternity . . . begin

BLANK: Inspired! Black Orpheus!

BAMBOOLA: Black man like abstract art. The man of the hour has set his clock.

INNOCENTI: Yes, but who —

BLANK: Yes, who —

BAMBOOLA: *(Smiles.)* Not me . . .

(Blank gives a frightened denial with a shake of his head. Innocenti shrugs.)

BLANK: You know him?

BAMBOOLA: I have that honor.

INNOCENTI: Who? Who?

BAMBOOLA: An imbecile.

INNOCENTI: An innocent?

BAMBOOLA: I said an imbecile.

BLANK: Go on! — but he's supposed to —

INNOCENTI: — To unleash a catastrophic event!

BAMBOOLA: Uh-hum. Don't worry, it couldn't be in better hands.

INNOCENTI: An imbecile! Do you think a revolution is a barbecue? *(Bamboola smiles.)* A revival meeting?

BLANK: *(Rhapsodic.)* It's a poem.

INNOCENTI Fool!

BLANK: Hey, where is he, then?

BAMBOOLA: He'll come.

BLANK: Perhaps he's come in without our knowing it. Let's look.

INNOCENTI: Every moment is precious.

(They search around the cafe never seeing Creep, they look under the tables, finally disappear behind the counter. Creep, missing them, calls out.)

CREEP: Waiter!

(A groan of fear from behind the counter. Three heads appear, stare at Creep.) *(Bamboola shakes his head no. They groan again.)*

INNOCENTI: O God! *(He stands up, approaches.)* What would you like, sir?

BLANK: That him?

CREEP: A half pint of beer, carefully drawn, no head.

INNOCENTI: At your service, sir.

(He absentmindedly pours a glass of port, gives it to Creep.)

CREEP: I ask for a beer, you give me a port. Is something on your mind?

INNOCENTI: *(Forced smile.)* Overworked is all. Forgive me for not noticing you right away. Have you been waiting long?

CREEP: Quarter of an hour.

INNOCENTI: *(Under his breath.)* Damnation!

BAMBOOLA: *(Sniffs, mutters.)* Bamboola smell wild beast.

BLANK: *(Mutters.)* Queer face. No soul. Bad karma.

CREEP: *(Drinks.)* Watching you, I observed to myself, "This waiter and his customers seem a trifle overexcited." What transpires?

(Innocenti shrugs.)

CREEP: You can trust me . . . I'm just curious. Besides, I'm up on current events. I read the papers, eh?

(No answer. Creep smiles benevolently, sips.)

CREEP: I've come to town to see the big event. *(Blank pokes Bamboola in the ribs.)* Doesn't happen often, eh?

INNOCENTI: Not often. But it's been known to happen . . .

CREEP: No, in my opinion, the world won't end today. *(Blank clutches Bamboola, trembling.)* Get rid of your medieval ideals — Nothing to be terrified of.

BLANK AND BAMBOOLA: Terrified?

INNOCENTI: Who's terrified? I welcome this big event, I bare my breast to it!

CREEP: How quaint — a local custom, no doubt. But the sun won't see your naked breast —

INNOCENTI: The sun?

CREEP: The eclipse will really drive you out of your mind.

INNOCENTI: The eclipse? *(Enlightenment.)* Of course, the eclipse — this morning. *(Meaningfully.)* The total eclipse! So!

BAMBOOLA: *(Taking it in.)* The total eclipse . . . shur' nuff! Bamboola good nigger, Bamboola afraid of eclipse.

BLANK: Me too — I'm sensitive to change. Can you picture it? The Death of Light. Medieval times? We're still in them.

CREEP: *(Soothing.)* Now, now, be calm. We're in the twentieth century, remember. Science, gentlemen. Here, let me read you the details. *(He reaches for the paper.)* Waiter, a glass of port, please.

INNOCENTI: At your service, sir. *(He draws a glass of beer.)*

CREEP: I ask for port, you give me beer. Oh, well, I'll put it down to the eclipse. *(He unfolds his paper, which completely obscures his face. The trio begins to signal each other. Bamboola produces a knife to slit Creep's throat. The others stop, calm him. Footsteps. Banger, a man with a limp, enters from the outside, carrying a heavy object wrapped in a cloth. The trio moves toward him, to cut him off.)*

BAMBOOLA: Banger!

BANGER: Huh?

(The three signal him to be careful. Banger looks at their antics, bursts into laughter, depositing his bundle.)

BANGER: You're off your rockers, acting like a bunch of frigging apes. Trying to put on a floor show? *(More signals.)* Cut the comedy, you clowns, orders are orders. *(More violent signals. Threatening signals.)* A bunch of ballerinas. *(He turns away, sees his covered object.)* Hey, you faggots, take a look at this. *(He pulls off the cover, revealing a huge submachine gun. The trio step back, terrified.)* That's my kind of art. Yeah, I call that friggin' poetry! *(He sees Creep.)* Who's he?

(Bamboola stands dead center, mimes a cop directing traffic.)

BANGER: You could've warned me. *(He hides the gun under a table, asks casually.)* Well, how's tricks, guys?

INNOCENTI: Quite well, thank you.

BAMBOOLA: Bamboola very well. Bamboola happy.

BLANK: Poetry's doing well, too, gimp. *(He looks meaningfully at Banger, leaps up onto a table.)* Lend me your ears. *(Very fast.)* Whom do we await in this astronomic blackness? Elephant, chair leg oculist, birdbath, handbag? No, flower-beard! An imbecile, it would appear. So it appears. When will he appear? I, the oracle, reply to unasked questions.

BANGER: The metaphor's a lot of laughs, but I don't get the friggin' scansion. An imbecile, you say? They chose an imbecile from the whole herd of humanity? *(Blank nods.)* Shit, he could be any creep. *(Creep jumps.)* Any poor slob in the world. Hell, he could be the next sucker to walk in that door.

(At these words, Pantagleize walks in the door.)

BAMBOOLA: *(A whispered gasp.)* It's him!

ALL: Him?

PANTAGLEIZE: *(To himself.)* Perhaps it's my eyes. Perhaps they're failing me. People don't have their usual look about them, today. I step out of doors — dazzling weather! Just right for walking about a lot, and thinking very little. Yet everything has another look, every sound has a strange new resonance. What do I see? Parades forming, newsboys screaming incomprehensible words, curbstone astronomers, military patrols. It's a holiday . . . the day of the great eclipse. The mob is unbearable . . . restive. Absurd to have a public holiday when there's an eclipse. Now, to escape this combustible crowd, I betake myself to a cafe, and what do I find? A collection of questionable, not to say shady, individuals who stare at me as if they owed me money. Why do they stare? Can they, perhaps, read signs of my destiny on my forehead? Well, I'll rise above it . . . be debonnaire . . . order a drink while I'm waiting for the eclipse or the parade — whichever comes first. Garçon, if you please, may I trouble you —

INNOCENTI: *(Low voice.)* So . . . you're the imbecile.

PANTAGLEIZE: Oh, I confess ignorance of what I really am —

INNOCENTI: Then you are . . . *the* imbecile.

PANTAGLEIZE: *The* imbecile? *(He stares back.)* This waiter is quite mad — I mustn't arouse him. *(Firmly.)* Yes, indeed, I'm the imbecile. I am whatever it pleases you to see in me. Holy shit! *(Sees Bamboola.)* Bamboola! Just the man to vouch for my imbecility!

BAMBOOLA: Yeah, Bamboola vouch for his little boss. You know these comrades?

PANTAGLEIZE: I haven't made their acquaintance. On the other hand, why should I? I'm the fool, and sufficient unto myself.

BLANK: Sometimes the fool wakes up a poet — that's the case with me. You dig poetry?

PANTAGLEIZE: I was a poet, once. In those days the avant-garde wrote about reinforced concrete and the internal combustion engine. *(Drinks.)* Recite. I'm listening — but I can already tell, I'll like your work.

BLANK: *(Oratorical, but very fast.)* Pinhead or pighead sweet fool from your head of wood is born the electric word, or ravisher of eclipse and merchant of parades the constellations and howitzers make Confucius laugh.

PANTAGLEIZE: *(Oratorical, but very fast.)* Confucius stuffed with straw in ancient history you are as handsome whippersnapper as a hairdresser whom a pipe makes ill climb the ladder quickly and see on Olympus if I am there.

BLANK: Wheeee! That's wild! Who would have thought — you're a primitive poet! Hey, poet, with all that inspiration zapping around inside your head can't you . . . slip us the word? Elliptically, I mean. Speak, and prodigies shall spring forth from your mouth.

PANTAGLEIZE: If it will make you happy. *(He takes out a little notebook. Silence.)* I speak. I pronounce. "Oh, what a lovely day." I have spoken.

(A stunned silence. Then an eruption, a triumphal chord.)

BLANK: Holy shit!

(The revolutionaries stare at one another.)

THE FOUR REVOLUTIONARIES: The signal, the signal!

The die is cast!

I happy, I happy!

I happy at last!

He's spoken the words

He's led the way

Comrades, to arms,

This is the day!

Oh, what a lovely day!

PANTAGLEIZE: *(Dazed, modest.)* It's not that original.

INNOCENTI: But you meant it?

PANTAGLEIZE: Why not?

INNOCENTI: So. When, comrade? Where?

PANTAGLEIZE: Here. Now. Everywhere. On the avenues and boulevards, where we're going to watch the parade — and the eclipse, whichever comes first.

BAMBOOLA: Everybody look sharp! Synchronize watches!

BANGER: Shit! I'll return to my post!

PANTAGLEIZE: So soon?

BLANK: Fellow poet . . . good luck!

PANTAGLEIZE: I thought we might all stay and chat . . .

INNOCENTI: Slaves, arise! The blood of the enemies will flow. The day of justice is at hand.

PANTAGLEIZE: It is a holiday after all . . .

BAMBOOLA: Pantagleize, boss . . . so long. Take care. See you at the top, in the finite . . . excelsior!

PANTAGLEIZE: Maybe it was something I said. All those nice people gone up in smoke. Perhaps I'm hallucinating. Oh, well . . . Waiter . . . Waiter.

CREEP AND PANTAGLEIZE: WAITER!

PANTAGLEIZE: It seems we call in vain. I think the only waiter left — he looked a trifle unsettled like the others.

CREEP: It's the eclipse, sir. The smallest thing will set them off today. For example, that little expression you read them: "Oh what a lovely day." What can it mean?

PANTAGLEIZE: It's merely a catchphrase. But, to paraphrase: "What fine weather we're having."

CREEP: (To himself.) Too simple! Right under our noses! An idiot could have — (Bows to Pantagleize.) Delighted to meet an intellectual. Your name, please.

PANTAGLEIZE: Pantagleize.

CREEP: Pantagleize? Enchanté. Mon plaisir. Mon honneur. Pas de tout. Oui, d'accord. And you're planning to watch the eclipse?

PANTAGLEIZE: Oh, sir, it would be wrong to sit inside a stuffy cafe on such a lovely day.

CREEP: (Thoughtfully.) Ah, too true. (He bows.) A thousand thanks, sir.

PANTAGLEIZE: (Bows.) A thousand pleasures, sir. So long.

CREEP: Hasta la vista.

PANTAGLEIZE: Arriverderci.

CREEP: Ciao.

(They both bow again. Pantagleize exits with dignity. At once Creep leaps to the telephone.)

CREEP: Hello! Hello! 1324 . . . Police headquarters? This is Chief Inspector Creep.

(Rachel Silberchatz bounds into the cafe.)

RACHEL: Comrades, hurry! Hurry!

CREEP: The Jewess . . . Well well well, what have we here . . .

> (*Creep reaches for his revolver. After she sees him, Rachel snatches up a stool, which she hurls at the policeman's head. Creep collapses, unconscious.*)

RACHEL: Son of a bitch! (*She runs out.*)

> (*Blackout.*)

SCENE THREE

The promenade. A wall. A street lamp. Broad daylight. Background noise of crowds, the Balladmonger rushes in.

BALLAD-MONGER: (*Sings.*) Thirty-two choruses for a franc!
All of your old favorites, folks
Buy a ballad, try on a song
All the latest hits, folks
(*Pantagleize enters with newspaper, umbrella.*)

PANTAGLEIZE: Ha! The daily papers — written by practical jokers! What right have they to conjure up the Middle Ages? I could die laughing. True, in the Middle Ages I'd have died of fright. Or plague, perhaps. (*He bumps into the Ballad-monger.*) Selling songs? You know the one my mother used to sing? (*Ballad-monger shakes her head.*) Probably not, she was an unwed mother. (*He clears his throat, sings.*) Then I'll sing it for you!
Little cuckoo, go to sleep
Little cuckoo do not weep
Mama made a slip one day
You popped out the first of May
Baby . . .

BALLAD-MONGER: Wait! What's your favorite song? Your song moves me to the bowels of my being. You're a man of the people.

PANTAGLEIZE: Of course! I am a bastard, ma'am. A love child.

BALLAD-MONGER: A man of the people. Buy a song — how about this one? The *Internationale*? (*Hands him a song.*)

PANTAGLEIZE: Is it a love ditty?

BALLAD-MONGER: It's about the love of the masses . . . about the last struggle of all, for — (*Sings.*)
Arise, ye children of starvation
Arise, ye wretched of the earth —

PANTAGLEIZE: Thank you, it sounds very nice. *(Puts it in his pocket.)*
BALLAD-MONGER: Thirty-two choruses for —
PANTAGLEIZE: *(He looks up.)* Oh, what a lovely day, eh?
BALLAD-MONGER: *(Stares.)* What? What did you say? *(She rushes off.)*
PANTAGLEIZE: Wait! Here's my franc — I was going to buy — It's the eclipse.
(He shrugs, opens up his paper, reads.) Who would have thought this ce-
lestial phenomenon would infect people's brains? It's still light out, but
they're already behaving like lunatics. Lun-a-tics. Moon madness, that.
Sun seizures. *(He looks up at the sun.)* Hello to you, sun! Classic star! Ben-
eficient gaseous fixed-point. *(Confidingly, to sun.)* They're afraid of the dark!
Oh well. *(He turns back to the paper.)* A serious, edifying occupation,
reading the papers. It provides you with irrefutable popular opinions on
all events. This morning's headlines: "Great People's Parade." *(He shrugs.)*
Why not? Walking's good for you. But I shan't join in — if everyone
marched, there'd be no one left to watch the parade, hence there would
be no point in having a parade. On the other hand, if everyone watched
and no one paraded — *(He reads.)* I've seen them all, this morning. Epilep-
tics, visionaries, madmen . . . I'll bet the next passerby will be —
(Rachel runs on, stops in front of Pantagleize.)
RACHEL: Comrade, what do you think of the day?
PANTAGLEIZE: I . . . I think, Miss . . . it will be a lovely day.
RACHEL: Stand fast! Courage! Conquer! *(She runs out.)*
PANTAGLEIZE: *(Beside himself.)* That's what I mean! Mass hysteria! Blame the
journalists — with their horrific predictions. *(He waves the paper.)* If I
were editor, I'd hearten the people with my sunny philosophy. *(He looks
at the Sun.)* Sun . . . little Sun . . . shhh . . . you're about to turn a somer-
sault. But be careful, they may misconstrue your antics. *(He glances at
paper.)* And if it is the end of the world? We'll all go down singing hymns
like stoics. *(Sings.)* Farewell, Earth . . . adieu, Sun. *(He looks up.)* When
all is said and done, you do have a pronounced effect on one.
*(Enter an astronomer in a robe, pointed hat, false beard. He sets up his tel-
escope and directs it toward the sky. It is Bamboola. He watches Pantagleize,
then makes signs to unseen people over the wall. Then he puts on dark glasses,
waves a picture of the eclipse.)*
BAMBOOLA: Eclipse, eclipse, she the only true eclipse . . . fifty pesos, authentic eclipse — all other imitation.
PANTAGLEIZE: What a disguise! Tell me, you charlatan, what's it all for?
BAMBOOLA: Oh, hello, Boss. — Public adore claptrap.
PANTAGLEIZE: Bravo, Nostradamus. So you're selling the eclipse. And sunglasses,

to take a dark view of life? I prefer to see life in a soft blue. It is a lovely day, today, and the sky has a positively prehistoric look. *(He puts on a pair of blue-tinted sunglasses.)* Well, is the world going to end today?

BAMBOOLA: Who knows, Boss . . . it will or it won't.

PANTAGLEIZE: That's safe. What's the parade?

BAMBOOLA: Proletarian parade. Oppressed sovereign people. Men and women on the march.

PANTAGLEIZE: *(Sings.)* I love a parade. They'll march around the city?

BAMBOOLA: They'll march around the centuries . . . through history . . . toward the ideal of brotherhood.

PANTAGLEIZE: I prefer the eclipse. *(He removes his sunglasses.)* The Sun parades across the universe, and he always returns to the place he started. Go, peddle your claptrap.

BAMBOOLA: Eclipse . . . Eclipse . . . *(Selling.)* The only authentic eclipse . . . made in the observatory. Also, a fine line in grenades . . . Saturday night specials . . . Molotov cocktails . . . Eclipse . . . Eclipse . . .

CREEP: *(Off.)* Eclipse . . . eclipse . . . forty-five marks. Beware of imitations. The official, endorsed eclipse. To try one is to buy one.
(Bamboola is taken aback. Creep enters as Astronomer, with top hat, dark glasses. He too sets up shop.)

CREEP: The wonders of the sky, sir.

BAMBOOLA: For fifty centimes.

CREEP: For forty-five marks.

BAMBOOLA: The grand event — come buy sir.

CREEP: The guaranteed, the true eclipse.

PANTAGLEIZE: A second Nostradamus? They must be brothers. *(To Creep.)* Here's forty-five sous — tell me if the end of the world is coming.

CREEP: No, sir, the world has taken its precautions.

PANTAGLEIZE: *(To Bamboola.)* Your colleague is a droll one.

BAMBOOLA: Look out, boss, he not come here to sell eclipse.
(Rachel enters in dark glasses.)

RACHEL: Comrade!!

PANTAGLEIZE: Oh, mademoiselle, are you looking for the eclipse? Allow me to buy you a glimpse of it —

RACHEL: The real spectacle isn't up there — it's in the street. *(To Bamboola, conspiratorially.)* How long until the eclipse?

BAMBOOLA: Five minutes . . . thirteen seconds.

CREEP: *(Correcting.)* Twenty-seven seconds.

RACHEL: I didn't ask you.

PANTAGLEIZE: What pretty eyes she must have behind her glasses. I'd like to say something gallant to you.

RACHEL: Say what you did before . . . about the weather.

PANTAGLEIZE: I said, "Oh what a lovely day."

RACHEL: Your words are golden!

PANTAGLEIZE: It was nothing.

RACHEL: Comrade, greetings! Salute! *(She leaves.)*

(Pantagleize is crestfallen. Music mingles with the din.)

PANTAGLEIZE: The lady is precipitous — eclipses don't promote tranquility.

CREEP: Too true.

BAMBOOLA: *(Annoyed.)* Boss, the eclipse is coming!

PANTAGLEIZE: I'm counting on it. But I shan't watch it through your telescopes . . . No, no . . . *(He climbs up the wall, stands on the top. The two telescopes immediately focus on him.)* Oh, the vastness . . . the parade . . . the flags moving toward us! Splendid view! What a crowd — like an army. Hip hip — hooray! Oh, they're waving back. How friendly! *(Rumbling in the crowd.)* Heavens, I came to watch them, but you'd think . . . I was the attraction. Maybe I'm the eclipse? They sound like a pack of snarling dogs — come on, good people, smile! *(Rumble grows stronger.)* But the flags — they're all black! Like a funeral! *(Inspiration.)* Ah, perhaps it's to harmonize with the eclipse.

(The light grows dimmer.)

CONFUSED VOICES IN THE CROWD: You! Up there on the wall! It's him. That's the man, the man of the hour! *(Etc.)*

PANTAGLEIZE: Yes, it's me, folks. Here I am. Funny, you find a clever catchphrase, you launch it, and suddenly you're a celebrity. *(He looks up.)* They weren't joking . . . the Sun's burning out. *(Rumbling grows.)* Someone should put the searchlights on. *(Airplane noise.)* Look, an airplane circling the sun — a good omen or a bad one? *(Basses start. Music grows nearer.)* It'll be a parade of shadows . . . ghosts. How pale they look. Like tiny ants . . . insects, down there. They're waiting, marking time. I think it's time I went.

BAMBOOLA: *(A voice like thunder.)* Stay! The eclipse!

(The light grows dimmer.)

PANTAGLEIZE: Yes, I suppose so. Someone must stay and reassure the crowds. Someone must given the lie to the newspapers. Why not me? *(He climbs up to lamppost.)* Look, everyone, I don't give a rap for the eclipse! I dance! Dance, good people!

(Black flags slowly pass on the other side of the wall. Cries, threats, jeers.)

PANTAGLEIZE: Listen! The sky won't fall in — I'll be responsible for that. *(Singing starts. Aside.)* I think it's working. *(To the crowd.)* I am he who shall give heart to humanity on this fateful day! *(To himself.)* Perhaps this is my destiny! *(He gestures to the crowds, darkness closes in. Rachel enters as an onlooker.)* This is my rostrum. I shall give heart to them. I shall speak!

BAMBOOLA: Speak!

PANTAGLEIZE: No, I shall sing.

    (N.B.: The mob song — or anthem — has a continual chant of.)

MOB: Forward, forward
    Forward, forward
    (Interspersed with their growing chorus.)
    Citizens, arise, arise
    The people shall prevail
    Oppressors' blood will fill the skies
    Our battle shall not fail
    Citizens, arise, arise
    March in freedom's name
    Revolution never dies
    Our cause a sacred flame
    (Etc.)

PANTAGLEIZE: *(Sings, contrapuntally.)* Ladies and gents,
    Friends of the proletariat,
    I've come to ease your fears,
    I'll make you merry, yet.
    The Sun, our little Sun
    Tells me he's sound at heart,
    The world won't end today,
    The Earth won't fall apart,
    Fear not the propaganda
    Of the local press
    Forget your worries,
    Your profound distress.
    In case you didn't know,
    Today's the first of May,
    The daffodils are popping —
    It's a lovely day!
    (Dead silence from the crowd.)

PANTAGLEIZE: *(Sings.)* Oh, what a lovely day!

(An explosion. The crowd screams. Shots, fighting. Bamboola stashes his astronomer's costume.)

PANTAGLEIZE: What did I do? I didn't do it? What's happening?

BAMBOOLA: Revolution! Resurrection!

REVOLUTIONARIES: Long live . . . forward . . . death to . . . to arms . . . *(Etc.)*

RACHEL: *(Runs forward.)* Come! Follow me!

PANTAGLEIZE: Excuse me, Miss? I'm ignorant!

RACHEL: Nonsense! You're wonderful. You're magnificent! You're a superman! *(She kisses him on the mouth.)* I love you! Follow me!

PANTAGLEIZE: Excuse me, miss, but you mustn't tease. *(But he follows her off, as the pandemonium crescendos.)*

RACHEL: Follow me.

(Blackout.)

SCENE FOUR

Rachel's room. Darkness. The eclipse is still running, but by the end of the scene there is a bit of light in the sky outside. A table. A chair. A lamp. Voices from offstage.

RACHEL: *(Off.)* Come on!

PANTAGLEIZE: *(Off.)* Where?

RACHEL: This way.

PANTAGLEIZE: Which way?

RACHEL: Can you see?

PANTAGLEIZE: See what?

RACHEL: Look out!

PANTAGLEIZE: For what — ow!

RACHEL: Fool!

(She switches on the lamp. Huge shadows. An explosion far away.)

RACHEL: That's the arsenal. That *was* the arsenal.

PANTAGLEIZE: There'll be trouble.

RACHEL: Fool!

PANTAGLEIZE: As soon as we dare speak out loud, I'll ask for more light. It's gloomy here —

RACHEL: Hush!

PANTAGLEIZE: Why —

RACHEL: Do as you're told! I'm counting —

PANTAGLEIZE: — But —

RACHEL: Ten.

PANTAGLEIZE: — I shall answer you the same way —

RACHEL: Twelve.

PANTAGLEIZE: — The general at Waterloo answered the —

RACHEL: Thirteen. *(She staggers suddenly. He catches her.)* Oh . . .

PANTAGLEIZE: What's wrong, Miss? Where are the smelling salts?

RACHEL: Never mind, it's passing. Nerves, I guess.

PANTAGLEIZE: I blame the eclipse.

RACHEL: The eclipse? *(She laughs harshly.)* Oh, yes, the eclipse.
    (Pantagleize giggles hysterically.)

RACHEL: Why are you laughing?

PANTAGLEIZE: Reaction.

RACHEL: You're pale — are you ill?

PANTAGLEIZE: Dizzy.

RACHEL: Smelling salts?

PANTAGLEIZE: Whiskey. *(She fetches a bottle.)*

RACHEL: Here. *(She pours.)*

PANTAGLEIZE: Thank you, Miss. *(He drinks.)*
    (Rachel takes the bottle, swigs from it, stares at him.)

RACHEL: I don't know you.

PANTAGLEIZE: *(Crushed.)* You don't?

RACHEL: You are the —

PANTAGLEIZE: Yes?

RACHEL: The one who gave the — who are you? *(He shrugs.)* Never mind, it
    really doesn't matter, does it?
    For the inevitable has been accomplished — and you did it. Whoever
    you are, you've saved humanity today, with one phrase. And I, a humble
    member of the working class, I have saved you. I am proud of that.

PANTAGLEIZE: Me, too.

RACHEL: But we've no time for sentiment. To be brief about it, I must tell you —

PANTAGLEIZE: — What?

RACHEL: That I love you.

PANTAGLEIZE: Really?

RACHEL: I never lie. Do you love me?

PANTAGLEIZE: I —

RACHEL: You love me! We all love each other — we are entering an era of love!

PANTAGLEIZE: In that case, shouldn't we go to bed?

RACHEL: The love of man for mankind! Born of blood and destruction. A new world! A new Eden! I shall be Eve —

PANTAGLEIZE: *(Quickly.)* I'll be Adam.

RACHEL: We shall move toward the promised land —

PANTAGLEIZE: Where *is* the bedroom?

RACHEL: It lies wherever the flesh has suffered. It lies wherever the soul has wept! Overthrow . . . annihilate . . . deliver! Our revolution shall, like a cyclone . . .

PANTAGLEIZE: *(News to him. Pause.)* Revolution?

RACHEL: *(Nods.)* Yes revolution. And it's all your doing! You are the saviour! *(Pause.)*

PANTAGLEIZE: *(Moved.)* I . . . my destiny . . . I am . . .

RACHEL: You are my brother! *(He gives her a confused look.)* Come to my arms! *(He perks up. She flings herself into his arms.)*

PANTAGLEIZE: My dearest!

(She disengages herself.)

RACHEL: *(Out of breath.)* I'm on fire when there's a cause. *(The phone rings. Into phone.)* Hello? Hello? Yes, yes. *(Places her hand on her heart.)* What ecstasy! *(She hangs up.)*

PANTAGLEIZE: I'm so glad.

RACHEL: Of course, we're all glad! When the eclipse is over, the capital will be in our hands.

PANTAGLEIZE: Bravo! My dearest —

RACHEL: There's no time for daydreaming now — we must go to our posts. . . . Look here — *(She unfolds a map, they lean over it, their faces illuminated.)* Zone eight: terminated. Strategic road: We block it. Here, the bridge: We decimate it. Look outside — see the tower? *(He crosses to the window.)* Is there a light on it?

PANTAGLEIZE: Yes.

RACHEL: Good, another triumph. *(Phone rings.)* Hello? What? The government in flight? Wonderful — now *we* are the government! *(She hangs up. She becomes lyrical.)* O race of Israel, your time has come! Persecuted people, you shall be the equal of all nations. O ancestors, despised of the ghettos, may the Eternal God give strength to my arm! May he gird my loins with steel! *(Businesslike.)* Okay, to work! You write the committee — no, never mind, I'll do that. You must go to —

PANTAGLEIZE: Go! But, Rachel, I've only just arrived, and you were speaking of love. *(She stares.)*

RACHEL: You called me Rachel. That is my name. You called my name. And you? You are . . .

PANTAGLEIZE: Pan — pan — pantagleize.

RACHEL: Pan — pan — pantagleize? Never heard of you. And yet, on this glorious day, we all know each other. Sit down! *(She pushes him down.)* Answer me: Where were you last night?

PANTAGLEIZE: At home.

RACHEL: Who was the first person you saw, this morning?

PANTAGLEIZE: A black man.

RACHEL: Anyone else?

PANTAGLEIZE: Don't tell me. A poet. A Waiter. Also, a lame fellow with a package.

RACHEL: *(Intimately.)* And tell me . . . how did you know?

PANTAGLEIZE: Know what? I don't understand.

RACHEL: We mustn't expect to. Events first, enlightenment later. I obey. You obey.

PANTAGLEIZE: Who? Whom? Whom do we obey?

RACHEL: It is forbidden to know. It's difficult, not knowing. Having to wait. Last night — that endless night of waiting . . . horrible! The revolution was ripe, every detail worked out, everything was set for this morning, all our people massed, each at his post. But throughout the night — no orders. No word of attack. Nothing. So we wait. Nothing. Are we done for? Spies? The army tipped off? Still . . . nothing. And where is the man, this unknown man, this special person who will either give — or not give the signal?

PANTAGLEIZE: Where? *(He really wants to know.)* It's so thrilling!

RACHEL: At last — the appointed hour. And suddenly — the word flashes out like lightning! The mysterious comrade has come! The man of the hour! And it is my task — my honor — to follow and protect him. *(Pause.)* You. *(Pantagleize reacts in surprise.)* We don't know who you are. We don't know who to look for. Police are everywhere. But suddenly . . . I recognize you. Something there . . . too natural, too naïve, too stupid. You play the part marvelously — see, you're still doing it, acting surprised. You *are* modest — unwilling to admit even to yourself the grandeur of your destiny —

PANTAGLEIZE: Yes, but dearest, allow me to confess that —

RACHEL: No need. We're wasting time —

PANTAGLEIZE: I agree — *(He lunges toward her.)*

RACHEL: Check the tower — how many beacons?

PANTAGLEIZE: Two.

RACHEL: Action!

PANTAGLEIZE: *(Misunderstanding.)* Action?! *(He lunges.)*

RACHEL: Take this revolver.

PANTAGLEIZE: *(Arrested, panicked.)* Wha-ha-whoa!

RACHEL: You must leave.

PANTAGLEIZE: *(Numb.)* I must leave.

RACHEL: D'you have your instructions about the treasure?

PANTAGLEIZE: The treasure. But that's you.

RACHEL: Fool! Listen to instructions. And if you don't go, I have orders to blow your head off.

PANTAGLEIZE: And you say you love me?

RACHEL: Above all, I love humanity! Listen: *(Reads.)* You are to go to the State Bank. It is heavily guarded — soldiers inside and out, and on the roof.

PANTAGLEIZE: Is that all?

RACHEL: It's vital that you gain access to this stronghold of capitalism. Unfortunately I don't know the password to the safe . . . you'll have to work that out for yourself. But you will — you have a kind of genius!

PANTAGLEIZE: I have a kind of genius.

RACHEL: If necessary, kill. If you're caught — kill yourself. Your assignment: *(She reads.)* Seize the imperial treasure; deliver it in forty-five minutes to the Objective Bar, where our committee sits. If you fail — farewell!

PANTAGLEIZE: Dearest Rachel —

RACHEL: No emotion — just get the treasure. Good luck. You know, under those stupid antics, you're a splendid fellow — don't think I'm not aware of it.

PANTAGLEIZE: I'm flattered.

RACHEL: That's it, then. Good-bye for now . . . or forever.

PANTAGLEIZE: *(Putting on his hat.)* Rachel . . . I fear I shall never see you again . . .

(He sighs, but his sigh brings no reaction. He goes. Alone, Rachel gives a hollow laugh. She picks up the phone, dials.)

RACHEL: Hello? What? The man? He's gone to the bank. He's what? An imbecile? He's the saviour, the chosen one. What? I'm being shadowed? Who? No, I'll be careful. I'll stay here. Courage, comrades.

(She puts the phone down, looks about, a noise.)

VOICE OF CREEP: Rachel Silberchatz?

(Rachel drowns the light as soon as she sees the curtain move. She shoots. In

the pale light a man leaps forward. Hand-to-hand struggle. Silence. A gruff male voice laughs in little bursts. Blackout.)

SCENE FIVE

Cannon.

MACBOOM: *(Blustering.)* Hear that? Cannon! *(A corporal nods.)* I've been sol-diering for fifty years — never heard the damned things go off before! I'll bet they're firing at us. Me. Oh. Gentlemen, prepare to die. *(Deaf-ening cannon.)* We're dead! Dead! *(He sags.)*

CORPORAL: *(Holding him up.)* Not yet, General, don't be afraid.

MACBOOM: Afraid? My boy, old soldiers never die. *(Cannon.)* Tell Mrs. Mac-boom, Anastasia, that I died for her.

CORPORAL: Pull yourself together, General.

MACBOOM: Great garrisons! Go to your post, soldier. *(To the Corporal.)* These revolutionaries . . . what are they up to?

CORPORAL: They're firing cannons, sir.

MACBOOM: Just as I thought! But, Great grenades! Why don't they aim for our artillery?

BANK MANAGER: I think they want the treasure, General.

MACBOOM: The treasure! Then let 'em come! Fifty years of experience at the front tells me that it's gonna be bloody. *(Cannon.)* They *are* aiming for the safe! Gentlemen, prepare for the battle. *(He stumbles over the Man-ager.)* You civilians are always in the way — you ought to be at home.

BANK MANAGER: Even civilians have orders, general. The governor of the bank has ordered us to stay — if necessary we must die defending the treas-ure.

MACBOOM: That's life! But I have orders too, from the minister of war: to shoot any civilians who stand in my way.

(He pulls out a revolver.)

BANK MANAGER: Mercy, General! Have pity!

MACBOOM: If you can't stand the heat, stay out of the kitchen. *(Putting re-volver away.)* Well . . . are you two good at anything?

BANK MANAGER AND ASSISTANT: I'm (he's) the bank manager.

MACBOOM: You must be able to read and write. *(Manager nods.)* Good, you can write my report. Describe our heroic stand, put it down for posterity. And you *(To the Assistant Manager.)* — you correct him. *(The Bankers glare at each other.)* Brisk military style, like this. Etc. etc. *(The Bankers start scribbling. Macboom turns to sentry.)* Tell me, boy, who are these revolutionaries?

CORPORAL: People who . . . who want to steal the government's treasure, sir.

BANK MANAGER: Discontented people, sir.

MACBOOM: Discontented? Great grenades, you think I'm content? Have you ever seen Anastasia? *(To the Manager.)* How's the report coming?

(The Managers clear their throats.)

MACBOOM: Rousing! Rousing! That's stimulating stuff! Carry on, and be sure you write in a nice round hand. And don't forget, put the password at the top of the page! *(A long pause.)* Blazing bazookas! I've forgotten the password! *(Calls.)* Sonny, tell me the password.

CORPORAL: Go to hell, sir.

MACBOOM: *(Stunned.)* What'd you say, boy? Repeat that, and I'll have you shot with ignominy — not to mention bullets.

CORPORAL: That's the password, sir, "Go to hell."

(Macboom thinks. Enlightenment.)

MACBOOM: So it is. I pardon you, soldier, and compliment you on your sterling memory. *(To the Manager.)* Put that in the report. "A Father to His Troops." Etc. *(He moves toward the gate.)* Let's hear that password — and put a lot of spirit into it! Sentry number Ten, you start it —

SENTRY NINE: Go to hell!

SENTRY EIGHT: Go to hell!

(The voices call out the password, receding into the distance.)

MACBOOM: Tell me, boy, how long does a revolution take? My dinner is probably getting cold. Anastasia's nerves must be a wreck.

CORPORAL: You see, General, it's like this: How long would depend on the artillery, sir. On their aim. If their side has been practicing, it'll be over pretty soon. And if our side has better aim, it'll be over even sooner. Either way someone wins, sir.

MACBOOM: So that's how it works.

(The password becomes audible again.)

SENTRIES: Go to hell!
Go to hell!
Go to hell!
Go to hell!
Go to hell!

CORPORAL: Go to hell.

MACBOOM: Now hold on, boy. Go to hell — oh, it's the password again. The password? The enemy must be at hand. My sword! Atten-shun! Forward March/About Face/Halt/Take Aim/No No Don't Shoot. Shoulder Arms! Or whatever — It might be the minister of war . . . or his replacement. It might be the revolutionary minister of war —

CORPORAL: Shall we shoot him, sir?

MACBOOM: Which one? Don't shoot — salute. That way we'll be safe.

SENTRIES: Go to hell!

Go to hell!

Go to hell!

Go to hell!

Go to hell!

MACBOOM: *(Losing his head.)* Attention. Forward March/Halt/About Face/Forward March/Halt/About Face/Oblique March/Halt/Inwards Turn/Forward March/ FALL OUT!!!

(The soldiers try madly to comply with these orders. In the midst of this, Pantagleize enters. Macboom salutes him with his sword nervously.)

PANTAGLEIZE: *(Aside.)* More soldiers? At least a hundred men have asked me for the password.

MACBOOM: My respects, Excellency. Notice how well we're guarding the treasure?

PANTAGLEIZE: My compliments.

MACBOOM: Men, his Excellency compliments you. And will his Excellency permit us to ask the password, according to orders?

(Pause.)

PANTAGLEIZE: The password? *(He takes a deep breath.)* I repeat, without ceremony, without equivocation, what I said to your men when they asked me the same question outside: Go to hell!

MACBOOM: Thank you, Excellency.

PANTAGLEIZE: Don't mention it. *(Aside. He shrugs.)* I see our soldiers are ready for action, General. But perhaps they shouldn't exhaust themselves before the showdown. Squad-Shun/Shoulder Arms/Forward March/Take Post/Take Post/Squad Halt/About Face/Order Arms/Stand at Ease. *(They obey.)*

MACBOOM: So that's how it's done.

PANTAGLEIZE: Well, then, General, I've come on a mission, a command mission.

MACBOOM: About the treasure?

PANTAGLEIZE: Exactly . . . the treasure. *(He takes out his gun, opens the chamber, counts the bullets, counts the sentries.)*

MACBOOM: Ah . . . er . . . excellency, you're holding a firearm. You might kill someone if you don't know how to use it.

PANTAGLEIZE: And if I do, I still might kill someone. Especially on a mission. *(He puts it away.)* It's merely a precaution. With all these rioters and murderers running around the streets —

MACBOOM: True, Excellency. Meanwhile, what are your orders for the treasures?

PANTAGLEIZE: *(With sang froid.)* I'm taking it.

MACBOOM: Good, good, very smart. God knows it's not safe here. What a load off my hands, Excellency. *(Cannon.)* They're going to storm the bank any minute.

(Cannon. The Bankers make frantic signals to Macboom.)

PANTAGLEIZE: Quick, General, the treasure!

MACBOOM: Yessir, I call this a deliverance! Civilians, the combination — I say, open the safe. Open it or I'll have you under arrest.

BANK MANAGER: We need confirmation, sir.

MACBOOM: Trembling torpedoes, who's in charge here? *(Telephone rings.)* There's your confirmation. *(Pantagleize takes out his revolver again.)* Hello? Yes, yes, Macboom here. The bank . . . yes, yes . . . the treasure . . . yes, yes. I understand. I'll see to it. No no . . . no need to explain. I am master of the situation. *(He puts down the phone.)* He says that you should — *(Cannon.)* Open it, I say — it's high time!

(Bank Manager, very disturbed, opens the safe. Pantagleize peers inside, hooks a small valise with his umbrella.)

MACBOOM: It's all yours, Excellency.

PANTAGLEIZE: Yes.

MACBOOM: Worth about three hundred million. Crown jewels.

PANTAGLEIZE: I can't thank you enough.

MACBOOM: Where are you taking them?

PANTAGLEIZE: Oh, to the Obj — that's a military secret. Thank you, General, I shall commend your courtesy. Would you like a receipt?

MACBOOM: *(Cannon.)* Don't bother. Is it safe out there?

PANTAGLEIZE: It's quite busy. Shooting. Looting. Temperature in the low sixties, partly cloudy but clearing. *(Phone rings.)* It's for you. Meanwhile, I have my orders, as you have yours. Good day, general — don't bother, I know the way out. *(The Bank Manager leads him out.)*

MACBOOM: My pleasure! All ease. *(He calls after Pantagleize.)* Watch out for

bullets. Good riddance to that! Yes, Macboom here. Yes. But . . . You already phoned me about all that. Of course, of course, he's already been here. Hello? What? The person coming for the treasure was a revolutionary? Stop thief! Anastasia . . . Anastasia, Help!
(Blackout.)

SCENE SIX

The Objective Bar. Curtains and a large potted palm. Outline of a double bass. Boisterous entry of the four revolutionaries.

BANGER: Waiter!

BAMBOOLA: Boy!

BLANK: There's a quarter in it for ya —

INNOCENTI: Comrades, the Provisional Committee is now in session.

BAMBOOLA: You're fuckin' right it is!

INNOCENTI: *(He bangs on a table.)* The Provisional Committee, in possession of full power to —

(Bamboola gives a hoot, Banger a raspberry, the three B's laugh at Innocenti, who moves a little away, annoyed.)

INNOCENTI: — Possessing full power to convene —

(Bamboola bangs for order — but rhythmically.)

BAMBOOLA: It's time to start our dialectic debate!

BLANK: Right! This is no time to celebrate.

BANGER: Sure, little buddies, we must ponder and think. But first, I say we all need a drink!

(The three B's cheer, jeer at Innocenti.)

INNOCENTI: What are you morons talking about? There's serious work to do — we've waited too long to do it! Why spoil it by acting like fools?

BANGER: 'Cause no one has a right to speak —

BLANK: In the name of the poor, with the voice of the meek!

BAMBOOLA: Pray, lower your sights without more ado,
This Provisional Committee isn't headed by you!

(The three B's laugh again.)

BANGER: *(Calls out.)* Waiter! Waiter!

INNOCENTI: I'm a waiter but you call me Comrade Innocenti. It will be a pleasure to serve such prestigious comrades. What will you have?

BAMBOOLA: Bourgeois champagne, please.

I proclaim a state of siege. I proclaim martial law. I proclaim death to the villains. I proclaim myself president.

INNOCENTI: Why you?

BAMBOOLA: Cause I good nigger . . .

INNOCENTI: Good for nothing.

BAMBOOLA: I will be president. And minister of war.

BLANK: I modestly agree to being minister of arts and culture.

BANGER: I'll take finance. Yep, I'll be minister of the proletariat's inviolable cash. Hey where's the treasure?

INNOCENTI: Frauds. The police must be laughing themselves sick. Your class war has taken place on a movie set.

BANGER: What do you mean?

INNOCENTI: I mean that the revolution should not have commenced today. *(Pause.)*

BLANK: Who cares — so long as it's successful.

INNOCENTI: Who says it's been successful? We've lived in a dream.

BLANK: I think *you're* dreaming, buddy —

BANGER: — Or else you want to screw it all up. Traitor! Shithead! *(He lunges.)* *(Bamboola, very much the president, separates them.)*

BAMBOOLA: Right, now — peace on earth, comrades. Let's have a drink — we can quarrel tomorrow.

(Innocenti picks up the phone, dials, listens.)

INNOCENTI: Rachel Silberchatz doesn't answer. Three o'clock . . . but Rachel doesn't answer. *(He replaces the receiver.)* Who's going to keep us in touch with the outside world, now? *(Pause.)* And where's that funny little fellow who gave the signal? He must know something more than we do. *(Pantagleize enters carrying the valise and umbrella.)*

PANTAGLEIZE: The Objective Bar? Good. I'd like a drink. *(No one moves for a moment.)*

BAMBOOLA: *(Softly.)* Pantagleize.

PANTAGLEIZE: Good lord, Bamboola! *(He looks at the four revolutionaries.)* What is it, a class reunion! *(To Bamboola.)* What's new?

BAMBOOLA: I've just been elected president of the republic. Have a drink.

PANTAGLEIZE: Yes, a drink — anything. I've just snatched this from under the nose of a general. *(He opens the valise.)*

INNOCENTI: Why do that? Revolution has nothing to do with the Imperial Treasure.

PANTAGLEIZE: It was an act of chivalry . . . I stole these to please a young lady. *(Recognizes Innocenti.)*

INNOCENTI: Have you seen her?

PANTAGLEIZE: *(Smiling.)* She told me she loved me. Then she ordered me to bring the treasure here.

THE THREE B'S: Bravo Pantagleize! Hurrah! Comrade!

INNOCENTI: Shut up! *(To Pantagleize.)* Tell me, the signal — where did you get it?

PANTAGLEIZE: I made it up.

INNOCENTI: Do you just imitate an imbecile, or are you the real thing?

PANTAGLEIZE: This morning you all decided I was the real thing. But now that I've been clever enough to steal the treasure, you're reassessing me. But let me tell you: Only fools are smart enough to pull off such feats! *(He drinks.)* As for the signal, "What a lovely day," believe me, I'll never utter that one again! *(He drinks.)* And my destiny! I'm still waiting. And the wicked bourgeois class has been eclipsed — poof! *(He takes a breath.)* And the sun, recovered from its brief indisposition, shines on an awe-inspiring scene of ruination, ashes, Babylon! *(He exhales.)* Comrades, it is indeed a lovely day.

THE THREE B'S: Hurrah! Bravo! Victory!

PANTAGLEIZE: It's just like the French revolution — remember that one? — but without a guillotine.

THE THREE B'S: Bring back the guillotine! Bravo! We want a guillotine!

PANTAGLEIZE: Then we could guillotine the property owners, the chiropodists, the art critics. We'll strip 'em naked and make 'em do gymnastic exercises — let's call 'em collective movements. One two three four, one two three four —

BAMBOOLA: *(Inspired.)* You'll be minister of gymnastics!

PANTAGLEIZE: My fiancée will be proud.

INNOCENTI: Rachel — was she alone when you left?

PANTAGLEIZE: Call me "Excellency." When I left, she was calling out to the God of Israel. I didn't see anyone else — but I think I heard a quarrel, somewhere. *(Innocenti rushes to the phone, dials, waits, nothing.)*

PANTAGLEIZE: But what does it matter, friends. It's time to celebrate this success to which, I modestly confess, I have contributed. Let us drink, waiters more champagne. *(Two waiters rush in.)* Waiters! Serve all the excellencies . . . me too. And cigars. *(The waiters pour, station themselves behind the ministers' chairs.)*

BANGER: Shit, that's more like it. Here's to the Provisional Committee!

BLANK: Please . . . call us the Council of Ministers. *(Innocenti groans, head in hands.)*

BAMBOOLA: We are in session.

(A third waiter rushes in, passes cigars, moves behind the revolutionaries.)

PANTAGLEIZE: O brave new society! May I take the floor?

(Banger stares drunkenly down at the floor. Innocenti answers, listens, starts, puts down the phone, controlling himself.)

BANGER: Who was that?

INNOCENTI: Nothing, Everything's fine. *(To Pantagleize.)* Break camp, comrade. Leave, please, it's time.

PANTAGLEIZE: Why? I like it here.

(Innocenti is hit over the head by a waiter. Unseen by the revolutionaries, he props Innocenti up.)

BLANK: And we like you. *(Poetry.)* Adventurer chief cook and bottle washer glow equally on your forehead you dance on a rope and say shit to the archangel it is ten to four and the lotus eats itself defusing your delight leaves Hell a-weeping.

(He waits for applause. The others laugh. Pantaleize drinks, climbs on top of the table.)

PANTAGLEIZE: Perhaps we'll guillotine poets as well. Waiter, more light.

(Drum rolls off.)

PANTAGLEIZE: Send for harps and cymbals! Give me a trident and the tablets of the law! Don't forget the laurel crown. Tonight I shall perform marvels! Behold the marvel of my equilibrium *(He totters.)* When I sway the nation sways . . . when the nation sways the people sway with it. Only first, we must invent the people. Next, after that, we must destroy the only true god and manufacture idols in rubber in triplicate. Happenings are on sale — discounts on happenings. History at bargain prices! Yessir! *(Dizzy.)* O I have seen lepers and boogey men commanding the legions of the proletariat, legions of impertinent skeletons wearing saucepans and chamber pots on their heads. For liberty, comrades, liberty to spit on the ceiling and piss on holidays. But never forget, you must give the earth unto the beasts and unto man his misery. So we must live. You are too swinish, too sick to die; you will turn into statues. And the People? When the People have been invented, and when we have tasted their resistance to our speeches, and to our bullets, we shall crown them with pajamas, tennis racquets, matching luggage and three pounds of international sausage per capita, and they will be bought. And they will stay bought. The rest — that's our business. The deluge. The masses. Humanity. My fellow ministers, humanity was ugly and passionate. It was wise and foolish. I now propose —

BAMBOOLA: *(Half rising.)* — The publication of your speech!
(Bamboola is knocked out by the waiter behind him, and sinks back into his chair, unconscious.)

BLANK: — for posterity. Errors, of course will be deleted, if you like —
(The waiter behind him knocks Blank out.)

PANTAGLEIZE: If I like? I'd like to find a South Sea island where I can be a god, edit an artistic review — I'd like to find a men's room.

BANGER: But before you sail, lay in a good supply: beer, pickles, beer, caramels —
(Banger is banged on the head. He sinks.)

PANTAGLEIZE: We'll lay in a good supply of crutches and shrouds. We'll lay in a gross of sociological studies, plus pneumatic hearts, and automatic back-sides with vinyl covers to receive the boots of the new masters. And best of all, I shall reorder the heavens, so we can have eclipses! *(He looks at his companions in surprise.)* Asleep? All? This is the last time I'll make a speech to you! Snoring through their heyday!
(The four waiters grab their respective bodies and drag them off.)

PANTAGLEIZE: Now I'm master here. *(He laughs.)* What's become of my puppets? Am I dreaming? *(Silence.)* If I had stayed in bed this morning . . .?
(He jumps off the table, pours out a glass of champagne.) No point in finishing the speech — I'd be the only one here to applaud. To my health.
(The palm tree begins to move toward Pantagleize.)

PANTAGLEIZE: Peekaboo. I see you! Are you a part of the green revolution? *(He bows formally to the palm.)* Tell me, what does a palm tree feel when it sees someone else drinking champagne?

PALM/CREEP: It feels the satisfaction of a job well done. But its satisfaction will not be total until the handcuffs are on the wrists of the champagne drinker.

PANTAGLEIZE: I ought to uproot you for a remark like that.
(He knocks the tree over. Creep blows his whistle. Pantagleize grabs the valise.)

PANTAGLEIZE: See you at the next eclipse! *(He runs out. The waiters return.)*

PALM/CREEP: Quick, that way! *(Two waiters stand Creep on his feet.)*

CREEP: I want that imbecile dead or alive.
(Blackout.)

SCENE SEVEN

Rachel's room. It is a wreck, with maps and papers strewn about. Rachel sits in the armchair, apparently asleep. Whiskey bottle, note on the table. Light slants through the window. Voice of Pantagleize on the stairs.

PANTAGLEIZE: *(Off.)* Pearls, gold, platinum, diamonds, radium, emeralds, rubies and — I don't know what. All yours, you enchanting daughter of kings and prophets. *(He enters carrying the valise, very drunk.)* Oh Rachel — alone together at last! *(He looks at her.)* Fast asleep? After such a day, one needs a good nap. I'll keep watch, and tell you a story, the kind you might hear in a dream. The treasure, the Golden Fleece, I've captured for you — I place it at your feet. We can live on the interest! But what is this treasure against the jewel of my love! *(He opens the valise, looks inside.)* I'd rather have brought you rarer things: a moonbeam, a necklace of dewdrops, the secret of perpetual motion. My child, my love, I am shattered with fatigue. But . . . *(He holds his head.)* . . . I must sort out today's wanderings. A calendar, a black man, a street lamp, then an eclipse. Whirling dervishes and shooting galleries. And you, Rachel, who saved my life. My destiny pursued its course. Then came . . . the theft of the treasure! Then I became minister of gymnastics. Then I met a talking palm tree. Then I ran away — which is the sanest thing I've done all day. What next? Is it all over? I bet it will end in a marriage. Marriage — *(He gets up.)* I'm rich and in love with a sleeping beauty? *(He tiptoes round the chair.)* How white she is. *(To Rachel.)* May the genies of the night surround you. *(He sighs.)* Such a contrast. Before, you were agitated, like a goat. Now you're silent as a statue, quiet as a painting. Strange, but suddenly I am without desires. I wish for nothing but to drown in sleep, anonymous, without memory, severed from past and future. I await nothing but your awakening. *(He moves away, to the maps and papers, makes a desultory effort to tidy them.)* Papers? Maps? Rachel a mess! Order is needed — Rachel, you have such splendid qualities. You're gifted, capable, modern — but your room is like an office! What room have you left for love? This is no Eden. Rachel, you must be a woman! Yes, and we shall live in nature with the birds and little beasts, far away from the barbarities of city life. You shall be Eve. And I . . . I . . . I shall be your . . . *(He trembles, suddenly, deeply moved.)* I can't bear strong feelings — no more can you. For proof, look at you, dear and lovely one. *(He drinks from the bottle.)* That revolution only had one end . . . to bring us together. — So much joy! *(He bursts into tears.)* Look at me, a former minister, crying. Pull yourself together. *(He searches for a lamp. He lights a candle.)* I must waken her. Rachel my love, my little Rachel. *(Silence.)* Cuckoo! Rachel? Comrade! *(He becomes a bit nervous.)* What a sleep — I'd better shake her — no, first I'll place the butterfly of my kiss on the flower of her brow. *(He kisses her, then draws back, wiping his mouth.)* No don't panic. Rachel, it's not nice.

(He moves.) What is there in this room? *(He crosses back to her, takes hold of her. He lets her fall back.)* My betrothed — she's had an accident! *(He sees the note on the table.)* A note . . . with blood on it. For me? "They've murdered me." *(He drops the note, embarrassed.)* Oh, like that is it? Murdered? *(He stands for a moment, moves away.)* Excuse me, dearest, I didn't mean to intrude. Accept my . . . maybe you'd like to be alone — *(He grabs the valise, babbling away hysterically.)* Good-bye, good-bye Rachel. I hope we . . . *(He exits quickly, without looking back.)*
(Blackout.)

SCENE EIGHT

A street. Debris. Light from fires and searchlights. A body lying face downward. Pantagleize runs in, clutching his valise. He runs round and round the body, talking as he runs.

PANTAGLEIZE: One two. One two. I'm running. I'm flying. Where? Where am I going? My destiny is to gallop! I'm breaking records. One two. One two. My birthday. Running is exhausting. So is having a destiny. So is being minister of gymnastics. One two. One two. *(A shot.)* Still at it? One two. One two. *(He stumbles over the body.)* Whoops, beg your pardon. You're dead, too, no doubt. But those bullets are live. *(Two shots.)* If they hit me, there won't be much difference between us. *(He sits on the body.)* Death must have a profound effect on you. *(Shots.)* Here we are, you dead and me rich. Please understand, it's not that I value life so highly, but *(Shots.)* this treasure . . . sudden wealth is a sweet surprise. You know, the day was to end with a wedding. Nevermore. I'm like a widower . . . a widower. She's dead. *(Almost whispers.)* She . . . listened to all the poetic nonsense I murmured in her ear and never laughed at me, or blushed. Why didn't I die with her?

Everyone's dead — it's the fashion! However, if any of my friends are left, I shall assemble them, and transport them all to my beautiful desert island. We'll each be allowed to take our favorite book and our favorite flower. *(He thinks of books, smiles.)* And I shall be the patriarch. *(He pats the valise.)* The philanthropist. I shall spend my fortune resurrecting *(Pause.)* . . . the ideals of all those . . . innocents; and my reward will be to recapture, to remember, to recollect in tranquility, the shining eyes of that woman who dreamed of a universal love. *(He stops for a moment.)*

My love was not enough for her, sir. *(Noise of a patrol coming.)* Play dead. So shall I — death makes one a neutral. *(He lies face downward.)*

VOICE OF MACBOOM: Forward, right dress, to the rear, forward, present arms, march!

MACBOOM: Left, face, fall forward, spring back company. Halt. Corpses everywhere . . . Two more.

CORPORAL: Shall we fire on them sir? To make sure they're dead?

MACBOOM: I know a corpse when I see one. Oh, the peace of total victory. "Keep the home fires burning." They don't write 'em like that any more. Blazing bayonets, did you hear that? About-face wait cancel that order, the police are mopping up. About-face once more into the breech. Forward hut one, two, etc. etc. Anastasia!

(Macboom and patrol exit in several directions. Pantagleize stands up, moves toward the fighting at right.)

PANTAGLEIZE: Courage is an enduring quality. *(He gazes toward the battle.)* *(Silently the corpse rises, rubs its back, posts itself behind Pantagleize.)* I've always admired the army. The police, on the other hand, are . . . creepy.

CREEP/CORPSE: So you do not like the police?

PANTAGLEIZE: *(Starts.)* — There was a corpse, here.

CREEP: Goodness, where can it have gone?

PANTAGLEIZE: *(Shrugs.)* Elsewhere, perhaps. God knows it's not safe here. But . . . wasn't that fat cadaver you?

CREEP: Voila, — a resurrection.

PANTAGLEIZE: *(Shakes Creep's hand.)* Congratulations on your recovery. You look familiar, actually. This morning . . . a little cafe? Enchanté. Yes. How've you been?

CREEP: Not bad, thanks. Oh, I did, in the course of the day, receive a blow on the head. I was left for dead.

PANTAGLEIZE: Oh, the wickedness!

CREEP: And you, dear sir?

PANTAGLEIZE: A touch of nerves — bullets are stressful. *(Creep nods.)* Otherwise, fine . . . I got rich today.

CREEP: Aha! Can we go halves?

PANTAGLEIZE: Unfortunately —

CREEP: — You won't go halves. Ah . . . your name —

PANTAGLEIZE: — Hasn't changed. Pantagleize.

CREEP: Creep here. I've had the pleasure of meeting you several times today, a day some called "lovely"! I ran into you on a street lamp, and again, going into a bank. I heard you delivering a speech in a bar where a certain committee was sitting. Oh, yes, I believe I bumped into you in the room of a Jewess.

PANTAGLEIZE: *(Surprised.)* Indeed, you're remarkably observant, sir.

CREEP: Elementary! And: Happy Birthday!

PANTAGLEIZE: You're too kind. *(Pause.)* The day has been like a dream . . . so strange.

CREEP: It was only a small revolution.

PANTAGLEIZE: But it was a real one?

CREEP: Near enough. During which you showed great courage, sir.

PANTAGLEIZE: You flatter me, sir.

CREEP: Alas, I have only one regret. That your destiny must separate us. A pity: With your looks and your talent, I might have made something of you on the police force.

PANTAGLEIZE: You honor me.

CREEP: Yes sir, you've got everything it takes, even the umbrella. Where is your umbrella, by the way?

PANTAGLEIZE: Here. *(Instinctively he clutches the valise tighter.)*

CREEP: That? That's a valise. What's inside, may I ask?

PANTAGLEIZE: Nothing . . . a little jewelry.

CREEP: What? No cigars? I could use a good cigar.

PANTAGLEIZE: No, but if you'd like to come along to my desert island, we can smoke oriental pipes and chew on drowsy plants. *(Running.)* Bring your favorite recipe, a good book, and a scouting knife.

CREEP: Wait!

PANTAGLEIZE: You're after my valise — you really oughtn't you know.
(He moves to right. A burst of fire stops him.)

PANTAGLEIZE: Ah, more bullets.

CREEP: You draw them to you.

PANTAGLEIZE: I'll find other roads. *(He tries the left. Bullets.)* The artillery is not courteous, not kind. *(He comes back center, Creep too. They bump into each other.)* We are both risking our lives, sir.

CREEP: True, we must learn to be more careful.

PANTAGLEIZE: Help each other in time of need. Blood brothers. I'll hide behind you.
(The shooting is redoubled.)

CREEP: Where are you going?

PANTAGLEIZE: I'd hate to see you shot in the back.
(Creep moves behind him.)

CREEP: Blood brother.

(He hits Pantagleize on the back of the head. Creep takes the valise, drags Pantagleize.)

PANTAGLEIZE: Look at the stars — the stars! No, no, the world has turned upside down — it's my diamonds that have rolled up into the sky. Don't lose me on the way.

CREEP: Count on me.

(They go out, Creep dragging Pantagleize. Blackout.)

SCENE NINE

A bare room. A table. Autopsy of Rachel.

FIRST SOLDIER: There was a soldier boy,

SECOND SOLDIER: Who did his girl enjoy,

FIRST: And when he marched away,

SECOND: His girl, she cried all day,

TOGETHER: Come back to me, O soldier true
And screw me like you used to do.
(They march a few steps more, sing the next verse.)
There was a soldier boy
The foe he did destroy
He rose high in the ranks
And thus he earned his thanks

ALL: Come back to me, O soldier true
And screw me like you used to do.
(A bugle call outside. The two soldiers snap to attention. A light from above hits the tribunal table. The Distinguished Counsel enters.)

DISTINGUISHED COUNSEL: Hello, boys. Do you think this evening's hearing will be over by midnight? They're expecting me at the Club. We shall try for brevity. By the way, what was that you were singing? *(Sings.)* There was a soldier boy . . .

FIRST SOLDIER: There was a soldier boy,

SECOND: Who killing did enjoy,

FIRST: He piled the corpses high,

SECOND: They mounted to the sky,

EVERYONE: Come back to me, O soldier true
And screw me like you used to do.
(Tribunal members march in.)

DISTINGUISHED COUNSEL: Gentlemen of the tribunal, my humble respects. *(The Generalissimo enters silently.)* We have an unpleasant task before us, judging these scoundrels. But duty, gentlemen, duty! *(The Distinguished Counsel gives a grin of utter salaciousness.)* Good. We understand each other. *(Pause.)*

GENERALISSIMO: The tribunal is now in session. I demand the full rigor of law in sentencing these swine! —

DISTINGUISHED COUNSEL: No, no, Generalissimo, we can't sentence until we have tried them. My job — I have to appear as counsel, first. Well, that's what it says in the book!

GENERALISSIMO: The book! You — and this tribunal — are mere pomp and decorum. I am the law! Book! *(To the sentries.)* Bring them in one at a time. *(Gong.)* First!

(Blank is flung in, whimpering.)

BLANK: Mercy, mercy, I'll never do it again!

GENERALISSIMO: Well, well, well, who is this? *(He circles Blank, and the tribunal follows, asking the same question.)* Speak dog! What do you do?

BLANK: I — I — I am a poet.

GENERALISSIMO: Perhaps you misunderstand, what do you do for a living?

BLANK: I'm a poet, a modern poet. My name is Blank . . . *(Panicked smile.)* I write in blank verse, get it?

GENERALISSIMO: *(With a kick.)* Enough! *(The tribunal murmurs "enough!," kicks, returns to table.)*

GENERALISSIMO: So, cur, a revolutionary poet?

BLANK: *(Giggles in terror.)* Yes, sir. Right. "Blank verse?"

GENERALISSIMO: Not content with overthrowing society, you must overthrow syntax, too! Recite one of your . . . "modern" poems, please.

BLANK: *(In one terrified breath.)* Sip on the crater is the first confession of the chilled pumpkin losing all its stuffed marrow the lovely child sucking and the mauve star of the Arab had melted the worm lonely and blue —

GENERALISSIMO: Enough! *(The tribunal echoes him.)* "Sucking the mauve star of —" Decadent art! Art to be burned. Here is poetry *(He takes a heroic stance.)*

Across the sky the thunders crack,
The trumpet calls, "Attack, attack!"
And then the soldier, bold at heart —
Di dum di dum di dum di dum —

That's poetry! Yours is not fit to be recited in a pigpen.

BLANK: Hey, I'm sorry.

GENERALISSIMO: You're mixed up with this Provisional Committee, yes? *(Blank sighs in resignation.)* Defend yourself, cur!

BLANK: I was only . . . it looked like a lot of laughs.

GENERALISSIMO: Ha, ha. *(The tribunal echoes his "Ha, ha.")*

DISTINGUISHED COUNSEL: Gentlemen, regard this youth! No revolutionary, but, rather, a child of our time, brainwashed by pernicious literature, whose only rebellion is against his parents. Send him back home — he'll be a good boy. Cut his hair, don't spare the rod, and by all means revoke his poetic license. But send him home!

GENERALISSIMO: *(To Distinguished Counsel.)* Most moving . . . touching. But the charge remains! He has attempted revolt against the state! Administer the punishment laid out! *(He bangs on the table. The tribunal bangs on the table.)*

BLANK: P-punishment? Don't punish me — not even with a flower!

DISTINGUISHED COUNSEL: Don't worry, lad, they won't do it with a flower.

BLANK: Help, they're going to — *(One of the soldiers seizes him, begins to drag him off.)* God damn you — God damn you all.

DISTINGUISHED COUNSEL: Courage!

BLANK: *(Going.)* FUCK YOU!

GENERALISSIMO: Next *(Gong.)* Speed it up!

(Banger limps in, wild and arrogant.)

GENERALISSIMO: Another revolutionary minister? We'd have a lame government with you at the helm. Ha. Ha. Ha. *(The tribunal echoes his laughter.)*

BANGER: Shit!

GENERALISSIMO: You acknowledge taking part in —

BANGER: — Shit!

GENERALISSIMO: Precisely. What have you to say in your defense?

BANGER: Shit! And shit again!

GENERALISSIMO: Eloquent . . . but lacking in legal — *(To Distinguished Counsel.)* Lawyer, will you —

DISTINGUISHED COUNSEL: *(Quickly to Banger.)* What shall I say in your defense?

BANGER: Shit!

DISTINGUISHED COUNSEL: You see, gentlemen, he knows only his name and his destination. I beg you, put no obstacle in his way —

(A volley of shots outside.)

GENERALISSIMO: To the wall! *(The dismissing gesture is parroted by tribunal.)*

BANGER: To — shit! *(He is marched out.)*

GENERALISSIMO: Next. Next!

(Bamboola enters. Distinguished Counsel sees him and does a double take.)

DISTINGUISHED COUNSEL: Good grief!

GENERALISSIMO: *(Reading from a folder.)* Fraud . . . white slavery . . . counterfeiting . . . criminal assault . . . murder . . . aha, here it is, "revolution."

BAMBOOLA: Bamboola good nigger. There is another, a doppleganger. Bad Bamboola. I good, he bad.

GENERALISSIMO: And what has good Bamboola been doing since dawn?

BAMBOOLA: Nothing, Boss. A leisurely stroll. I visited the museums, took in the parade for a while, then a chamber music concert —

GENERALISSIMO: And at the Objective Bar?

BAMBOOLA: A few whiskeys and soda, a dance or two. Black man love to dance! *(A volley of shots outside.)*

BAMBOOLA: No . . . not die . . . Bamboola good nigger.

GENERALISSIMO: *(Reading.)* A fine collection of weapons in your arsenal. Rifles: one hundred and forty-seven. Hand guns: forty-eight. Machine guns: twelve. You have a weakness for weaponry, eh?

BAMBOOLA: *(Helpfully.)* I could join the police.

GENERALISSIMO: Lawyer!

(Bamboola sees Distinguished Gentleman for the first time.)

DISTINGUISHED COUNSEL: I crave the indulgence of the Tribunal. Bamboola, he good nigger. I rest my case.

GENERALISSIMO: The legal penalty! *(He pounds on the table, the Tribunal follows suit.)*

(The soldiers start to lay hands on Bamboola. He shakes them off, pulls himself up.)

BAMBOOLA: Don't touch me! *(They move toward him again.)* I said, don't sully me with your greasy white hands! — Keep away! My holy rage makes me too pure to suffer your touch! Keep off scum, yes! *(He turns back to Generalissimo.)* Watch me go!

(He walks off, followed at some distance by soldiers.)

GENERALISSIMO: Next. Next!

(After a moment, Innocenti walks in calmly.)

GENERALISSIMO: You? Name? Profession?

INNOCENTI: Innocenti. Waiter.

GENERALISSIMO: Is that an alias?

INNOCENTI: Let's say . . . yes.

GENERALISSIMO: And you are not a waiter, you are, in fact, a doctor of law, a former university professor. What are you doing before this tribunal, mixed up with a bunch of criminals?

INNOCENTI: *(Shrug.)* My convictions.

GENERALISSIMO: Intelligent men don't have convictions. You're a revolutionary? You admit it? *(Innocenti nods.)*

GENERALISSIMO: You don't deny you were mixed up in this revolution?

INNOCENTI: I was mixed up in this revolution — on principle, yes? Revolution is my sole ideal. Now, I do not hide the fact that I find this particular revolution unfortunate — it has miscarried, as it was doomed to. But that in itself is a good thing for the revolutionary ideal. And that ideal . . . is a never-ending process of revolution, it is an anarchic eruption which comes again and again, to wash in blood a society which is by nature corrupt! So. All that remains is for me to share the fate of my comrades, if you please.

GENERALISSIMO: You are asking for death?

INNOCENTI: Yes, and I wouldn't mind a cigarette. *(He takes a cigarette from Generalissimo.)* My death will save me from the humiliating act of suicide. *(He puts the cigarette out.)*

GENERALISSIMO: Lawyer, offer your services to this gentleman —

INNOCENTI: Don't bother, just show me the way out. *(Going, he turns back, smiles sweetly at Generalissimo.)*

DISTINGUISHED COUNSEL: *(Bewildered.)* To the left, sir.

INNOCENTI: Naturally. My dear enemy, next time the ocean will be filled with your blood. *(He exits. Troubled silence.)*

GENERALISSIMO: Painful. *(He sighs.)* The session is over gentlemen. *(The tribunal rises.)* It's like surgery. If the limb is diseased . . . *(He mimes ax, the tribunal does the same.)* Thank you for attending.

(Creep enters with Pantagleize. Creep carries the valise, the umbrella, and the street lamp.)

DISTINGUISHED COUNSEL: Too late, they're not trying any more today.

CREEP: We're set down for this session.

GENERALISSIMO: Well, take your places and be quick about it. *(The tribunal sits down.)*

CREEP: I've caught a rare bird, sir, take it from Creep. This one's an oddball.

GENERALISSIMO: *(Turns, impressed.)* Ah, so you are the famous Creep. Your conduct has been superb. Bravo. *(He claps his hands. Echo from the tribunal.)* Let's have a closer look at your prize. *(He circles Pantagleize.)* Creep, you've made some mistake. This is a clown.

CREEP: *(Offended.)* Clown? Tremble, Generalissimo, tremble, for you see before you the most dangerous arch-criminal of history. Examine him well: full-face, three-quarter view, profile. It is enough to strike terror in the

heart of a Goliath! Gentlemen, it was he who gave the signal for the revolution to start — whisper his name! *(He whispers.)* Pantagleize!
(General amazement, horror. Pantagleize looks up at last, at his name, sees them staring at him.)

PANTAGLEIZE: Delighted to meet you all.

CREEP: Pantagleize! *(He sets up the street lamp.)* Do you recognize this illuminating device? Yes. Did you climb on it for an oration? Yes. What did you say to the crowd from your perch above the city?

PANTAGLEIZE: I said, "Oh, what a lovely day."
(General sensation.)

CREEP: After which you received orders from a Jewess. After which you went to the bank. After which you appeared at the Provisional Committee's meeting place, the Objective Bar, where you were appointed minister and delivered a speech.

PANTAGLEIZE: What's happened to my friends, please?

GENERALISSIMO: Ha! So you admit it!

CREEP: And you recognize this object? *(He holds up the umbrella.)*

PANTAGLEIZE: Ah, found again! Wherever did I leave it? *(He takes the umbrella, cradles it to him.)*

GENERALISSIMO: His behavior is baffling. Furthermore, our records make no mention of him —

PANTAGLEIZE: Pantagleize.

GENERALISSIMO: Traitor!

PANTAGLEIZE: Me? No, indeed, I write for a fashion magazine.

GENERALISSIMO: Explain, then. What do you know?

PANTAGLEIZE: *(He gives an eloquent shrug.)* What do I know? I know only that I know nothing. *(Volley of shots.)* I know that noise, that's how people amuse themselves on such a peaceful night.

GENERALISSIMO: Facts, please. You admit you used that phrase, "What a lovely day." You knew its significance?

PANTAGLEIZE: It's my custom to be witty . . . the art of the epigram —

DISTINGUISHED COUNSEL: We cannot continue this. The man's a lunatic.

GENERALISSIMO: You think so? On the contrary, I find him sane, even dangerous!

DISTINGUISHED COUNSEL: He understands nothing — he's nature's accident, an incredible innocent.
(Pantagleize looks up in mid-yawn.)

PANTAGLEIZE: Imbecile.

DISTINGUISHED COUNSEL: I am saying that this man is stupid!

GENERALISSIMO: And I maintain that he's acting stupidly.

PANTAGLEIZE: Let me reconcile you. The issue of stupidity is merely relative. According to some I'm a bonafide imbecile, according to others, a superman. I have been called philosopher, journalist, rioter, robber, minister of gymnastics, millionaire, lover. What do I call myself? *(He thinks for a minute.)* Solitary. Lost. She is dead, gentlemen, dead. Twisted and bleeding — that's how she last appeared to me. Young girls should not die that way!

DISTINGUISHED COUNSEL: You see, he's mad.

GENERALISSIMO: Society wouldn't lose much if it lost you.

PANTAGLEIZE: Oh, I was planning to bid it farewell, anyway, nevermore to return.

GENERALISSIMO: Bon voyage, then. *(He bows, rises.)* Gentlemen, I believe . . . the prescribed . . .
(His voice trails away. The tribunal rises. Follows him off.)

PANTAGLEIZE: He has a way of not completing his conversations.

DISTINGUISHED COUNSEL: Well, client . . . *(Distinguished Counsel shakes Pantagleize's hand.)*

PANTAGLEIZE: Which way out?

CREEP: That way.

PANTAGLEIZE: And can I trouble you . . . the time?

CREEP: A quarter to midnight.

PANTAGLEIZE: Past my bedtime. Thank you. We certainly kept running into each other today, but we remain good friends in spite of it, eh? *(He shakes Creep's hand.)* I'll drop you a postcard from my island. The exit? *(A soldier pushes him out left.)*
(Afterward, Creep and the Distinguished Counsel look at each other, and laugh. Creep goes out right.)

DISTINGUISHED COUNSEL: Well, this day's over, I hope. Lovely day. Hey, soldier, how did that song go? *(He leaves.)*

FIRST SOLDIER: That soldier boy so true

SECOND: Wrote to the girl he knew

FIRST: Three cheers and hip hooray

SECOND: I've won the war, today.
(Blackout.)

EPILOGUE

A yard, bare and dark and cold. Four bodies lie against the wall, looking like fallen scarecrows. An officer, wrapped in a long cloak and carrying a lantern, moves among the bodies. A shadow glides in. It is the Generalissimo. The Officer starts.

GENERALISSIMO: Captain!

OFFICER: Who goes there!

GENERALISSIMO: Come over here.

OFFICER: *(Nervous laugh.)* General!

GENERALISSIMO: All finished? *(The Officer shines his lantern on the bodies.)* How did they die?

OFFICER: It was comical, sir. They looked like puppets on strings! Jerked about like dancers . . . sleepwalkers. Yes sir, a man's soon done for!

GENERALISSIMO: Quite. *(Pause.)* Chilly for May.

OFFICER: A touch of snow. My feet are cold.

GENERALISSIMO: It will warm up.

OFFICER: Yes, sir.

GENERALISSIMO: Where's the firing squad?

OFFICER: Dismissed for the night.

GENERALISSIMO: Call them back.

OFFICER: But — *(He sighs, shouts.)* Sound the fall-in!

SOLDIER: *(Off.)* Fall in! Bugler, fall in!

GENERALISSIMO: Well . . .

(He exits. A bugle sounds in the distance. A soldier enters.)

OFFICER: Where's the man?

SOLDIER: Behind me.

OFFICER: Wait for the squad — I'll be right back.

SOLDIER: *(To Pantagleize.)* Come along, friend. It's not far.

PANTAGLEIZE: *(Off.)* I'm cold. Lovely night, but frosty. *(He enters.)*

SOLDIER: Worried about catching cold? *(He laughs.)* Walk around a bit . . . exercise to get the blood circulating.

PANTAGLEIZE: Good advice. Walking warms you up. *(He stumbles in the dark.)* How black it is — can you see in this blackness? *(He shivers.)* I'm chilled to the bone! Even though I'm sweating. And there's that stench, again. How I want to sleep! *(He shivers again.)* Courage! It won't be long — I'm planning to take a trip, far away. I've made up my mind to do it — you won't see me around any more. My last night in Europe . . . tomorrow, the ocean . . . then another world! I'll be dozing on a peaceful island — *(He bumps into a body.)* Who's there? *(He bends down.)* Ho! It's you . . . my friends. What, asleep? Collapsed like broken puppets! But I asked you to follow me, and you wouldn't. You are not men of good will . . . still, I love you. Are you dreaming? What are you dreaming of? The fight is over. Aren't you going to get up again? *(Silence.)* I'm tempted to sleep with you, lost in an egalitarian darkness. *(He moves away.)* But it smells like a butcher shop here, and I cannot live with memories any longer. No, I'll leave — excuse me.

VOICE: Squad, halt!

PANTAGLEIZE: *(Listens.)* Soldiers!

OFFICER: *(Sees Pantagleize.)* Well, my friend.

PANTAGLEIZE: I beg your pardon?

OFFICER: You've dropped your umbrella.

PANTAGLEIZE: Have I? *(He stoops to pick it up.)* Thank you, officer. And could I trouble you to show me a practical way out of here? It's so dark.

OFFICER: *(Laughs.)* Right in front of you. Right, you're getting close . . . a little that way. Yes, you're getting toward the edge.

PANTAGLEIZE: Thank you. I don't see it . . .

OFFICER: Feel for the edge, it's there. *(Harshly.)* Squad, present!

PANTAGLEIZE: *(Turns.)* Yes?

OFFICER: Fire! *(Discharge. Flash. Silence.)* Shoulder arms/about-face/forward march.

OFFICER: Six bullets. Poor imbecile! *(He lights a cigarette.)*

PANTAGLEIZE: Oh . . . Oh . . . The sky has fallen on my head! I've been damaged, somehow. I've made up my mind. Friends — I'll come and sleep with you.

OFFICER: Still talking?

PANTAGLEIZE: The sky has fallen on my head! *(He supports himself on his elbows.)* Good evening, sir . . . I've had a little accident. I must tell you . . . I met a girl today, a very nice girl. So beautiful, so disturbing, so sorrowful that you would say she was humanity itself . . .

OFFICER: I know what you need.

(He pulls out a revolver, moves in back of Pantagleize.)

PANTAGLEIZE: It was a lovely . . .

(The Officer fires the revolver into the back of Pantagleize's head. The lights black out. Twelve bells from a church tower.)

END OF PLAY

Marriage

AN ABSOLUTELY INCREDIBLE EVENT IN TWO ACTS

Translated from the Play by
Nikolai Gogol

To the memory of my mother, Esther Field

From left to right: Kochkariev (Alvin Epstein), Podkoloisin (Peter Michael Goetz, standing), Zhevakin (Randall Duk Kim), Agafya (Cara Duff-McCormick), Anuchkin (Jake Dengel), Poach'tegg (Jon Cranney), and Dunyashka (Margaret Silk, standing) in a scene from the 1978 Guthrie Theater production of Gogol's *Marriage* adapted by Barbara Field and directed by Anatoly Efros, with set and costume design by Valery Leventhal. Photo credit: Pat Swifka.

CONTEXTUAL NOTES ON *MARRIAGE*

Alvin Epstein started his tenure as the Guthrie's Artistic Director by inviting the renowned Soviet artist Anatoly Efros to direct his acclaimed production of Nikolai Gogol's *Marriage* on our stage, which was to open on October 18, 1978. Alvin invited me to do the translation. At the time I neither spoke nor read Russian; I contracted a literal translation and began taking Russian lessons. I knew that because Efros spoke no English, my English-language acting text must be as close to the Russian original as possible. Hence, *Marriage* as it appears here is really not an adaptation at all, but a rather strict translation. All the variations in the script are from Efros' wonderfully theatrical soul.

No one knew what to expect when Efros arrived. The Cold War was still going strong. He was accompanied by an official interpreter (who eventually confessed that she was there to "keep an eye on" Efros). Efros also brought the superb Bolshoi Theater designer, Valery Leventhal.

There never was a "first reading" of the script. Efros pulled the actors out of their seats and kept them racing from day one. He explained the technique he wanted for acting the play: "The words are funny. But the actors must play it seriously. You must play it as if it were *Oedipus* or *Hamlet*." In rehearsal, nothing was held in reserve, and the effect was dizzying . . . and exhausting. Efros had been allowed an eight-week rehearsal period, but we only did two or three hours of rehearsal a day — everyone was too tired to do more. Language differences began to melt away, and by the third week of work, the actors began to grasp his meaning before the translators could utter it.

Gogol was born in 1809. *Marriage: An Absolutely Incredible Event in Two Acts* premiered in 1842, the same year that his great novel *Dead Souls* was published. His highly stylized language was combined with a vision of the human condition that was at once tragic and comic. In his idiosyncratic characters, he depicted the excesses of mankind with a clarity that sometimes bordered on the surreal. His grotesque sense of situation made him, in both his stories and plays, a direct forebearer of the modern Absurdists.

MARRIAGE
Adapted for The Guthrie Theater by Barbara Field

Director .... Anatoly Efros
Scenic and Costume Designer .... Valery Leventhal
Lighting Designer .... Ronald M. Bundt
Stage Manager .... Michael Facius
Interpreter/U.S.A. .... Julia Kocich
Interpreter/U.S.S.R. .... Elena Perfilova
Design Coordinator .... Jim Guenther

CAST

AGAFYA .... Cara Duff-MacCormick
IVAN KUZMICH PODKOLIOSIN .... Peter Michael Goetz
STEPAN .... David Cecsarini
FIOKLA .... Barbara Bryne
ILYA FOMICH KOCHKARIEV .... Alvin Epstein
ARINA .... Rosemary Hartup
DUNYASHKA .... Margaret Silk
IVAN PAVLOVICH POACH'TEGG .... Jon Cranney
NIKANOR IVANOVICH ANUCHKIN .... Jake Dengel
BALTAZAR BALTAZROVICH ZHEVAKIN .... Randall Duk Kim
THE MERCHANT .... Don R. Fallbeck
AKINF STEPANOVICH PANTELEYEV .... Peter MacNichol

SETTING
The action of the play takes place in St. Petersburg during a day in early spring
in the nineteenth century.

MARRIAGE

PROLOGUE

The stage is empty, except for a very long banquet table that is covered in snowy white linen and laden with a variety of festive food, including a wedding cake and several bottles of champagne. Agafya enters in her wedding gown. She looks around shyly, whirls in a circle, raptly watching her skirt billow. Podkoliosin enters after a moment. She feigns surprise. He begins to pursue her around the table — a little game. At one point he ducks under the table, and she searches for him, growing alarmed. Finally, he leaps out, startling her. He catches hold of her little hand, which he holds to his breast for a moment, then releases it. In a dream of happiness, she whirls around by herself and whirls offstage. Podkoliosin stares at his hand, the one which had captured hers, looks around for her, but she is gone. The lights fade.

ACT I
SCENE ONE

A bachelor's room. Podkoliosin alone, lying on a sofa, smoking a pipe.

PODKOLIOSIN: Yes indeed, when you really take the time to think it over, you realize that Man must come to it, in the end. Man must marry. Yes indeed, you go on and on and on . . . and on, living in filth, until you're sick to death of it! I've let winter slip away. Ash Wednesday's around the corner. The matchmaker's been showing up for three months. Honestly, I'm beginning to be ashamed of myself—hey, Stepan! *(Stepan, a surly servant, appears.)* Has the matchmaker shown up yet?

STEPAN: No one's showed up.

PODKOLIOSIN: But you've been to the tailor, right?

STEPAN: Right.

PODKOLIOSIN: And he's working on my tailcoat?

STEPAN: Right.

PODKOLIOSIN: How far has he got?

STEPAN: Far enough. He's starting the buttonholes.

PODKOLIOSIN: He didn't ask why your gentleman needs a new tailcoat?

STEPAN: Nope.

PODKOLIOSIN: He didn't ask, maybe, if your gentleman's planning to get married?

STEPAN: He didn't say a word.

PODKOLIOSIN: But you saw other tailcoats, there? He's working for others, as well?

STEPAN: There are lots of tailcoats hanging in his shop.

PODKOLIOSIN: But they're not as fine as mine?

STEPAN: Nope, they're not like yours.

PODKOLIOSIN: Good. —And the tailor didn't ask why the gentleman needed such an unusually fine tailcoat?

STEPAN: Nope.

PODKOLIOSIN: He didn't utter a word? For instance: "So, I hear Podkoliosin's thinking of marriage."

STEPAN: Not a word.

PODKOLIOSIN: You don't say. — But you mentioned my rank to him, and the location of my office?

STEPAN: Right.

PODKOLIOSIN: What did he say to that?

STEPAN: He said, "I'll speed it up."

PODKOLIOSIN: Good. Good. You may go. *(Stepan goes.)* In my opinion, there's nothing as grand as a black tailcoat. Yes indeed. Colors may suit petty officials, and mere clerks; but those of higher rank must maintain a certain . . . a certain . . . a certain . . . what-do-you-call-it? *(He grows fearful and agitated .)* — my God, I've forgotten the right word!! *(He tries to compose himself.)* Yes indeed, Podkoliosin, a Court Councilor is as good as a Colonel any day — only without the epaulets. Hey, Stepan! *(Stepan enters.)* Did you buy my shoe polish?

STEPAN: I bought it.

PODKOLIOSIN: Did you get it in that little shop in Voszhnesenski Street?

STEPAN: Right.

PODKOLIOSIN: Is it any good?

STEPAN: Good enough.

PODKOLIOSIN: You've tried polishing my boots?

STEPAN: Right.

PODKOLIOSIN: And they shine?

STEPAN: Enough.

PODKOLIOSIN: And when he sold you the polish, he didn't ask what on earth your gentleman wanted it for?

STEPAN: Nope.

PODKOLIOSIN: He didn't suggest . . . he didn't hint . . . that your gentleman might be thinking of getting married?

STEPAN: He didn't say a word.

PODKOLIOSIN: Well. Well well. You may go, Stepan. *(Stepan goes.)* Boots might look like a trivial part of one's life, but if they weren't stitched with the best thread, if they weren't well-polished, one simply wouldn't be treated with proper respect in society. No indeed. — And there's the matter of bunions. I can stand anything, God knows, but I can't stand bunions! Hey, Stepan!

(Stepan appears.)

STEPAN: You called?

PODKOLIOSIN: Did you tell the shoemaker not to give me bunions?

STEPAN: Of course.

PODKOLIOSIN: What did he say to that?

STEPAN: He said, "All right." *(Stepan goes.)*

PODKOLIOSIN: The fuss and bother connected with this whole marriage business — to hell with it! Do this, do that, don't forget the other — getting married is easier said than done. Hey, Stepan — *(Stepan enters.)* I wanted to ask you —

STEPAN: — The old woman's here.

PODKOLIOSIN: She is? Show her in. *(Stepan goes.)* Yes, indeed, when you think of it, this marriage business is too much! *(Fiokla enters.)* Ah, here you are! Come in, come in, Fiokla Ivanovna. How are things progressing? Pull up a chair and tell me everything. What's her name again, Masha?

FIOKLA:. Agafya. Agafya Tikhonovna.

PODKOLIOSIN: Oh yes, Agafya Tikhonovna. She's a fortyish spinster, right?

FIOKLA: Not at all, not at all. Once you marry her, you'll learn to love her more each day. You'll thank God for giving her to you.

PODKOLIOSIN: You're a liar, Fiokla.

FIOKLA: I'm too old to lie. Young dogs tell lies.

PODKOLIOSIN: Now tell me about her dowry . . . again.

FIOKLA: *(By rote.)* The dowry: a brick house in the Moscow district — two stories high, fully occupied. It's a treasure, that house, with such tenants! One tenant pays seven hundred a year in rent. Then there's a beer cellar in the basement that's a real social gathering place. And two annexes, one wood, the other on a brick foundation — four hundred a year in rent, each. Then there's a vegetable garden in the Viborg district — a greengrocer's been raising cabbages there for three years; he's a decent man, doesn't touch a drop; and he's got three sons, two already married, and the baby — the greengrocer says, "He's still young, let him help in the shop for a while." He minds the shop, see?

PODKOLIOSIN: And what about her, what's she really like?

FIOKLA: A prize! Pink and white, like milk mixed with blood. Such a beauty — words fail me! From this moment on, if you're not fully satisfied — *(She draws her finger across her throat.)* You'll never stop thanking me. "Fiokla, I'll never be able to thank you enough."

PODKOLIOSIN: Maybe. But on the other hand, she's not exactly an admiral's daughter —

FIOKLA: — She's the daughter of a merchant, a third-guild merchant! An admiral would be proud to marry her. But she's not interested in just anyone. No merchants for her. "For me," she says, "outward appearances are unimportant. Who cares if he's not handsome? It's the inner man that counts. He must be a "gentleman." Yes indeed, she's got real class—you should hear her silks crackling on a Sunday! She's a jewel, a princess!

PODKOLIOSIN: Yes, indeed. But I'm a Court Councilor, if you take my meaning —

FIOKLA: She's already been offered one Court Councilor, but she turned him down flat . . . just didn't take to him. Well, he was a touch peculiar — whenever he opened his mouth he lied. I don't know what God had in mind when he made him. But the poor fellow couldn't help himself, he couldn't stop lying. It was God's will.

PODKOLIOSIN: Tell me . . . have you got anyone beside her?

FIOKLA: What's wrong with her?

PODKOLIOSIN: I mean, is she the best you've got?

FIOKLA: Go! Wander the wide world! You won't find her equal.

PODKOLIOSIN: Well . . . I'll think it over, Fiokla, my sweet. I'll think it over. Come back day after tomorrow, and we'll talk about it. I'll lie on the sofa, and you'll tell me about her . . . again.

FIOKLA: Just a minute! I've been coming here for three months and how far have we got? All you do is lie around in your bathrobe and puff on that damned pipe!

PODKOLIOSIN: If you think, my good woman, that marriage is a trivial ho-hum affair — if you think it's just, "Hey, Stepan, fetch me my boots!" . . . then . . . then . . . a man's got to ponder. He's got to examine things meticulously.

FIOKLA: Of course, of course, ponder. Examine — this merchandise is worth pondering, I promise. Get your coat on right now, and off we go!

PODKOLIOSIN: Now? It's so gloomy outside. As soon as we leave it'll probably start to rain.

FIOKLA: You know, your hair's turning gray. Soon you won't be able to hold up your part of the bargain, even if you are a Court Councilor! We can do lots better than you, you know — we won't give you a second thought soon.

PODKOLIOSIN: Me?! Gray hair — ??!! I've never noticed any —

FIOKLA: — Of course you've got gray hair, it comes to all men. Check it yourself. Meanwhile, I may turn my attention to this captain — so tall you wouldn't reach to his shoulder, with a voice like a trombone.

PODKOLIOSIN: Liar! Liar! Show me in the mirror, where did you see a gray hair? Hey, Stepan, bring my mirror! No, wait!! I'll get it myself! What next? This is worse than smallpox! *(He gets off the sofa at last, goes. Kochkariev enters.)*

KOCHKARIEV: Where's Podkoliosin? *(He sees Fiokla.)* You! You! You! What are you doing here, you — do you realize what a demon you married me to?!

FIOKLA: Please, marriages are made in heaven.

KOCHKARIEV: But you found my wife in the other place. Send her back there, I beg you.

FIOKLA: You were the one who kept pestering me. "Find me a wife, Fiokla, find me a wife."

KOCHKARIEV: You old she-rat. Anyway, what are you doing here? Say . . . Podkoliosin isn't thinking about . . .

FIOKLA: God has sent me to do good.

KOCHKARIEV: That scoundrel never said a word about it to me. How deceitful of him! *(Podkoliosin enters carrying a mirror. He gazes into it frantically.)*

PODKOLIOSIN: All right, show me the gray hair! You old liar, there's not one gray hair in my head. *(Kochkariev creeps up behind him.)*

KOCHKARIEV: Boo! *(Podkoliosin drops the mirror with a shriek.)*

PODKOLIOSIN: Are you crazy? What a stupid trick — my heart's in my mouth!

KOCHKARIEV: It was a joke.

PODKOLIOSIN: Some joke — you nearly scared me to death. You made me break the mirror. It was very expensive, you know, I bought it in the English Shop.

KOCHKARIEV: I'll buy you another mirror.

PODKOLIOSIN: I can imagine the mirror you'll buy me. It'll make me look ten years older, and distorted to boot.

KOCHKARIEV: Listen, I'm the one who should be angry. You've been keeping secrets from your best friend. You've decided to get married.

PODKOLIOSIN: Quite wrong, I haven't decided a thing.

KOCHKARIEV: *(He points to Fiokla.)* Here's the evidence, the proof. Why else would this old bird roost here? Not that there's anything wrong with marriage, no indeed. It's a man's Christian duty, it's a man's patriotic duty. But it's a matter I shall take into my own hands. *(To Fiokla.)* Well, tell me: who, when, where, and so on. Is she the daughter of a nobleman? Of a civil servant? A shopkeeper? What's her name? Out with it!

FIOKLA: Agafya Tikhonovna.

KOCHKARIEV: Agafya Tikhonovna Brandakhlistov?

FIOKLA: No, Agafya Tikhonovna Kuperdiagina.

KOCHKARIEV: Oh yes, of course. And she lives in Seven-Shop Street?

FIOKLA: Wrong again, she lives in Soap Street, near the Peski district.

KOCHKARIEV: Of course, in Soap Street! The small wooden house just behind the store?

FIOKLA: Not behind the store, above the beer cellar.

KOCHKARIEV: Above the beer cellar? I don't know her.

FIOKLA: You see, you turn into Soap Street, then on your right you see a sentry box, and you go past the sentry box, and on your left, right in front of your eyes, you see a wooden house — that's where the dressmaker lives, the one who used to be the Senator's mistress? Anyway, you go past her, and next door you see a brick house. That's where she lives. I mean the bride, Agafya Tikhonovna.

KOCHKARIEV: Why, thank you very much. I can take the reins now, leave it to me. Your services are no longer needed.

FIOKLA: What?! You want to arrange this marriage yourself?!

KOCHKARIEV: That's it, by myself. You needn't meddle any longer.

FIOKLA: Why, you shameless son of a bitch! That's no job for a man! Step aside, vermin, step aside!

KOCHKARIEV: You'd better go peacefully. Each to his own task, right? Clear out, granny!

FIOKLA: Taking the bread out of my mouth! You—atheist! *(She exits in a rage.)*

KOCHKARIEV: Well, brother, we mustn't waste any time. Let's go.

PODKOLIOSIN: Wait —! Nothing's settled! I've just started to think things over.

KOCHKARIEV: Nonsense, don't be afraid. I'll marry you off so fast you won't even know what's happened. Let's go meet the bride and you'll see how painless it is.

PODKOLIOSIN: You mean — go now?

KOCHKARIEV: Why not? Look, see what comes of not being married? Look at this room: unpolished boots, tobacco all over the table, and you! You lie on the couch like a sloth, turning from side to side.

PODKOLIOSIN: I admit it, Kochkariev, there's no sense of order in my life.

KOCHKARIEV: But once you've got a wife, you'll never recognize the place . . . or yourself. You'll have a nice couch over here, with a cunning lapdog lying on the cushions. Picture yourself on the couch, listening to an adorable little canary in a cage, when suddenly — the lady of the house comes to sit by you, with her soft dainty hands.

PODKOLIOSIN: Soft, dainty hands? Yes . . . yes, they're as soft as milk . . .

KOCHKARIEV: And they don't have just hands, you know, they have . . . God knows what!

PODKOLIOSIN: I'd like it . . . a little lady sitting next to me.

KOCHKARIEV: You've got the picture! We have only to work things out, you needn't worry about a thing — the wedding supper, and so on — I'll take care of everything. Champagne — a dozen bottles won't be enough! And Madeira — half-dozen at least. The bride must have a whole flock of aunts, and they mustn't be served cheap Rhine wine, must they? Now as far as the supper is concerned, I know a caterer — he fills you up! You can't even get out of your chair!

PODKOLIOSIN: Calm down, Kochkariev, you're racing ahead as if we were already at the altar!

KOCHKARIEV: Why retreat now? You agree, don't you?

PODKOLIOSIN: Not exactly. Not yet. No, I haven't agreed at all.

KOCHKARIEV: But you said not one minute ago —

PODKOLIOSIN: — I only said it mightn't be a bad idea.

KOCHKARIEV: But we just worked it out. What's the matter, don't you like the idea of marriage?

PODKOLIOSIN: No, I like the idea, but —

KOCHKARIEV: So? What's wrong with you?

PODKOLIOSIN: Nothing. It's just . . . strange.

KOCHKARIEV: What's strange?

PODKOLIOSIN: It is strange. I was always a bachelor; and then, in a flash, I'm married!

KOCHKARIEV: You ought to be ashamed! I see I'll have to have a heart-to-heart talk with you, father to son. Look at yourself. Closely, like you're looking at me. What do you see? Who are you? No, you don't have the answer, there is no answer. What do you live for? Examine yourself in the mirror. What do you see? The same bored, stupid face, and not much else. But now, imagine yourself: children surrounding you — two, three, maybe half a dozen — all exactly like you. Peas in a pod. Right now, you're nothing but an unmarried Court Councilor. But picture yourself at the center of a family of teeny-weeny civil servants, itsy-bitsy court councilors, all pulling on your whiskers. And you'll be barking at them, barking like a dog, bow wow wow! What could be lovelier?

PODKOLIOSIN: But if they turn into little monsters, they'll wreck everything. They'll mix up all my legal papers.

KOCHKARIEV: Let them mix — remember, they look just like you.

PODKOLIOSIN: Damn, it's funny . . . little ones, looking just like me!

KOCHKARIEV: Funny? It's wonderful. Let's go, then.

PODKOLIOSIN: All right, let's go.

KOCHKARIEV: Stepan! Stepan! Help your master! We've got to get him dressed — fast! *(Stepan enters.)*

PODKOLIOSIN: Wait, I think I ought to wear my white vest.

KOCHKARIEV: Don't bother with that now.

PODKOLIOSIN: Damned laundress didn't starch my collar! Again! It won't stand up properly. Tell her, Stepan, tell her if she continues doing my laundry like this I'll find someone new. She carries on with her boyfriend instead of starching my collars.

KOCHKARIEV: All right, all right, but hurry up!

PODKOLIOSIN: One more second. *(He puts on his frock coat, sits down.)* Listen to me, Ilya Fomin Kochkariev, I've got a good idea. You go by yourself.

KOCHKARIEV: By myself — are you out of your mind? Who's getting married, you or me?

PODKOLIOSIN: You're right. But suddenly I don't feel quite like it. Tomorrow will be better.

KOCHKARIEV: The man doesn't have an ounce of brains! Idiot — you're all dressed, and suddenly you "don't feel quite like it"! You're a complete fool.

PODKOLIOSIN: *(He whispers.)* Why are you yelling at me? I haven't done anything to you.

KOCHKARIEV: You're an idiot! Everyone knows it. They all say, "Podkoliosin's an idiot, even though he is a Court Councilor." Why the hell I bother — why, you can't even cross the street by yourself. You're just a damned, lying, lazy bachelor! You're a damned — no, I can't bring myself to use the word that describes you, you . . . damned old woman! Old bed socks!

PODKOLIOSIN: You're not so appealing yourself. *(He whispers.)* Are you out of your mind, cursing me in front of my own servant? You might have done it in private! And such foul language.

KOCHKARIEV: Why shouldn't I swear at you? Who could resist swearing at you? You decide, like any normal human being, to follow my mature advice and get married. And then, out of cowardice, you—

PODKOLIOSIN: All right, I'm coming, I'm coming. Why are you shouting?

KOCHKARIEV: He's coming, he's coming, he's coming! Hey, Stepan! Quick, bring his hat and coat. *(He looks back at Podkoliosin.)* Strange creature. I wouldn't want to play cards with him — he'd keep changing his bid. All right, my dear, it's all over now. I'm not swearing at you any more. *(Exeunt.)*

SCENE TWO

A room in Agafya Tikhonovna's house. Agafya is sprawled on the ground, using cards to read her future. Her Aunt Arina looks on.

AGAFYA: Look, Auntie, another journey! And the King of Diamonds is showing some interest! Tears . . . a love letter . . . what's this? My God, am I going to stay a spinster forever? There's not a single suitor here, not one! They've all disappeared — like a plague came and killed them all. *(She looks up.)* Once upon a time, refined suitors went looking for their brides. But nowadays they wait for you to come to them! That's why I asked Fiokla to — but will she find anyone? Oh, there's no respect left for women, it's God's truth. *(She prays.)* Lord, please let it be a gentleman. From a respectable family. It's scary, when you think of it. He'll arrive. My heart will be pounding and — very well, let him come, I'm prepared. I won't be afraid! *(She peers at the cards again.)* Look, Auntie, on the right . . . the King of Clubs!

ARINA: And who is this King of Clubs?

AGAFYA: I don't know.

ARINA: I do.

AGAFYA: Who?

ARINA: A substantial merchant in the clothing business. Aleksei Dmitrievitch Starikov.

AGAFYA: I doubt that. It would never be him.

ARINA: Don't argue, Agafya. Isn't his hair dark? There's no other King of Clubs here.

AGAFYA: You're quite wrong. The King of Clubs indicates a gentleman. I'd hardly call a merchant a King of Clubs.

ARINA: Oh Agafya, if your dear father were still alive you'd speak differently.

I can see him now, sitting at the table and shouting, "I'll spit on anyone who's ashamed of being a merchant!" And he'd say, "I wouldn't marry my daughter off to a Colonel! And I won't allow my son to enter the civil service! You ask me why? I ask you: Don't merchants serve the state as well as anyone?" And then he'd pound on the table with his fist — his fist was the size of a coal shovel! With that shovel of a fist he'd pound on the table and — to tell the truth, he was the death of your sainted mother. If it weren't for him, she'd be alive still.

AGAFYA: You see? That's why I'll never marry a merchant. He might turn out to be as bad as my father.

ARINA: Aleksei Dmitrievitch Starikov is different.

AGAFYA: I won't do it! I won't! He's got a big beard, and whenever he eats, the food gets into his beard! No, I absolutely won't have him!

ARINA: You'll never find a better gentleman — search the streets, you won't find one.

AGAFYA: Fiokla Ivanovna will find me one. She promised to find me the very best. *(Fiokla enters in time to overhear Arina.)*

ARINA: But she's a known liar, my child.

FIOKLA: I see. I work my fingers to the bone, Arina Panteleimovna, and this is my reward? Shame!

AGAFYA: Fiokla! Come in, tell me what's going on. Have you found anyone yet?

FIOKLA: Well well, let me catch my breath. I was in a terrible hurry to get here. On your behalf, my dear, I've combed every house, every government office, even the military barracks. On your behalf. *(Arina laughs.)* Let her laugh. You know, sweetheart, they almost beat me up. On your behalf. That old matchmaker, the one who married the Aferovs, she actually screamed at me: "You so-and-so, trying to take the bread out of my mouth! Stay in your own district!" "All right, all right," I yelled back, "but for my client, I'd go through fire!" And have I picked husbands for you! The world has never known such gentlemen! Some of them are dropping by today, so I ran ahead to warn you.

AGAFYA: Today? Dear God! Fiokla, I'm terrified.

FIOKLA: Don't be afraid, sweetheart, it's all routine. They come here, take a look at you. You take a look at them. If you don't like what you see, they leave.

ARINA: A nice bunch of suitors she's picked.

AGAFYA: How many? A lot?

FIOKLA: Six. Six men.

AGAFYA: *(Screams.)* Ooooh!

FIOKLA: I don't understand, what's scaring you? You only have to pick the best. If you don't like one, try another.

AGAFYA: You say they're all gentlemen?

FIOKLA: They're all choice! They're so choice, their equal doesn't exist anywhere.

AGAFYA: What do they look like?

FIOKLA: Words are inadequate, my dear.

ARINA: I believe that!

FIOKLA: First, we have Baltazar Baltazarovitch Zhevakin . . . what a gentleman. He served in the Navy, and now he's all yours. He tells me he wants a bride with some meat on her bones — he can't bear the skinny type. *(She consults her list.)* And then we have Ivan Pavlovitch Poach'Tegg, he's an assessor for the government. Now he's a huge man. He roars at me, "Don't tell me about the bride, just tell me how much she's worth in cash, and how big the estate is!" "She's worth this much, Ivan Pavlovitch Poach'Tegg, see for yourself." "This much? You've got to be a liar, you old whore!" His language was so foul I knew he had to be very important.

AGAFYA: And who else?

FIOKLA: There's Nikanor Ivanovitch Anuchkin. He's the cream! Floats right to the top. You should see his lips — raspberries, perfect raspberries. He tells me, "For me, the bride must be refined. She must be well-educated, and of course she's got to speak French." Very classy, very delicate, this Anutchkin. And his legs are so fine and slender.

AGAFYA: I don't like men with fine, slender . . . I don't care for them.

FIOKLA: If you like them bigger, you'd better take Poach'Tegg. He's a tremendous man — I bet he can't squeeze through this door!

AGAFYA: How old is he?

FIOKLA: Quite young. Fifty — maybe less.

AGAFYA: And what did you say his name was?

FIOKLA: Poach'Tegg. Ivan Pavlovitch Poach'Tegg.

AGAFYA: That's his last name?

FIOKLA: That's it.

AGAFYA: My God, Fiokla, if I married him, my name would be Agafya Tikhonovna Poach'Tegg. Mrs. Poach'Tegg.

FIOKLA: There are some pretty peculiar names in Russia. Some are so odd you want to spit and cross yourself when you hear them. But sweetheart, if you don't like his name, you'll want to take Baltazar Baltazarovitch Zhevakin, he's a national treasure.

AGAFYA: What's his hair like?

FIOKLA: Nice hair.

AGAFYA: And his nose?

FIOKLA: His nose is all right, too. Everything seems to be in the right place. He's a perfect gentleman. Only he doesn't own any furniture, not a stick. His sole possession is a pipe.

AGAFYA: Who else do you have on your list?

FIOKLA: Akinf Stepanovitch Panteleiev. Court Councilor. But nothing much comes of it. He stammers.

ARINA: So he's a councilor, so what? I hear he drinks a lot.

FIOKLA: I won't argue. He's a Court Councilor, but he's also drunkard. That's why he stammers.

AGAFYA: I don't want a drunkard!

FIOKLA: I don't see what harm there is in taking a drop once a while. But I told you, if you don't like one, pick another.

AGAFYA: Who else do you have?

FIOKLA: One more left. He's kind of . . . well, God's been less kind to him than the others.

AGAFYA: Who is he?

FIOKLA: I didn't want to bring him up. He . . . he's another Court Councilor. But he's kind of a stay-at-home . . . hard to get him out of the house.

AGAFYA: We've only got five so far. You said six.

FIOKLA: Five's not enough? You've turned greedy — a few minutes ago, you were terrified.

ARINA: And what good are they?! Civil servants! One solid merchant would be worth all five of them.

FIOKLA: You're wrong, Arina, a gentleman counts for much more.

ARINA: Take Aleksei Dmitrievitch Starikov, in a sable cap, driving through town in his sleigh —

FIOKLA: — So a gentleman with epaulets meets him and says, "Hey, you silly shopkeeper, get the hell out of my way!" Or the gentleman says, "Show me your best velvet, shopkeeper." "With pleasure, sir," says Starikov. And the gentleman roars, "And take off your sable cap, you son of a bitch!" That's what my gentleman roars.

ARINA: But my merchant doesn't have to sell him the velvet, so your gentleman goes naked!

FIOKLA: So my gentleman stabs your merchant to death!

ARINA: So my merchant files a complaint against your gentleman with the police!

FIOKLA: So my gentleman files a complaint against the merchant with a senator!

ARINA: So the merchant goes to the governor!

FIOKLA: So the gentleman goes to —

ARINA: — Liar! Liar! A governor's higher than anyone. Anyway, a gentleman must learn to take his hat off, like anyone else. *(The doorbell rings.)* The bell!

FIOKLA: Goodness, here they are.

ARINA: Who?

FIOKLA: The gentlemen. *(Agafya screams.)*

AGAFYA: Lord have mercy on me! *(Fiokla goes out.)*

ARINA: The room's a complete mess! *(She runs around the room in circles.)* The tablecloth's filthy! Coal black! Dunyashka, Dunyashka! *(Dunyashka, the servant, enters.)* Quick, straighten things up!

AGAFYA: Auntie, Auntie, what shall I do? I'm not even dressed.

ARINA: Well, get dressed. *(Arina and Dunyashka rush about.)* Dunyashka, run out and tell them I'm coming. *(Dunyashka rushes out, shouting, "I'm coming!")*

AGAFYA: Auntie, my dress isn't ironed.

ARINA: Good grief, child, put on another one. *(Fiokla runs in.)*

FIOKLA: Where are you, Agafya Tikhonovna? Hurry up! *(The bell rings again.)* My God, he's still waiting.

ARINA: Dunyashka, ask him to wait. *(Dunyashka runs off to the hallway.)*

POACH'TEGG: *(Off.)* Is she home?

DUNYASHKA: *(Off.)* She's at home. Please step into the parlor. *(Agafya is peeking out.)*

AGAFYA: My God, he's so fat!

FIOKLA: Here he comes! *(They all run out. Dunyashka enters with Poach'Tegg.)*

DUNYASHKA: Wait here, sir.

POACH'TEGG: I'll wait. *(She goes.)* Why should I wait? I leave my office for one minute. As soon as I'm gone, the general is sure to ask, "Where has the assessor gone?" "He's gone to look over a prospective bride." He'll adore that! Oh well, I'm here. Let's have another look at the dowry. *(He pulls out a paper, reads.)* "A two-story brick house." *(He looks around.)* That's true, anyway. "Two annexes, one wood, one with a brick foundation." Wooden one's not worth a damn. "One chaise. One two-horse sleigh, handcarved, with two lap robes, one big, one small." Could be a lot of junk. But that old woman insists it's all top quality. Let's say it is. "Two dozen silver spoons." Every house should have silver spoons. "Two fox fur coats." Hmmm. "Four large goose-down feather beds, and two small ones." *(He purses his lips significantly.)* "Six silk dresses, six cotton ones, two nightgowns . . ." *(He turns the page.)* And this page is empty. "Napkins, tablecloths . . ." That's her business. But I'd better make sure it's all here. They promise a house and a sleigh, but once you're married you might wake up to find yourself stuck with nothing but a feather bed. *(The bell rings. Dunyashka runs into the hallway. Voices off.)*

ANUCHKIN: *(Off.)* Is she in?

DUNYASHKA: *(Off.)* She's in. *(Dunyashka enters with Anuchkin.)* Wait here, sir. They'll be out any minute.

POACH'TEGG: Good day, sir.

ANUCHKIN: Have I the honor of addressing the young lady's beloved papa?

POACH'TEGG: No, sir. I'm no one's papa. I haven't got any children.

ANUCHKIN: Oh, forgive me. Forgive me, good sir.

POACH'TEGG: *(Aside.)* Something odd about this fellow's face. I have a feeling he may be here for the same reason I am. *(To Anuchkin.)* You have some business with the lady of the house, sir?

ANUCHKIN: No sir . . . no business, sir. I just happened to be passing by, so I dropped in.

POACH'TEGG: *(Aside.)* Liar! He just happened to be passing by — ha! He wants to get married too! *(The bell rings. Dunyashka runs through the room. Voices off, Dunyashka and Zhevakin, as above. Dunyashka leads him in.)*

ZHEVAKIN: My dear young lady, will you please brush me off? It's so dusty out there in the street: so . . . thank you. Look, isn't that a spider on my coattail? No? Good. Now the sleeves. *(He notices the other suitors.)* Cloth's English, see? Wears forever. I bought this back in . . . in '95, when our squadron was serving in Sicily. At the time I was a midshipman, and I had a uniform made up of this cloth. Then in . . . in '01, when I was serving under Pavel Petrovitch, I was promoted to lieutenant — cloth looked as good as new! Then in '14, I sailed around the world . . . and it was only a little frayed at the seams. In '15 I retired. I had it turned then. Been wearing it that way for ten years, and so far it's good as new. Thank you, my pretty. *(He blows Dunyashka a kiss, she goes.)*

ANUCHKIN: I beg your pardon, sir, did you say Sicily? Is Sicily a pleasant country?

ZHEVAKIN: Wonderful! Spent thirty-four days there. Ravishing views, I tell you, and those mountains! Those pomegranate trees. And those Sicilian girls — rosebuds! You want to kiss them all.

ANUCHKIN: Are they well-educated?

ZHEVAKIN: Superbly educated. Our own countesses are seldom as well-educated. I'd stroll down the streets with my epaulets shining — lots of gold thread, you know, and those dark-eyed little beauties . . . Every house had its own balcony, and on every balcony I'd see one of those little rosebuds sitting. Well, of course I . . . *(He gestures, bows.)* And she . . . *(He gestures.)* Dressed up in silks and trinkets, and other feminine accoutrements. Words can't paint the picture!

ANUCHKIN: And if I may be permitted to ask, what language did they speak in Sicily?

ZHEVAKIN: Oh, French, French.

ANUCHKIN: The ladies all spoke French?!

ZHEVAKIN: Every one of them. Maybe you won't believe me, but we were there thirty-four days, and during that time I never heard a word of Russian spoken!

ANUCHKIN: Not one word?

ZHEVAKIN: Not a word. And I'm not just speaking of the nobility, but even the peasants. The simplest fellow hauling garbage — just say to him, "Hey, brother, give me some bread." And by God, he won't understand a word. Then try it in French: "Dateci del pane." Or "Portate vino." He'll bring you what you want in a flash!

POACH'TEGG: Sicily must be a fascinating country. Tell me about those Sicilian peasants, are they like the Russian ones? I mean, big and broad-shouldered? Do they plow the fields?

ZHEVAKIN: Don't know whether they plow or not, but I can tell you, they all smell of tobacco. Don't smoke it, though. They chew it. In their mouths. Really! Transportation's excellent there . . . cheap. Almost all water . . . gondolas everywhere . . . and each with a little Italian rosebud, floating along — little darlings! Met some English officers too, sailors. Couldn't understand each other at first . . . hard, at first. Later we got friendly, began to understand each other. You know, you point at a bottle or a glass — and right away they know it means drinking; or you put your hand to your mouth, lips go puff puff, and they know it's smoking. All I can say is . . . language isn't so hard. In three days our sailors understood each other perfectly.

POACH'TEGG: Life abroad sounds interesting. I'm pleased to make your acquaintance. To whom have I the honor?

ZHEVAKIN: Zhevakin. Naval lieutenant, retired. Excuse me, to whom have I the honor — ?

POACH'TEGG: Collegiate Assessor Ivan Pavlovitch Poach'Tegg.

ZHEVAKIN: Thank you, I've already eaten. Knew I'd have a long way to go, this morning, and the weather's nippy, so I ate some pickled herring —

POACH'TEGG: — No, no, that's my name. Ivan Pavlovitch Poach'Tegg. *(He bows.)*

ZHEVAKIN: Forgive me, I have a little trouble with my ears. I thought you said, "Have a poached egg."

POACH'TEGG: What can I do? I asked the general to call me Poachedeggovitch, but he says it would be like calling me Sonofabitch.

ZHEVAKIN: It happens. In our squadron there were officers and sailors with the most peculiar names. Our commander used to say, "A fiend concocted your names." Let's see, there was a Boozikov . . . a Slopnik . . . and a Stinkovitch. One midshipman had a very simple name: Hole. Hole. And the commander would yell, "Hey, Hole, come here!" And he'd tease poor Hole — *(The bell rings. Fiokla runs through the room to open the door.)*

POACH'TEGG: Hello, mamutchka. Wait —

ZHEVAKIN: How are you, my dear?

ANUCHKIN: Bonjour, Fiokla Ivanovna.

FIOKLA: *(Running through.)* Fine, fine, thank you, perfect health . . . *(Voices in the hallway.)*

KOCHKARIEV: *(Off.)* Is she home?

FIOKLA: See for yourself. *(She enters with Kochkariev and Podkoliosin.)*

KOCHKARIEV: Remember — courage! *(He looks around, amazed. He bows.)* My Lord, what a collection! What does it mean? Are they all after her? Would-be bridegrooms? *(He nudges Fiokla.)* Where did you find these old vultures?

FIOKLA: There are no vultures here, no odd birds at all. These are perfect gentlemen.

KOCHKARIEV: "Uninvited guests stay forever."

FIOKLA: They're invited! Besides, "the man with the biggest feather in his cap has the least gold in his purse."

KOCHKARIEV: On the other hand, "the fattest purse may contain the biggest hole." *(Turns to the others.)* Well, where is she? I suppose this door leads to her bedroom? *(He crosses to it.)*

FIOKLA: I told you, she hasn't finished dressing. Shameless!

KOCHKARIEV: *(Peeking through the keyhole.)* No harm intended, I just want to have a look.

ZHEVAKIN: May I have a glance too?

POACH'TEGG: I'd like a little peek.

KOCHKARIEV: Nothing to see, gentlemen. I can't tell if it's a woman or a pillow — *(The others rush at the door.)* Wait — someone's coming. *(They all move away from the door. Agafya and Arina enter. The men bow.)*

ARINA: To what do we owe the pleasure, gentlemen?

POACH'TEGG: I learned from the newspaper that you wanted to sign a contract for the sale of timber, and being the assessor in the department concerned, I came to inquire about details: what kind of timber, what quantity, and where you plan to sell it.

ARINA: You've got the wrong contract. We don't own timber, but I'm glad you came. Your name, sir?

POACH'TEGG: Collegiate Assessor Ivan Pavlovitch Poach'Tegg.

ARINA: Please have a seat. And you, sir?

ZHEVAKIN: I too read an announcement . . . of something-or-other. I thought to myself, why not stop by? Weather seemed nice . . . road clear . . .

ARINA: What's your name?

ZHEVAKIN: Baltazar Baltazarovitch Zhevakin, the Second. I knew another Zhevakin . . . navy . . . retired before me . . . wounded just below the knee. Bullet hit him, passed right through the tendon, threaded it like a needle. When you stood beside him, you worried that he'd unintentionally kick you with his game leg.

ARINA: Have a seat, sir. And you? What brought you here?

ANUCHKIN: Pure neighborliness. I'm a neighbor —

ARINA: Are you the one who's taken over the Tulobov's house across the street?

ANUCHKIN: No, actually I live across the river in the Peski district. But I've been toying with the idea of moving into this neighborhood.

ARINA: I see. Please sit down. And you—?

KOCHKARIEV: You already know me, madam. *(To Agafya.)* And you too, don't you remember me?

AGAFYA: I don't think I've ever seen you before . . .

KOCHKARIEV: Try to remember where . . .

AGAFYA: Honestly, I don't recall. It wasn't at the Biryushkins'?

KOCHKARIEV: That's it! At the Biryushkins'!

AGAFYA: Have you heard the news? Something dreadful's happened to Madame Biryushkin.

KOCHKARIEV: I've heard. She got married.

AGAFYA: No, no, she broke her leg!

ARINA: And badly, too. On her way home, quite late one night, her coachman was drunk and turned the carriage over in the road.

KOCHKARIEV: That's right, now I remember. I knew it was something awful, either marriage or a broken leg.

ARINA: And what did you say your name was?

KOCHKARIEV: Kochkariev, Ilya Fomin Kochkariev, at your service. I think we're related. My wife's told me all about you. Permit me . . . *(He looks for Podkoliosin.)* Permit me to introduce my friend . . . *(He pushes Podkoliosin toward the women.)* Ivan Kuzmitch Podkoliosin, Court Councilor in the civil service. There is a nominal head of his department, but believe me, it's Podkoliosin that makes all the decisions.

ARINA: I see. Please have a seat. *(The suitors are now all seated on the chaise. There is a long silence.)*

POACH'TEGG: Strange weather we're having. This morning it looked like rain, but now it's clearing up.

ARINA: Yes, it's unusual. One moment clear, the next moment wet. It's positively inconvenient.

ZHEVAKIN: We were in Sicily in springtime, my dear. Our squadron. It was February, but they called it spring. You'd look out the window — sunny day. So you'd go out and — rain! Have to go inside again.

POACH'TEGG: It's fine as long as you're not alone in weather like this. If you're married, it's one thing, you're not bored. But if you're single—

ZHEVAKIN: It's death, it's positively death!

ANUCHKIN: Yes, one could call it that.

KOCHKARIEV: Simply torture! How can you enjoy life that way? May God keep us from such a situation.

POACH'TEGG: And what, young lady, if I may pursue the subject, what kind of man interests you? Forgive me for being direct, but I don't beat around the bush. What branch of service would you consider appropriate in a husband?

ZHEVAKIN: Would you consider, my dear, a husband who's sailed the stormy seas?

KOCHKARIEV: In my opinion, a husband who can run a government department would be best.

ANUCHKIN: I sense some prejudice here. One ought to consider a man who, although he did serve in the infantry, nonetheless appreciates the finer things in society.

POACH'TEGG: *(To Agafya.)* Well, you have the floor. What do you say? *(Agafya is silent.)*

FIOKLA: Answer, my dear, say something to them.

POACH'TEGG: What's on your mind, little lady?

KOCHKARIEV: Just tell us what you think, Agafya Tikhonovna.

FIOKLA: *(Whispers.)* Say something, for God's sake! It's not polite to sit there like that.

AGAFYA: *(Aside.)* Oh, I'm so ashamed, so ashamed. I'm going, Auntie, I must go — you can handle this better than I can —

FIOKLA: Don't make a scene, don't embarrass yourself. What will they think?

AGAFYA: I'm leaving — I've got to get out of here! *(She runs from the room, Fiokla and Arina run after her.)*

POACH'TEGG: There they go and here we sit! What does it all mean?

KOCHKARIEV: Something must have happened.

ZHEVAKIN: Probably something to do with her dress. They've all gone to pin something up. *(Fiokla enters.)*

KOCHKARIEV: What's going on?

FIOKLA: What should go on? Nothing. Nothing's happening.

KOCHKARIEV: Then why did she run away?

FIOKLA: She was embarrassed, she's so shy she simply couldn't sit still another minute! She begs your forgiveness and asks you to return for a cup of tea later. *(She goes out.)*

POACH'TEGG: A cup of tea! That's what I hate about matchmaking. Today won't do, but please come again tomorrow — then the day after tomorrow — for a cup of tea! "We need time to think it over." Think it over — dammit, I'm a busy man, I haven't time for such nonsense.

KOCHKARIEV: *(To Podkoliosin.)* Our hostess isn't bad-looking is she?

PODKOLIOSIN: No, not bad.

ZHEVAKIN: Our hostess is damned good-looking.

KOCHKARIEV: *(Aside.)* Damn, this idiot's fallen in love with her — he'll confuse the issue for her. *(To Zhevakin.)* You call that good-looking?

POACH'TEGG: Her nose is big.

ZHEVAKIN: I didn't notice her nose. She is a perfect rosebud.

ANUCHKIN: I agree. Still, one wonders whether she's familiar with cultural matters and social customs. One wonders if she's fluent in French. One wonders if she even speaks French . . .

ZHEVAKIN: Then why, if I may be so bold, didn't you ask her yourself — in French?

ANUCHKIN: You think I speak French? Alas, I was never given the opportunity to become acquainted with that language. I have never had the advantage of such an education. My father was a brute. It never occurred to him to teach one French. And as a child, one might have been taught so easily . . .

ZHEVAKIN: But if you don't speak it, why is it so important to have her speak — ?

ANUCHKIN: No no no no no, a woman is another matter entirely. She should — she must know French. Without it she'd be . . . no. A woman who doesn't know French is not a woman!

POACH'TEGG: Who gives a damn either way? I'm going out and take a look at the house, the courtyard, the annexes. If everything's in order, I'll come back later. These fellows are no competition — young brides never choose men like that. *(He goes.)*

ZHEVAKIN: Well, I'm going now . . . light up my pipe. Anyone going my way? Where do you live, sir, if I may ask?

ANUCHKIN: I live in the Peski district, my dear sir, on Petrovski Street.

ZHEVAKIN: Well . . . a bit out of my way — I live on the island, Eighteenth Avenue. But I'll go along with you. *(Zhevakin and Anuchkin go.)*

PODKOLIOSIN: What are we waiting for?

KOCHKARIEV: Isn't she sweet?

PODKOLIOSIN: As a matter of fact, I'm not impressed.

KOCHKARIEV: You're — what?! You already admitted she was good-looking!

PODKOLIOSIN: But her nose is too big. And she doesn't know French.

KOCHKARIEV: Come on, why does she have to know French?

PODKOLIOSIN: All brides should know French.

KOCHKARIEV: Why?

PODKOLIOSIN: Because . . . I don't know why . . . because it's appropriate.

KOCHKARIEV: Another fool puts it into his head, he makes his own! She's a beauty, a real beauty — you'll never find another like her.

PODKOLIOSIN: Yes, she seemed attractive at first, but then they started with that long nose, big nose — and when I looked at her, all I could see was her nose.

KOCHKARIEV: But you can't see the nose in front of your own face! They were carrying on like that just to put you off the scent. I was trying to bluff them, telling them I didn't know what they saw in her. But take a look at her, brother. What a girl! Her yes — devilish eyes, melting, whispering eyes. And that nose — pure alabaster, smooth as a monument! Take a closer look.

PODKOLIOSIN: *(Smiling.)* Yes, I can see it now, she's quite pretty.

KOCHKARIEV: Of course she's pretty. Listen: now they've all left, let's find her. We'll sit down and talk it over, and close the deal.

PODKOLIOSIN: Oh, I couldn't do that.

KOCHKARIEV: Why not?

PODKOLIOSIN: It's not fair to the others. She ought to choose for herself.

KOCHKARIEV: Why think about them? Are you afraid of them? Or what? I'll get rid of them all, don't worry.

PODKOLIOSIN: How?

KOCHKARIEV: That's my business. You just give me your word that you won't renege later.

PODKOLIOSIN: Why would I do that? I'm not a liar. And besides, I want to get married.

KOCHKARIEV: Give me your hand.

PODKOLIOSIN: *(After a moment of painful hesitation.)* Here. *(They shake hands.)*

KOCHKARIEV: That's all I need to hear. That's all I need to hear! *(They both go out.)*

END OF ACT I

ACT II

Agafya Tikhonovna is alone.

AGAFYA: It's impossible to choose! If it were only one gentleman, or two. But four! I simply don't know which one. Nikanor Ivanovitch Anuchkin isn't bad looking . . . he's thin, of course. Ivan Kuzmitch Podkoliosin's not so bad either. On the other hand, Ivan Pavlovitch Poach'Tegg may be fat, but he is impressive. Baltazar Baltazarovitch Zhevakin's a strong contender . . . oh, it's too hard to make such a crucial decision. If you put Anuchkin's lips under Podkoliosin's nose . . . or combined Zhevakin's manners with Poach'Tegg's solidity — then there'd be no question of choice. But as things stand, the whole business is giving me a headache! Perhaps it would be best to draw lots and leave it in God's hands. I'll write their names on scraps of paper, fold them up and . . . and Thy will be done! *(She tears up a sheet of paper, writes names on the scraps, folds them as she talks.)* What a miserable position for a young girl, particularly if she's in love. Men are never placed in such a position — they can't begin to grasp the difficulty of her situation. Done. Well, let me put them in my purse . . . I close my eyes . . . and what will be will be. *(She places her hand in the purse.)* I pray I get Nikanor Ivanovitch Anuchkin. Wait, why do I want him? Ivan Kuzmitch Podkoliosin's a better choice. Podkoliosin? No, he's worse than all the rest. No . . . no . . . let fate decide. *(She draws all the scraps out at once.)* All of them? Impossible! My heart's beating like a drum. I can only have one. *(She puts the scraps back into the purse. Kochkariev sneaks up behind her.)* Ah, if I could pick Baltazar Baltazarovitch — I mean Nikanor Ivanovitch —

KOCHKARIEV: Take Ivan Kuzmitch, he's the best. *(Agafya screams, covers her face with her hands.)* What are you frightened of? Don't be afraid, it's only me. Yes, indeed, you take Ivan Kuzmitch.

AGAFYA: *(Peering through her hands.)* I'm so ashamed that you overheard.

KOCHKARIEV: Ashamed? Of your old Cousin Kochkariev? Let's see your little face.

AGAFYA: I am ashamed.

KOCHKARIEV: Ivan Kuzmitch, Ivan Kuzmitch — *(She screams, hides her face again.)* He's a capable fellow, at work and at home.

AGAFYA: *(Through her fingers.)* How about the rest? Take Nikanor Ivanovitch Anuchkin, for instance, he's a nice man too.

KOCHKARIEV: Next to Podkoliosin, they're all trash.

AGAFYA: No!

KOCHKARIEV: It's clear as day, Podkoliosin is a man . . . a man . . . a man you don't run into every day.

AGAFYA: What about Ivan Pavlovitch Poach'Tegg?

KOCHKARIEV: Poach'Tegg's trash. They're all trash.

AGAFYA: Why?

KOCHKARIEV: Judge for yourself. Compared to Ivan Kuzmitch, they don't add up to much.

AGAFYA: They've got nice manners.

KOCHKARIEV: Manners? They're hoodlums! Hooligans! A collection of bullies — you'll probably be whipped the day after the wedding.

AGAFYA: My God, what a dreadful thought!

KOCHKARIEV: And that's probably not the worst you've got in store for you.

AGAFYA: Then you really think I should take Ivan Kuzmitch?

KOCHKARIEV: Ivan Kuzmitch. Certainly, Ivan Kuzmitch. *(Aside.)* It's working! Podkoliosin's waiting in the cafe. I'd better run and get him.

AGAFYA: You're absolutely sure Ivan Kuzmitch is the one?

KOCHKARIEV: Absolutely. Positively.

AGAFYA: What about the others?

KOCHKARIEV: Send them away.

AGAFYA: But how? I can't face it.

KOCHKARIEV: How? Just tell them you've thought it over. You're too young, and you're not ready for marriage.

AGAFYA: But they'll never believe that — they'll start questioning me.

KOCHKARIEV: Simply tell them to get the hell out.

AGAFYA: I could never.

KOCHKARIEV: If you try very hard . . . I'm sure you can manage it. I assure you, they'll clear out and leave you alone.

AGAFYA: It might lead to hostility —

KOCHKARIEV: — If you never see them again, what does it matter?

AGAFYA: It's so rude . . . they'll be cross.

KOCHKARIEV: So what if they're cross?! At worst, one of them will spit in your face. That's not so terrible —

AGAFYA: — Spit in my face — ?!

KOCHKARIEV: So what? It happens. Some people have been spat on more than once. I recall a certain young man who kept pestering his boss for a raise. Naturally the boss didn't appreciate that, but the fellow persisted, so finally the old man couldn't stand it any longer: He spat in the young man's face. "Here," he said, "here's your big raise, you devil!" But to his surprise, when the next payday came around, there was his raise after all. So it was worth it. You see, it doesn't matter if someone spits in your face, so long as you've got a handkerchief in your pocket. *(The bell rings.)*

AGAFYA: Oh, I'm shaking!

KOCHKARIEV: Don't worry — just breathe deeply. Breathe deeply. Good-bye for now! *(Aside.)* I've got to drag Podkoliosin back here! *(He goes. Poach'Tegg enters.)*

POACH'TEGG: I'm back early. I wanted to speak to you alone. Well, madam, as for my status with the government, I presume you know all about that. I serve as Collegiate Assessor. I'm smiled upon by my superiors, and I'm obeyed by my subordinates. There's only one thing missing in my life: a loving partner.

AGAFYA: Yes.

POACH'TEGG: And now I've found that partner — it's you. Tell me, is it yes or no? *(Aside, as he stares at her.)* Oh, this one is far from skin and bones . . . this one's got everything!

AGAFYA: I — I'm still too young. I'm not ready to marry yet.

POACH'TEGG: I beg your pardon, madam, then why is that matchmaker running around? Perhaps you meant something else — *(The bell rings.)* Dammit, I'll never be allowed to get down to business! *(Zhevakin enters.)*

ZHEVAKIN: Perhaps I'm a bit early. *(He notices Poach'Tegg.)* Ah, Ivan Pavlovitch, it's a pleasure.

POACH'TEGG: *(Aside.)* To hell with your pleasure! *(To Agafya.)* Well, what will it be? One word: yes or no? *(The bell rings. Poach'Tegg spits crossly. Anuchkin enters.)*

ANUCHKIN: I suspect, dear madam, that I may be a bit on the earlier side than is usual in high society, but — *(He sees the others.)* Gentlemen, my respects.

POACH'TEGG: *(Aside.)* Keep your respects to yourself! Fellow turns up like a bad penny! I'd like to break those matchstick legs of his. Well, what's your answer, madam? I'm a busy man and my time is running out.

AGAFYA: I don't know . . . I don't know what I'm saying . . . I don't know . . .

POACH'TEGG: Don't know what? Well?

AGAFYA: Never mind . . . it isn't . . . I mean . . . *(She suddenly pulls herself together, turns on them all.)* Get the hell out! *(She covers her face with her hands.)* Oh my God, what have I said?

POACH'TEGG: Get the hell out? What do you mean, "get the hell out"? Allow me to ask what you mean by that? *(He approaches her menacingly. Agafya looks into his face and screams.)*

AGAFYA: Help! He'll beat me, he'll beat me! *(Agafya runs from the room. Poach'Tegg stands open-mouthed. Arina runs in, looks at him, screams, and runs out.)*

POACH'TEGG: This whole thing is a nightmare! *(The bell rings. Voices off.)*

KOCHKARIEV: *(Off.)* Come on, come on, what are you waiting for?

PODKOLIOSIN: *(Off.)* You go ahead. I've got to fix my trousers, one second.

KOCHKARIEV: *(Off.)* You want to run away again.

PODKOLIOSIN: *(Off.)* I won't. I swear I won't.

KOCHKARIEV: *(Off.)* Have you fixed them yet?

PODKOLIOSIN: *(Off.)* Just a minute, just a minute. *(Kochkariev enters.)*

KOCHKARIEV: It's crucial for him to fix his damned trousers!

POACH'TEGG: Tell me, is the bride crazy, or what?

KOCHKARIEV: Why? What's going on?

POACH'TEGG: Confusion and chaos. She ran out screaming, "He'll beat me, he'll beat me!" What the hell does that mean?

KOCHKARIEV: Well . . . yes. It's been known to happen to the poor girl, from time to time. She's a bit simpleminded. *(To Podkoliosin, off.)* Are you ready yet?

POACH'TEGG: You're related to her?

KOCHKARIEV: Yes, I am.

POACH'TEGG: How are you related, may I ask?

KOCHKARIEV: To tell you the truth, I'm not sure. My mother's aunt is something to her father. Or my father is something to her mother's aunt. My wife could tell you all about it, she makes it her business to know these things. *(To Podkoliosin, off.)* How are the trousers?

POACH'TEGG: How long has she been like this?

KOCHKARIEV: Oh, since she was born.

POACH'TEGG: It would be better if she were normal. But all other things being equal, if the dowry settlement's in order, it'll be all right.

KOCHKARIEV: But she hasn't got a thing, you know.

POACH'TEGG: What about this brick house?

KOCHKARIEV: Only the paint holds the walls together. The walls — one thickness of brick, filled with rubble, garbage, litter and wood chips.

POACH'TEGG: No!

KOCHKARIEV: Yes! You know how houses are built nowadays — any garbage will do, just to secure a mortgage.

POACH'TEGG: But — this house isn't mortgaged?!

KOCHKARIEV: Who told you that? Not only is it mortgaged, but there's been no interest paid on it for two years! She's got a brother in the Senate who has his eye on this house — he'd rob his own mother of her last blanket. *(To Podkoliosin, off.)* What's going on with the trousers?

POACH'TEGG: But that old woman, the matchmaker, told me — what a beast she is, one of God's mistakes! *(Aside.)* Of course it might be him that's lying. I'll question the old woman. If it's even partly true, I'll teach her to sing a different tune!

ANUCHKIN: Forgive me for disturbing you with a question, sir. Admittedly, when one does not know the language oneself, it's difficult to ascertain whether the young lady has the ability to speak French or not . . . whether the lady of the house can . . .

KOCHKARIEV: Not a word.

ANUCHKIN: Really?

KOCHKARIEV: It's true. She went to school with my wife, and she was well known for her laziness. She always had to sit on the dunce's stool. And that poor French teacher was forced to beat her with a stick.

ANUCHKIN: Amazing . . . from the moment I met her, I had a feeling she didn't speak French.

POACH'TEGG: To hell with the French — what about the matchmaker? That old witch — if you knew how she built the girl up! The brick house, the two annexes — brick foundation! The silver spoons, the sleigh! She practically had me driving that sleigh! You won't find such well-written fiction in novels. That rotten old woman fed us pure romance! Just wait till she runs into me. *(Fiokla enters. All turn to her at once.)* Ah, here she comes. Come here, you old hag, you old sinner!

ANUCHKIN: You have deceived me, Fiokla Ivanovna.

KOCHKARIEV: Prepare for your punishment, you old crow!

FIOKLA: What? I can't hear a word, you're all babbling at once.

POACH'TEGG: One thickness of brick, you old whore, and you're painting pictures of mezzanines and terraces and God knows what!

FIOKLA: How should I know? I didn't build this house. One thickness of brick — go talk to the architect!

POACH'TEGG: And it's mortgaged! May the devil devour you, you old witch!

FIOKLA: Listen to him — anyone else would be grateful for my efforts.

ANUCHKIN: But you told me, Fiokla Ivanovna, that she spoke French!

FIOKLA: She does, my dear, she speaks everything, even German. Languages, everything — she knows it all!

ANUCHKIN: Apparently she speaks nothing but Russian.

FIOKLA: So what's wrong with that? At least you can understand her when she speaks Russian. That's why she speaks Russian. If she spoke Mesopotamian it wouldn't do you much good. Besides, what's wrong with Russian? You all speak Russian, don't you? All the holy saints spoke Russian —

POACH'TEGG: Let me catch you, you old witch, just let me — *(Fiokla walks slowly to the door.)*

FIOKLA: I'm going now. As for you, you're a big, fat, over-grown, foul-tempered man who'd as soon beat a woman as look at her!

POACH'TEGG: You don't care for the idea, do you, my little dove? If I take you to police headquarters, you'll think twice about cheating honest men! Wait and see. And as for the bride, tell her for me, she's a real bitch! *(Poach'Tegg leaves.)*

FIOKLA: Look, he's gone. That fat pig — always thinks he's in the right!

ANUCHKIN: I'm forced to admit, my dear lady, I never believed you'd be such a deceiver. If I had an inkling about the bride's education, I'd never have set foot inside her door. Such a pity. *(Anuchkin leaves.)*

FIOKLA: *(Calls after him.)* Go to hell! Your father begat you in a fit of amnesia! *(To Kochkariev.)* This is the result of compulsory education! *(Kochkariev laughs loudly, points a finger at her. She exits in a rage. Kochkariev's laughter grows out of control. It is almost frightening, and he cannot stop.)*

KOCHKARIEV: I can't . . . I can't . . . I swear I can't stop . . . my sides are splitting . . . I may die laughing . . . *(Zhevakin looks at him, also starts to laugh. Kochkariev sinks exhaustedly into the chaise.)* I'm exhausted. If I go on laughing, my heart'll burst!

ZHEVAKIN: I like to see a cheerful disposition. When our squadron served under Captain Boldirev, we had one midshipman . . . Petukhov, Anton Ivanovitch Petukhov . . . he had the same cheerful nature. You only had to wag a finger at him, he'd be off, laugh all day long. And you'd have to start laughing, yourself.

KOCHKARIEV: May God have mercy on our sinning souls. *(He becomes businesslike.)* The old woman's run off. Well, now I can take over.

ZHEVAKIN: You can arrange marriages?

KOCHKARIEV: Of course. I can marry anyone to anyone you like.

ZHEVAKIN: Really? Could you marry me to the lady of the house?

KOCHKARIEV: You? Why do you want to marry?

ZHEVAKIN: That's an odd question, if I may say so. Marriage is a very popular institution, that's why.

KOCHKARIEV: You heard with your own ears, she's got no dowry.

ZHEVAKIN: That's a pity, of course . . . an inconvenience. But the little lady's so delightful, we can get along without the dowry, I do believe. Tiny little room . . . *(He indicates the size with his hands.)* . . . Tiny little window looking out on the backyard. . . tiny . . .

KOCHKARIEV: What do you like about her?

ZHEVAKIN: To be perfectly honest, I like her because she's womanly. And I've always been a great admirer of women. Womanly women . . .

KOCHKARIEV: *(Aside.)* Poor fellow, he looks like an empty tobacco pouch. *(To Zhevakin.)* No, no, you mustn't get married, sir.

ZHEVAKIN: Why not?

KOCHKARIEV: Because (and this is just between us) your legs look like a chicken's.

ZHEVAKIN: Like a chicken's . . . legs?

KOCHKARIEV: That's right.

ZHEVAKIN: Excuse me, aren't you getting a bit personal?

KOCHKARIEV: I'm speaking honestly because I know you're sensible. I wouldn't say it to just anyone. Look, I'll marry you off, I promise, only it must be to another lady.

ZHEVAKIN: But I don't want another lady. I want this one.

KOCHKARIEV: All right, I'll marry you. But on this condition: that you won't interfere, you won't even let the young lady glimpse you. I'll fix things for you.

ZHEVAKIN: Leave it all to you? But don't I have to present myself to the bride?

KOCHKARIEV: Quite unnecessary. You just go home. I'll let you know tonight. *(He leads Zhevakin out, returns.)* What the hell — where's Podkoliosin? He can't still be fixing his damned trousers!
(Agafya enters, looks around the room.)

AGAFYA: They're all gone? None left?

KOCHKARIEV: Not a single soul.

AGAFYA: If only you knew how I trembled. It's never happened to me before. And that Poach'Tegg — he'd be a real tyrant to his wife. I'm afraid he'll be back any minute.

KOCHKARIEV: He's got nothing to come back for. I'll bet neither of those two will stick his nose in here.

AGAFYA: And the third?

KOCHKARIEV: Which third? *(Zhevakin pops his head back in, unnoticed.)*

ZHEVAKIN: I'm dying to hear what she says about me with her pretty little rose-bud mouth.

AGAFYA: I mean Baltazar Baltazarovitch.

ZHEVAKIN: Ah, here it comes, here it comes.

KOCHKARIEV: That old fool? I didn't know who you meant. That one's a complete dolt!

ZHEVAKIN: What's he saying? I don't understand.

AGAFYA: He seemed such a pleasant-looking man.

KOCHKARIEV: He drinks.

ZHEVAKIN: I don't understand a word.

AGAFYA: Drinks? Really?

KOCHKARIEV: And worse, I assure you. *(Zhevakin steps into the room.)*

ZHEVAKIN: Excuse me, sir, but I didn't ask you to say that. I asked you to speak in my behalf. That would have been one thing, this is quite another. I begin to suspect you're not my friend.

KOCHKARIEV: Back so soon? Look at him! His legs can hardly support him. Send him away. Launch him on the high seas. Put the wind in his sails. *(Aside.)* Where the hell is Podkoliosin? Fool! I'd better go get him. *(He goes out.)*

ZHEVAKIN: He promised to speak for me, then insulted me. Nasty fellow — don't believe him, dear lady.

AGAFYA: Forgive me, I don't feel well at all. I've a headache.

ZHEVAKIN: Maybe there's something about me you don't like? *(He points to his head.)* Small bald patch here, but it's nothing, the result of a fever. New hair will grow soon enough.

AGAFYA: I don't care what you have up there, it's all the same to me.

ZHEVAKIN: And as for my complexion, my dear lady, when I wear a black coat my complexion has more character.

AGAFYA: Good for you. I really must leave now. *(She goes.)*

ZHEVAKIN: Dear lady, tell me why. Is there a reason? Is there something wrong with me? She's left me . . . peculiar. It's happened again. Seventeen times it's happened to me, and each time it's always the same. Things start off well enough, but when it gets close to the crux, I'm rejected. *(He paces with a heavy heart.)* Seventeenth bride . . . can't understand her objection . . . complex, very complex . . . if I were homely, then . . . *(He looks in the mirror.)* But there's nothing to complain about. Nature has showered her gifts on me, so I don't understand. Maybe I ought to go home, look in my trunk. I had a poem there . . . a poem no woman could resist. My God, it's incomprehensible! It went so well at the beginning. Well, I've just got to steer a new course, but it's a pity . . . a real shame . . . *(He leaves. Podkoliosin and Kochkariev enter, looking at him as they pass by.)*

KOCHKARIEV: He didn't notice us. Did you see how sad he looked?

PODKOLIOSIN: Perhaps she turned him down too.

KOCHKARIEV: Him too.

PODKOLIOSIN: *(A bit smug.)* Damned hard thing, being turned down.

KOCHKARIEV: That's right.

PODKOLIOSIN: I still can't believe she told you she preferred me.

KOCHKARIEV: And how she prefers you! She's mad about you! It's love — she's in the grip of an unbridled passion.

PODKOLIOSIN: *(Smiles contentedly.)* There are no little nicknames a woman in love won't murmur. She'll call me her little bear cub, her little wolf.

KOCHKARIEV: That's before the wedding. After two months, words can't describe what other names she'll call you! It'll melt your heart.

PODKOLIOSIN: Really?

KOCHKARIEV: Would I lie? But listen, you've got to get started. Talk to her, open your heart and ask for her hand.

PODKOLIOSIN: This minute?

KOCHKARIEV: This instant! Here she comes. *(Agafya enters.)* I have brought you, madam, this mortal whom you see standing transfixed before you. Never has man been so enchanted, never has —

PODKOLIOSIN: *(Aside, to Kochkariev.)* Slow down, brother, slow down!

KOCHKARIEV: I beg your pardon, he's so shy. You'll have to be more free-and-easy with him. Wink at him; gaze at him through half-lowered lids; then brush him with your shoulder — why didn't you wear a short-sleeved dress? Anyway, I promise you, he'll turn into a wolf! He won't be able to resist . . . Well, I'll run along, leaving you in pleasant company. I've got to check your kitchen and dining room, to arrange for the caterer. He'll be bringing in the supper. Perhaps the wine's already been delivered. *(To Podkoliosin.)* Courage! *(He goes.)*

AGAFYA: Please have a seat. *(They both sit in silence for a long time.)*

PODKOLIOSIN: How do you feel about boating?

AGAFYA: Boating?

PODKOLIOSIN: It's very pleasant, rowing around in the summertime.

AGAFYA: In summer I often go on walking trips with friends.

PODKOLIOSIN: Summer . . . God knows what it'll be like . . .

AGAFYA: I hope it will be warm . . . *(They sit in silence.)*

PODKOLIOSIN: What's your favorite flower, madam?

AGAFYA: Whatever has the strongest scent . . . carnations, I suppose.

PODKOLIOSIN: Flowers suit women.

AGAFYA: Yes, flowers are woman's work. *(Pause. Silence.)* Where did you go to church last Sunday?

PODKOLIOSIN: Voznesenski Chapel. The Sunday before I went to Our Lady of Kazan. No matter which church we choose, we can still pray.

AGAFYA: Yes!

PODKOLIOSIN: Our Lady of Kazan's got more decoration. *(Silence. Podkoliosin drums the table with his fingers.)* Soon Carnival will be here.

AGAFYA: In a month.

PODKOLIOSIN: Less than a month.

AGAFYA: It should be nice this year.

PODKOLIOSIN: Today is . . . let's see, the eighth. *(He counts on his fingers.)* Ninth . . . tenth . . . eleventh — in twenty-two days, to be exact.

AGAFYA: So soon!

PODKOLIOSIN: Not counting today. *(Pause. Silence.)* How brave the Russian peasant is!

AGAFYA: I beg your pardon?

PODKOLIOSIN: The Russian peasant. Fearless. They stand at the very top. On my way to work I passed a house, and I noticed a carpenter working on the roof — no fear at all.

AGAFYA: Really? Where was that?

PODKOLIOSIN: On the way to my office. I go to work every day. In my office. *(Silence. He begins drumming again. Finally he picks up his hat and bows.)*

AGAFYA: Going already?

PODKOLIOSIN: Yes, forgive me for boring you.

AGAFYA: Boring me? Quite the opposite, I want to thank you for a pleasant time.

PODKOLIOSIN: But I suspect I was boring you.

AGAFYA: No, I swear you weren't.

PODKOLIOSIN: Then perhaps you'll allow me to drop in again . . . this evening?

AGAFYA: With pleasure. *(They bow to each other. He starts out. To herself.)* What a nice man.

PODKOLIOSIN: What a marvelous woman.

AGAFYA: Now that I've spent a little time with him, it's hard not to fall in love with him. He's genteel and clever.

PODKOLIOSIN: What an incredible woman!

AGAFYA: His friend was quite right. Only . . . it's too bad he left so soon. I could have gone on talking to him much longer. On the other hand, no one could accuse him of being a chatterbox.

PODKOLIOSIN: What a marvelous, incredible woman!

AGAFYA: I wanted to speak with him longer, but I was so shy, my heart was pounding like a mallet. He is an agreeable man. I'll have to go tell Auntie.

(She runs past Podkoliosin, without seeing him. Kochkariev enters, taps him on the shoulder.)

PODKOLIOSIN: I'm going home now.

KOCHKARIEV: Now? Why?

PODKOLIOSIN: Why should I stay here? I've said everything I had to.

KOCHKARIEV: You poured out your heart to her?

PODKOLIOSIN: Pour? No, well, I didn't exactly pour it out. Yet.

KOCHKARIEV: So why not?

PODKOLIOSIN: You expect me to just walk in and say, "Good afternoon, madam, let's get married?"

KOCHKARIEV: What did you two talk about for half an hour?

PODKOLIOSIN: We chatted about any number of things. I admit it was very pleasant.

KOCHKARIEV: You haven't much time left to settle it. In one hour the church bells will begin to ring for you.

PODKOLIOSIN: Are you crazy? Marry her today — ?!

KOCHKARIEV: You gave your word. You swore you'd do it the minute the others were out of the way. So now you're ready to get married.

PODKOLIOSIN: I'm a man of my word. Only . . . not right now. Give me a month to prepare.

KOCHKARIEV: You must be out of your mind.

PODKOLIOSIN: Less than a month's impossible.

KOCHKARIEV: I've ordered the supper from the caterer, you fool. Listen to me, Ivan Kuzmitch — do it!

PODKOLIOSIN: I couldn't, right now.

KOCHKARIEV: Ivan Kuzmitch, I beg you — if not for yourself, do it for my sake.

PODKOLIOSIN: I can't.

KOCHKARIEV: You can, my dear, you will. Don't hesitate.

PODKOLIOSIN: Impossible. The time's not right.

KOCHKARIEV: Why? Why? Look, you're a sensible man, I'm appealing to you, not only as a Court Councilor, but as a friend. My dear, try to look at it rationally.

PODKOLIOSIN: Well . . . perhaps I . . .

KOCHKARIEV: Ivan Kuzmitch, darling! Must I get down on my knees before you? *(He kneels.)*

PODKOLIOSIN: Why would you do that?

KOCHKARIEV: I am on my knees! See? I'll be indebted to you forever, my dearest, only don't be pig-headed.

PODKOLIOSIN: But I can't, I can't! *(Kochiariev rises in a rage.)*

KOCHKARIEV: Pig! Pig!

PODKOLIOSIN: Go on, work yourself up.

KOCHKARIEV: The world has never known such stupidity.

PODKOLIOSIN: Go on, go on!

KOCHKARIEV: Why did I go to the trouble? For you! I did it for you! And now I wash my hands of you!

PODKOLIOSIN: Who asked you to go to the trouble in the first place? Please do wash your hands of me.

KOCHKARIEV: Without me you'll never get anywhere. You'll stay an idiot.

PODKOLIOSIN: So what?

KOCHKARIEV: I did it as a mission of mercy, you feebleminded fool!

PODKOLIOSIN: You needn't have taken the trouble.

KOCHKARIEV: Good, then go to hell.

PODKOLIOSIN: I'm going!

KOCHKARIEV: Bon voyage!

PODKOLIOSIN: Good-bye!

KOCHKARIEV: And may you break both legs on the way. You're a clod, not a Court Councilor. It's all over between us — I hope I never set eyes on you again!

PODKOLIOSIN: You won't. *(He goes.)*

KOCHKARIEV: Good riddance! The world has never seen such stupidity! *(He paces back and forth.)* But I'm no prize either. I'm as stupid as he is. Why was I working so hard? Shouting till I'm hoarse? Why? Am I my brother's keeper? We're not even related! But I act like his aunt, his cousin, his wet-nurse. For what? God knows for what — I've no peace of mind left. You'll come begging for my help, next time, but forget it, you can help yourself. What a filthy crook, what a face! I'd like to twist your nose off! Punch out all your teeth, poke out your eyes! What hurts me is the way he just walked out. Not a twang of remorse, just water over the dam. Filthy beast. I've seen nasty fellows, but he's a unique specimen. God never created him in His own image! I know what I'll do — I'll go find him! He won't get away with this! *(He runs out. Agafya enters.)*

AGAFYA: My heart's still pounding. No matter which way I turn, Ivan Kuzmitch seems to be standing there. That's it, then, there's no escaping one's fate. I must get him off my mind. But no — I try to wind my wool or embroider my purse, and Ivan Kuzmitch always seems to seize my hands and stop me. Maidenhood, adieu. They'll call for me, lead me to the altar, then leave me all alone with . . . a man! Oh, I'm trembling. Farewell to innocence, to my beautiful girlhood. *(In tears.)* How many years have I spent in peace, and now I must end it all. I must marry. There'll be nothing but trouble: noisy, quarrelsome little boys. And little girls who must be cared for, so that they can grow up and get married (may their husbands be kind men!). But they might marry drunkards . . . no, I can't bear it! I haven't had enough time to enjoy my girlhood. I've only had twenty-seven years as a virgin . . . *(Voices off.)* Why is Ivan Kuzmitch so late? *(Podkoliosin is pushed through the door by Kochbariev.)*

PODKOLIOSIN: *(Stammering.)* I've returned . . . to clear up one little matter . . . one little thing. But first, I want to know whether you'll find it strange?

AGAFYA: What's it about? *(She lowers her eyes.)*

PODKOLIOSIN: No, madam, first you must say if you find it strange . . .

AGAFYA: *(Still with downcast eyes.)* I don't know what it is yet.

PODKOLIOSIN: Admit it, you're going to find what I'm about to tell you strange.

AGAFYA: Of course not. How could it be strange — anything you have to say is pleasing to my ears.

PODKOLIOSIN: But you haven't heard this yet. *(Agafya lowers her eyes again. At this moment, Kochkariev tiptoes into the room to listen.)* It's this . . . *(Pause.)* I'll tell you another time.

AGAFYA: Tell me what?

PODKOLIOSIN: Well, I wanted to tell you . . . but I hesitate . . .

KOCHKARIEV: Good grief, he's a parody . . . a parody of manhood!

AGAFYA: What are you hesitating for?

PODKOLIOSIN: There is some doubt — *(Kochkariev leaps out.)*

KOCHKARIEV: Buffoon! Parody! Actually, my dear, he's asking for your hand. He's trying to explain that he can't live without you, and above all, he wants to have your consent!

PODKOLIOSIN: *(Whispers to him.)* What have you done?

KOCHKARIEV: What will it be, my dear? Will you make him the happiest man alive?

AGAFYA: I cannot presume . . . that I might make him happy . . . but yes, yes, I agree.

KOCHKARIEV: Good, it's a deal! Give me your hands.

PODKOLIOSIN: Wait a minute — *(He tries to whisper into Kochkariev's ear. Kochkariev shakes his fist. Podkoliosin gives his hand, and Kochkariev joins it to Agafya's.)*

KOCHKARIEV: God bless you both. I consent to your union. Marriage is quite an event, you know. It's not like calling a carriage and taking a ride. It's a responsibility, a real responsibility — I haven't got time now, I'll tell you about the responsibility later. Ivan Kuzmitch, kiss the bride — it's permitted from now on. In fact, it's your duty. No, my dear, it's quite proper, stand still and let him kiss you.

PODKOLIOSIN: Yes, madam, allow me. Let me kiss you. *(He takes her hand and kisses her.)* What a beautiful little hand. Where did you get such lovely hands? Let the wedding take place at once!

AGAFYA: So soon?

PODKOLIOSIN: I can't wait! I want the wedding to take place this very minute!

KOCHKARIEV: Brave! Excellent! Wonderful man, he can't wait — and won't wait in the future, either, let me tell you. You'd better hurry and dress, my dear. I've already sent for the carriage, and invited the guests. They'll be coming straight to the church. I assume your wedding dress is ready?

AGAFYA: Oh yes, it is. It's been ready for a long time. *(She goes.)*

PODKOLIOSIN: Thank you very much, brother, I'm grateful for your help. My own father couldn't have been kinder to me . . . and you acted out of generosity and friendship. I swear, I'll never forget your help. Next spring I'll certainly visit your father's grave.

KOCHKARIEV: Don't mention it, friend. I'm so happy for you. *(He kisses him on both cheeks.)* May God bless you, and bring you great joy. May he brighten your life with lots of children.

PODKOLIOSIN: Thank you, thank you. I've only begun to realize what life's all about. A new world is opening for me, I can see it changing, bubbling, fermenting, germinating. Until now I understood nothing. I was a sleep-walker, just going through the motions of living with my eyes closed.

KOCHKARIEV: I'm so glad. I'd better check on the tables they're setting up — I'll be back in a minute. *(Aside.)* And just to be on the safe side, I'll take his hat with me. *(He grabs Podkoliosin's hat, goes.)*

PODKOLIOSIN: Yes indeed, what have I been, until this moment? Have I grasped the essence of life? No. I haven't grasped a thing. How dull I've been . . . done nothing, good-for-nothing. I merely existed . . . went to my office, had dinner, slept — in other words I've been the most boring, mundane man on earth. Yes indeed, the man who refuses to marry is a fool, and there are many such blind fools. If I were the Tsar, I'd order every bachelor to marry immediately — there wouldn't be an unmarried man left in the whole country! When one considers . . . that one will be married in a matter of hours . . . minutes . . . in a matter of minutes one will taste the ecstacy that is the stuff of fairy tales . . . a joy which no words can express . . . *(A pause.)* On the other hand . . . it's odd, when one takes the time to consider . . . binding oneself for life . . . all those years. And afterward, no retreat, no turning back . . . nothing. Nothing. Yes indeed, everything's settled, everything's over. Fini. Why, even now it's too late to back out — you can't run away. The supper's ready, everything's prepared. And really, it would be impossible to escape — there are people at all the doors, watching — I can't — no, I mustn't — but here's an open window. No, no, I would never — it's so . . . undignified. And besides, it's too high up — *(He crosses to the window.)* Well, it's not really so high. Just one story, as a matter of fact. No — and I don't have my hat. How could I leave without my hat? It's unheard of. On the other hand, if I can't leave with my hat . . . I ought to try to leave without it . . . eh? I might try. . . . *(And he climbs onto the window ledge.)* Heavens, what a height! *(And he jumps.)* Looord deliver meeee!

PODKOLIOSIN'S VOICE: Hey, driver!

DRIVER'S VOICE: Where to, eh?

PODKOLIOSIN'S VOICE: Take me past the Semenovski Bridge — to the Kanavki district!

DRIVER'S VOICE: That'll be ten kopeks — not a penny less!

PODKOLIOSIN'S VOICE: It's yours! Let's go! Drive on! *(Noise of the carriage driving away. Agafya enters timidly, in her wedding gown.)*

AGAFYA: I feel shy again. I don't know what's the matter. Oh, if only he weren't here in the room, if he had just left for a moment to fetch something . . . *(She looks up timidly.)* No one's here. Where did he go? *(She calls into the hallway.)* Fiokla? Fiokla Ivanovna, where did Ivan Kuzmitch go?

FIOKLA'S VOICE: He's there.

AGAFYA: Where? *(Fiokla enters.)*

FIOKLA: Here. He was sitting in this room.

AGAFYA: He's not here, see with your own eyes.

FIOKLA: Well he didn't leave the room. I've been sitting in the hallway all this time.

AGAFYA: Then . . . where has he gone?

FIOKLA: How should I know? Perhaps he's gone out by the back stairs. Maybe he's in Arina Panteleimovna's room?

AGAFYA: Auntie? Auntie? *(Arina enters, all dressed up.)* Is Ivan Kuzmitch with you?

ARINA: Isn't he in here? He didn't come into my room.

FIOKLA: Well, he didn't come into the hallway either. I was sitting there the whole time.

AGAFYA: He's not here — see for yourself. *(Kochkariev enters.)*

KOCHKARIEV: What is it? What's going on?

AGAFYA: Ivan Kuzmitch has disappeared.

KOCHKARIEV: What? He's left?

AGAFYA: He hasn't left. But he isn't here.

KOCHKARIEV: Not here and not gone?

FIOKLA: I can't guess where he is. I can't figure it out. I was sitting in the hall the whole time.

ARINA: And he couldn't leave by the back stairs.

KOCHKARIEV: Damn it! If he didn't leave the room, he must be somewhere. He's hiding. Ivan Kuzmitch, where are you? "Come out, come out, wherever you are!" It's not a very good joke, Ivan Kuzmitch. It's time to go to church. *(He looks under the chaise.)* I don't get it — he can't have escaped, he's got to be here in this room. Why, his hat is still on the chair out there — I put it there myself.

ARINA: Let's ask the maid, she was standing in the street, maybe she'll know. Dunyashka! Dunyashka! *(Dunyashka enters.)* Have you seen Ivan Kuzmitch anywhere?

DUNYASHKA: Yes, madam. The gentleman just jumped out the window.

EVERYONE: Out the window?!

DUNYASHKA: Yes, then he climbed into a cab and drove off.

ARINA: Are you telling the truth?

KOCHKARIEV: You must be lying — it's impossible.

DUNYASHKA: In God's name — I swear he jumped out! Even the man in the store across the street saw him. He gave the driver ten kopeks and drove off.

ARINA: *(To Kochkariev.)* You made fun of us, eh? You wanted to make us look ridiculous. I'm sixty years old, and till now I've never lived through such humiliation! For this I'll spit in your face — Even though you call yourself a gentleman. *(She spits at him. He flinches.)* And you've made a laughingstock of this poor girl — in front of the world. I'm not a highborn lady, but I'd die before I'd do such a thing to anyone. Shame! Shame! *(She runs out of breath, turns to Agafya, who has started to sob quietly. Kochkariev doesn't hear a word of it.)*

KOCHKARIEV: I'll bring him back!

FIOKLA: Some manager you are! Thinks he can arrange a marriage without the matchmaker. My gentlemen may have been a peculiar bunch but, pardon me, I have never had any window-jumpers!

KOCHKARIEV: It's impossible! It can't be true! I'll bring him back — I'll run after him and bring him back!

FIOKLA: You just try bringing him back! You don't know an earthly thing about marriage, do you? If he had simply strolled out the door, it would be

one thing. But when your bridegroom jumps out the window, then . . .
then . . . good luck! *(Lights fade out.)*

END ACT II

EPILOGUE

Empty stage. Agafya alone, sobbing, in her wedding gown. Suddenly, the banquet table with its wedding cake and champagne appears. It is wheeled on by Stepan. Agafya gasps, moves out of the way. The table begins to pursue her. She swivels and tries to avoid it. It continues to follow her; she keeps trying to elude it. Finally, she screams and runs off. Stepan saunters off in another direction. The table stands alone, for a moment. Then, suddenly, all the champagne corks start to pop. Lights fade out.

END OF PLAY

Monsieur de Molière

Translated and Adapted from the Play by
Mikhail Bulgakov

To the memory of Anatoly Efros

Molière (Jan Triska, center) with Charles Varlet de La Grange (Jon Cranney, left), Zacharie Moirron (Larkin Malloy, top), Gilbert Du Croisy (John Spencer), and Bouton (Jake Dengel, right) in a scene from the 1979 Guthrie production of Bulgakov's *Monsieur de Molière*, adapted by Barbara Field, directed by Anatoly Efros with set and costume design by Valery Leventhal. Photo credit: Boyd Hagen, New York.

Director Anatoly Efros's political troubles with the censorship of the Soviet government in the 1970s inspired him to revive a play Bulgakov had written in the 1930s, a play that had expressed Bulgakov's own frustrations with the repressive regime of Joseph Stalin.

The play tells the story of Molière, who also had political problems. In his case, it was that sly, tyrannical art lover, Louis XIV, and with the monarch's corrupt minions within the Catholic Church. This play is about art, censorship, absolute power, and, most of all, fear.

The company members in this play were real; they were the actors in Molière's troupe. And the playwright did have a long affair with Madeleine Béjart, but eventually married her young sister Armande. The speculation that Armande, unbeknownst to him, was really his daughter is apocryphal. The banning of *Tartuffe* was very real, as was the fact that Molière died backstage after a performance of *The Imaginary Invalid.* Jean-Baptiste de Poquelin, Monsieur de Molière, was one of the world's great playwrights. Because he spoke the truth, he also became the mortal enemy of the Church.

Ironically, shortly after Anatoly Efros' Minneapolis production in 1979 of *Monsieur de Molière,* the Soviet government removed Efros from his beloved theater and acting company, the Malaya Bronnaya in Moscow, and assigned him elsewhere. He died a few years later.

(This play is known in English by several titles, *Monsieur de Molière, A Cabal of Hypocrites,* and *The Black Cross.*)

Monsieur de Molière
Adapted for The Guthrie Theater by Barbara Field

Director	Anatoly Efros
Scenic and Costume Designer	Valery Leventhal
Lighting Designer	Ronald M. Bundt
Interpreter	Julia Kocich
Music Director	Dick Whitbeck
Stage Manager	Robert Bye
Asstistant Stage Managers	Diane DiVita, Sharon Ewald

CAST

JEAN-BAPTISTE POQUELIN DE MOLIÈRE	Jan Triska
MADELEINE BÉJART	Jacqueline Bertrand
ARMANDE BÉJART	Amy Nissen
MARIETTA RIVALE	Virginia Ness
CHARLES VARLET DE LA GRANGE	Jon Cranney
JEAN-JACQUES BOUTON	Jake Dengel
ZACHARIE MOIRRON	Larkin Malloy
GHILBERT DU CROISY	John Spencer
A CHARLATAN	Don R. Fallbeck
RENÉE	Naomi Hatfield
LOUIS XIV	Gerry Bamman
MARQUIS D'ORSINI	Justin Deas
MARQUIS DE LESSAC	Richard Hilger
THE HONEST COBBLER	Peter MacNichol
FATHER BARTHOLOMEW	Ken Risch
ARCHBISHOP CHARRON	Robert Pastene
BROTHER FORCE	Tom Hegg
BROTHER FIDELITY	Richard Grusin
UNKNOWN WOMAN	Linda Gehringer
COURTIERS, MUSKETEERS, MEMBERS OF THE CABEL:	Erik Anderson, Richard Ayd, Joel Dossi, Sean O'Phelan

SETTING

The action of the play takes place in Paris, from February 17, 1663, to February 17, 1673.

Monsieur de Molière

SCENE ONE

Backstage, Palais Royal. Above, on the stage of the Palais Royal, a perform-
ance of The Miser *is concluding. Anselmo says to Valere: "Come, let us go*
to dinner and share our happiness!" The actors start trooping down the spi-
ral staircase toward the dressing rooms. Alone on stage, Harpagon/Molière
kneels lovingly before his little cask of gold. He caresses a few coins, lets them
trickle through his fingers. Then he chooses one, kisses it, and holds it up in
a gesture of love. He holds the pose.

PROMPTER: *(From below.)* Curtain!

> *(Bouton pulls on some ropes, and the "stage" curtain shuts. Thunderous ap-*
> *plause off, as lights cross-fade from the above to the deck below, where the ac-*
> *tors are murmuring, taking off costumes, removing makeup.*

> *This cellar/dressing room contains mirrors, a couple of dressmaker's dum-*
> *mies, a costume rack, wig stands, a large harpsichord. At one dressing table*
> *hangs a crucifix, with many candles burning. At another table, La Grange*
> *sits, remote from the others, his face illuminated by a lantern. Everyone else*
> *in the dressing room shows signs of unusual excitement.*

> *Molière comes pounding down the spiral stair, carrying a metal cask and*
> *a cane. He sports a false nose with a large wart. He is clutching his chest, like*
> *a man with heart trouble. The makeup is dripping off his face. He throws*
> *off his cloak.)*

MOLIÈRE: *(Gasps.)* Water!

BOUTON: At once. *(He hands him a glass.)*

> *(Du Croisy, who is playing Jacques tonight, turns to address them all tri-*
> *umphantly.)*

DU CROISY: The king is applauding! *(He goes behind the clothes rack.)*

MADELEINE: The king is applauding!

MOLIÈRE: Towel! *(Boutin hands him the towel.)*

BOUTON: The king is applauding —

MOLIÈRE: Yes, yes, I hear, I'm coming. *(He crosses himself.)* Holy Virgin, holy
Virgin — *(To Bouton.)* Open up the curtain!

> *(He races up the stairs, and Bouton slowly opens the curtain above. Candles*
> *burn brightly in the chandeliers. There is a row of footlights. We cannot see*

the audience, but we can feel them. Their watchfulness. Molière walks forward toward them, with catlike steps. One pair of hands begins to clap, quickly joined by others — then a thunder of applause. Then silence.)

MOLIÈRE: Your . . . your Majesty, your Majesty . . . Most Radiant Ruler . . .
(He pronounces these first words almost with a stammer [in real life, he does occasionally stammer] but his speech gains confidence, and from his opening words, it is clear that (onstage at any rate) he is topnotch. His smile is infectious.)
Your majesty, the actors of our troupe, your faithful and humble servants all, beg me to thank you for the extraordinary honor you have done us all by visiting our theater. And now sire . . . now . . . I . . . lost my —
(A ripple of laughter in the dark. Not pleasant.)
Sire!
O Muse! O Thalia, my naughty queen,
You beg me each evening, behind the scene
To put on my false nose, my wart, and my wig,
And you lure me onstage, where I mince and I jig.
The groundlings have each paid their thirty-five sous
To see this poor clown who's inspired by a muse.
I bow to thee, Thalia, and bow reverently low
To my king — how I chatter, my head's spinning so —
So today, my sweet Thalia, please help me be clever.
(This brief intermezzo is taking forever!)
To amuse our most Radiant Sun King of France
Isn't easy for me in this tense circumstance —
(Thunderous applause.)

BOUTON: *(Below.)* What a brain — France/circumstance!

CHARLATAN: When did he compose this poem?

BOUTON: *(Haughty.)* Never — it's extemporaneous.

CHARLATAN: Impossible —

BOUTON: For you. Shhh —

MOLIÈRE: *(His tone changes abruptly.)* Sire, you bear the burden of ruling fair France;
I'm only a clown — I can sing, I can dance.
But lit up by your glory, my poor words take wing,
My Louis the Great — Thou noblest French King!!
(He throws his hat in the air. The audience goes mad with cheers. Then silence.)

LOUIS: *(A voice from on high, the voice of God, the ultimate authority, courteous and banal.)* Thank you, Monsieur de Molière.
(Molière bows deeply, and in the process, his cane knocks down one of the footlight candles. Laughter from the "audience" off. The Prompter calls out, "Curtain!" and the laughter is sliced off abruptly. Molière runs back down the stairs in a rage.)

MOLIÈRE: He bought it! The bloody tyrant bought it — he ate it up! Maybe he'll eat me up! And God knows I deserve it, grovelling before him, like a worm in the dirt!
(Bouton hands him the towel.)
I'll kill him — I'll chop his head off!

BOUTON: Whose head do you plan to chop off in your hour of triumph?

MOLIÈRE: *(Grabs him roughly.)* Yours!

BOUTON: Help, help! He's murdering me — at a command performance!
(La Grange moves toward his lamp, then becomes still again. At Bouton's shout, Du Croisy and Rivale come to rescue him. Rivale is half-naked. They grab Molière, he kicks at them. Finally, they manage to pull him off Bouton, along with a piece of Bouton's shirt. Molière sinks into a chair.)

DU CROISY: Have you lost your mind? They can hear you out there.

MOLIÈRE: So what?

RIVALE: Jean-Baptiste . . .
(She closes his mouth. The frightened Charlatan peers from behind his harpsichord. Bouton notices his torn shirt.)

BOUTON: Well done. Simply splendid. *(To Molière.)* What did I ever do to you?

MOLIÈRE: Scoundrel! How long have I harbored this torturer in my company? We play it perfectly forty times in a row — but let the king sit in the house and — and a candle falls onto the stage. Idiot!

BOUTON: Who was alone onstage? Who was making all those fancy flourishes with his stick? Who knocked the candle out?

MOLIÈRE: Liar! Lazy scoundrel!
(He lunges at Bouton again. La Grange puts his head in his hands and weeps.)

RIVALE: Bouton's right, Jean-Baptiste. You caught the candle with your stick.

MOLIÈRE: They're laughing at me, out there. The king's dumbfounded.

BOUTON: The king's the most refined personage in France and, trust me, he didn't notice any candle.
(A pause. Molière looks up slowly.)

MOLIÈRE: The king's a capricious monster. So I hit the candle? Me? Then why was I screaming at you?

BOUTON: I'm at a loss to say.

MOLIÈRE: Did I tear your shirt? Here, take my shirt.

BOUTON: Thank you.

(He takes off his pants and shirt, quickly slips one leg into a pair of Molière's lace-trimmed pantaloons.)

DU CROISY: *(To Rivale.)* Rivale, I'm famished. Let's go get supper.

(She nods, they start to go, then she looks down at herself.)

RIVALE: Oh my God, look how I'm dressed!

(She grabs a skirt, pops it over her head, fastens it as she goes out. Molière turns to the mirror, mutters to himself. Madeleine hovers, waiting to talk to him.)

MOLIÈRE: *(Bitter.)* So he finally turned up at the theater. Louis le Grand! His divine radiance must have struck me temporarily insane, to grovel so — hey, who said anything about the pants?!

BOUTON: Surely you can see, master, it would be the acme of bad taste to wear such a fine shirt with my wretched old pants. They're a disgrace! *(He sticks his hand in a lace-trimmed pocket.)* How odd, master. Two coins of a truly insignificant denomination have just been discovered in the pocket. *(An expectant pause. Finally.)* What shall I do with them?

MOLIÈRE: Donate them to charity, you swindler.

BOUTON: Charity begins at home, if you catch my drift.

MOLIÈRE: Thief.

BOUTON: Me? Never. I'm the soul of honor. That's because I'm French — by descent.

MOLIÈRE: You're French by descent, and a scamp by profession.

BOUTON: You're an actor by profession, but by nature you're a cranky old boor! *(He leaves.)*

MOLIÈRE: I must have sinned constantly in my youth, and as punishment, God inflicted that idiot on me . . . *(He thinks back.)* While I was playing the city of Limoges, long ago . . .

MADELEINE: Jean-Baptiste, we must talk —

CHARLATAN: Monsieur Director —

MOLIÈRE: What? Oh, Charlatan, you've some new act to show me?

CHARLATAN: It's a magic harpsichord.

(Madeleine sighs in exasperation, picks up her cloak and goes, unnoticed.)

MOLIÈRE: Show me, how does it work?

CHARLATAN: Allow me.

(The Charlatan moves the bench far from the harpsichord, sits, starts to "play" the instrument, at a distance. Magically, music sounds. Molière tries to grab at invisible wires, but there are none. He is nonplussed.)

MOLIÈRE: It's a second-rate trick, Charlatan. Still, I might try it out for a week. Here's your advance. *(He hands him a coin. Very casually.)* By the way . . . how do you do that?

CHARLATAN: Professional secret.

(He leaves.)

MOLIÈRE: Damn! There must be a hidden spring somewhere. Madeleine, did you want to speak to me? *(He looks around, but of course she's left.)* Madeleine — damn!

(He wraps himself in his cloak, goes out looking for her, still in his false nose. La Grange rises, as if he wanted to stop Molière, then sits down again, to write in his journal. After a moment, Armande enters. Her pretty face resembles Madeleine's. She is seventeen. La Grange rises, calls out.)

LA GRANGE: Armande!

ARMANDE: *(Starts.)* Ah, it's you, Chronicler.

LA GRANGE: Don't call me "chronicler."

ARMANDE: Everyone else does . . . because of your journal, I suppose. But if you don't care for the title, I'll call you —

LA GRANGE: Call me Charles Varlet de la Grange, that will do. I've been waiting for you.

ARMANDE: Have you?

LA GRANGE: Today's the seventeenth of February.

ARMANDE: So?

LA GRANGE: That's always been our unlucky day in this troupe —

ARMANDE: You're the historian, you ought to know.

LA GRANGE: See, I've put a black cross in the diary.

ARMANDE: Has someone died?

LA GRANGE: It's an evil day — Armande, refuse him!

ARMANDE: Who gave you the right to —

LA GRANGE: Don't marry him!

ARMANDE: Why? Are you in love with me too?

LA GRANGE: To be quite frank, I can't bear the sight of you.

ARMANDE: Leave me alone then.

LA GRANGE: You've no right to marry him — he's too old!

ARMANDE: Has everyone in this troupe gone mad? What business is it of yours?

LA GRANGE: I can't tell you — but what you're doing is a sin.

ARMANDE: All that gossip about him and my sister? So what? So Madeleine had an affair with him years ago. That's got nothing to do with me —

(She tries to pull away.)

LA GRANGE: Refuse him!

ARMANDE: No.

LA GRANGE: Then I'll have to draw my sword —

ARMANDE: Crazy — murderer —

LA GRANGE: You don't love him. You're a child and he's an old man.

ARMANDE: I do — I love him!

LA GRANGE: Refuse him — or I'll kill you.

ARMANDE: I can't. You see, I'm pregnant.

(Slowly he puts up his sword.)

LA GRANGE: Forgive me, I wanted to save you. Forgive me.

(He wraps himself in his cloak and goes out, taking his lantern. Armande sits fuming in Molière's chair.)

ARMANDE: Monstrous!

(Molière enters, sneaks up on her.)

MOLIÈRE: Aha! *(He embraces her.)* My lovely Armande . . . *(Bouton appears.)* Damn! *(To Bouton.)* Listen, Bouton, will you run and check the candles in the lobby?

BOUTON: *(Brandishing a wick trimmer.)* I did.

MOLIÈRE: Then listen — go out to the buffet and bring me a decanter of wine.

BOUTON: *(Holds up a bottle.)* Here it is.

MOLIÈRE: Then how about this: Clear out!

BOUTON: Why didn't you say so in the first place? *(Going.)* Master, please tell me, how old are you?

MOLIÈRE: What's that supposed to mean?

BOUTON: Nothing at all. Someone was speaking about senility and —

MOLIÈRE: Get out!! *(Bouton goes. Molière locks the door.)* Kiss me.

ARMANDE: You're still wearing your nose. *(He removes it, kisses her.)* I've got some news. I'm . . . *(She whispers in his ear.)*

MOLIÈRE: My darling girl. *(He frowns. Then smiles.)* No, it's all right, I've made up my mind, I'm not afraid anymore. Only swear you love me.

ARMANDE: I love you, I love you, I love you.

MOLIÈRE: And you'll never deceive me? Look at me, love, I've got wrinkles, I'm getting old. And I'm surrounded by enemies —

ARMANDE: Enemies?

MOLIÈRE: If you deceived me, the shame would kill me.

ARMANDE: How can you think I'd —

MOLIÈRE: I promise you'll never be sorry, I'll make you an actress — the greatest actress of all.

ARMANDE: Better than Madeleine? *(He nods.)* I see no wrinkles on your brow — you're so brave and splendid, you'll never have wrinkles. You are Jean!

MOLIÈRE: I am Baptiste!

ARMANDE: You are Molière! *(She kisses him.)*

MOLIÈRE: We'll be married tomorrow. *(A knock at the door.)* What a life! Don't go home, my love. I must speak with Madeleine, I want to tell her about us, myself. Wait for me in the garden. After Bouton puts out the lights we'll sneak back in here. There's no moon —

(More furious pounding on the door. From the other side, Bouton yells frantically.)

BOUTON: Master, master, open up, open up!

(Molière opens the door. Bouton, La Grange, and One-Eye enter. One-Eye wears the uniform of the Black Musketeers, and a black scarf that covers one eye. He wears a red wig.)

ONE-EYE: Monsieur de Molière?

MOLIÈRE: Your obedient servant —

ONE-EYE: Yes, yes, the king has asked me to reimburse you for his seat in the theater tonight. Thirty-five sous. *(He hands Molière a few coins on a pillow. Molière kisses the coins.)* But to express this delight in your extempore poem, His Majesty has asked me to give you a little something extra: five thousand livres —

MOLIÈRE: O King! *(To La Grange.)* Five hundred livres for me, then divide the rest among the company.

LA GRANGE: On behalf of the actors, I thank you.

(He takes the money, exits. In the distance, a military march sounds.)

MOLIÈRE: The king is leaving. Excuse me, but I must thank him —

(He runs out.)

ONE-EYE: Yes, yes. *(To Armande.)* Mademoiselle, how kind of fate to furnish the opportunity: I am Captain D'Orsini, of the Black Musketeers.

ARMANDE: D'Orsini? You're the swordsman?!

ONE-EYE: And you, mademoiselle? An actress in this company?

ARMANDE: Armande Béjart.

BOUTON: *(Mutters.)* It begins. Oh, my foolish master.

(One-Eye notices him, particularly the lace on his trousers, and looks at him, amazed.)

ONE-EYE: Did you say something, my good man?

BOUTON: Who, sir? Me, sir? No, sir.

ONE-EYE: Then it would appear you're in the habit of talking to yourself.

BOUTON: That's it, sir! You know, I once talked to myself in a dream.

ONE-EYE: You don't say.

BOUTON: As God is my witness.

ONE-EYE: Idiot! *(To Armande.)* Your lovely face, mademoiselle —

BOUTON: I screamed wildly in my dream. Eight of the finest doctors in Limoges treated me.

ONE-EYE: I trust they did you some good?

BOUTON: They did not. They bled me eight times in three days, after which I lay down and took the last rites.

ONE-EYE: You're quite an original, my good man. *(He slowly pulls out his sword.)* Say your prayers. *(To Armande.)* I flatter myself, mademoiselle, that you're not indifferent to my — who is this little man?

ARMANDE: Our candle-snuffer, Jean-Jacques Bouton.

ONE-EYE: Some other time, my good man, I'll be delighted to hear how you bellowed in your sleep, but right now I —

(Molière enters. One-Eye bows to him.)

ONE-EYE: Your obedient servant, monsieur. I must catch up with the king. *(He leaves.)*

MOLIÈRE: *(To Bouton.)* Ask Madeleine Béjart to come see me. Then put out the lights and go home.

(Bouton exits. Molière embraces Armande.)

ARMANDE: I'd better go, master.

MOLIÈRE: I'll meet you in the garden. There's no moon . . .

(She leaves. Molière starts to take off his makeup. Madeleine enters.)

MOLIÈRE: Madeleine, listen, I've something important to say.

(She clutches her heart, sits.)

MOLIÈRE: I want to get married.

MADELEINE: *(In a dead voice.)* To whom?

MOLIÈRE: Your sister.

MADELEINE: Tell me you're joking.

MOLIÈRE: Believe me, I'm not.

MADELEINE: And me?

(The lights in the theater begin going out.)

MOLIÈRE: You're my faithful friend, but there's been no love between us for a long time.

MADELEINE: When they put you in prison, who brought you food?

MOLIÈRE: You did. That was twenty years ago!

MADELEINE: And who's cared for you in the twenty years since?

MOLIÈRE: You, you!

MADELEINE: No one drives out a dog that's spent its life guarding the house. No one but you — you're a frightening man.

MOLIÈRE: Don't torment me — I'm possessed by passion.

MADELEINE: Change your mind, Jean-Baptiste, eh? We'll act as if this conversation never took place, eh? Let's go home. You'll light a candle, and I'll come to you. You'll read me the third act of *Tartuffe*. I — I think it's a masterpiece. And if you need someone to talk to, who do you really want? Look, she's just a little girl; and you, Jean-Baptiste, you're old. Your hair's going gray, you like hot water bottles! I'll make it nice for you. Think, the candles burning, and we'll light a fire and . . . everything will be nice.

And if you really can't, with me, take a look at Rivale, is she so bad? What a body —

MOLIÈRE: What?!

MADELEINE: Yes, I'll even pimp for you! Take Rivale, I won't say a word, anyone you want, but not Armande! I curse the day I brought her to Paris!

MOLIÈRE: Hush, Madeleine, I beg you. I have to marry her, it's too late, it's my duty, you understand? *(A pause.)*

MADELEINE: So that's it, then. I release you, and I pity you. *(He moves toward her.)* No, keep away. I shall leave the troupe.

MOLIÈRE: Why, for revenge?

MADELEINE: I'm tired, I need rest. *(Sharply.)* I've sacrificed too much for this company!

MOLIÈRE: Oh yes, you paid a tavern bill once, in Lyons, but the wine was stale and sour even then. Sorry. What will you do?

MADELEINE: I'll go to church and pray.

MOLIÈRE: The theater will give you a pension — God knows you've earned it. You'll come visit?

MADELEINE: No. Jean-Baptiste, Armande must know nothing, you understand? Nothing.

MOLIÈRE: It's late. I'll see you home.

MADELEINE: No thank you. Let me sit here for a moment.

MOLIÈRE: But —

MADELEINE: I'll leave soon enough, don't worry. For God's sake, go away!

MOLIÈRE: Good-bye.

(He goes. After a moment, La Grange enters with his lantern.)

LA GRANGE: Who's still here? Is that you, Madeleine Béjart? So. It's happened? Yes, I know.

MADELEINE: I'm thinking, Chronicler.

LA GRANGE: You didn't have the strength to tell him?

MADELEINE: Too late for that.

LA GRANGE: I tried to stop her . . .

MADELEINE: You're a chivalrous man, Charles Varlet de la Grange. You alone know my secret.

LA GRANGE: You honored me with your trust. I'll keep your secret. Let me see you home now.

MADELEINE: No need, La Grange. Thank you. *(She smiles.)* I left the stage today. Good-bye.

(She vanishes. La Grange returns to his table. He opens his diary, writes.)

LA GRANGE: February seventeenth. Command performance. To signify this honor I inscribe a fleur-de-lis. After the performance I came upon Madeleine Béjart, in the dark, in anguish. She has given up the stage. *(He puts down his pen.)* The reason? A terrible thing has happened. Jean-Baptiste de Molière, unaware that Armande is not the sister, but the daughter of Madeleine — and perhaps his own, as well — has agreed to marry the girl. It must not be written down, but to signify this horror I now inscribe a black cross. An end to the seventeenth of February.

(He picks up his diary and lantern, and exits. Darkness and silence. Then a light appear in the cracks of the harpsichord. The lid is suddenly flung open, and out crawls Moirron. His eyes dart about like a thief's. He is a boy of fifteen, with a handsome, dirty, vicious, exhausted face. He is in rags.)

MOIRRON: Gone! At last! May you all rot in hell — demons! *(He shivers.)* I'm unlucky . . . dirty . . . haven't slept for two days . . . never get to sleep . . . *(Weeping, he falls to the floor, asleep. After a moment, Armande and Molière enter, giggling, with a lantern. Moirron stirs in his sleep. Armande screams, Molière collars him.)*

MOLIÈRE: Who are you? Confess!

MOIRRON: Don't kill me, Monsieur Director, I'm not a thief! I'm Zacharie Moirron, I'm the unfortunate Moirron. I live in the harpsichord!

(Molière looks from him to the harpsichord.)

MOLIÈRE: Aha! I see, I understand. You're the trick. You're the magic trick! *(He bursts into laughter.)* Oh, that Charlatan! That damned Charlatan!

SCENE TWO: AT THE PALACE

The King's reception room. Lights everywhere. A stairway leading who knows where. Courtiers look on, anxious and unctuous. At a card table. Louis XIV is playing cards with the Comte de Lessac. One-Eye actually holds and plays the King's cards for him. Lessac has a pile of gold in front of him, and there are gold pieces scattered on the floor. Lessac is sweating. Only the King is seated, guarded by a Musketeer who never takes his eyes off the King. Louis is a man to be afraid of, despite his pleasant-seeming banalities.

LESSAC: Three knaves and three kings.

LOUIS: Aha. You don't say.

ONE-EYE: *(To Louis.)* I beg your pardon, Sire, but these cards are marked. *(To Lessac.)* Say your prayers!

(The Courtiers freeze in terror.)

LOUIS: You don't say!

ONE-EYE: I swear it.

LOUIS: *(To Lessac.)* You actually tried to play against me with marked cards, Lessac?

LESSAC: Your Majesty, the impoverished state of my finances, my taxes, my pathetic estates —

LOUIS: *(To One-Eye.)* Tell me, Marquis, according to the rules that govern card-playing, how must I proceed? It's an odd case . . .

ONE-EYE: Sire, as for the correct course of action: First you may strike the Comte de Lessac in the face with a candelabra —

LOUIS: Distasteful rule . . . *(He picks up a candelabra.)* This thing must weight fifteen pounds! Perhaps I could use a lighter one?

ONE-EYE: Allow me, Sire.

LOUIS: Don't trouble yourself. *(He lifts the candelabra high above Lessac's head, Lessac cowers. Louis turns back to One-Eye.)* And the second rule?

ONE-EYE: Curse him like a dog.

LOUIS: You don't say. Splendid. Send for that little fellow, what's-his-name? *(The Courtiers rush about in all directions, shouting, "The cobbler, the cobbler!", "Send for the Honest Cobbler!," "The Honest Cobbler!," etc. Louis turns pleasantly to Lessac.)* Now tell me, Comte de Lessac, how do you do it?

LESSAC: With my fingernails, Your Majesty. On the queens, for example, I carve little zeros.

LOUIS: Aha. And the knaves?

LESSAC: Slanted crosses, Sire.

LOUIS: Fascinating. And how does the law view all this?

LESSAC: Negatively, Sire.

LOUIS: *(Sympathetically.)* And what can the law do to you for this?

LESSAC: Put me in prison?

LOUIS: You don't say.

(The Honest Cobbler bursts in noisily.)

COBBLER: I come! I run! I fly! I'm near! I've arrived! Greetings, Your Majesty!

LOUIS: Greetings, Honest Cobbler.

COBBLER: So, who do you want me to curse, Mighty King?

LOUIS: The Comte de Lessac has been playing with marked cards.

(The Honest Cobbler takes a long, distressed look at Lessac, takes a deep breath, addresses him.)

COBBLER: Have you lost your mind, or what? What on earth were you thinking of? In the marketplace they'd smash your face in for trying a trick like that! *(To Louis, with a sense of accomplishment.)* There, did I put him in his place, Sire?

LOUIS: Thank you very much.

COBBLER: I'll just take this . . . apple?

LOUIS: Help yourself. And you, Comte de Lessac, pick up your winnings. *(Lessac pockets the gold.)*

COBBLER: Hold on there — I get an apple and the thief keeps the gold?

LOUIS: *(Staring into space, to One-Eye.)* Marquis, if it's not too much trouble, place the Comte de Lessac in the dungeon for a month. Make sure he has a candle and a deck of cards. He can pass the time scratching little zeros and crosses on the cards. If he can keep the rats from eating them. *(Afterthought.)* If he can keep the rats from eating him. When the month's up, send him home, with his gold. *(To Lessac.)* Straighten up your life! And don't ever play cards again. Next time you might not be so lucky.

LESSAC: O Sire —

(He is led out. The Honest Cobbler yells after him, bitterly.)

COBBLER: Get out of the palace, you — you —

ONE-EYE: Villain?

COBBLER: That's good.

(The servants move about, placing a small dining table set for one before Louis. The Archbishop approaches.)

CHARRON: Your Majesty, will you permit me to present an itinerant preacher to you? His name is Father Bartholomew.

LOUIS: *(Eating soup.)* I love all my subjects, even the vagrants. You may present him, Archbishop.

(Father Bartholomew's strange singing can be heard even before he appears at the door. He is ragged and barefoot, with the eyes of a madman.)

BARTHOLOMEW: We are all fools in Christ.

(All but Louis are shocked. Louis continues to eat soup. Brother Fidelity, who has a sour, sanctimonious face, sidles up to Charron, whispers.)

ONE-EYE: *(To Bartholomew.)* Say your prayers, you grotesque dunce!

BARTHOLOMEW: Most radiant Regent of the Earth! I am come to warn you: The antichrist has been seen in your fair land.

(The Courtiers are stupefied.)

BARTHOLOMEW: And who is this poisonous worm who gnaws at the very foundations of your throne? His name is Jean-Baptiste de Molière. Burn him, Sire! And burn his blasphemous new play, *Tartuffe.*

LOUIS: What's this new play?

CHARRON: *Tartuffe.*

LOUIS: Haven't caught it yet.

BARTHOLOMEW: Burn Molière, burn the play, burn it all! Every true believer demands this of you!

(At the word demands, Louis drops his soup spoon, One-Eye draws his sword, Brother Fidelity clutches his head, and Charron hisses.)

LOUIS: Demands? Demands? Of whom do they demand this?

BARTHOLOMEW: Of you, Sire.

LOUIS: Aha, you don't say. Archbishop —

CHARRON: Forgive me, Sire, he's obviously quite mad today, I didn't realize — it's entirely my fault —

(Louis stares into space. To One-Eye.)

LOUIS: Marquis, if it won't disoblige you, place Father Bartholomew in the dungeon.

(One-Eye gestures to guards who lead the priest out.)

BARTHOLOMEW: *(Going.)* It's the fault of the antichrist — the devil in player's clothing — the antichrist — the blasphemer —

(His screams fade away. Louis' soup is replaced by a fowl course.)

LOUIS: You may approach, Archbishop. Is that fellow mad?

CHARRON: Quite mad, Sire. But his heart is the heart of a true servant of God.

LOUIS: And you, Archbishop, you really believe Molière's dangerous?

CHARRON: Sire, he is Satan.

LOUIS: Aha. So you agree with the madman?

CHARRON: Sire, hear me out. Nothing has darkened your cloudless reign, nor will it, so long as you love —

LOUIS: Whom?

CHARRON: God.

LOUIS: Oh, but I do, I love him.

CHARRON: He sits up there, you sit down here, and there is no one else.

LOUIS: I like that.

CHARRON: Your power knows no limits, Sire . . . so long as the light of the Church shines on your throne.

LOUIS: I like the Church.

CHARRON: Which is why I, along with poor mad Bartholomew, beg you to defend it from that . . . viper.

LOUIS: Surely there are plenty of defenders of the faith? You've got that mysterious cabal — what do you call them, the Black Cross? They're enough to scare anyone . . . God knows they scare me. (He smiles at Charron.) You're convinced Molière has offended the Church?

CHARRON: In *Tartuffe*, he holds me — I mean religion — up to ridicule, he accuses us of hypocrisy — he could destroy us! And after us, what's left to destroy but . . . (Whispers.) your reign, Sire.

LOUIS: (Reflective.) He may be a devil. But he's a gifted devil, he can enhance the glory of my court —

CHARRON: But Sire —

LOUIS: That ecstatic madman, does he love the king?

CHARRON: Yes, Sire.

LOUIS: Release him after three days, Archbishop. And explain to him that when conversing with a King of France, it's unwise to use the word *demands*.

CHARRON: May God bless you, Sire; and may he bring your chastening hand down upon the head of the atheist!

VOICE: (From off.) "Your Majesty's servant, Monsieur de Molière."
(Charron and Fidelity glare at each other.)

LOUIS: Let him come forward.
(Molière enters, bows to Louis, walks past the curious Courtiers. He has aged considerably. His face is sick and gray.)

MOLIÈRE: Sire!

LOUIS: Monsieur de Molière, I'm dining. You've no objection?

MOLIÈRE: O, Sire.

LOUIS: And will you join me? (He speaks into space.) Marquis, a chair.
(One-Eye snaps his fingers, a chair appears.)

MOLIÈRE: Your Majesty, I cannot accept this honor —

LOUIS: (Into space.) Marquis, dishes. (Dishes appear. Molière sits nervously on the edge of his chair.) Have you met the Marquis D'Orsini? Known to some as One-Eye. Known to others less fortunate as Say-Your-Prayers.

MOLIÈRE: I — I've had the honor.

LOUIS: Do you like chicken?
(One-Eye beckons, food appears before Molière.)

MOLIÈRE: Oh, my favorite, Sire. Please, Sire, allow me to stand —

LOUIS: Eat. Go on. How's your wife . . . what's-her-name?

MOLIÈRE: Armande, Sire. She's well.

LOUIS: Handsome woman; good actress, too. You've been married —

MOLIÈRE: Ten years, Sire.

LOUIS: Ten years — has it been that long?! And how is my godchild?

MOLIÈRE: To my sorrow, the child has died.

LOUIS: What? The second one died too?

MOLIÈRE: My children do not live, Sire.

LOUIS: Aha. Don't be depressed. Eat.

MOLIÈRE: Your Majesty, never before has anyone dined with the king. It makes me nervous.

LOUIS: Monsieur de Molière, France sits before you in a chair. France is eating chicken and he's not a bit nervous.

MOLIÈRE: O Sire, only you can speak like that.

LOUIS: Rumor has it that you've finally finished that play *Tartuffe* is it called? Is it funny? *(Molière gives a modest shrug.)* Aha, you're a clever writer. And I've been generous with my patronage, haven't I?

MOLIÈRE: I'd be nothing without Your Majesty.

LOUIS: I know. Art, monsieur . . . Art and Patronage go hand in hand, but we both know that Patronage leads the dance, eh? There are certain topics which must be approached with caution by the artist, agreed? *(He smiles.)* I trust you've been circumspect with *Tartuffe?* You know the clergy, so sensitive. You've got to give them proper respect or they . . . you know, they come running to me to complain and I'm forced to oblige them, or else they start to pout, and then they don't pay their taxes. I hope you're not an atheist?

MOLIÈRE: *(Terrified.)* For pity's sake, no, Your Majesty!

LOUIS: Aha. Good. And since I'm confident you plan to tread the path of righteousness in the future, I hereby grant you permission to perform *Tartuffe* at the Palais Royal.

(Everyone is dumbfounded, Molière most of all.)

MOLIÈRE: My king — I love you!

(Louis stands.)

LOUIS: And tonight you've the honor of preparing my bed.

(Another gasp from the court. Louis departs, Molière grabs the candelabra, calls out.)

MOLIÈRE: Make way for the king! Make way for the king! *(He turns back to Charron.)* See, Archbishop, you can't touch me! *Tartuffe* has been permitted! *(Going.)* Make way for the king! Make way for the king!

(He disappears after Louis. The Courtiers follow. Charron turns to Brother Fidelity.)

CHARRON: Strengthen my arm against this atheist. And let him fall off the stage and break his neck! Why, Brother Fidelity? Why did you send me a madman? You promised that this Bartholomew would make an impression on the king . . . and he did.

FIDELITY: How could I guess he'd use the word *demand*.

CHARRON: Demand.

FIDELITY: Demand. *(A pause.)*

CHARRON: Tell me, have you got the woman?

FIDELITY: She's over there.

(He points to a nun who stands with her back to them (and us). Slowly she turns, to reveal a masked face. The mask is red, and somewhat lewd-looking. She turns away again.)

FIDELITY: She'll send the message to the fellow in question. She'll find some innocent dupe to deliver it.

(The Honest Cobbler, napping on his stool, gives a little snort.)

FIDELITY: Perhaps the king's jester.

CHARRON: But will One-Eye follow her?

(The Masked Nun crosses to the Cobbler, wakes him, whispers, hands him a note and a coin, then leaves as.)

FIDELITY: This woman? Archbishop, I think you may count on it.

(One-Eye appears at the top of the stairs. Fidelity catches sight of him, slips away. Charron starts to follow, but One-Eye stops him, bows ironically.)

ONE-EYE: The mad priest went hunting the antichrist, and all he caught was a trip to the dungeon. I despise the clergy, malicious eunuchs all. *(To the heavens.)* Ah, God in heaven, say Your prayers! *(Charron turns and goes.)*

COBBLER: Say-Your-Prayers?

ONE-EYE: The Marquis D'Orsini to you.

COBBLER: I've got a message for you.

ONE-EYE: From whom?

COBBLER: Who knows? She was masked.

ONE-EYE: *(Reads the note.)* Hmmm. What kind of woman?

COBBLER: I don't know; loose, I suppose.

ONE-EYE: Why loose?

COBBLER: Because she sends notes.

ONE-EYE: Does she have a good figure?

COBBLER: See for yourself.

(He nods at a fashionable woman who wears a lewd red half-mask.)

ONE-EYE: Quite right.

(One-Eye makes no eye contact with the woman, but follows her offstage at

a distance. The lights begin to dim. A voice: "The king is sleeping." Another: "The king is sleeping." And a third, a fourth. The Honest Cobbler lies down on a card table, wraps himself in a portiere.)

COBBLER: And I'll sleep too.

(Only his boots stick out. The palace swims in darkness, and disappears.)

SCENE THREE: MOLIÈRE'S APARTMENT, DAY

The harpsichord is open and Moirron plays softly. He is now a handsome, elegantly dressed young man of twenty-five. Armande sits pretending to read a manuscript, but she never takes her eyes off his face.

MOIRRON: Don't you like the way I play, little Mama?

ARMANDE: Must I ask you again, Monsieur Moirron, to stop calling me "Mama." Please.

MOIRRON: And how many times must I remind you, I'm not Monsieur Moirron, but Monsieur de Moirron.

ARMANDE: Oh yes, how forgetful of me, you got your title by sitting inside a harpsichord.

MOIRRON: Good God, woman, I was a little boy then. Today all Paris is at my feet —

ARMANDE: Which you owe to my husband, or have you forgotten that too? He dragged you out of that harpsichord by your dirty ear.

MOIRRON: No, by my dirty feet. Father Molière's good-hearted, but he's jealous, and as cross as a bear.

ARMANDE: My poor husband, he adopted an incredibly insolent son.

MOIRRON: Insolent? Well, I admit I may be. But why not? I'm the greatest actor in Paris, eh?

(He grows even merrier, like a man begging for misfortune.)

ARMANDE: The arrogance! What about Jean-Baptiste?

MOIRRON: All right, all right, there are three great ones: the master, and myself —

ARMANDE: And who's the third?

MOIRRON: You, my renowned darling — *(He grabs her script, reads.)*
"To please you is my joy, my only goal;
Your love is the restorer of my soul — "

ARMANDE: Give me my script back, you villain!

MOIRRON: "Madam, no happiness is so complete

As when, from lips we love, come words so sweet."

(She grabs the script away, he grabs her.)

ARMANDE: "Why be in such a hurry? Must my heart
  Exhaust its bounty at the very start?" *(He lifts the hem of her skirt.)* Jean-Baptiste will be —

MOIRRON: He's with the King of France, remember?

ARMANDE: Oh. Where's Bouton?

MOIRRON: He's gone to the market. *(He bends, kisses her foot.)*

ARMANDE: Leave me alone. *(He kisses her knee. She shudders.)*

MOIRRON: Mama, let's go into my room.

ARMANDE: I swear by the holy Virgin, nothing could induce me. *(He kisses her other knee.)* I curse the day he dragged you out of that damned harpsichord!

MOIRRON: Come to my room.

ARMANDE: I won't go — never! *(They enter his room, close the door.)* Ah, you'll ruin me . . . ruin me . . .

(A pause. Bouton enters with a basket of vegetables. He listens, puts the basket down softly.)

BOUTON: Strange. *(He takes off his shoes, tiptoes to the closed door, listens.)* Thief! *(To an imagined jury.)* But gentlemen, I've seen nothing, I've heard nothing, I'll say nothing.

MOLIÈRE: *(Off.)* Armande!

BOUTON: Good God, here he comes!

(He leaves his shoes and the basket of vegetables and hides. Molière bursts in.)

MOLIÈRE: Armande, the news is good! The king will permit *Tartuffe!* We play it next week! And Armande, I met that ridiculous one-eyed fellow, D'Orsini — he's the perfect model for Don Juan! I really must write a play about him, and . . . Armande?

(He looks around, studies the vegetables and shoes. Then the key slowly turns in the closed door. Molière flings it open, Armande screams. Noise. Moirron runs out, wig in hand.)

MOIRRON: How dare you! How dare you! *(Molière pursues him.)*

MOLIÈRE: Villain! I don't believe it! Can't believe my own eyes!

(He slumps in a chair. The key turns, as Armande locks herself in.)

ARMANDE: *(Off.)* Jean-Baptiste, you're not being fair!

(Bouton pops out, hides again.)

MOLIÈRE: So, you eat my bread, and in return you dishonor me.

MOIRRON: I challenge you. *(He pulls out his sword.)*

MOLIÈRE: Oh please. Drop the sword.

MOIRRON: I challenge you! You're cuckolding yourself!

MOLIÈRE: Just get out of my house.

MOIRRON: You've put the horns on your own head!

MOLIÈRE: Bastard, I gave you shelter, but I can hurl you back into the abyss. Zacharie Moirron, I banish you from the company of the Palais Royal. Go!

MOIRRON: You're dismissing me from the company?

MOLIÈRE: Get out, you adopted thief.

ARMANDE: *(Desperate, behind the door.)* Jean-Baptiste!

MOIRRON: You were dreaming it, Father. We were rehearsing *Tartuffe* — don't you recognize your own lines? Why are you ruining me?

MOLIÈRE: Get out, before I run you through.

MOIRRON: Very well, but I'm curious to know who'll play Valère tonight. Bouton? Ha ha. *(A pause.)* Monsieur de Molière, you will regret this madness. I know your little secret — one overhears things, monsieur. Have you forgotten Madeleine Béjart?

MOLIÈRE: What about her?

MOIRRON: Madeleine's near death now, she's always praying. And don't forget, in France there is a king!

MOLIÈRE: What are you raving about, you —

MOIRRON: Raving? I'm going to visit the Archbishop now.

MOLIÈRE: Thank you both for betraying me. Now — get out, you wretch!

MOIRRON: *(Going.)* Cuckold!

(Molière grabs a pistol, Moirron leaves. Molière rattles the door, yells into the keyhole.)

MOLIÈRE: Whore! *(Armande cries, behind the door.)* Bouton! *(Bouton appears.)* Pimp! What are your shoes doing here?

BOUTON: Sir, I —

MOLIÈRE: You're lying! I see from your eyes, you're lying!

BOUTON: In order to lie, one must be allowed to speak. I can't get a word in edgewise. I took off my shoes because . . . look, see the nails? Curse all shoes with heel-plates. I was making a racket with my shoes, see? And they were rehearsing, those two, so they locked the door to get rid of me. Of the shoes.

ARMANDE: *(Off.)* Yes, that's it!

MOLIÈRE: And what about the vegetables?

BOUTON: The vegetables? Oh, the vegetables, to be honest, play no part in the affair. I've just been to market.

MOLIÈRE: *(Through the keyhole.)* Are you trying to kill me? You know I've got a bad heart.

BOUTON: *(Through the keyhole.)* Are you trying to kill him? You know he's got a bad heart.

MOLIÈRE: *(Kicks the basket.)* Get out! *(Bouton goes. Molière sits on the floor by the door.)* Armande? Be patient, you'll soon be free of me. Armande? I don't want to die alone. *(She opens the door, enters, tear-stained.)* Swear to me — ? Say something.

ARMANDE: A dramatist like you . . . great, but here in your own home you act like a —

MOLIÈRE: You're right.

ARMANDE: How dare you even think such a thing? The scandal you cause!

MOLIÈRE: You're right, you're right. Now that little worm will start running all over town. And I hit him — ridiculous!

ARMANDE: What did he mean, he's going to visit the archbishop?

MOLIÈRE: God knows. He probably went to gossip about *Tartuffe.*

ARMANDE: Bring Moirron back. Bring him back!

MOLIÈRE: Let him go to the devil — for a day. Then I'll bring him home.
(Lights fade out.)

SCENE FOUR: A CELLAR

A three-branched candelabra and some manuscripts rest on a table with a red cloth. Around the table sit members of the Order of the Black Cross. They wear masks. Charron, without a mask, sits apart. Two dour men lead Moirron in, blindfolded. His hands are tied behind his back.

MOIRRON: Where have you brought me? *(They remove his blindfold.)*

CHARRON: That's none of your business. Will you, in front of these virtuous brothers, repeat your denunciation?
(Moirron is silent. He looks around.)

BROTHER FORCE: Are you deaf, Actor?

MOIRRON: I — Holy archbishop, it happened ten years ago, I was a little boy and I couldn't hear too well at the time. It might be better if I didn't say anything.

CHARRON: You mean, you slandered Monsieur de Molière when we spoke this morning?

BROTHER FORCE: Answer the archbishop, you gorgeous dunghill. *(Silence.)*

CHARRON: It saddens me that you slandered him.

BROTHER FORCE: Lying is dangerous, Actor. We'll have to put you in the dungeon, my beauty, where you'll feed the bedbugs for a long time. But we'll finish up this business in any case, with or without your help.

MOIRRON: *(Hoarse.)* I didn't slander him!

BROTHER FORCE: Then don't make me lose my temper! Tell us. *(Moirron is silent. Two unpleasant-looking men enter.)* Why look, such pretty shoes you're wearing, Actor. But there are even prettier ones. Perhaps you should try one on? *(To the torturers.)* Bring in the Spanish Boot.

MOIRRON: No!! Years ago — I was a boy — I used to sit in the Charlatan's harpsichord.

BROTHER FORCE: Whatever for?

MOIRRON: I played a keyboard hidden inside, it was a trick, as if the harpsichord played itself.

BROTHER FORCE: So?

MOIRRON: So while I sat in the harpsichord — no, I can't, Holy Father, I can't! I was drunk this morning, I can't remember what I told you —

BROTHER FORCE: This is the last time I'll ask you.

MOIRRON: I . . . one night I heard a voice say that Monsieur de Molière married — that she wasn't Madeleine Béjart's sister, she was her daughter.

BROTHER FORCE: And whose voice did you hear?

MOIRRON: I don't — I think I dreamed it.

BROTHER FORCE: Well then, whose voice did you dream?

MOIRRON: The actor La Grange.

(The Inquisitors smile at each other.)

CHARRON: Thank you, my friend. You've performed your duty with honor — no, don't reproach yourself. Every loyal subject of the king, every faithful son of the Church should be honored to supply information about a crime.

(Brother Force re-ties the blindfold.)

Now, as a reward, you're going to spend a little time in a safe place. You'll be well taken care of. Then you'll come with me to see the king.

BROTHER FORCE: He's not such a bad little fellow, after all. At first I didn't care for him, but now I can see he's a good Catholic.

(Moirron is led out.)

CHARRON: And now, my good brethren, we're about to receive another guest. I'm afraid he knows my voice, so I'll ask Brother Fidelity to speak with him. *(A knock. Charron draws his cowl over his face. Brother Fidelity opens the door. The Woman in the Red Mask leads in One-Eye, who is blindfolded.)*

ONE-EYE: Well, my charmer, when may I take off this blindfold? You might have trusted me. It feels damp in your room . . . it smells musty . . .

WOMAN-IN-MASK: Just one more step, Marquis. So. Remove the blindfold. *(She hides. He removes the blindfold, looks around him.)*

ONE-EYE: Ah, say your prayers! *(He grabs his pistol in one hand, his sword in the other, stands with his back to the wall.)* Well, well, well, what a charming reception. The tips of your swords are peeping out from your cloaks. If you try to kill me, I'll take a few of you with me. They call me Say-Your-Prayers! — don't move! Where is the whore who lured me into this trap?

WOMAN-IN-MASK: *(From the darkness.)* Here, Marquis, but I'm no whore.

BROTHER FORCE: Sir, she is a lady.

FIDELITY: Rest easy, Marquis, no one will attack you.

BROTHER FORCE: Put away your sword, it impedes our conversation.

ONE-EYE: Where am I?

FIDELITY: In a room. In a great church.

ONE-EYE: I'm not much of a churchgoer.

FIDELITY: You're free to leave whenever you wish.

ONE-EYE: Then who bother to lure me here? Say your prayers . . . but first, is this a plot against the king?

FIDELITY: God forgive you, Marquis. These men are devoted supporters of His Majesty. You are attending a meeting of the Order of the Black Cross.

ONE-EYE: The Black Cross, well, well. And what does it want of me?

FIDELITY: Sit down, I beg you. *(He sits.)* We grieve for you, Marquis.

CHORUS OF THE "ORDER": We grieve.

ONE-EYE: I can do without your grief. Explain.

FIDELITY: We merely want to inform you, you're about to be ridiculed at court.

ONE-EYE: I told you, I'm called Say-Your-Prayers.

CHORUS: *(Whispers.)* Say your prayers.

FIDELITY: All France knows of your remarkable skills. That's why they whisper behind your back.

ONE-EYE: Who dares? What's his name?! *(He pounds with his sword.)*

BROTHER FORCE: Why such a racket, Marquis?

FIDELITY: The whole court is whispering.

ONE-EYE: Explain, or I'll lose my temper.

FIDELITY: Have you seen a certain depraved play by Jean-Baptiste de Molière? I think it's called *Tartuffe*.

ONE-EYE: No, but I've met the fellow. He's a clown, a performing ape.

FIDELITY: In *Tartuffe*, the atheist-clown ridicules religion and its faithful servants.

ONE-EYE: *(Shrugs.)* And?

FIDELITY: He's preparing a new piece, with you as the model for its — I hate to use the word "hero."

ONE-EYE: Me?

FIDELITY: He makes you swagger, he makes you leer, and worst of all, he makes you a coward.

BROTHER FORCE: He calls this play *Don Juan*.

ONE-EYE: I see. Thank you very much.

(His face twitches. Fidelity picks up a manuscript.)

FIDELITY: If you wish to read it . . . ?

ONE-EYE: No thank you. Why, my friends, should I be portrayed in so an unflattering a light? Answer?

FIDELITY: Silence is your answer. And now —

ONE-EYE: And now, you can guess how I'll proceed with this clown.

FIDELITY: We ask only that you keep this visit a secret.

ONE-EYE: *(Nods.)* Where is the lady who brought me?

WOMAN-IN-MASK: Here. The blindfold, if you please, Marquis.

(She reties it.)

ONE-EYE: I owe you a profound apology.

WOMAN-IN-MASK: God will forgive you, Marquis, as I do. Now I'll deliver you back to the spot where we met.

(She leads him out. Charron emerges from the shadows.)

CHARRON: That manuscript, the one you suggested the Marquis read?

FIDELITY: The pages were blank. He's not much of a reader.

CHARRON: Lucky for us. Well, the snare has been sprung. I declare this meeting of the Order of the Black Cross closed. Let us pray.

CHORUS: Laudamus tibi, Domine, rex eternae gloriae . . . *(Etc.)*

SCENE FIVE: A CATHEDRAL

The Archbishop's confessional. Two dark figures walk past. A hoarse whisper: "Have you seen Tartuffe?" *Armande and La Grange lead Madeleine in. She is sick and gray.*

MADELEINE: Thank you, Armande. And thanks, La Grange, old friend.

(An organ starts to play.)

LA GRANGE: We'll wait for you. *(They move into shadow. Madeleine enters the confessional.)*

CHARRON: Come closer, my daughter. You are Madeleine Béjart? *(The organ stops.)* You are one of the truly devout of this cathedral. You are dear to my heart.

MADELEINE: You honor this sinner. *(He blesses her, covers her head with her veil.)*

CHARRON: Poor woman, you're ill? *(She nods.)* Do you wish to leave this world?

MADELEINE: With all my heart, Father.

(The organ plays on high.)

CHARRON: What is your sickness?

MADELEINE: The doctors tell me my blood is poisoned. I see the devil and I am afraid of him.

CHARRON: My poor child. What are you doing to save yourself from the devil?

MADELEINE: I pray.

(The organ falls silent.)

CHARRON: For that God will raise you up and love you. Tell me, have you sinned?

MADELEINE: I've sinned all my life, Father. I lied. And I was a terrible wanton. For years I was an actress — I seduced them all.

CHARRON: And is there, perhaps, some particularly burdensome sin that comes to mind?

MADELEINE: I . . . don't recall, Father.

CHARRON: People are mad, they're mad! You'll travel with a red-hot nail in your heart, and when you arrive down there, no one will be able to remove it. Never! Do you know the meaning of the word *never?*

MADELEINE: Oh, I am so afraid.

(Charron turns into the devil.)

CHARRON: You shall see the fires burning, and in their midst —

MADELEINE: The sentinel walks and walks —

CHARRON: And he whispers, "Why didn't you abandon your sin in your lifetime? Why have you brought it with you?"

MADELEINE: And I wring my hands, I cry out to God —

CHARRON: But by then God won't be able to hear you! And so your limbs will be plunged into the fire . . . forever. Do you know the meaning of the word *forever?*

MADELEINE: I'm afraid to — if I did, I'd die right now. *(She cries out weakly.)* I do understand! And if I abandon my sin here?

CHARRON: You shall hear the eternal choir.

(Children's voices sing above. A processional passes with candles. Then it all vanishes. Madeleine reaches out in the dark.)

MADELEINE: Where are you, Holy Father?

CHARRON: I am here, I am here.

MADELEINE: I want to hear the eternal choir.

CHARRON: Confess!

MADELEINE: Once, long ago, I lived with two men. And I gave birth to a daughter, Armande. And all my life since, I've been tormented, not knowing whose child she was.

CHARRON: My poor soul.

MADELEINE: That was long ago, in the provinces. When she grew up I brought her to Paris and passed her off as my sister . . .

CHARRON: Well?!

MADELEINE: One day, one of those two men, consumed by passion, became one with her. But he was innocent, I had never told him a thing about my child. And now, because of me, he has . . . perhaps . . . committed a mortal sin. And now I am condemned to Hell. I want to fly up to the eternal choir!

CHARRON: I, Archbishop of Paris, now absolve and release you.

MADELEINE: *(Tears of joy.)* And I may fly?

(The organ plays.)

CHARRON: Fly, fly! *(The organ is silent.)* Is your daughter here? Call her. I shall also forgive her unwitting sin. Go.

(Madeleine emerges from the confessional.)

MADELEINE: Armande, Armande, my sister, the Archbishop wishes to bless you too! I'm happy, so happy!

(La Grange leads her out. Armande enters the confessional. Charron appears demonically, with a horned miter. He makes the sign of the cross over her several times, with an inverted devil's cross.)

CHARRON: Tell me, do you realize who that was?

ARMANDE: You mean my sister?

CHARRON: Your sister?

(Suddenly, in horror, Armande understands.)

ARMANDE: No, no, she is my sister, my sister!

CHARRON: She is your mother! I will absolve you, but you must run from him this very day! Run! Run!

(With a weak cry, Armande falls to the ground. Charron disappears into the darkness. The organ plays. Blackout.)

SCENE SIX: THE KING'S AUDIENCE CHAMBER

Louis sits at a table. Before him stands the exhausted Charron. The Honest Cobbler sits on the floor, mending a shoe.

CHARRON: Madeleine Béjart confirmed the boy's story, Your Majesty. It was her last confession. She's dead.

LOUIS: Pity.

CHARRON: Sire, Molière has sullied his name with this crime. But it's up to Your Majesty to judge.

LOUIS: Thank you, Archbishop. *(He speaks into space.)* Summon the director of the Palais Royal immediately. *(To Charron.)* Meanwhile, I'll speak to this actor, Moirron.

CHARRON: Yes, Sire. *(He goes.)*

COBBLER: Mighty Ruler?

LOUIS: Yes, Honest Cobbler?

COBBLER: I suppose no state can exist without squealers?

LOUIS: Don't you like squealers?

COBBLER: What's there to like about them? Bastards!

LOUIS: Be still, fool, and fix your shoe.

(Moirron enters, his eyes are those of an animal at bay. He's frightened, and looks as if he's slept in his clothes. He is overwhelmed by the King.)

LOUIS: *(Politely.)* Zacharie Moirron?

MOIRRON: Yes, Your Majesty.

LOUIS: You were in the harpsichord?

MOIRRON: Yes, Sire.

LOUIS: And Monsieur de Molière adopted you? *(Moirron is silent.)* I've asked you a question.

MOIRRON: Yes.

LOUIS: He taught you the actor's craft? *(Moirron begins to cry.)* I've asked you a question.

MOIRRON: He did.

LOUIS: Aha. Why did you address this denunciation to the king? Look, it says here, "desiring to aid in the administration of justice — "

CHARRON: "Desiring to aid in the administration of justice — "

MOIRRON: Yes, desiring to . . .

LOUIS: Is it true he struck you in the face?

MOIRRON: It's true.

LOUIS: Why? Well? Speak up.

MOIRRON: I was betraying him with his wife.

LOUIS: Simply answer "for personal reasons."

MOIRRON: For personal reasons.

LOUIS: How old are you?

MOIRRON: Twenty-five.

LOUIS: We've got good news for you. Your information has been confirmed by our investigators. What do you wish from your king, money perhaps?

MOIRRON: Please, Sire, allow me to work in your Royal Theatre at the Hotel de Borgogne?

LOUIS: No.

MOIRRON: No?

LOUIS: It's been reported that you're a bad actor.

MOIRRON: I . . . bad? What about the Theatre de Marais?

LOUIS: No to that too.

MOIRRON: But . . . what shall I do?

LOUIS: Why do you need this dubious acting business? You're a man with a spotless reputation. If you like, you can go into the King's service . . . in the Secret Police. When you apply, don't hesitate to mention my name. They know me there. You may go.

(Moirron rises, leaves with Charron.)

COBBLER: Go to the gallows, squealer, to the gallows.

LOUIS: Fool.

(Off, a guard shouts, "Monsieur de Molière!" La Grange appears, leading Molière, who looks odd. His collar is askew, his wig dishevelled, his face gray, his hands trembling. His sword hangs crookedly at his side.)

MOLIÈRE: Sire.

LOUIS: Who is he? You were asked to come alone.

MOLIÈRE: My faithful student, the actor La Grange . . . helped me. If you please, I've had some sort of heart attack, I couldn't get here on my own. I hope . . . I haven't angered Your Majesty? *(A pause.)* If you please, I've been struck by . . . bad luck. Forgive my appearance, Madeleine Béjart died yesterday, and my wife . . . ran away from home. She left everything behind. Gowns, think of it, a chest of drawers filled with . . . things and . . . scarves, rings. She left a crazy note too. *(He takes a scrap of paper from his pocket, smiles pleadingly.)*

LOUIS: *(Pleasantly.)* The Archbishop was right after all. Not only are your plays blasphemous filth, but you yourself are a disgusting, incestuous criminal. *(Molière freezes.)* We hereby pronounce our decision in the matter of your marriage: We forbid you to appear at Court. We forbid you to perform *Tartuffe*. In order that your company not die of starvation, we permit your light farces to be played at the Palais Royal, but nothing else. And from this day forward, take care not to remind us of your existence. We deprive you of the King's Patronage!

MOLIÈRE: Your Majesty, this is disaster — worse than death. Why?

LOUIS: Because the shadow of a scandalous marriage has darkened the king's name. *(Molière sinks to the ground.)*

MOLIÈRE: Forgive me, I can't . . . seem to get up . . .

LOUIS: This audience is over.

(He rises, exits. La Grange pulls Molière to his feet.)

LA GRANGE: Master —

MOLIÈRE: Get the carriage, take me away — *(La Grange disappears.)* I must see Madeleine, I can get her advice. But she's . . . dead. What's it all about?

COBBLER: You don't know either, eh? So you don't believe in God? What a mess — have an apple. *(Molière takes it.)*

MOLIÈRE: Thank you.

(Charron enters, stares at Molière, his eyes gleaming with satisfaction. At the sight of Charron, Molière begins to wake up. He rises from his chair, eyes glittering.)

MOLIÈRE: Ah, Holy Father, satisfied? You think you've evened the score for *Tartuffe?* Yes, you guessed right, Your Reverence. Friends used to tell me, "You ought to describe some vulture of a monk, some day, for a comedy." Yes. And guess who I chose for my model? I could never find a better vulture than you, Your Reverence.

CHARRON: I grieve for you. A man who's chosen your path must surely end on the gallows, my son.

(Molière pulls out his sword.)

MOLIÈRE: Don't call me your son, I'm not the son of the devil.

COBBLER: What are you two barking about?

CHARRON: In fact, you won't have to wait for the gallows.

(One-Eye enters, approaches Molière, pushes him down.)

ONE-EYE: Sir, you pushed me, and you haven't asked my pardon. You, sir, are a boor.

MOLIÈRE: *(Mechanically.)* I'm sorry. No, wait, you pushed me!

ONE-EYE: Liar.

MOLIÈRE: What do you want from me?

(La Grange enters.)

LA GRANGE: Master, leave right now. Right now! Marquis, Monsieur de Molière is unwell.

ONE-EYE: I found him with his sword drawn, he's well enough. *(To Molière.)* My name's D'Orsini. You, sir, are a scoundrel.

MOLIÈRE: I challenge you, you bragging buffoon!

LA GRANGE: Leave, master, I beg you, this man is Say-Your-Prayers!

CHARRON: *(Delighted.)* Gentlemen, what are you doing? And in the king's chambers —

MOLIÈRE: I challenge you!

ONE-EYE: Good, the matter's settled; I need not insult you further. *(Merrily.)* May God judge me, and if He finds me lacking, which I doubt He could, may the Bastille claim me! *(To La Grange.)* You, sir, are the witness. *(To Molière.)* Give him any instructions regarding your estate. *(He tests the top of his sword.)* No instructions?
(He crosses the air with his sword, starts to parry with Molière. Charron cheerfully munches an apple.)

CHARRON: *(Calmly.)* Gentlemen, use your heads. Gentlemen!

ONE-EYE: Say your prayers!

LA GRANGE: Ruthless murderer —

COBBLER: Help, people are hacking each other to pieces in the king's audience chamber!
(One-Eye grabs the Cobbler to shut him up, then rushes again at Molière, who waves him away with his sword. Molière hides behind a table, One-Eye jumps on top of the table.)

LA GRANGE: Throw down your sword, master. *(The sword is discarded.)*

ONE-EYE: Pick up your sword.

LA GRANGE: You can't fight a man who doesn't have a sword.

ONE-EYE: True. Pick it up, you coward, so I can kill you.

MOLIÈRE: Please don't kill me. There's something here I don't understand . . . I have a sick heart, and my wife's left me — her diamond rings are lying on the floor — she didn't even take her linen . . . disaster.

ONE-EYE: What's he raving about?

MOLIÈRE: And now you attack me. I've only met you twice in my life — you brought me that money. La Grange, see that it's distributed among the troupe . . . but that was years ago. I'm sick. And now, please don't hurt me again.

ONE-EYE: *(Slips his sword back into its scabbard.)* I shall kill you after your next performance.

MOLIÈRE: Good, good, it doesn't matter . . .
(The Honest Cobbler manages to break away, runs out. La Grange lifts Molière from the floor, carries him out. Charron crosses to One-Eye, eyes blazing.)

CHARRON: Why didn't you kill him?

ONE-EYE: None of your business!

CHARRON: Afraid?

ONE-EYE: He threw down his sword.

CHARRON: Coward. Idiot.

ONE-EYE: Devil's own priest — say your prayers!

(Charron suddenly spits at him. One-Eye is so amazed that he can only spit back. Charron replies in kind. One-Eye spits. Charron spits. Etc. The Honest Cobbler runs in, followed by Louis. But the Archbishop and the duelist are so involved in their spitting contest, that they can't stop immediately.)

LOUIS: Aha. Forgive the interruption.

(Blackout.)

SCENE SEVEN: BACKSTAGE AT THE PALAIS ROYAL

Molière wears a bathrobe over his costume for The Imaginary Invalid. *Bouton sits glumly in a chair. On a table are two swords, a pistol, a bottle of wine. La Grange, wearing a dark cloak over his doctor's costume, paces. He makes a little sound halfway between a hum and a moan. On the wall behind him is the shadow of a knight. The prompter runs through, carrying props. Du Croisy enters nervously. He is also in costume.*

DU CROISY: The audience is coming in.

LA GRANGE: Cancel the show.

DU CROISY: They've paid for their tickets.

LA GRANGE: The whole place is ready to explode — the audience is filled with enemies. *(He takes his journal off a dressing table.)* Look. See? February the seventeenth. It was exactly ten years ago today —

DU CROISY: What was?

LA GRANGE: Our unlucky day. Ten years ago — that little Judas was in the harpsichord, and he overheard me writing — so it was my fault, it was me —

(Du Croisy goes out to check the house.)

MOLIÈRE: You had nothing to do with it. Fate entered my house without an invitation, and stole it all.

BOUTON: I've had a tragic fate too. There I was, selling pies in the town of

Limoges. No one was buying, so I ran away with the strolling players instead. And ended up here.

MOLIÈRE: Shut up, Bouton.

BOUTON: I'm shut up.

(A pause. The stairs creak, a door opens, and Moirron enters. He is unshaven, wears a dirty shirt, carries a lantern. La Grange grabs the pistol. Molière hits La Grange on the arm, he drops the pistol, which discharges into the air. Moirron looks apologetically at the bullet hole. La Grange breaks a jar, attacks Moirron. He knocks him to the ground, starts to strangle him.)

LA GRANGE: Punish me, Your Majesty, but first — Judas!

MOLIÈRE: Bouton, help me —

(They drag La Grange off Moirron.)

La Grange, do you want to kill me? All that screaming, you'll be the death of me, both of you.

(La Grange glares at Moirron.)

LA GRANGE: Zacharie Moirron, do you know me? Wherever you go tonight, expect death. You'll never live till morning.

(Moirron nods, then kneels before Molière.)

MOLIÈRE: Why have you come, my son? My crime has been proclaimed to the world. There are no more secrets to unearth about me — unless I've forgotten something. Maybe I'm a forger? Go, search my desk, I give you permission.

(Moirron bows down his head.)

MOIRRON: Esteemed and beloved teacher —

MOLIÈRE: No bowing! Just tell me what you want.

MOIRRON: I've come to comfort you with the thought that by midnight, I'll have hanged myself. My life can't go on. Here's the rope — *(He pulls it from his shirt.)* And here's a letter: "I am going to Hell."

MOLIÈRE: Now that's a comfort.

BOUTON: As a famous philosopher once said —

MOLIÈRE: Shut up, Bouton.

BOUTON: I'm shut up.

MOIRRON: But even if I were to live, I'd never look at Madame Molière again, not once.

MOLIÈRE: You won't have to. She's run off, and I'm alone . . . forever. I'm impetuous, that's why I always act first and think later. But having thought and grown wise, I forgive you, and take you back into my house. Come in. *(Moirron weeps.)*

LA GRANGE: You're not a man, master, you're a rag that people wipe the floor with.

MOLIÈRE: Don't try to judge things you can't understand. *(To Moirron.)* You'll wear holes in your pants, get up. Where's your coat?

MOIRRON: I pawned it in the tavern.

MOLIÈRE: For how much? *(Moirron shrugs.)* Dreadful, leaving satin coats in taverns. Bouton, go buy back his coat.

BOUTON: But this evening's performance —

MOLIÈRE: Plenty of time. Go. *(Bouton goes out. To Moirron.)*
They say you've been wandering all over town. I hear you even dropped in on the king.

MOIRRON: And the king told me to join the Secret Police — the Secret Police! He said I'm a bad actor.

MOLIÈRE: Ah, the human heart. The king's wrong, you're a first-rate actor. But you're not cut out for the Secret Police, your heart's not cut out for that. I've only one regret: that I shan't be acting with you much longer. *(He has a coughing spell.)* What's the play tonight? Oh yes, *Imaginary Invalid.* You'd better get into your costume.
(Moirron starts to change.)

MOLIÈRE: Did you hear the news? They've sic'd the one-eyed dog on me. The king's deprived me of his patronage, so now One-Eye and the Archbishop are free to kill me.

MOIRRON: While I'm alive, they'll never touch you. I can handle a sword.

LA GRANGE: Before you face Say-Your-Prayers, you snot-nose worm, you'd best buy yourself a requiem mass.

MOIRRON: I'll wait and stab him in the back.

LA GRANGE: Yes, we know you can do that well.

MOIRRON: *(To Molière.)* I'll watch over you always, it's why I've come back. At home, in the streets, day, night —

LA GRANGE: Just like the Secret Police.

MOLIÈRE: *(To La Grange.)* Go stuff your mouth with lace.
(The crowd in the theater starts to grumble and whistle. The sound grows menacing.)

MOIRRON: Please listen, Chronicler: If you kill me, they'll hang you, and our master will be defenseless against the Black Cross.

LA GRANGE: You've grown wiser since you left home. Too bad it took so long.
(Du Croisy enters nervously.)

DU CROISY: Black Musketeers are in the stalls — they're causing trouble.

MOIRRON: They're above the law.

(Bouton enters with Moirron's coat.)

MOLIÈRE: It's Mardi Gras! The chandeliers in the theater have been broken often enough, the audience is having fun.

DU CROISY: One-Eye is in the theater.

MOIRRON: *(To La Grange.)* Take your pistol and let's start the play.

(La Grange and Moirron arm themselves and go to the stage with Du Croisy. Pause.)

MOLIÈRE: *(Mutters.)* Tyrant, tyrant . . .

BOUTON: Who's a tyrant, master?

MOLIÈRE: The King of France —

BOUTON: Sshhh!

MOLIÈRE: Louis the Great — tyrant!

BOUTON: Well, that does it! We're both as good as hanged! They'll hear you in the theater.

MOLIÈRE: I nearly died of fright today. The golden idol — would you believe it, Bouton, his eyes are emerald green . . . and in my head he comes closer and closer, choking me . . . the idol is choking me.

BOUTON: Both of us as good as hanged, including myself, side by side in the square.

MOLIÈRE: Why? Why?! I don't understand, Your Majesty.

BOUTON: You'll swing this way, and next to you, me, the murdered innocent, Jean-Jacques Bouton —

MOLIÈRE: Perhaps I've praised you too little? Perhaps I haven't crawled enough? But Your Majesty, where will you find another bootlicker like Molière?

BOUTON: Are we dead? Where are we? In heaven? I never thought we'd end up here —

MOLIÈRE: Why?! I grovelled because of *Tartuffe*. I thought I'd find an ally in the king — never grovel, Bouton.

BOUTON: They'll erect a monument to you, a fountain with the statue of a girl, water gushing out of her mouth — I promise you, it will make you immortal, but now, for the love of God, be quiet!

MOLIÈRE: Tyrant, tyrant!

BOUTON: Shut up.

MOLIÈRE: But Your Majesty, I am a writer. I think. No, I protest, she's not my daughter, no — please, ask Madeleine Béjart to see me, I need her advice.

BOUTON: Master?

MOLIÈRE: Oh yes, she died. But . . . why didn't you tell me the truth, old dear? Why didn't you teach me? Why didn't you beat me? Light a candle, she

said, and I'll come to you. The candles are burning, but she's not here . . .
(To Bouton.) I tore your shirt, didn't I? Here's some money to buy a new
shirt —

BOUTON: That was ten years ago! What's happening?

(Molière rises, suddenly energetic.)

MOLIÈRE: Pack up everything! Tonight I'll perform for the last time, then we'll
escape to England! *(He smiles.)* How stupid of me. The wind blows from
the sea, and besides, they speak a foreign language there. But really, the
problem's not England, the problem is —

(The Prompter sticks his head in.)

PROMPTER: A nun is asking to see you.

MOLIÈRE: *(Terrified.)* What kind of nun?

PROMPTER: You asked her to pick up some clothes to be laundered.

MOLIÈRE: You scared me, you fool. Tell her to come back tomorrow.

(The Prompter goes out.)

MOLIÈRE: Now, where were we? Ah yes, your shirt, I tore it —

BOUTON: Master, go to sleep, for pity's sake.

(Molière pulls a blanket over his head.)

Almighty God, don't let anyone hear what he said about the king. Anyway, he's not the only actor around here. Now it's my turn. *(Very, very
loud.)* What's that you say, master? That our king is the wisest, most bril-
liant monarch in the whole world? Well, yes, I share your opinion.

MOLIÈRE: *(From under the blanket.)* No talent.

BOUTON: *(Viva voce.)* Yes, I shouted. I do shout. I shall shout: long live the king!

(The Prompter sticks his head in.)

PROMPTER: What's going on?

BOUTON: Nothing. I was conversing with Monsieur de Molière and I just happened to exclaim, "Long live the king!" Doesn't Bouton have the right
to exclaim any more? I exclaimed "Long live the king!!!"

MOLIÈRE: *(Under the blanket.)* Oh God, what a talentless imbecile!

*(Rumbling and yells from the auditorium. La Grange, Moirron, and Du
Croisy come down from the stage.)*

LA GRANGE: Musketeers have just killed one of our guards.

BOUTON: Oh my God.

LA GRANGE: The theater's filled with armed musketeers. As secretary of this
company, I forbid this performance to continue —

MOLIÈRE: He forbids, he forbids! Don't forget who you are! Next to me you're
a boy! I've got gray hair, that's what I've got. What else did I want to
say . . . ?

BOUTON: My cherished master —

MOLIÈRE: Bouton —

BOUTON: "Shut up." I know. I've been with you thirty years and all I've ever heard is "shut up" or "get out." I'm used to it. You love me. And master, in the name of that love, I beg you on my hands and knees — don't finish the performance. Run! The carriage is waiting.

MOLIÈRE: What makes you think I love you? You're raving. No one loves me. The archbishop's edict has been published. I can't be buried in the cemetery. I'm barred from holy ground! The rest of you get to lie inside the fence, but I'll be on the outside. Well, I don't need their cemetery, I spit on it! All my life you've tortured me, you're all my enemies.

DU CROISY: For God's sake, dear master —

LA GRANGE: How can we go out there and act? *(Rumbling from the audience.)* Well?

MOLIÈRE: Where's Moirron?

(He runs to Moirron, hides under his cloak.)

DU CROISY: We should call a doctor.

MOLIÈRE: *(Peeks out.)* All doctors are bloodsuckers. That's why I wrote the play we're doing tonight. *(A beat.)* That's it! One-Eye can't touch me on stage, I'm safe so long as I'm on stage.

(Silence. Rivale runs in, wearing a costume with a doctor's hat and eye glasses like wheels. As usual, she's half-naked.)

RIVALE: The entr'acte can't be stretched out any longer. Either we go on, or —

LA GRANGE: He wants to go out there and act. What shall we do?

(Rivale looks at Molière for a long time.)

RIVALE: Act.

MOLIÈRE: Magnificent! Come here my brave girl, let me kiss you! We can't start the last performance and not finish it. She knows. Twelve years she's been with me, and I've never seen her dressed, she's always naked.

RIVALE: Will you listen to me? Right after your last speech, we'll lower you through the trap. We'll hide you in my dressing room until morning, then at dawn we leave Paris. Agreed?

MOLIÈRE: Agreed.

(They all put on the masks, hats, and glasses. It's hard to tell them apart.)

MOLIÈRE: Let's start the last scene. What's the play? Oh yes, *Imaginary Invalid*.

(One-Eye walks through the door. His sword is drawn. Moirron slowly reaches for a sword on the table.)

ONE-EYE: Say your prayers! *(He looks from one to the other.)* Which one are you? Answer, damn it! I want the putrid old clown, I'm here to kill him.

MOIRRON: Go away, we're busy.

ONE-EYE: Busy — ha!

MOIRRON: We're actors. Our audience is waiting.

(And the five actors, indistinguishable in their masks, mount the stairs to the stage. One-Eye watches, then leaves, frustrated.)

LA GRANGE: *(Calls out.)* "Curtain!"

(A gong sounds. The curtain above opens slowly. Candles are lit in the prompter's box. On "stage" are a chair and a large statue. Molière takes off his hat and mask, moves to the chair with ease. He begins to snore. He has become Argan. La Grange, as a doctor, prods him awake.)

MOLIÈRE/ARGAN: What the hell — ? Get out! Be gone!
   Why are you in my room at night?

LA GRANGE: I'm Doctor Purge, my dear Argan,
   I'm sorry I gave you such a fright.

(Du Croisy now looms over Molière.)

MOLIÈRE: Another doctor? What can it mean?
   Who else is lurking behind that screen?

DU CROISY: I am a popular court physician,
   With little talent but much ambition.

RIVALE: And I am called Doctor Pancreas
   From the Collegium Medicus.

MOIRRON: Doctor Diaforis is my name,
   A diagnostician of great fame.

(The four doctors dance toward Molière.)

LA GRANGE: Whose stomach gets the best of care?

MOIRRON: The king of enemas, sitting there.

MOLIÈRE: But — wait —

RIVALE: Argan, we've come with news for you.

DU CROISY: You shall become a doctor too!

(They pull Molière up into the dance.)

MOLIÈRE: Hold on —

DOCTORS: Gloria, enema, medica quack
   Gloria, medica, aching back
   Gloria, enema, medica quack
   Gloria, medica, aching back — *(Etc.)*

(Molière stops, stares out at the audience.)

MOLIÈRE: Send Madeleine Béjart to see me . . . I need her advice . . .

(He collapses. The audience laughs. He turns to them.)

MOLIÈRE: Audience, don't laugh, don't laugh . . . hold on . . . hold on . . .

LA GRANGE: Ladies and gentlemen, go home. Tonight's play is over.

(The audience grows quiet. Molière dies.)

LA GRANGE: I beg you, gentlemen, leave. It's over. Disperse . . .

(Moirron bends, closes Molière's eyes, kisses his forehead, then turns to glare at the audience. He thrusts his sword into the stage, goes down the stairs, and out. Rivale and Du Croisy each bless Molière, as.)

LA GRANGE: Gentlemen . . . gentlemen, please . . . *(To Bouton.)* Curtain! For God's sake, curtain!

(Rivale, Du Croisy, and La Grange slowly leave the stage. Bouton climbs up to the stage, kneels by the body. Du Croisy, Rivale, and Moirron disappear into the darkness. La Grange sits down to his table, takes out his diary, as Bouton starts to put out the footlights, one by one.)

LA GRANGE: *(Takes up his pen.)* Seventeenth of February. Fourth performance of the play *The Imaginary Invalid* by Monsieur de Molière. At ten in the evening, Monsieur de Molière, who was playing the role of Argan, collapsed on stage, and was claimed by unmerciful death. *(A pause.)* To mark this, I shall inscribe the largest black cross of all. And so I shall set it down. *(By this time, the footlights are out. Bouton is seated on the stage floor, guarding the body. Lights fade out.)*

END OF PLAY

Camille

ADAPTED FROM THE NOVEL BY
ALEXANDRE DUMAS, *FILS*

To the memory of Garland Wright

Marguerite Gautier (Margaret Whitton), Comte de Guiche (Richard Russell Ramos), and Prudence Duvernoy (Barbara Bryne) in the 1980 Guthrie Theater production of *Camille,* adapted by Barbara Field from the novel of Alexandre Dumas, *fils,* and staged by Garland Wright with set design by Jack Barkla and costumes by Lewis Brown. Photo credit: Bruce Goldstein.

CONTEXTUAL NOTES ON *CAMILLE*

From 1979 to 1980, the Guthrie was between artistic directors, which meant we operated by committee. Because of this, our selections for the following season were somewhat haphazard. Once in a while, that turns out to be the best way, for one decision can change the course of the theater.

Camille was mentioned as a possibility for the Guthrie's 1980 season. Dumas, *fils,* had adapted his novel for his own stage version, and of course there was *La Traviata,* but I thought I ought to have a look at the source before I trod the well-worn path.

When I finally acquired a copy of the novel itself, it was very different from what I expected. For one thing, poor Marguerite Gautier did *not* die in her lover's arms — to my relief. Also, the novel seemed riddled with numbers — it was about the economics of Marguerite's life, as well as a love story. The novel starts at the end, a flashback, with the auctioning of Gautier's possessions after her death. (Armand Duval, her lover, arrives too late for the auction, a nice irony.) This obsession with pricing everything fascinated me, and so the auctioning of all her goods, the reduction to mere *francs* of her existence became the central metaphor for this adaptation.

Because there was no one at the helm of the theater, I was allowed to pick a director for this project. I chose a stranger to me, Garland Wright, whose work I had admired from afar. I sent an outline to Garland, and I asked him to read the novel before I traveled to New York to meet with him. Little did I know that meeting would be the first step leading to his appointment as the Guthrie's artistic director a few years later.

Ours was a fortuitous partnership from the beginning, for we shared a sensibility about the play, and we were eager to explore matters of style in the production. How did nineteenth-century actors breathe and speak lines that were highly colored and far from our modern naturalistic TV-style of acting? How did they move across a ballroom? We were looking for something *large* in the rhetoric and the very breathing of the thoughts from the actors we hired.

The result was a highly praised, handsome production — and it was the beginning of a friendship that lasted until Garland died.

CAMILLE
Adapted for The Guthrie Theater by Barbara Field

Director .... Garland Wright
Scenic Designer .... Jack Barkla
Costume Designer .... Lewis Brown
Lighting Designer .... John McLain
Composer .... Hiram Titus
Sound Designer .... Terry Tilley
Choreography .... Robert Moulton
Vocal Consultant .... Marjorie Phillips
Conductor .... Dick Whitbeck
Assistant Director .... Richard Edwards
Research Historian .... Joann Cierniak
Production Secretary .... Melanie Spewock
Stage Manager .... Sharon Ewald
Assistant Stage Manager .... Jann Iaco
Orchestra . . .Matt Barber (percussion), Brian Grivna (woodwinds)
Eileen Reagan (piano), David Straka (cello), Dick Whitbeck (horn)

CAST (IN ORDER OF APPEARANCE)

AUCTIONEER .... Richard Hilger
COMTE DE GUICHE .... Richard Russell Ramos
BARONESS DE MONTREUX .... Jane MacIver
ALPHONSINE FIDEAUX .... Peggy Schoditsch
A YOUNG GIRL .... Priscilla Entersz
AUCTIONEER'S ASSISTANT .... Gary Kingsolver
LUCIEN CLEMENT .... Russell Leib
OLYMPE .... Wanda Bimson
GASTON RIEUX .... Jeffrey Alan Chandler
A DANDY .... Jason McLean
A YOUNG LADY .... Kristine Nielsen
BAILIFF, MAJOR DOMO .... Peter Thoemke
PRUDENCE DUVERNOY .... Barbara Byrne
ARMAND DUVAL .... William Converse-Roberts
MARGUERITE GAUTIER .... Margaret Whitton
COMTE DE NIRAC .... Alan Brasington
NANINE .... Pamela Danser
WAITER .... Todd Murken

JOSEPH .... Gilbert Cole
MONSIEUR DUVAL .... Richard M. Davidson
PRIEST .... Armin Shimerman
WAITERS, DANCERS, AUCTIONEER'S ASSISTANTS, ETC.: George Everett
Kate Fuglei, Steve Gronwall, Donald Martin,
Brian Poffenberger, Ric Purdue,
Neil Spencer, Cynthia White.

SETTING

The action of the play takes place in and around Paris, 1842–1843

CAMILLE

AUCTION ONE

Early spring, 1842. An auction is in progress. The crowd of curious onlookers jostle each other in their eagerness to examine the objects for sale in the room . . . while they examine each other.

The Comte de Guiche watches the crowd with detached amusement. Gaston Rieux, as high-spirited as ever, chats with the venerable Baroness Montreux. Prudence Duvernoy sniffs conspicuously into a black-bordered lace handkerchief whenever she thinks someone might be watching. When she believes she is unobserved, she is both greedy and tragic. Lucien Clement is there with his dazzling young mistress, Olympe. And there's a shy young girl, whose name we'll never know.

The Auctioneer gestures for his assistant to hold up a small landscape by Greuse. He raps his gavel.

AUCTIONEER: And now, mesdames, messieurs, we'll open bidding on the next item, a country landscape by Greuse. Bidding to start at eighty francs.

A VOICE: Eighty-two.

ANOTHER: Eighty-five.

ANOTHER: Ninety.

AUCTIONEER: Ninety francs? Ninety francs, I hear ninety —

DE GUICHE: God, it's hideous.

BARONESS: Hello, De Guiche, it's not a bit hideous, I quite like it.

DE GUICHE: Baroness, enchanted.

BARONESS: You're too discriminating for my taste, De Guiche.

DE GUICHE: I haven't had a glimpse of you since New Year's Eve at the Café Anglais. You're looking radiant.

BARONESS: Such a charming liar! Tell me, what are you doing at a public sale?

DE GUICHE: I knew her.

BARONESS: Her? All this belonged to a woman?

DE GUICHE: Don't be coy, Baroness, you know it was a woman, and a "kept" one at that.

BARONESS: And you, did you ever "keep" this person?

VOICE: One hundred ten.

DE GUICHE: One hundred twelve.

AUCTIONEER: One twelve? One twelve?

BARONESS: One hundred fifteen francs.

AUCTIONEER: One hundred fifteen? One hundred fifteen? Sold to the Baroness de Montreux. And now, mesdames, messieurs, a comb, brush and mirror set backed with gold filigree.

BARONESS: A hairbrush?!

AUCTIONEERS: Bidding to open at one hundred fifty-one francs.

VOICE: One fifty-one.

AUCTIONEER: Really, ladies and gentlemen, these items are of particular interest! The brush hasn't been washed since her death. Why, a diligent collector might gather up enough strands of hair to put in a locket!

A VOICE: One hundred sixty.

YOUNG GIRL: *(To the assistant.)* Heavens, they must have been a special gift to her.

ASSISTANT: To a courtesan nothing's a gift — it's all barter.

VOICE: One eighty-five.

YOUNG GIRL: How much will this little clock bring?

ASSISTANT: The expected price is five hundred francs.

YOUNG GIRL: Goodness!

ASSISTANT: But everyone's been asking, so it might go as high as 100 percent up. Did you know her?

YOUNG GIRL: No, but I worshipped her.

(Prudence stands by a little Saxe statuette. She tries to slip it into her bag, but it won't fit. The Assistant sees her, taps her on the shoulder.)

AUCTIONEER: A fine Sèvres urn, eighteenth century, mint condition, Chinese motif, considered rare. Bidding to start at four hundred francs.

ASSISTANT: If you please, madame.

VOICE: Four hundred twenty.

PRUDENCE: Eh?

ASSISTANT: I believe something tumbled into your bag — quite by accident, I believe. A little Saxe statue . . . ?

VOICE: Four fifty.

PRUDENCE: What's that? Peculiar . . . I've no idea how that happened, I was merely examining . . .

(She places it reluctantly in his hand.)

VOICE: Four hundred seventy-five.

BARONESS: Gaston Rieux, is that you?

GASTON: Enchanted, Baroness.

BARONESS: You knew the lady too?

GASTON: We all knew her. *(He nods at De Guiche.)* Some of us better than others, to be sure. Her life was a sensation.

BARONESS: And now her death is, as well. There are carriages lined up all the way to the Rue de Rivoli — was the traffic this heavy during her life?

DE GUICHE: Don't be naughty, Baroness.

VOICE: Five fifty.

ANOTHER VOICE: Six hundred.

AUCTIONEER: Six hundred. Six hundred. Sold to the gentleman in gray for six hundred.

DE GUICHE: *(To Gaston.)* One face is missing, at any rate.

GASTON: Hers?

DE GUICHE: Don't act like a bigger fool than you are, Rieux!

GASTON: I beg your pardon?

DE GUICHE: No, I beg yours. I was referring to him.

GASTON: I suspect he doesn't even know she's dead.

AUCTIONEER: And now, mesdames, messieurs, two cashmere shawls: They graced the whitest shoulders in Paris. Bidding to start at sixty-five francs.

VOICE: Sixty-six.

VOICE: Seventy-three

(Lucien pinches the cheek of the shy Young Girl.)

LUCIEN: Who knows, little one, you might grow up to be as famous, someday.

YOUNG GIRL: Do you really think I might?

(Olympe sweeps up, and whirls Lucien away.)

OLYMPE: Lucien . . .

LUCIEN: Ah, here you are, my dear. That little girl reminds me of you, when we first met . . . last year.

OLYMPE: How sweet. Come, Lucien, I want you to have a look at some crystal. Not that I covet any of her used merchandise.

(She leads him away.)

DE GUICHE: Prudence, my pet, I saw that man catch you in the act.

PRUDENCE: He made a mistake, De Guiche, he has no respect. After all, I'm in mourning.

DE GUICHE: Indeed you are . . . considering all you've lost.

PRUDENCE: I do consider it, constantly. What's to become of me?

DE GUICHE: Poor Prudence, doesn't know where her next opera ticket's coming from —

PRUDENCE: — You forget yourself! I also lost a friend.

DE GUICHE: I'm sorry. I'm glad someone's mourning her, my dear.

PRUDENCE: He didn't come back, he didn't come back.

DE GUICHE: Perhaps he never got your letter.

VOICE: Seventy-six.

VOICE: Eighty.

BARONESS: Eighty-five.

AUCTIONEER: Eighty-five, eighty-five, sold to the Baroness de Montreux. And now, ten Baccarat wine glasses, one with a slight chip on the stem.

DE GUICHE: Still, Prudence, you should envy Marguerite Gautier.

PRUDENCE: Why on earth — ?

DE GUICHE: Because she managed to escape the courtesan's first death: old age.

PRUDENCE: Really, De Guiche, you've no feeling at all!

(She starts to go. The Young Girl touches De Guiche on the arm.)

YOUNG GIRL: Pardon me, monsieur, did you know her? The Lady of the Camellias?

DE GUICHE: I was her friend. Do you like flowers?

YOUNG GIRL: Roses. She was mad about camellias, they say. They were delivered fresh each day, masses of them.

VOICE: Thirty-eight.

ANOTHER: Forty-one.

DE GUICHE: She carried them in a little silver bouquet holder. Twenty-five days a month they were white, the other five they were red.

YOUNG GIRL: Why? Oh yes, of course. I love roses. Camellias have no fragrance.

DE GUICHE: That's why she chose them. The lady suffered from a chest disease. The smell of roses offended her.

YOUNG GIRL: Well, I still like them best.

VOICE: Fifty-four.

VOICE: Fifty-five.

VOICE: Fifty-six.

BARONESS: *(To De Guiche.)* I haven't heard you bid on a thing.

DE GUICHE: I'm merely observing. As usual. I'm a student of human behavior.

BARONESS: I'm looking for bargains. But I can't find exactly what I had in mind.

DE GUICHE: I don't think you will, Baroness. Because this auction contains only what is for sale since the lady's death, and nothing of what was for sale during her life.

VOICE: Sixty-two.

VOICE: Sixty-four.

VOICE: Sixty-six.

(By this time, all of the objects and furniture have been carried away, and the last of the gawkers are gone. The stage is empty. Lights cross-fade to Scene One.)

AT THE OPERA COMIQUE

From off, the finale of Act I, The Daughter of the Regiment. *Then applause. A few members of the opera audience drift into the lobby. Gaston and Armand Duval enter with their capes and hats.*

GASTON: It looks as if we missed Act I. Pity.

ARMAND: Never mind, I'm told the intermission's good, too.

GASTON: Let us study the scene, Duval. Who's here? Anyone you know . . . or wish to know?

(Prudence, Marguerite, and Nirac have come out, above. Prudence catches sight of Gaston and yoohoos. He waves back.)

ARMAND: So, your circle of acquaintances includes dowagers?

GASTON: She wouldn't appreciate being called a dowager.

ARMAND: My apologies to the lady.

GASTON: Oh, she's not precisely a lady. Prudence Duvornoy was a courtesan before I was born.

ARMAND: That means she was a Napoleonic tart — how delectable.

GASTON: Now she calls herself a "milliner": but she's a parasite of considerable talent, that's how she gets to the opera.

(At that moment Marguerite turns around, and Armand catches sight of her. She raises her opera glasses to have a better look at him.)

GASTON: Dazzling, eh?

ARMAND: What's her name?

GASTON: Duval, you confound me — that's Marguerite Gautier, the reigning queen of the night.

ARMAND: Marguerite . . .

GASTON: Pierced by the arrow so quickly? They say she reads Voltaire in her spare time! Let's buy them some *raisins glacés* and join their party.

(Gaston buys a paper cone of raisins glacés *as: Nirac leads Marguerite down the stairs. Prudence already headed down. A poor, simply dressed young girl stands gazing at Marguerite. It is Olympe. Marguerite accidently drops her program on the stair, and before Nirac can reach it, Olympe races up and retrieves it. She hands it to Marguerite shyly. Marguerite takes it, touches Olympe's cheek.)*

MARGUERITE: Pretty child.

(She presses the program into Olympe's hand, then continues down the stairs. Olympe looks as if she's just received the Grail.)

PRUDENCE: *(To Gaston.)* The opera's unbearable tonight. Hello, my dear. The soprano's flat as stale champagne, so we three are deserting the Daughter of the Regiment. You've met Marguerite Gautier? The Comte de Nirac? Gaston Rieux.

GASTON: Madame Gautier, enchanted. Monsieur le Comte. Let me present my friend — my stricken friend — Armand Duval. Prudence Duvornoy, Madame Gautier, Comte de Nirac.

ARMAND: I . . . oh God . . . I . . .

(Marguerite laughs with swift cruelty, then sweeps out with Nirac in her wake.)

PRUDENCE: What's wrong, is he epileptic?

GASTON: Not when he came in, but . . .

PRUDENCE: If he recovers, perhaps you'd like to drop in at Marguerite's for a little supper. Is he often subject to these fits?

GASTON: Usually, he's a model of decorum.

PRUDENCE: A bite of supper might do wonders, eh, monsieur?

ARMAND: What? Oh, enchanted, madame.

PRUDENCE: It's settled, then. What's in the cornet? Oh, *raisins glacés. (She helps herself.)* Stale. *(Going.)* Number nine, Rue d'Antin — you know, next to the Rue Louis le Grand.

GASTON: You're sure it's quite convenient?

PRUDENCE: Marguerite always welcomes new friends. And me, I enjoy a good party!

(She grabs a few more raisins glacés, goes. Gaston glances at Armand, who is still transfixed.)

GASTON: Fate! Fate — accompanied by a sonorous C minor chord!

ARMAND: Don't be silly.

GASTON: Me?! You look like a sixteen-year-old choirboy who's just received divine enlightenment about women. Why? I mean, it's not as if you haven't had your share.

ARMAND: For a moment, it was as if we'd met each other . . . somewhere.

GASTON: Longchamps, no doubt.

ARMAND: As if . . . we had an affinity of the fluids.

GASTON: I beg your pardon?!

(Armand suddenly bursts into laughter.)

ARMAND: What can I possibly mean?

GASTON: God knows. Poor Duval, for someone who's always been the picture of propriety, temperance . . . even tedium —

ARMAND: — You're too kind —

GASTON: You're bewitched. Well, let's go call on the sorceress.

ARMAND: Willingly. Lead me to my fate.

(The orchestra begins to tune for the second act. As they start out, they encounter Olympe, still clutching her program.)

GASTON: Do you like sweets?

(He stuffs the cornet into her hands. And goes. Clement enters.)

CLEMENT: Mademoiselle.

OLYMPE: She called me pretty.

CLEMENT: Quite right, too. Who?

OLYMPE: Marguerite Gautier. And she gave me her opera program!

CLEMENT: Do you like Donizetti?

(She looks at him blankly.)

CLEMENT: Mademoiselle, would you care to join me in my box?

(He offers his arm as the lights fade.)

AT MARGUERITE GAUTIER'S

As the furniture is shifted in, we hear the auction continuing:

AUCTIONEER'S VOICE: Mesdames, messieurs, the bidding is now open on a pair of fine mother-of-pearl opera glasses with silver frames, made in Switzerland. Leather case. Forty francs.

A VOICE: Forty-two.

A VOICE: Forty-four.

ANOTHER: Forty-five.

ANOTHER: Forty-eight.

ANOTHER: Fifty.

Marguerite is seated at the spinet, playing a tune in a lazy way. The Comte de Nirac stands fawning over her. Prudence is spread out on the chaise and looks as bored as Marguerite, who strikes a wrong note.

NIRAC: C sharp.

(She doesn't acknowledge him, plays on. Nanine admits the two young men.)

NANINE: They're expecting you, messieurs.

PRUDENCE: I was afraid you might not come!

GASTON: No fear.

PRUDENCE: I hope you plan to be very clever tonight. The opera was so dull . . .

MARGUERITE: And we've not been overwhelmingly amused here at home, either.

GASTON: I shall aspire to brilliance.

MARGUERITE: Monsieur Duval, have you recovered from your affliction?
(Her laughter stings him again.)
Does the opera always render you speechless?
(Again, Armand is speechless.)

GASTON: Donizetti affects him that way.

MARGUERITE: Ah. But you must say something, Monsieur Duval, if you want to get acquainted.

GASTON: Don't trouble yourself. According to this poor benighted creature, you've already met.

MARGUERITE: Really?

ARMAND: I feel as if we . . . as if I'd known you always.

MARGUERITE: Charming.
(Nirac steps forward nervously.)

NIRAC: Good evening again. Nirac, last but not least —

MARGUERITE: That's debatable.

PRUDENCE: Marguerite!

MARGUERITE: Did you hear M. Duval, Nirac? He's so eloquent, he "feels he's known me always." Why can't you say enchanting things like that?

NIRAC: But I've only known you two months.

MARGUERITE: M. Duval has only known me two minutes.
(Prudence groans.)

GASTON: You were playing when we came in. Please, give us some music.

MARGUERITE: No, no, that's all very well when I'm alone with Nirac. You two don't deserve such punishment.

NIRAC: You show me that preference?

MARGUERITE: Don't reproach me for it, Nirac, it's the only one.

PRUDENCE: *(Aside.)* I don't believe this!

NIRAC: Marguerite, I pray you —

MARGUERITE: — My head is splitting!

ARMAND: We've intruded, madame. M. Rieux and I will —

MARGUERITE: — Don't go, please, I insist you stay.

NIRAC: It seems I'm the one who must go . . . to my club.

PRUDENCE: Don't be silly, Nirac, this party's for you.

NIRAC: Gentlemen. Madame. *(He bends over Marguerite's hand.)* Adieu, Marguerite.

MARGUERITE: Oh dear, are you leaving so soon?

NIRAC: I fear I've bored you.

MARGUERITE: No more than usual, Nirac.

(Another groan from Prudence.)

MARGUERITE: When shall I see you again?

NIRAC: When you permit me.

MARGUERITE: Well then. Nanine, light Monsieur le Comte, to his carriage.

(Nanine leads Nirac out.)

MARGUERITE: At last! Good God, how that fool gets on my nerves.

PRUDENCE: You're the fool, for treating him so cruelly. *(She appeals to Armand.)* He's good to her, good as gold. He bought her that ormolu clock today, it must have cost 500 francs; and last week, that charming little Saxe monkey.

(She eyes the statuette.)

MARGUERITE: It's hideous! He's hideous! Take it home if you like it so much, take the monkey and Nirac and —

PRUDENCE: — Heartless! He loves her, poor man.

MARGUERITE: When I weigh what he gives me against what it costs me to listen to him, I find he buys his visits here very cheap. Dear Prudence, stop nagging me. If I had to be kind to every man who loved me, I'd never have time to eat.

PRUDENCE: Did you mention eating? I'm quite sure I'm starving to death, aren't you?

MARGUERITE: Nanine!

PRUDENCE: Perishing for a bit of supper, a little pâté, perhaps a morsel of chicken.

(Nanine enters.)

MARGUERITE: You're like an aged infant. Nanine, it's time for Mme. Duvernoy's feeding. Cold supper. The gentlemen are staying. *(She pulls a little shawl over Prudence's shoulders to mollify her.)* Do you fancy this shawl? It suits you, my dear. Let me give it to you? *(She crosses to the piano.)* M. Rieux, help with this waltz? I can start it, but I don't have any luck with the fast part — all those loathsome sharps!

(He joins her at the piano. Prudence sidles over to Armand.)

PRUDENCE: Still in a trance, M. Duval? Perhaps your collar's too tight, let me loosen it.

(He backs off.)

PRUDENCE: No? Perhaps Nanine will bring oysters — to liven you up.

(Marguerite starts to play a waltz: Chopin's A minor. Gaston takes over at the "fast part," and Marguerite begins to waltz around the room. Armand

watches, spellbound. She stops in front of him. Prudence, by now, has moved in on Gaston.)

MARGUERITE: So you've known me always, monsieur. How can I repay you for your charming words?

ARMAND: By letting me visit you.

MARGUERITE: I'm at home between five and six each evening. Except Wednesdays, I take piano lessons on Wednesdays. Do you find it strange for a grown woman to study piano? Six years ago, I could neither read nor write, Monsieur Duval. I never laid eyes on a piano before I came to Paris. But I love music, music excites, consoles. *(She returns to the piano bench, starts to play the waltz with Gaston.)* Monsieur Liszt assures me I'd be quite accomplished if I took time to practice. I can't sit still that long. *(She falters, misplays.)* The devil take all sharps and flats!

(She moves away. Gaston starts to pick out a tune, an old army song, "Psalms." He sings the verse, and the ladies join in.)

CHORUS: Blessed Saint Symphorien,
  Hark to my confession.
  It's true, dear saint, that I have sinned,
  But only with discretion.

VERSE: The girl who goes to early mass
  Slips a pillow 'neath her knee;
  The priest, he slips one 'neath her ass,
  And prays, "Remember me."

(Marguerite has come tauntingly close to Armand as she sings. He grabs her arm.)

ARMAND: Please! Don't sing that.

MARGUERITE: What, a Puritan in our midst?

ARMAND: Not for my sake, for yours.

PRUDENCE: All cuckolds shall be drowned today,
  Declared the Duke d'Yquem.
  "Dear Lord," his wife began to pray,
  "Does he know how to swim?"

GASTON: You're a wicked old creature.

PRUDENCE: I'm in my prime, you barbarian.

GASTON: Are you? *(He tickles her.)* Are you? I earnestly hope so.

(Marguerite coughs lightly.)

MARGUERITE: M. Duval is not amused, Prudence.

PRUDENCE: Perhaps he should have been a priest.

GASTON: They rejected him. Even the Jesuits find him too upright.

ARMAND: *(Trying to smile.)* I take after my father.

MARGUERITE: Monsieur is not from Paris?

ARMAND: From Rouen.

MARGUERITE: From Rouen. Of course. You'll learn, though, I did. I came from the country.

(She crosses back to the piano. Prudence and Gaston are quite engrossed in each other. Marguerite sings.)

MARGUERITE: The Duchess of Lyons is known
　　For fits of pious prayer;
　But fifty cocks their seed have sown
　　In madame's charming snare.

(Prudence, Gaston, and Marguerite burst into raucous laughter. Marguerite's cough becomes uncontrollable. Prudence pulls Gaston up, he takes a candelabra and, arm in arm, they climb up the stairs singing Blessed Saint Symphorien. *In the darkened room, Marguerite gasps for air. She takes the napkin from her mouth. It is stained with blood. She crosses to the chaise, lies down, closes her eyes. She opens them again to find Armand staring at her.)*

MARGUERITE: You're pale as a ghost, Monsieur Duval, are you ill? I think it's you who should be lying down.

ARMAND: Don't speak, I beg you.

MARGUERITE: I'm quite all right.

ARMAND: No, you're ill.

MARGUERITE: So you're a doctor! Doctor Duval. Pray, what do you prescribe, bed rest? Twelve hours of sleep at night? That would be the death of me, indeed, because I'm restless. The doctors say I've a nervous temperament, but they don't tell me what to do for this affliction. So I amuse myself in the small hours — a few friends, a little wine and music. It calms me. Besides, a girl like me, what does one of us more or less matter?

ARMAND: Please —

MARGUERITE: The doctors pretend that the blood I spit up comes from a sore throat, and I pretend to believe them, so we're all happy.

ARMAND: Mocking, mocking — you realize you're killing yourself? You must stop.

MARGUERITE: I find you much too proprietary, for a new acquaintance.

ARMAND: You trouble me.

MARGUERITE: Don't be. See how much notice the others take of me? Come, finish your supper. This medical consultation bores me to the soul.

(He seizes her hand, kisses it. She touches his cheek, pulls back in surprise.)

MARGUERITE: Tears! Why, what a child it is, to cry.

ARMAND: I must seem foolish indeed.

MARGUERITE: Let's cheer up. The only sin in this world is to be dull, Armand Duval. Do you sing?

ARMAND: Not the songs you know. Dull, yes, but patient. Please rest, and I'll sit with you.

MARGUERITE: Will you talk to me? Tell me everything, all about Rouen. Have you a fat, jolly mama back in Normandy?

ARMAND: No, she was small and frail. She died when I was twelve. My father's alive, and I've got a little sister, Blanche, a pretty little thing, sixteen.

MARGUERITE: I was sixteen when I came to Paris. Tell me more.

ARMAND: Let's see . . . my father's a judge, very upright.

MARGUERITE: That's where you get it!

ARMAND: Yes. He's strict, but fair and kind. I look up to him.

MARGUERITE: That explains why you're still in Paris.

ARMAND: What?

MARGUERITE: One keeps a safe distance from people one looks up to!

ARMAND: I came to Paris to study, earned my degree in law. But somehow I wasn't ready to go home to Rouen. So I've hung on here, drifting.
(He smiles suddenly. She smiles back.)

ARMAND: At home·we've an enormous apple orchard. My father keeps trying to breed the perfect apple. He prunes and grafts and . . . tries to impose his own order on nature.

MARGUERITE: Not much like my father. He grew weeds. I used to feel his boot in the small of my back, if I wasn't up at five to milk. Now I go to bed at five.

ARMAND: You're from a farm?

MARGUERITE: Not what you'd call a proper farm, a little heap of stones. I wonder what it's like . . . having a father who raises apples — for a hobby! Now you've made me sad.

ARMAND: I want to make you happy. Let me care for you and I will, I swear it! Listen to me, Marguerite, I don't know what influence you're to have over my life, but at this moment there is no one, not even my little sister, who has ever moved me so. I know I mean nothing to you, but if you'd let me care for you —
(She laughs.)

ARMAND: You think I mean only for a few hours? I mean forever, I'd never leave your side!

MARGUERITE: Day and night?
(He nods.)

MARGUERITE: Such monumental devotion. I suppose you're going to tell me you love me? Spare me that revelation, I beg you.

ARMAND: If I love you, tonight's not the night for me to say so.

MARGUERITE: You'd do better to forget the whole thing. Either I shan't accept your kind offer, and your feelings will be hurt; or I shall accept, and then, my friend, then! You'll have a wonderful mistress, who sleeps till noon, who spends a hundred thousand francs a year, who spits up blood . . . qualities which will hardly endear me to your upright father in Rouen.

ARMAND: Don't underestimate me.

MARGUERITE: Are you rich?

ARMAND: I beg your pardon?

MARGUERITE: Are you rich?

ARMAND: I have a small income from my mother. Very small.

MARGUERITE: Then let us be friends. Friendship costs nothing, we can afford it. In that way you won't exaggerate my value.

ARMAND: Will you stop talking about money!

MARGUERITE: Poor man, how can I make you understand? You're too young and tender to live in my world.

ARMAND: I'm no younger than you —

MARGUERITE: — In years, yes. But you're a carefully bred plant. No one's ever placed a boot in the small of your back!

ARMAND: Marguerite.

(A pause.)

MARGUERITE: Nirac is taking me to the Bois de Bologne tomorrow afternoon in his new carriage.

(Armand rises, extends his hand.)

ARMAND: Then you must try to get some rest.

MARGUERITE: Oh dear, are you leaving so soon?

ARMAND: Precisely the words you used to Nirac not an hour ago. How amusing. Naturally, I couldn't expect you to stop your social engagements for me —

MARGUERITE: — Have you never had "social engagements"?

ARMAND: I have had women.

MARGUERITE: Then we're quits. But there's a difference, Armand: I do what I must to live. I have several lovers, I live by them. They're my trade, like your father's is the Law.

ARMAND: You have never had a lover who feels for you what I do. I don't want the same thing —

MARGUERITE: — Of course, of course, what is it you want?

ARMAND: Love me a little.

(Pause.)

MARGUERITE: Tell me, my friend, if I said yes, would you do all I ask? Without question, without opinion?

ARMAND: Anything! Anything you wish!

MARGUERITE: You'd be discrete? Submissive? You'd leave me free to do as I please?

ARMAND: I swear!

MARGUERITE: Swear away, for all the good it will do. There's no man alive who can love without judging, no man who'll let me love him without demanding that as his right.

ARMAND: I am that man.

MARGUERITE: Are you? We shall see.

ARMAND: When shall we see?

MARGUERITE: Tomorrow.

ARMAND: Why not tonight?

(She removes a red camellia from her bouquet, slips it into his buttonhole.)

MARGUERITE: You can't always expect delivery on the day of purchase. Come back when the camellias are white. Tomorrow night, between eleven and midnight. Then we'll see. *(She kisses him on the cheek.)* It's late. Come, disentangle your poor friend from Prudence and take him home. Prudence! *(She turns back to Armand.)* I shan't live long, you know; that's why I must live faster.

ARMAND: Don't speak that way!

MARGUERITE: My friend, I promise I shall live longer than you will love me. Prudence!

(Gaston comes down the stairs, disheveled.)

MARGUERITE: Aha, here's Monsieur Rieux, looking the worse for wear. We've been having a nice chat, M. Duval and I. Nanine's fast asleep by now, I'll fetch your hats.

(She goes out.)

GASTON: Well? Is it fate?

ARMAND: Yes.

GASTON: And you told her so?

ARMAND: Yes.

GASTON: And she accepts her fate?

ARMAND: No, alas. What about Prudence?

GASTON: We abandoned rhetoric early on. Dear old Prudence, she's still not half-bad.

(Marguerite returns with hats and cloaks.)

GASTON: May I come again and play the piano?

MARGUERITE: By all means, any afternoon between five and six —

GASTON: — Except Wednesdays. *(He kisses her hand.)* Altogether a delightful evening, madame.

(He and Armand start off, Marguerite starts up the stairway. She turns back, to find Armand gazing at her. They turn away as the lights fade.)

AT MARGUERITE'S

We hear the voices from the auction again.

AUCTIONEER: Now offered for sale: a fine Playel spinet, rosewood inlaid with ebony. Bidding will open at eight thousand francs. Only qualified buyers will be invited to participate.

VOICE: Eight thousand.

ANOTHER: Eight thousand two hundred.

ANOTHER: Eight thousand five hundred.

ANOTHER: Eighty-seven.

ANOTHER: Nine thousand.

Lights up on Marguerite's salon. The next evening. Prudence is pacing up and down, trying to talk with Marguerite, who is offstage.

PRUDENCE: You haven't the brains you were born with — stop hiding in your dressing room and come listen to me! Marguerite!

MARGUERITE: *(Off.)* I'm not hiding, I'm in the bath.

PRUDENCE: *(To herself.)* I don't care if you're in the Seine, my dear.
(She yells.)
You'll catch pneumonia, bathing at this time of night!

MARGUERITE: *(Off.)* What?

(Prudence spots the little Saxe monkey and tries to squeeze it into her purse.)

PRUDENCE: You haven't a care for your future — not to mention my future. A selfish woman, that's what she's become. And I ask myself, is he so unattractive? Of course not, he's a perfectly reasonable figure of a man — and a count to boot! And he's burning with the desire to make all our lives comfortable. But madame has grown finicky. Madame says no thank you, Monsieur le Comte de Nirac, I don't care for your hair, your nose

— *(She yells again.)* You haven't the brains you were born with! *(To herself.)* I fail to understand. He's not so bad. If she'd seen some of the men I . . . when I was young —
(Nanine has entered with Armand.)

PRUDENCE: — What are you doing here?

ARMAND: Madame Duvernoy, enchanted. Where's Marguerite?

PRUDENCE: Madame Gautier is enthroned in her bathtub. Well, what are you doing here?

ARMAND: Paying a call. I happened to be in the neighborhood.

PRUDENCE: At midnight?

ARMAND: You're here at midnight.

PRUDENCE: I come and go as I like. Marguerite and I are like sisters. Besides, there's a small business matter I settled for her this evening. And you?

ARMAND: Most decidedly not business.

PRUDENCE: Certainly. When women like us entertain a poor young man late at night, it's never business. We do it for a lark, for a change . . . *(She remembers something long past.)* For consolation. But business comes first, I always say —
(Marguerite enters above.)

MARGUERITE: — Prudence, were you able to bring it? *(She sees Armand, feigns surprise.)* M. Duval, are you here too?

ARMAND: I thought you were expecting me.

MARGUERITE: Was I? Perhaps — I've forgotten. Prudence, did you see him? And you got it?

PRUDENCE: Six thousand.

MARGUERITE: Amen!! I hope he wasn't annoyed, I've neglected him lately.

PRUDENCE: He was charming, my dear, butter wouldn't melt.

MARGUERITE: Dear, generous, patient de Guiche! Do you need any cash, Prudence?

PRUDENCE: No thanks. Well, perhaps I might. As a matter of fact the fifteenth is coming round, my dear, and I wouldn't refuse three or four hundred, just to tide me over.
(Marguerite peels off a few bills.)

PRUDENCE: Dear, generous, patient Marguerite.

MARGUERITE: Will you join us for supper?

PRUDENCE: No, I'm engaged, but I'll drop by tomorrow. I want to talk with you seriously.

MARGUERITE: Not again.

PRUDENCE: Then too, if I stay, someone else in this room might murder me. Au revoir, M. Duval. Until tomorrow, Marguerite.

(She goes.)

ARMAND: Have I offended her?

MARGUERITE: Your poverty has. Forgive her, her greed is born of fear. I shan't be like her when I grow old, because I won't grow old!

(Nanine enters with a decanter, glasses.)

MARGUERITE: I won't need anything else, Nanine.

NANINE: Shall I lock up then, Madame?

(A pause. Armand feels his life depends on the answer.)

MARGUERITE: Yes, do.

(Nanine leaves, grinning. Marguerite pours wine.)

MARGUERITE: I presume you still love me?

ARMAND: Yes.

MARGUERITE: And you swear to love me forever, naturally?

ARMAND: Yes.

MARGUERITE: To the grave?

ARMAND: And beyond.

MARGUERITE: You needn't go that far. Look, you've spilled your wine, you're trembling, poor child. Have you honestly had other women?

(He nods, puts his glass down.)

ARMAND: It's you, you're trembling.

MARGUERITE: Me?

(She looks down at her hands, then away.)

ARMAND: Don't be afraid, Marguerite, don't be afraid.

(He sweeps her into his arms, and starts to carry her up the stairs. The lights fade.)

THE RUE D'ANTIN

Exterior. During the first part of the scene, a waiter carries out a couple of sidewalk café tables and chairs. De Guiche strolls in, with Lucien Clement and Olympe. At this point Olympe's clothing is only a little improved, perhaps by the addition of a small fur muff.

LUCIEN: You don't mean you traveled all the way to London and never saw the Tower?

DE GUICHE: I was pursuing other treasures — less ancient and certainly softer to the touch. I'm sure mademoiselle will forgive me, but women, Clement, women . . . very paradoxical: smooth and warm outside, inside as cold and hard as ice.

LUCIEN: I take it your trip to London wasn't a success.

(De Guiche stops in front of the stairway.)

DE GUICHE: Alas. Well, we must part company, here.

LUCIEN: I trust you'll find it warmer up there.

DE GUICHE: I have reason to believe I shall. Adieu, Clement.

(He runs up the stairs, rings. Nanine appears, and he follows her out of sight.)

LUCIEN: Au revoir, de Guiche.

(He turns back to Olympe.)

Now what were you saying, Olympe?

OLYMPE: Only that it was the most amazing shade of blue. The lady in the shop said it matched my eyes.

LUCIEN: Then it must have been very blue indeed. May one venture to ask how much . . .?

OLYMPE: One hundred twenty francs, Uncle Lucien. *(She looks up.)* So this is Marguerite Gautier's house! I do believe I'd like to have my apartment in this street.

(Gaston enters. Clement is glad for the distraction.)

LUCIEN: Rieux! Beautiful day, isn't it?

GASTON: Come, have a coffee with me. Mademoiselle.

(He sits at a table. Olympe curtsies.)

LUCIEN: I'm afraid not, we're shopping.

GASTON: Shopping! Shopping, indeed . . .

(Clement and Olympe stroll off. The waiter brings a cup of coffee for Gaston. Armand passes, heading for the stairs. Gaston's call stops him.)

Armand!

ARMAND: Good morning, Gaston. Sleep well?

GASTON: Good afternoon, Armand. I needn't ask you the same question.

ARMAND: I'll answer, nonetheless: well. Very well, indeed.

GASTON: Thus Gautier makes another conquest.

ARMAND: No, my friend, it's I who've conquered.

GASTON: Are we speaking of the same Marguerite Gautier — the renowned demi-mondaine who's trampled half the hearts of Paris?

ARMAND: Your imagination was always limited. For you, deflowering a virgin is a feat on the order of tumbling the walls of Jerico. No, Gaston, to be loved by a virgin, to be the first to reveal the secrets of love to her, is a trivial matter. You wage a little war and capture a heart that's unfortified because it has no experience of the battle called love. But to be loved by a courtesan, that's conquest, truly!

GASTON: Mad, quite mad.

ARMAND: All those little endearments we murmur they've heard a hundred times before. Such women are better guarded by their experience than any virgin by her convent.

GASTON: So you claim to have captured Gautier's heart?

(Armand grins.)

Ah, the smirk of triumph.

ARMAND: She doesn't know it yet.

GASTON: Aha.

ARMAND: She still thinks of me as her "caprice" — courtesans use that word to describe a bit of romance after business hours, they all have caprices.

GASTON: Professor Duval.

ARMAND: But if the caprice grows into love, a miracle occurs.

GASTON: What miracle's that?

ARMAND: Why, her love becomes a kind of absolution for her past.

GASTON: Father Duval. Look, I'm hardly devout, but I was raised to believe you had to do penance before you won absolution. What's Gautier's penance to be?

ARMAND: Me. Me. With all my soul, I intend to bury her past.

GASTON: Absolution, penance, soul — help, he's in the throws of a religious crisis! *(He seizes Armand's arm with sudden urgency.)* But knowing how the world turns, I can guess who'll play the martyr in the end. Gautier. And somewhere on that great canvas entitled *The Martyrdom of Sainte Marguerite,* way down in the lower left corner, there I'll be. The art historians will dub me The Accomplice.

ARMAND: Really, Gaston.

GASTON: I'm a simple man. I simply like women. Feed 'em and flatter 'em and they'll show you affection, the darlings. You're talking about matters too complicated for me.

(He rises, throws a few coins on the table.)

ARMAND: I'm going to call on her now.

GASTON: You only left her a few hours ago!

ARMAND: I can't wait till midnight. I'll surprise her.

(They go in different directions.)

GASTON: Let's hope the surprise will be all hers.

(He goes. Armand bounds up the stairs, rings. Nanine appears.)

NANINE: Well? Oh, it's you.

ARMAND: I've come to see Mme. Gautier.

NANINE: I'm sorry, sir, madame has a visitor, she's asked not to be disturbed.

(A pause. Below, Prudence has entered the Rue d'Antin. She listens.)

ARMAND: I see, I see.

NANINE: I believe she's expecting you at midnight.

ARMAND: I see. *(He backs down the stairs.)* Tell her I called, Nanine. Tell her I apologize for the few tedious hours I gave her. Alas, I can't tell her myself; I'm leaving for Rouen.

NANINE: I'll give madame your message.

(She goes back in. Armand finds himself face-to-face with Prudence.)

PRUDENCE: What an ugly temper you have.

ARMAND: Who's up there?

PRUDENCE: Not that it's any of your business . . . the Comte de Guiche. Didn't you notice his carriage? It's blocking the entrance to the Rue d'Antin. . . . Why so petulant, M. Duval?

ARMAND: Do you think I enjoy cooling my heels while she services the Comte de Guiche?

PRUDENCE: Watch your tongue, you little swine!

ARMAND: Why should I — there are no ladies present!

(A pause.)

PRUDENCE: No indeed, I don't think you're going to work out at all.

ARMAND: I beg your pardon?

PRUDENCE: I told her you wouldn't work out, I warned her. You're as self-centered as a baby! How's she supposed to live? What's she to eat while she's being faithful to you? De Guiche gives her money — she took six thousand francs of his last night, while you were under her roof! Surely even you realize such a gift isn't exactly a charitable offering. — What do you earn? Seven or eight thousand a year? That's not enough to keep her carriage. It's a question of simple arithmetic. ·

ARMAND: Women of your sort reduce everything to simple arithmetic.

PRUDENCE: Carriage, horses, hairdressers, florists — she spends over a hundred thousand a year, not including the bills she never quite manages to pay. My dear young man, Marguerite Gautier needs three or four lovers like de Guiche, for even the richest of 'em can't advance her the entire sum, they've got their own expenses!

So where does that leave you? My answer may surprise you — I'm more your friend than you think. Let her love you. Buy her a few sweets and flowers — it will be a nice interlude for both of you. You see, women like us have our needs too. We deserve our . . . consolations. Only, don't expect more than she can give you —

ARMAND: — Give me, give me! I didn't come here for crumbs!

PRUDENCE: Crumbs? You expect her to give up de Guiche for you? Or Nirac? What equal sacrifice will you make for her? Eh? You'll love her for a little, while she gives you the best years of her life. Then one fine day you'll pack off to Rouen to marry the first bovine country lady your father finds you.

ARMAND: Then I shall spare her that pain. I'll return to Rouen tonight — perhaps my father's already found me a suitably bovine country wife. Au revoir, Mme. Duvernoy, your logic is irrefutable!

(He bows and goes. She stares after him, then sits down at the cafe table.)

PRUDENCE: It's a wonder, isn't it, that anyone survives youth. Oh the tears, the rapture! Was it ever worth the trouble? A caprice is fine, naturally, a warm caprice on a cold night . . . *(She smiles at a memory.)* But even warmth has its dangers — affection can ignite and consume you, leaving nothing but ashes. Yes, I do believe it's better — for Marguerite — if things go on as they are, for in this world you must hold on to what you already have. You dare not let go!

(She rises, takes a quick look around, then pockets the money Gaston left for the waiter. She goes. Lights fade out.)

ARMAND'S APARTMENT

Sounds of voices bidding, in the air. The lights come up slowly. It is evening. A chair, a desk, an open trunk. Armand and his manservant, Joseph, are packing clothes.

ARMAND: I'll want those extra shirts, Joseph. I don't know how long I'll be away.

JOSEPH: Is your father expecting you, monsieur?

ARMAND: No. How happy he'll be to see the prodigal back on his doorstep, how he'll love that!

(A knock at the door. Joseph goes.)

ARMAND: I'm not expecting anyone. I suppose I'd better take the green cravat, and something light. The weather's warming up, isn't it?

(Joseph reappears with Marguerite.)

MARGUERITE: I've come to say good-bye.

(Armand silently nods at Joseph, and the servant leaves.)

ARMAND: Why did you betray me?

MARGUERITE: My poor Armand. If I were a duchess with two hundred thousand a year, we might speak of betrayal. But I am who I am, which makes your question foolish and my answer unnecessary.

ARMAND: I've broken my promise to you already.

MARGUERITE: Yes.

ARMAND: It's because I love you.

MARGUERITE: My friend, try to love me less or else understand me better. Look at me, see me as I am. If you want me, the price is that I continue with them — it's a fair bargain.

ARMAND: A bargain!

MARGUERITE: Yes, don't you see? I can buy the satisfaction of my soul at the expense of my body, it's a small thing. Armand, last night I permitted you to come to me —

ARMAND: — Why? Why?

MARGUERITE: Because you wept for me. I had a puppy once who loved me in that way, without question, without judgment. When I coughed, he was sad for me. And when he died, I wept for him more than for my mother's death. Armand, if men knew what they could have for a tear . . .

ARMAND: Puppy! Can you understand the humiliation I feel at being your kept lapdog? It makes me little better than a whore —

(She slaps him on the face.)

MARGUERITE: Why don't you pay me, then, and there's an end to it! That will make you like all the rest, and you'll enjoy their privileges —

(Suddenly weeping, the two come together.)

ARMAND: Pardon me, Marguerite, pardon me, I pray you. I shall be your dog, faithful without question, humble without expectation . . .

MARGUERITE: Hush . . . hush . . . hush . . .

(Joseph enters.)

JOSEPH: Monsieur Armand, the carriage you ordered is waiting. If you wish to catch your train . . .

ARMAND: Send the carriage away.

(Joseph goes out.)

ARMAND: I forgot the only important part of it all, didn't I? That I've known you always. That I will be with you forever, to the grave and beyond.

MARGUERITE: My dear —

ARMAND: Joseph! Send out for some supper.

(Marguerite starts to pull away.)

MARGUERITE: *(Very quietly.)* I can't stay, Armand, someone's waiting at home.

ARMAND: Who?

MARGUERITE: Nirac.

ARMAND: Send your regrets.

MARGUERITE: I cannot.

ARMAND: Tomorrow will be fine — we'll drive into the country.

MARGUERITE: He's waiting.

(He pulls away from her. A significant pause. He decides.)

ARMAND: Go to him now. We'll talk tomorrow. But for the moment you must go, I understand it.

(She studies him, starts to go, turns back.)

MARGUERITE: Joseph!

(Joseph appears.)

JOSEPH: Madame called?

MARGUERITE: Send a message to my maid: number nine, Rue d'Antin. Tell her I won't be coming back tonight.

ARMAND: Tell her, Joseph, not to wait breakfast, either!

(Joseph bows and goes out. They embrace. He carries her out of the room. Lights fade out.)

RUE D'ANTIN

Exterior, day. Bare stage. Throughout the scene Nanine appears, hauling valises, bundles, hatboxes, etc. down the stairs and off. She makes several trips. Clement appears with Olympe on his arm. She is noticeably more elegant. As she speaks, de Guiche strolls on from the other direction.

OLYMPE: . . . And they were a perfect matched pair, perfect chestnuts, white between the eyes, Lucien. And handsome! They'd look quite elegant — you'd almost have to buy a new carriage to show them off.

DE GUICHE: Hello, Clement, Madame Olympe.

CLEMENT: De Guiche.

OLYMPE: *(Going.)* His tailor is inspired, don't you think?

(They are off. Nanine comes down with a hamper, and Prudence enters from another direction.)

DE GUICHE: Prudence, is our friend going somewhere?

PRUDENCE: Oh, it's you. To the country, if you please. A place called Bougival, on the river.

DE GUICHE: I know she loves clothes, but even so, isn't she taking a large wardrobe for a May weekend?

PRUDENCE: Who said anything about a weekend? She'll find more manure and fewer flowers than she remembered, in the country.

DE GUICHE: She's not retiring? Come to think of it, I haven't had a glimpse of her for weeks!

PRUDENCE: That shows how heartfelt your passion is! Skin-deep, eh?

DE GUICHE: You know me too well, my dear. Well, tell me about this . . . love in bloom.

PRUDENCE: It won't last, I assure you. They'll be back. You can't live on love, you know.

DE GUICHE: And what will you live on, till then?

PRUDENCE: Don't you worry, I've tucked away a little something, here and there. After all, practicality's a woman's greatest asset.

DE GUICHE: And all along I thought it was purity.

PRUDENCE: Purity? Something you can lose at one shot?

(She leaves. He stares after her.)

DE GUICHE: Poor old thing, out in the cold. You don't even get to play Strumpet-of-Honor in this affair.

(But suddenly he shivers a little, feeling a chill. He walks off as the lights fade.)

BOUGIVAL

A garden. Morning. There is a little bench on which lie pen, paper, and a ledger. But Marguerite and Armand are sprawled on a blanket on the ground. She is reading a novel, he is sketching her. She looks up sadly.

MARGUERITE: Love's too tragic in novels. Real life's much simpler, isn't it?

ARMAND: Hold still, your nose is very tricky.

MARGUERITE: How lazy you've grown. When we first came, you'd hike and fish. You were quite an inspiration for me. But in three short months you've degenerated into a sloth. You go nowhere!

ARMAND: I'd be a fool to step outside the boundaries of Eden.

MARGUERITE: Finish up my nose, so I can exercise you. *(A bird squawks.)* The crows and magpies are so quarrelsome today — that means autumn's on the way.

ARMAND: My country queen. The country's made you bloom — I see the trace of an enchanting double chin —

(She throws the novel at him. He picks it up.)

ARMAND: *Manon Lescaut* — again? You've read it a dozen times.

MARGUERITE: I love a good cry. Such undying devotion on his part. Such a shallow love of finery on Manon's. She's about to die in his arms . . . again. *(Armand settles his head in her lap.)*

ARMAND: You're right, real life's much nicer.

MARGUERITE: Oh thou indolence, all you do is recline.

ARMAND: But I do it so well. Look at that sky — not a cloud.

MARGUERITE: That may be good for the grapes, but the garden's parched. Armand?

ARMAND: Hmm?

MARGUERITE: I met the strangest little man this morning, early, when I was taking my walk. He was a caretaker, or grave digger —

ARMAND: A grave digger?

MARGUERITE: I was walking in the graveyard. It's so picturesque and romantic there.

(Armand tosses the novel far away.)

ARMAND: I absolutely forbid you to read these morbid novels!

MARGUERITE: Silly. Anyway, he was watering the flowers on a little grave. I asked whose it was. "A poor girl's," he said, "one who lived a bit too free and easy." And then he sighed, "I'm quite in love with her."

ARMAND: Had he known her?

MARGUERITE: No. But he said that folk who work in a place like that are obliged to love the dead — they've so little time to love anything else. And then, Armand, he began to speak to the dead girl! "Aye, love, I'll tend your garden, aye, with no one else to buy you so much as a flower, but me. I'll care for you." And then he blew his nose and laughed and said, "Isn't ours a merry trade?" Then he turned back to his watering.

ARMAND: Very strange.

MARGUERITE: And romantic — much more than *Manon Lescaut.* Poor dead girl.

ARMAND: Imagine a man in love with the dead. *(He sits up, takes up his sketch.)* If you promise to sit still, I'll attack your nose again. We can't leave until it's right.

MARGUERITE: *(Placidly.)* Oh dear.

ARMAND: It could take days. *(He draws.)* Years. We could grow old sitting in this garden. This is the happiest I've ever been in my life. Right here, in Bougival, watching you chase butterflies, listening to your dolorous stories and . . . trying to cope with your nose.

(As he draws, Nanine appears with the mail.)

NANINE: Postman's early today. Two for madame, one for monsieur.

(Armand frowns at his envelope.)

ARMAND: Here we go again.

MARGUERITE: Your father?

(They open their envelopes.)

ARMAND: Yes indeed. "My son: despite our unfortunate interview last month, I wish to speak with you again." I'll bet he does! "I shall be in Paris on the seventeenth —" That's today. " — And I'd be grateful if you'd agree to dine with me. I shall call at your apartment at six. Respectfully, your father, Charles Christian Duval."

MARGUERITE: *(Reading her letter.)* Go.

ARMAND: No, thank you.

MARGUERITE: Go, I beseech you. He's an old man, he adores you.

ARMAND: I'm a young man, I adore you. He doesn't understand. End of discussion. Who's your letter from?

MARGUERITE: Prudence.

ARMAND: I can guess. "My dear girl, renounce that young pauper and come home like a reasonable human being."

MARGUERITE: Something like that. *(She folds up the letter, opens the other one.)* Go see him, dear heart.

ARMAND: Georges Christian Duval? No thank you.

MARGUERITE: And while you're in Paris you can do an errand for me. I've a few trinkets for Prudence. If you go by the early train, you can drop them at her place before you meet your father.

ARMAND: Are you giving her a present? Is it her birthday?

MARGUERITE: I'm simply lending her a few things. For a ball. Please?

(She starts to read the second letter.)

ARMAND: Not today, I haven't the time. Today we're going to float down the river on a barge bedecked with wildflowers. And I'll gather all the passing waterlilies and weave them into a blanket for us to lie on, and then we'll —

MARGUERITE: — Please see him, my dear.

ARMAND: You're pale, suddenly. Who's your other letter from?

MARGUERITE: Prudence.

ARMAND: Two letters?

MARGUERITE: I'm chilled from sitting on the ground. Autumn's coming, after all.

ARMAND: What does she need this time, the dress off your back?

MARGUERITE: No, she forgot to tell me about her evening at the opera in the first letter . . . she's getting so absentminded, poor thing. Please, Armand, do me this little favor while you're in town? Nanine. Nanine! — I'm not so demanding a mistress, am I? Not like Manon Lescaut.

(Nanine appears.)

MARGUERITE: Ah, Nanine, fetch the little blue morroco box on my table, for monsieur.

(Nanine goes out.)

MARGUERITE: Please? Take the trinkets to Prudence, then be a good boy and make it up with your father. *(She flings herself at him suddenly.)* Then come home to me as quickly as you can, my love. — And bring some *raisins glacés* with you. I do crave them!

ARMAND: All right, I'll go, but more for the sake of your raisins glaces than for my father.

(Nanine appears with a small blue box. Marguerite takes it and presses it into Armand's hands.)

MARGUERITE: Thank you, Nanine. You see, it's not large. If you hurry, you can catch the two o'clock train. You'll be there by four, and have plenty of time to —

(She buries her head in his waistcoat.)

ARMAND: There, there, my dear, I shan't forget your sweets.

MARGUERITE: Do you love me?

ARMAND: I love you.

MARGUERITE: Forever?

ARMAND: I'll be back before midnight and prove it.

(He kisses her once more, then goes. She looks at the second letter again, crumples it. She sinks onto the bench, buries her head in her hands. Then she dries her tears, takes up her ledger and pen.)

MARGUERITE: Let me see . . . for the butcher, for August, forty-four francs. For the greengrocer, twenty-seven. That's sixty-one — no, seventy-one francs. If Prudence can get two hundred for that little bracelet . . . *(She stares absentmindedly for a moment, then.)* And the milk man, thirty-five. Why should the milkman want thirty-five, when the greengrocer only wants . . .

(Nanine enters.)

NANINE: A gentleman to see you, madame.

(Marguerite slowly closes her ledger. She seems to shrink in size. A tall man, somberly dressed, enters.)

DUVAL: Madame, my name is Georges Christian Duval.

(A silence.)

MARGUERITE: Yes, I've only now received your letter. You just missed Armand.

DUVAL: I know.

MARGUERITE: Have a seat, monsieur.

(But Duval declines, moves off a few feet to study her at length, almost rudely.)

DUVAL: So, you're the renowned Marguerite Gautier. Your reputation has traveled far and wide.

MARGUERITE: All the way to Rouen . . . fancy.

DUVAL: Bad news travels with amazing speed.

MARGUERITE: You're as rude as your son said you were, monsieur.

DUVAL: I'm honest, madame. And since I am, I must speak frankly: You are ruining my family.

MARGUERITE: Monsieur Duval, I wish you no harm. I'm not even rude.

DUVAL: Madame, you must release my son.

MARGUERITE: He's not my prisoner.

DUVAL: Oh, you have bound him with your own kind of chains. I demand you release him!

MARGUERITE: Don't mistake courtesy for weakness, monsieur. Bullying me won't work.

(A pause.)

DUVAL: I shall pay handsomely for you to release Armand.

MARGUERITE: Ah, bribery, I thought we'd come to that! I'd no more take money from you than I would from him. Did you know, I've never accepted a gift from your son, except the gift of his love — I'd rather die.

DUVAL: Then you've chosen to elevate Armand to a special category indeed, among your male acquaintances.

(She turns away.)

DUVAL: I apologize for that remark. You've made me lose my temper . . . I seldom do that.

(A pause.)

MARGUERITE: I love Armand.

DUVAL: You're certain? Yes, I can see you are. Then it's not by threats, but by entreaties that I must ask you for this sacrifice. I don't ask lightly, I can see it will cost you much.

MARGUERITE: I'm sorry I can't oblige you. I could not live without Armand.

DUVAL: If we both love him, surely we have the common goal of shielding him from unhappiness? We must decide which is the lesser of two evils —

MARGUERITE: — You or me, you mean?

DUVAL: I only wish to spare him pain.

MARGUERITE: What of my pain?

DUVAL: You're young and beautiful, and I've no doubt life will console you. You are intelligent — I mean it. *(He lifts her chin, studies her face.)* There are many so-called Good Women who would despise you for what you do, who you are. But I can see, my child, your heart is more generous and your soul more worthy than theirs.

(Marguerite suddenly looks confused and tired.)

MARGUERITE: Then why are you so resolute against me?

DUVAL: If you'd been my child, I would have given you every advantage. You'd have blossomed like a queen. But fate is cruel . . . my poor child, my poor child . . .

(He rocks her like a little girl.)

MARGUERITE: You're making me cry.

DUVAL: So brave, poor little girl, so brave. If only Armand had your courage. *(He breaks from her, a rhetorical move.)* Armand, Armand, what are we to do with him? He hates me for my hasty assessment of your character — he was right about that, and I was wrong. But he's weak by nature. I've heard he gambles now.

MARGUERITE: He did, to settle some debts, but he's stopped since we came to Bougival. You must believe me when I tell you I'd never take a sou from him.

DUVAL: I do. But Armand will gamble again when you are in debt again. I'm worried that he might gamble away his small inheritance. Having lost that, he might squander his sister's, and the little portion I've set aside for the repose of my old age.

MARGUERITE: I'd never allow that. *(She opens her ledger.)* Look, these are pawn tickets — I've been pawning my jewels, my silver — I don't need them any more, they do me no good, except to pay our bills in Bougival. I show them to you proudly, for they prove I come to Armand without the compromise of obligation.

(Now it is Duval who is confused. His confusion grows into horror.)

DUVAL: You're telling me *he* lives off of *you?!*

MARGUERITE: He doesn't know about these, it's my secret.

DUVAL: My God, the scandal! They'll say Armand has allowed a kept woman to sell all she possessed for him. They'll say *he* ruined *you!!* *(He pulls himself together, assesses her state of mind, and marshalls his final attack.)* Sit down, child, you look exhausted. *(He takes a little turn around the garden.)* It's beautiful here in Bougival, the Seine looks like it's made of silver. In Paris it's gray and dead-looking. I hate Paris.

MARGUERITE: He says you grow apples.

DUVAL: Some of the trees in my orchard are very old, some are so young they haven't even blossomed yet. I like to think of my grandchildren climbing up in those branches, picking the good apples. *(A beat.)* I'm growing old. I'd like to see that sight once, before I'm gone. May I call you Marguerite?

(She nods.)

DUVAL: I've a daughter, Marguerite. Her name is Blanche.

MARGUERITE: She's seventeen.

DUVAL: She's as beautiful and pure as an angel. This summer, Blanche came home from the convent — and fell in love. The boy's from an old and honorable family. It's a lovely sight, watching them together. Alas, poor Blanche.

MARGUERITE: *(Whispers, waiting for him to strike.)* Why?

DUVAL: The boy's family has heard of Armand's liaison. The marriage is off if he continues to offend their sense of propriety. Society is cruel.

MARGUERITE: *(Whispers.)* Yes.

DUVAL: So, there it is, it must be weighed. And suddenly you're the judge, not I. The future of a child who has never harmed a soul rests in your hands. She's innocent. She has the right to a happy future. Look at me, Marguerite. The time has come for you to render your decision: Have you the right to shatter her happiness?

(A pause.)

MARGUERITE: Armand told me once that you were just and honest. Will you answer one question, as truthfully as you can?

DUVAL: Of course.

MARGUERITE: Do you believe I love your son?

(A pause. His answer is honest.)

DUVAL: Yes.

MARGUERITE: With a disinterested love?

DUVAL: Implicitly.

(Pause.)

MARGUERITE: I shall rule in your favor. I can do nothing else.

(She is in obvious pain. She takes her pen and paper, sits and writes. Duval looks around the garden again, trying not to show his relief.)

DUVAL: The soil here is rich. This year's harvest should be splendid, according to all I've heard. — I'm sorry, Marguerite. I wish the rules were different, I wish no one got hurt. But if we didn't live by our rules, chaos would — you know what I'm trying to say, don't you? *(A pause.)* Before I got here I thought . . . *(A pause.)* I didn't think it would be this hard! *(She hands him the letter.)*

MARGUERITE: Give this to his manservant. Read it?

(He hesitates, then unfolds the letter.)

DUVAL: "By the time this letter reaches you, my dear Armand, I shall be the mistress of another man. Go back to your father, my friend, to a love purer than you have enjoyed with me. I am sorry to have hurt you, but I promise you will forget your pain sooner than I shall forget you. Marguerite Gautier."

MARGUERITE: You must be strong for him.

(Duval folds the letter and puts it in his pocket.)

DUVAL: What can I — ?

MARGUERITE: Embrace me, monsieur, as if I were your daughter.

(He crosses to her, kisses her on the brow.)

DUVAL: God will love you for this.

MARGUERITE: Your son will hate me.

(Duval goes. Marguerite stands, waiting, the lights fade out.)

END OF ACT I

ACT II

THE BALL

The orchestra plays, off. Couples dance through during the course of the scene. Wine is served by white-gloved waiters.

THE DANDY: How the champagne flows tonight!

DE GUICHE: If they pour much more, we'll have to build an ark!

GASTON: Our host's a very rich fellow. They say his money comes from railways. That makes it "new money."

(*Marguerite and Nirac appear at the top of the stairs.*)

DE GUICHE: One mustn't hold that against him, for his title is very old, I gather.

GASTON: Very old — I hear he bought it last year.

(*The Dandy spots Marguerite, waves.*)

DANDY: Now the party can begin! Marguerite!

(*Nirac whispers in Marguerite's ear, then bows and disappears in the direction of the gaming tables, off. The gentlemen raise their glasses.*)

DANDY: To Marguerite!

ALL: Marguerite!

DANDY: What a pleasure to find you gracing the old town. When did you get back?

MARGUERITE: Two months ago.

GASTON: Paris wasn't the same without her.

MARGUERITE: Gentlemen, you are too kind.

GASTON: Without you, the crystal loses its sparkle —

DE GUICHE: — The champagne is flat —

GASTON: — Nearly as flat as the reparté.

MARGUERITE: But one thing never changes.

DANDY: What's that?

MARGUERITE: The flattering, well-oiled tongue of society.

GASTON: You wound me to the soul!

DE GUICHE: I thought you had no soul, Gaston.

GASTON: It's an encumbrance I try to ignore.

DANDY: We're grateful to Nirac for bringing you, this evening.

MARGUERITE: Yes, he doesn't like to share his toys, usually. And how kind of our host to give this little dance.

GENTLEMEN: Here here! To our host! To the Duke!

DE GUICHE: By the way, where is he?

GASTON: Perhaps he forgot to come!

DANDY: Perhaps he's too busy playing with his trains!

DE GUICHE: Will you honor me with a dance, Marguerite?

MARGUERITE: As many as you like. Nirac dislikes dancing. Oh, it is good to be back in Paris!

GASTON: Think of all you missed, buried in the country.

MARGUERITE: I made quite a list — the music, the lights, the chocolate éclairs at the Café Anglais!

(They applaud her. Nirac heads toward them.)

There's no one to talk to in the country, only the livestock.

GASTON: Ah, Nirac, we were just speaking of you.

NIRAC: When you have a moment, my dear, I want you to come meet the Baron de Liège. He's simply fascinating on the subject of credit!

(He kisses her hand and leaves again.)

GASTON: "Simply fascinating on the subject of credit?" — think of it!

(They laugh.)

MARGUERITE: Where was I — oh, yes, when it gets dark in the country, there's nothing to do but sleep. In Paris, at night, the lights go on — and we live!

(As she says this, Olympe and Lucien enter, above. Olympe has become magnificent. The men gaze up at her, as she moves regally down the stairway. She has quite eclipsed Marguerite.)

DANDY: Olympe! How ravishing you look tonight! Now the party can begin!

(Marguerite crosses to her, they touch cheeks.)

MARGUERITE: My dear Olympe, it seems only yesterday you were a little girl. But here you are, not only grown-up, but perfection itself!

OLYMPE: You are my model.

MARGUERITE: You're too kind.

OLYMPE: But your cheeks are flushed — are you quite well, my dear?

MARGUERITE: Such a glorious gown — you've found a new dressmaker — but you mustn't be allowed to keep her to yourself.

(Armand appears above. People turn, surprised to see him. There is a murmur. De Guiche, Gaston, and Prudence edge toward Marguerite, as.)

OLYMPE: As a matter of fact, I was strolling down the Rue de Rivoli last week, and there was this little shop with a sign in the window, so Lucien said —

(Marguerite has spotted Armand at last.)

MARGUERITE: — My apologies, dear Olympe, but I seem to have had the tiniest catastrophe with a stocking, and I'd better go remedy it, my dear, before disaster sets in, I'd better —

(She rushes off. Olympe shrugs. The music starts again. Lucien arrives at Olympe's side.)

OLYMPE: Well well, so you've caught up with me at last, Lucien. I suppose you'll attempt to dance now? I wonder what possessed poor Marguerite?

CLEMENT: Not too fast, my dear, you know my heart —

OLYMPE: Your heart, your heart! Sometimes you make me feel like an attending physician!

(They dance off. Armand descends, snaps his fingers. A waiter appears, and Armand takes two glasses from the tray. He brings them over to Prudence.)

ARMAND: Champagne to slake your thirst?

PRUDENCE: What ill wind blows you back into town?

ARMAND: Recovery. I've been in Rouen, recovering from brain fever. Now it's my turn to ask a question. Who was that enchanting creature in white? I'm quite smitten.

PRUDENCE: That's Olympe. Awe-inspiring name, isn't it? Her mother was ravished by a Greek god — or so she says. I place her Olympian ravishment somewhat closer to home, in the neighborhood of Notre Dame, say. Do you want to meet her?

ARMAND: I'd be forever in your debt.

PRUDENCE: She's been taken up by an old banker, but I suspect she'd like the idea of a little caprice. Lucien Clement's a bit feeble, if you take my meaning. You see, I'm as considerate as ever about your financial situation.

ARMAND: And Marguerite?

PRUDENCE: what about her?

ARMAND: I trust she recouped her losses?

PRUDENCE: It was a close thing, my boy. The day before she left you, last summer, her creditors threatened to seize her furniture.

ARMAND: I'd no idea I was so costly.

PRUDENCE: Well, never mind, her debts have been settled.

ARMAND: And now I must settle mine. By the way, who came to her rescue?

PRUDENCE: The Comte de Nirac, and very generously. He got what he wanted, but it cost him eighty thousand —

ARMAND: Yes, well, I want to thank you.

PRUDENCE: For what, dear boy?

ARMAND: I owe it to you, partly, that I met her. And I certainly owe to you the fact we're no longer together.

PRUDENCE: Don't mention it. I did what was best for Marguerite.

ARMAND: And now I'll owe you double thanks, for here comes our Olympic goddess, and you promised an introduction.

(They cross to Olympe and Lucien.)

PRUDENCE: Madame Olympe, M. Clement: M. Duval.

LUCIEN: A pleasure.

ARMAND: Enchanted. May I have this dance?

(Olympe and Armand waltz away. Clement is fighting for breath.)

CLEMENT: I need some air — my heart —

PRUDENCE: Perhaps you're out of practice. *(She fans him.)* Waiter, bring monsieur a glass of champagne.

(She leads him off to the side, props him up against a wall, then beckons Gaston to take her away. Olympe and Armand waltz on.)

ARMAND: Enchantress . . .

OLYMPE: You're bold, M. Duval.

ARMAND: You've only yourself to blame: You set my blood racing, my heart pounding —

OLYMPE: Dear God, there's no end to this *Materia Medica!*

ARMAND: I beg your pardon?

OLYMPE: I was just being naughty, monsieur.

ARMAND: I hope you'll be a lot naughtier before the night ends.

OLYMPE: You may hope.

(They waltz out again. Prudence promenades with Gaston. They nibble a plate of hors d'oeuvres.)

PRUDENCE: There wasn't much future for me there, so I said to myself, go to Paris. You won't get mud on your skirts in Paris, because the streets are paved; and you won't have to muck out any barns because there aren't any barns. I was fourteen, you see, and the village schoolmaster had already taught me more than was in the curriculum. So I had nothing left to lose. I hopped aboard the first diligence to Paris. It's a city of miracles, truly.

GASTON: What miracle's befallen you, pray?

PRUDENCE: I haven't seen the inside of a barn from that day to this!

(They stroll out. De Guiche and Marguerite waltz on. She too has trouble breathing.)

DE GUICHE: You've got fever, haven't you?

MARGUERITE: I don't know.

DE GUICHE: Ask Nirac to take you home.

MARGUERITE: He's not ready to leave. Please, de Guiche, let's keep dancing. I'm afraid to stand still.

DE GUICHE: Why, my dear?

MARGUERITE: I'm afraid I might be overtaken. Why did he come back? Let's keep dancing.

(They start to waltz. Nirac appears, taps her on the shoulder.)

NIRAC: I thought I asked you to wait in the library.

DE GUICHE: Do let us finish this waltz, Nirac.

NIRAC: I think not. Her stamina's not what it ought to be.

(He starts to walk away. Marguerite follows docilely. De Guiche stares after them. The Baroness beckons a waiter.)

BARONESS: Please send someone into the Green Salon. A man has been sick on the Aubusson rug.

(The waiter departs hastily.)

CLEMENT: Who?

BARONESS: God knows who anyone is, anymore. A Monsieur le Grand — he looks like a butcher's assistant.

CLEMENT: Well, he's certainly behaved like one.

(Olympe and Armand walk on. He holds a small pouch filled with coins.)

OLYMPE: What a lot of money you've won — three hundred louis d'or. Such a clever boy.

ARMAND: It's only a game of chance.

OLYMPE: But the gods were with you.

ARMAND: Just one, a goddess. Here, take it, deity, to buy ambrosia.

(He presses the pouch into her hands.)

OLYMPE: I couldn't.

ARMAND: You could. Only one thing — let me stay with you tonight.

OLYMPE: I'm afraid I must decline.

ARMAND: I thought you fancied me. Is it that old man?

OLYMPE: Lucien? He's probably going straight home to his wife tonight, with palpitations. No, it's because you love Gautier — everyone knows it. If you become my lover you'll have a little revenge, eh? But M. Duval, I'm too young and pretty to be forced into so insulting a role.

ARMAND: Then consider another suggestion: Take me for nothing. *(He takes back the little pouch of coins.)* Let me be your caprice. No money will change hands. Well? What do you think?

OLYMPE: I think . . . that I just lost three hundred louis d'or.

(He dangles the pouch in front of her.)

ARMAND: Then reconsider. If I had used a go-between to offer you this, you'd have grabbed it quickly enough. Accept now, without probing my motives. Tell yourself, "Yes, I'm the fairest of them all, and Armand Duval is mad about me!" *(He jingles the coins tauntingly.)*

OLYMPE: You'd never have dared to speak to Gautier like that, it's too insulting. *(Her fingers start to creep toward the purse.)* Still . . . *(She grins, takes the purse.)* Heavens, what will you take me for?

ARMAND: We know what I take you for, Olympe. We've just been quibbling about the price.

(They dance off again, laughing. The Baroness dances on with Gaston.)

BARONESS: And there in the theater sat Victor Hugo, in a box, presiding over the riot his own play had created. And in the audience, the old guard was booing and hissing on behalf of dramatic decorum, and the young Romantics were cheering in support of artistic freedom. That's what I recall of the opening of *Hernani,* my dear

(They dance off, Armand and Olympe whirl back in.)

ARMAND: Out of breath so soon? You'll never survive the night.

OLYMPE: Is that a threat . . . or a promise?

ARMAND: Wait, I'll fetch you some sherbet.

(He goes out. Marguerite ambles toward Olympe. Olympe gives her a radiant smile.)

OLYMPE: I've been dancing with an old friend of yours.

MARGUERITE: Yes.

OLYMPE: He's about to become a new friend of mine.

MARGUERITE: Why are you doing this?

OLYMPE: He claims he's unattached, and he's very sweet. My dear Marguerite, you're looking tired. Nirac should take you home to bed.

MARGUERITE: How can you be so cruel?

OLYMPE: I only said you looked tired.

MARGUERITE: You know what I mean — Armand —

OLYMPE: Aren't you a bit late to be issuing territorial claims?

MARGUERITE: As my friend, I beg you —

OLYMPE: I'm not your friend, I'm your colleague. Friendship's a luxury women in our profession can ill afford.

MARGUERITE: Then we're lost souls indeed. What other solace will be left us in old age?

OLYMPE: That's too far away — I'm still young. As for solace, I hope I'll find that tonight. Such a charming boy . . . I cannot think why you ever gave him up.

MARGUERITE: Olympe, please.

OLYMPE: Perhaps we can have tea tomorrow, and compare notes —

MARGUERITE: — You're too vulgar, Olympe!

(By this time, Armand has come up behind Marguerite. Olympe smiles sweetly at her.)

OLYMPE: Vulgar, am I?

MARGUERITE: And cruel, trotting that old man around like a pet donkey. And attaching yourself to Armand, like a leech —

OLYMPE: Is there anything else you want to call me?

MARGUERITE: A whore! A whore with two purses! One where her heart should be, the other down below, where —

ARMAND: — Enough, madame! Cease your obscenities! You've insulted this lady —
(Prudence rushes over, grabs Marguerite.)

PRUDENCE: Stop it, my dear, the situation's dangerous. I beg you —

ARMAND: Well, madame. If you were a man, I'd call you out to duel, but it's clear I'm not to have that satisfaction. And I don't want to stoop to your level of invective to defend the lady. *(Wildly he turns to the others, who listen in horrified silence.)* What shall we do, throw her out into the street? *(To Marguerite.)* You, who peddle your love to the highest bidder; you, who can be bought and sold in the marketplace, like a stinking cabbage — your behavior disgusts me! Filth! Filth! I cannot fathom why God made you!
(Marguerite looks from Armand to Olympe, to the others who have gathered. She screams, starts to run up the stairs, and collides with Nirac. He puts his arm on her.)

NIRAC: Marguerite, what's come over you? You'd better apologize for your tantrum. *(To Prudence.)* What happened? Did she drink too much . . . again? *(To the assemblage.)* Whatever has happened, I truly regret madame's bizarre behavior. Come, Marguerite.
(He leads her out. A silence. Olympe smiles at Armand sweetly.)

OLYMPE: Well, have you gotten your money's worth?

ARMAND: — Pardon? Oh, no, not yet, my goddess. The night's still young.
(They go out, arm in arm. Murmurs. The music starts up again, and the dancing. De Guiche looks at Prudence and shakes his head in concern. Prudence nods.)

PRUDENCE: Usually I'm gratified when I'm proved right about a person.

DE GUICHE: But even you found his behavior surprising. Yes. Funny, I feel almost as sorry for him as I do for Marguerite.

PRUDENCE: Don't feel sorry for her, she's got Nirac, she's lying in the lap of luxury. I like Nirac . . . the little toad.

DE GUICHE: He is a toad. She keeps kissing and kissing him, wondering why he doesn't turn into a handsome prince.

PRUDENCE: He's a very handsome toad — think what he's done for her.

(De Guiche gives a short bitter laugh.)

DE GUICHE: I wouldn't dream of causing you distress, but I don't think Nirac will be around much longer.

PRUDENCE: Why? *(Sudden panic rises in her.)* Why?! You don't know what you're saying!

DE GUICHE: She uses paint cleverly, but it's there nonetheless: the circles under her eyes, the ugly flush on her cheeks — that's not rouge, you know.

PRUDENCE: I'll send the doctor round tomorrow.

DE GUICHE: By next month Nirac will be wearing a fresh flower in his lapel. And it won't be a camellia.

PRUDENCE: Don't even dream of such a thing, it would mean disaster! Dear God, I wish that damned duke had never given this party tonight! Disaster . . . !

DE GUICHE: By the way, I never saw our host.

PRUDENCE: Disaster!

(She staggers out, de Guiche continues to muse to himself.)

DE GUICHE: What a good idea, to give a party and not show up, yourself. On the other hand . . . he did miss the fireworks.

(The dancers waltz on and the lights fade.)

AT THE AUCTION

The Auctioneer appears above, holding aloft a silver bouquet-holder.

AUCTIONEER: Mesdames, messieurs, let us turn to Lot 495, a delicate silver bouquet-holder: Snap the little bracelet over the lady's wrist and she is chained to her flowers. Until now, this particular item has been used only for camellias. It is considered to be of great historic value. Bidding to start at one hundred francs.

A VOICE: One hundred ten.

ANOTHER: One twelve.

ANOTHER: One fifteen.

ANOTHER: One eighteen.

ANOTHER: One hundred twenty.

ANOTHER: One twenty-five.

AUCTIONEER: One twenty-five, one twenty-five . . .

(The light on him fades out.)

ARMAND'S APARTMENT

Armand is reading. Joseph enters.

JOSEPH: Monsieur?

ARMAND: Well, Joseph?

JOSEPH: Madame Olympe's maid is below. Madame wishes to know what time you'll be calling on her tonight.

ARMAND: Even God rested on the seventh day! Tell her my father's come to town. Tell her anything — I'll see her tomorrow.

JOSEPH: Will you dine at home, monsieur?

ARMAND: I suppose so.

(Joseph bows and leaves. Armand pours himself a glass of wine. He sinks back into his chair, staring at the glass. Marguerite appears. He senses, rather than hears, her come in. She looks ill.)

MARGUERITE: I'm . . . Joseph let me in . . . I've come to —

ARMAND: Well, what is it? What's the matter?

MARGUERITE: You've been so unkind. I've done nothing to you.

ARMAND: Nothing?!

MARGUERITE: Nothing but what circumstances forced me to do.

ARMAND: Of course.

MARGUERITE: I've come to ask two things of you.

ARMAND: Well?

MARGUERITE: First, pardon for what I said to Olympe last week at the ball. I didn't intend to insult your mistress.

ARMAND: And second?

MARGUERITE: I want to beg pity — pity for what you may yet do to me. Since that evening, I've borne such pain! When I've gone out alone in public, you've never failed to humiliate me. You've written me vile letters which hurt me more than I thought possible. Why? Why revenge yourself on a sad and sick woman like me? I've been ill again. I left my bed to come beg you . . . not for your friendship, but for your indifference.

(He drinks his wine off, then buries his head in his hands. Finally he rises, comes to her and takes her hand.)

ARMAND: Your hand's burning with fever. You're shivering. — Do you think I didn't suffer. I nearly went mad with grief.

MARGUERITE: You've a mistress, now, young and beautiful. They say you're happy.

ARMAND: And you, Marguerite, are you "happy"?

MARGUERITE: Please, don't mock my sorrow.

ARMAND: Once upon a time, in a garden near a river . . . why did you betray it all?

MARGUERITE: Circumstances were stronger than my will —

ARMAND: — Circumstances, circumstances! Damn all circumstances! Why did you leave?

MARGUERITE: I cannot tell you. *(She starts to leave.)* I'm so sorry . . .

(He watches her struggle with her cloak for a moment.)

ARMAND: Don't go. Stay. In spite of what you did, I still love you. Stay —

MARGUERITE: We're on quite different paths now, it would be folly to begin again, madness.

ARMAND: I am mad — obsessed.

MARGUERITE: And despite what you say, you despise me.

ARMAND: No, the past is dead, I swear it. We exist only in this moment, we two. *(He kisses her, she tries to pull away.)* Shall we go back to Bougival?

MARGUERITE: That was a century ago, we were children.

(He starts to pull off her cloak.)

MARGUERITE: I can no longer make you happy.

ARMAND: You're all I want, all I want.

(He kisses her again, she tries weakly to free herself, like a small animal in a trap.)

MARGUERITE: Don't — I'll be your slave, your dog. But you must stop . . . no . . . please don't hate me. I beg you —

ARMAND: Tomorrow we'll go home. Joseph! Send madame's carriage away. My dear, you're so feverish, so feverish and cold. Come, I'll warm you, only please don't cry.

MARGUERITE: No . . .

ARMAND: Don't cry, don't cry . . .

(Lights fade out.)

RUE D'ANTIN

The shy young girl enters with a priest.

PRIEST: — And suddenly mankind felt the heavy burden called sin. But alas, mankind grew used to it. That's why the seven deadly sins still flourish — habit! That's why you must never let your guard down, mademoiselle.

YOUNG GIRL: No, father.

PRIEST: This neighborhood is rife with sinners. Lust, avarice, the whole lot. Avert your eyes, undreamed of sin lurks behind these walls. And never let down your guard for a moment —

(From off, we hear Armand's voice calling, "Marguerite, Marguerite!" He runs in as the Priest and the Young Girl go off. He bounds up the stairs, rings the bell. Nanine appears.)

ARMAND: I've come for madame, she left before I woke up —

NANINE: I'm afraid she's engaged.

ARMAND: How engaged? With whom?

NANINE: The Comte de Guiche.

(Armand takes a small purse, counts out five coins, hands them to Nanine. Going.)

ARMAND: Give that to madame, five hundred francs — it slipped my mind last night.

NANINE: Wait — where are you going?

ARMAND: Away from Paris, away from France — I shall go to the devil!

(He flees. The lights fade.)

AT MARGUERITE'S

We hear the auction, sound only:

AUCTIONEER'S VOICE: Bidding to start at five hundred francs.

VOICE: Five hundred ten.

VOICE: Five hundred twenty-five.

(The voices begin to sound slightly warped and distorted.)

VOICE: Five fifty.

VOICE: Six hundred.

VOICE: Six hundred and thirty.

VOICE: Six hundred and eighty.

(Lights come up. Marguerite is lying on her chaise, de Guiche sits in a chair nearby, drinking tea. Nanine fusses over Marguerite with an afghan.)

MARGUERITE: She's like a mother cat, this Nanine. I'm afraid she's going to pick me up in her teeth and carry me off at any moment.

NANINE: I might, if you don't behave. The doctor told me to keep her warm.

MARGUERITE: If winter lasts much longer, Nanine, that aging tomcat over there will be forced to carry me off, to Italy, and the sun.

DE GUICHE: Nothing would delight me more. Only not next week, please.

MARGUERITE: Monsieur le Comte is getting married next week.

NANINE: Sir, you're never going to do it, are you?

DE GUICHE: The laudable Nanine expresses doubt. Why? — you think no one will have me?

NANINE: I can't see you tangling with the law that way.

DE GUICHE: The praiseworthy Nanine believes I'm not going to get enmeshed in something I can't undo by law. But marry I must. Her father's a duke. Will the righteous Nanine give me her blessing?

NANINE: I can't say. I haven't seen the bride.

(She exits.)

MARGUERITE: I'm happy for you, old friend. She's an enchanting child, and far too good for you.

DE GUICHE: Yes. And, let's face it, she's rich. Now I'll be able to buy you exquisite gifts — and afford them.

(They smile. A silence.)

MARGUERITE: You're an extraordinary man, de Guiche. I'll say it now, in case I'm not around to —

DE GUICHE: — Don't be absurd, you look splendid.

MARGUERITE: Oh yes, I'm to endure forever — at least as long as the pyramids, eh? See, I'm quite the ruin.

(She picks up a little mirror, studies herself.)

DE GUICHE: You're more beautiful than you were the day you came to Paris, seven years ago.

MARGUERITE: I'm twenty-three. I feel a hundred. Never mind, I was speaking of you, de Guiche. I believe you're the only man I've ever met who likes women.

DE GUICHE: Come, come —

MARGUERITE: No, who truly likes women. We're your friends. Other men feel lust for us, and scorn. They judge us. But always, your hand is open to us in simple friendship. I love that about you.

DE GUICHE: You give me too much credit. If I'm as amiable as all that, it's because I've never really mucked about in the business of loving and hating. I always stopped short. I told myself I was too fastidious for all that . . . feeling.

MARGUERITE: The Man of Detachment?

DE GUICHE: But often . . . I wonder what I've missed by so curious a . . . limitation.

MARGUERITE: Pain, de Guiche, pain.

DE GUICHE: And exaltation?

(She nods.)

MARGUERITE: But on a January day, when the sky is as gray and dead as my heart, I doubt the exaltation to have been worth the pain.

(A pause.)

DE GUICHE: Well, my dear, rest assured that my heart, however limited, is forever at your disposal.

(As he kisses her hand, Prudence enters.)

PRUDENCE: I've brought you the papers. — Look who's here, the sacrificial lamb, about to be led to the altar!

DE GUICHE: I'm the oldest, toughest lamb in the barnyard, my dear — I hope marriage softens me up.

PRUDENCE: Not a chance. I'm parched.

MARGUERITE: *(Rising from her bed.)* I'll have Nanine fetch another cup.

(De Guiche starts to go instead, but Prudence signals him to stay behind. Marguerite goes off slowly, as.)

PRUDENCE: When's the nuptial mass to be?

DE GUICHE: A week from Saturday.

PRUDENCE: I know! I'll gather all the ladies who used to be your special friends, and we'll come to your wedding together! We'll sit in the choir loft and send our blessings wafting down, as you kneel at the altar with your bride.

(Marguerite is off by now.)

DE GUICHE: What a grotesque idea!

PRUDENCE: I'm glad you've come. She doesn't get many visitors these days. Men are so fickle! I always knew that fool would bring her to grief.

DE GUICHE: Duval?

PRUDENCE: She's dying of love for him, no matter what the doctors call it. I wrote to him, to Alexandria. That's in Egypt. I told him he'd better hurry home if he wanted to see her alive.

DE GUICHE: Hush!

PRUDENCE: She looks more and more like a corpse every day —

DE GUICHE: Hold your tongue!

PRUDENCE: Well she does, it's as good as over for her. What man would want her, looking the way she does?

DE GUICHE: What does the doctor say?

PRUDENCE: He keeps insisting it's a sore throat, but I caught him in the foyer the other day, wiping away a few tears.

DE GUICHE: Perhaps a more detached doctor — ?

PRUDENCE: We haven't the money to pay this one! We've been pawning the jewels. The creditors are getting nasty.

DE GUICHE: You keep saying "we." Have you pawned your jewels? Have you sacrificed one sou of your little nest egg for her?

PRUDENCE: I've got my old age to consider. She's not going to have an old age! I'm good to her, I come here every day, I bring her the papers — I do love the girl, de Guiche. — But I have to live!

DE GUICHE: Don't worry, you will outlive us all!

(Marguerite enters on Nanine's arm.)

MARGUERITE: Is he trying to flatter you, Prudence?

(Marguerite's laugh turns into a cough. Nanine offers her a plate of cakes, which she waves away. Prudence helps herself.)

PRUDENCE: Yes, indeed, he's been positively showering me with compliments! All men are alike, when it comes to that. You keep repeating you esteem us, you worship us, you revere us. But it's only in your self-esteem that we come first!

(She laughs good-naturedly, and she eats cake.)

DE GUICHE: Touché, touché.

(Lights fade out.)

AT MARGUERITE'S

We hear the auction, again. This time, the voices are even more distorted, and they overlap each other.

AUCTIONEER'S VOICE: Lot 719. A Meissen tea service, complete. No chips or visible flaws. Bidding to start at three hundred francs.

A VOICE: Three ten.

ANOTHER: Three twenty.

ANOTHER: Three twenty-five.

ANOTHER: One thousand two hundred.

ANOTHER: Three thirty.

ANOTHER: Fourteen hundred.

ANOTHER: Three fifty.

ANOTHER: Two thousand.

ANOTHER: Three fifty-five.

ANOTHER: Twenty-five hundred.

ANOTHER: Four hundred.

ANOTHER: Three thousand.

(The sound fades out, the lights come up at Marguerite's. She is lying alone, asleep. A knock. Nanine crosses to answer. She returns with a stranger, and tries to prevent him from waking Marguerite.)

NANINE: Please, be a little quiet, monsieur.

BAILIFF: Number nine, rue d'Antin?

NANINE: Can I help you?

BAILIFF: I can help myself. Here's my orders. I'm the bailiff of this case. I've come to take the contents of the house.

NANINE: Are you mad?! You can't — there's a dying person here — dying! You can't touch a thing!

BAILIFF: The creditors want to make sure no one makes off with any of the goods. Dying?

(Nanine nods.)

BAILIFF: That's all right. I can wait.

(He walks over to Marguerite, peers down, then moves away. He pulls a chair over to a corner, and spends the rest of the scene waiting. Marguerite stretches, wakes up.)

MARGUERITE: Nanine? What's the weather like?

NANINE: Horrible . . . snowing.

MARGUERITE: Has the postman come?

NANINE: Just two bills today.

MARGUERITE: Only men are strong enough not to forgive.

NANINE: Hush, drink your medicine.

MARGUERITE: Who was at the door?

NANINE: A bailiff. Don't worry, I won't let him bother you.

(Prudence enters.)

PRUDENCE: Here are the papers. Well, what did the doctor say?

(Nanine shoots her a warning look.)

PRUDENCE: You'll never guess who I passed on the way over here! Olympe, as large as life and as grand as a duchess! She was riding in her new carriage with that little toad, Nirac. Prudence, I said to myself, that girl is fated to make a meal on Marguerite's leftovers.

(Marguerite turns her head away.)

PRUDENCE: It's God's truth, she never had an original thought in her head, especially about men.

MARGUERITE: Prudence?

PRUDENCE: What is it, my pet?

MARGUERITE: Did you go to the opera last night?

PRUDENCE: No, to the Variétés. Déjazet was superb, her singing melted my heart. But that Bouffe — he wasn't in voice at all! It must be the weather.

MARGUERITE: Did you see anyone, any of our friends?

PRUDENCE: No, no one. But I came late and left early.

MARGUERITE: How you lie to me!

PRUDENCE: Take your medicine, my dear. By the way, who's that man over there?

MARGUERITE: My watchdog. He's here to make sure I don't stroll off with any of the furniture. He's waiting for me to die.

PRUDENCE: Hush, that's a foolish fancy.

MARGUERITE: If I don't die soon, they'll sell the bed out from under me. Prudence?

PRUDENCE: What?

MARGUERITE: Ask Nanine for pen and paper. I must write Armand.

PRUDENCE: But you need your rest. Very well — Nanine!

(Prudence goes out.)

MARGUERITE: My dear Armand: The weather is dark and I am sad. I think of you, Armand. Where are you as I write these lines? Far, far from Paris, they tell me. Because I owe you the only happy moments in my life, I also owe you this explanation about the past. You will know I speak the truth, for by the time you read this letter, death will have sanctified it. I am ill. I shall die of this illness. Armand, do you remember that last day, in the garden at Bougival? A few minutes after I sent you off to Paris, a man presented himself to me. It was your father . . .

(We hear the little ormolu clock ticking. The light changes. Prudence enters and Marguerite hands her a sealed envelope.)

MARGUERITE: What time is it?

PRUDENCE: Six.

MARGUERITE: Give this to Armand after I'm gone. Swear it.

PRUDENCE: Take a little nap, now.

(Marguerite sinks back down and sleeps. The stillness is disrupted by Gaston, who enters with an abundance of camellias, in his usual boisterous good spirits.)

GASTON: I've brought her some flowers. I went round to ever florist and found as many as —

(Prudence hushes him crossly.)

GASTON: Oh, yes, hush. Shhh. *(He tiptoes over to look at Marguerite.)* Marguerite . . . oh my God.

PRUDENCE: You're not making jokes now, are you? Life doesn't seem quite so merry, eh?

GASTON: Suddenly it seems relentlessly grave and sour. Poor soul. I wonder if God will implicate me in this . . . The Accomplice, in the Martyrdom of St. Marguerite. Oh my dear, I am so sorry, so sorry . . .

(He leaves the room in tears. We hear the clock ticking away, and the lights change again. De Guiche is seated by the bed, reading aloud.)

DE GUICHE: "About daybreak, Manon whispered to me that she was at her last hour. Do not ask me to tell you what I felt, nor what were the last words she spoke to me. My soul did not follow hers. For two days and two nights I stayed with my dear Manon. I meant to die there —" *(De Guiche looks up in time to see Marguerite wipe away a tear. He puts down the book.)* My voice is tired. Look, the sun's trying to shine — I do believe the thaw has come at last. Next week, if the weather's fine, my wife would like to have tea with you.

MARGUERITE: What time is it?

DE GUICHE: Three. — Did Prudence tell you about the masked ball? All Paris was there. The orchestra was conducted by a man named Musard. He's got quite a following! His admirers think he's the devil, because when he conducts they can't stop dancing.

MARGUERITE: Did you dance?

DE GUICHE: My pumps hurt me, so I watched. This Musard fellow, he's the ugliest man I've ever seen, yellow and pock-marked.

MARGUERITE: Hand me my mirror.

DE GUICHE: I wish you could have seen him waving his baton, Marguerite. Next time there's a costume ball —

MARGUERITE: — I'll go as Death.

DE GUICHE: Hush.

MARGUERITE: Ask Nanine if the mail's come.

DE GUICHE: It hasn't, yet.

(Prudence enters.)

MARGUERITE: Tell me the truth, old friend, if I were to sell this body now, how much do you think it would bring?

(De Guiche smooths her hair, Prudence wipes her brow. They exchange a glance, then he goes. Nanine passes him, bringing the mail.)

NANINE: There's a letter just come.

MARGUERITE: Armand?

PRUDENCE: Let me see — it says Duval!

MARGUERITE: Open it, Prudence!

PRUDENCE: It's from his father. "Madame: I have only now learned of your illness. Were I closer to Paris, rest assured, my dear, that I would call upon you myself. Were my son here, I would delegate him to do so. But my duties prevent me from leaving Rouen, alas; and Armand is several thousand leagues away. Please believe in my sincere wishes for your recovery. I am yours most faithfully —" And he's enclosed five thousand francs. *(Softly, to Nanine.)* The pig! He was good for ten thousand, at least.

MARGUERITE: Armand, Armand, your father has a noble and forgiving heart. You must learn to love him, and do as he wishes . . .

PRUDENCE: Send for the doctor!

(Nanine runs out.)

PRUDENCE: Oh my God! Marguerite, listen, can you hear me? Can you — ? No, you mustn't do this to me — *(She seizes Marguerite's hand in a powerful grip.)* — No, no, I'll break your bones before I let you slip away from me — you have betrayed me! Deserted me! How dare you die without caring what will become of me? Selfishness! How dare you teach me what it is to have a friend, and then leave me friendless! Oh God, how I hate you for doing this to me! *(She sobs, then whispers.)* Oh, I'm sorry my sweet, I'm — Nanine! Nanine, the priest!! *(She rushes out of the room. Light change. The clock ticks relentlessly.)*

MARGUERITE: We must have done something very wicked before we were born, or else God means us to be very happy after we're dead. Why else would he make us pay and pay and pay for our lives? Open the window, Nanine, I can't breathe — You cried, and promised you'd follow me to the grave, and beyond, but only if you catch the early train back from Paris. *(The Priest enters to give the last rites. Marguerite sees him and shrinks back from him, in her bed.)*

MARGUERITE: If I recover, I'll make a pilgrimage — no, not to Lourdes, to Bougival. But you must understand, M. Duval, I am his fate, he calls me his fate. I promise I'll be good, only you must let me climb the apple trees as if I were your own little girl. What time is it? *(We hear, faint and distorted, voices calling out numbers: five, seventeen, two hundred thirty, etc. Marguerite is struggling frantically. She does not want absolution.)*

MARGUERITE: Pawn the necklace! Sell it! It's got sapphires and pearls, we might get a thousand francs, perhaps eleven hundred! Prudence, sell my hair! *(She stops her struggle, becomes seductively agreeable with the Priest.)* I suffer so, Armand, I'm going to die. Just like Manon. And your soul won't be able to follow mine. You'll bury me in the desert . . . The train is late,

the train is late. *(Suddenly she sees a very clear light.)* It was a wild, unreasonable dream, yes. But no one is unhappy always. Air . . . air . . .
(She dies. The Priest has completed the last rites. He packs up and leaves. Prudence and Nanine look down at her body. Lights fade out.)

THE AUCTION

The distorted numbers multiply, then slowly the sound fades away. As the lights come up, the auction is as it was at the beginning.

AUCTIONEER: Lot 535, a small boudoir clock. Swiss movement, onyx and malachite casing. This is a very beautiful ornament, fragile but accurate. Bidding will start at twelve hundred francs.

A VOICE: Twelve hundred ten.

ANOTHER: Twelve fifty.

ANOTHER: Fourteen.

ANOTHER: Fifteen hundred —

(Armand bursts in, breathless.)

ARMAND: Marguerite —

A VOICE: Sixteen hundred.

PRUDENCE: So you've come at last. She left you a letter.

(He tears it out of her hands, opens it and reads.)

A VOICE: Seventeen fifty.

ANOTHER: Eighteen hundred.

ANOTHER: Two thousand.

ANOTHER: Twenty-one hundred.

(Armand screams. The crowd turns to stare at him.)

AUCTIONEER: I beg your pardon, monsieur, but you're disrupting the bidding. Is there something you wished to buy?

A VOICE: Twenty-two hundred.

ANOTHER: Twenty-three.

ANOTHER: Twenty-four.

(The light and the sound fade.)

END OF PLAY

Great Expectations

ADAPTED FROM THE NOVEL BY
CHARLES DICKENS

To the memory of my father, Harry Field

Pip (Mitchell Lichtenstein), Miss Havisham (Henrietta Valor), and Estella (Kathryn Dowling) in the 1985 Guthrie Theater production of Charles Dickens's *Great Expectations,* adapted by Barbara Field with set design by Jack Barkla and costumes by Jack Edwards. Photo credit: Joe Giannetti.

CONTEXTUAL NOTES ON *GREAT EXPECTATIONS*

In 1985, the Guthrie production of *Great Expectations* reunited the creative team that had developed *A Christmas Carol* and *Pantagleize*. The script had originally been commissioned by the Seattle Children's Theatre in 1982. The Guthrie's plan was to play it on their main stage as part of the regular season, then send it on a national tour.

The novel travels to so many locations and tells such a complex story that it required a simple, almost austere style to communicate all the necessary information. I decided to give the actors in the play the shared task of narration, which enhanced its intrinsic sense of storytelling. The children, Pip, Estella, and Herbert, were played by the actors who played them as adults.

Because of limitations on running time and cast size, I eliminated a couple of ancillary characters and wrote some roles to be doubled — most notably Uncle Pumblechook, Wemmick, and Bentley Drummle, who were all dazzingly performed by one gifted actor, Richard Iglewski. It's an unabashedly theatrical device that is as much fun for the audience as it is for the actors.

Dickens wrote two endings for the novel. In the first version, Pip runs into Estella as he is strolling in Piccadilly with Joe Gargery's little boy. Pip and Estella greet each other, and then she rides away. Dickens was prevailed upon by his friends to do a second version. This time, Pip and Estella meet in Miss Havisham's ruined garden on a misty morning. They are reunited in the last elliptical sentence of the book: "I saw no shadow of another parting from her." Bernard Shaw disliked both endings. He felt the first was too matter-of-fact to be the right ending for a tragedy; he thought the happy ending was "a sentimental falsehood. . . . It is too serious a book to be a trivially happy one."

Shaw was right. I liked the misty ruined garden setting rather than Piccadilly, so I placed the ending there. However, although Pip and Estella have each won redemption, both have been too victimized during childhood and too damaged as adults to walk into the sunshine together — but must heal in their own time and on their own terms. So they meet, and so they part.

Adapted for The Guthrie Theater by Barbara Field

Director . . . . Stephen Kanee
Scenic Designer . . . . Jack Barkla
Costume Designer . . . . Jack Edwards
Lighting Designer . . . . Dawn Chiang
Composer/Musical Director . . . . Hiram Titus
Dialogue Coach . . . . Elizabeth Smith
Action Coordinator . . . . Bjorn Johnson
Sound Designer . . . . Tom Bolstad
Dramaturg . . . . Robert Cowgill
Stage Manager . . . . Russell Johnson
Assistant Stage Manager . . . . Mary Manthis
Production Assistant . . . . Lisa Anderson
Directing Intern . . . . Charles Smith
Stage Management Interns . . . . . Olivier Fournot, Todd Kauchich
Casting Consultants . . . . Stanley Soble, Jason LaPadura

CAST

PIP . . . . Mitchell Lichtenstein
MAGWITCH . . . . Allen Hamilton
MRS. JOE GARGERY/MOLLY . . . . Barbara Tirrell
JOE GARGERY/AGED PARENT/PORTER . . . . John Towey
JAGGERS/COMPEYSON/CLERGYMAN . . . . Richard Ooms
UNCLE PUMBLECHOOK/WEMMICK/BENTLEY

     DRUMMLE . . . . Richard Iglewski
HERBERT POCKET . . . . Mark Benninghofen
ESTELLA . . . . Kathryn Dowling
MISS HAVISHAM/MISS SKIFFINS . . . . Henrietta Valor
BIDDY/CLARA BARLEY/BARMAID . . . . Barbara Kingsley
SOLDIER/COACHMAN/PORTER/STABLE BOY . . . . Thomas Glynn
NARRATION . . . . Narration is shared among the cast

GREAT EXPECTATIONS

ACT I

The entire company is assembled onstage, except for the actor playing Magwitch, who is already hiding behind the tombstone.

NARRATION: His family name being Pirrip and his own name being Philip, in the beginning the boy could make of both names nothing longer than . . . Pip. So he called himself Pip, and came to be called Pip. The family name, Pirrip, he had on the authority of a certain tombstone, his father's, And on the authority of his older sister, Mrs. Joe Gargery, who was married to the town blacksmith. They lived in the marsh country of Kent, where the Thames ran down to the sea. In that dark, flat wilderness was a village churchyard where, one day, Pip found his parents.

• • •

Churchyard. A few tombstones. Pip kneels in front of one of them, reads haltingly.

PIP: "Philip Pirrip, late of this parish." *(Pause.)* "Also Georgiana, wife of the above . . ."

NARRATION: The boy, a small bundle of shivers, began to cry, when — *(Magwitch pops up from behind a tombstone.)*

MAGWITCH: Keep still, you little devil, or I'll cut your throat!

PIP: Oh don't, sir!

MAGWITCH: Tell us your name quick, then!

PIP: Pip, sir. *(Magwitch lifts him abruptly, sets him atop the stone, searches him. He finds a crust of bread, which he gnaws.)*

MAGWITCH: Lookee here, then — where's your mother?

PIP: There, sir. *(Magwitch starts.)* There — "Also Georgiana." That's my mother.

MAGWITCH: Hah. And that's your father, alonger your mother?

PIP: Yes, sir. "Late of this parish."

MAGWITCH: Hah. And who d'ye live with now, supposin' I kindly let you live, which I haven't made up my mind about?

PIP: My sister, Mrs. Joe Gargery. She's wife to the blacksmith.

MAGWITCH: Blacksmith, eh? *(He looks down at his leg irons.)* Lookee here: The question being whether or not you're to be let live — you know what a file is?

PIP: Yes, sir.

MAGWITCH: And you know what wittles is?

PIP: Wittles is food, sir.

MAGWITCH: You bring me a file and you bring me some wittles, or I'll have your heart and liver out. Bring 'em tomorrow at dawn — and don't say a word about having seen me — and I'll let you live. *(Pip nods.)* But mind, I'm not alone, if you're thinking that. No indeed, there's a young man hid with me, in comparison with which young man *I* am an angel. So you must do as I tell you.

MAGWITCH: *(Pulls out a little Bible.)* Swear — say "Lord strike me dead if I don't."

PIP: "Lord strike me dead if I don't." *(Magwitch gives him a dismissing nod. The boy backs away, then bolts. Magwitch huddles by the tombstone.)*

• • •

The forge kitchen.

NARRATION: Pip's sister, Mrs. Joe Gargery, was more than twenty years older than the boy. She had established a great reputation as a foster parent, because she had brought the boy up *by hand.*
(As Pip races in, Mrs. Gargery slaps him.)
She was neither a good-looking woman, nor a cheerful one.
(Joe steps in to protect Pip.)
Pip had the impression that she must have made Joe Gargery marry her *by hand,* too.
(She slaps Joe, as well.)

MRS. JOE: Where've you been, young monkey? I'm worn away with fret and fright over you.

PIP: I've only been to the churchyard.

MRS. JOE: Churchyard! If it weren't for me you'd have been in the churchyard long ago. Bad enough being a blacksmith's wife, and him a Gargery, without being your mother as well. You'll drive me to the churchyard one of these days, between the two of you. *(As she talks, she butters a slice of bread, hands it to Pip with another slap. He takes a bite, then when she isn't looking, he secrets the rest in his pocket. Joe notices, however. Mrs. Joe turns to*

Pip.) Where's your bread? Did you swallow it whole? This boy has the manners of a swine!

JOE: Oh no, my dear, I don't think he —

MRS. JOE: Don't "my dear" me! I'm not your dear. *(She hands Pip a slate, some chalk.)*

NARRATION: Pip felt little tenderness of conscience toward his sister. But Joe he loved.

(Joe watches Pip writing laboriously on the slate.)

JOE: I say, Pip, old chap, what a scholar you are!

PIP: I'd like to be. *(He writes.)* How do you spell Gargery?

JOE: I don't spell it at all.

PIP: But supposing you did?

JOE: It cannot be supposed — though I am oncommon fond of reading.

PIP: Are you, Joe? I didn't know that.

JOE: Oncommon — give me a good book and I ask nothin' better.

PIP: *(Pause.)* Did you ever go to school?

JOE: My father, he were given to drink, Pip; and whenever he were overtook with drink, he'd beat my mother and me, most onmerciful. We ran away a time or two, and my mother would find a job. "Joe," she'd say, "now you shall have some schooling, please God." And so I'd start school. But my father was such a good-hearted man, he couldn't bear to live without us, so he'd hunt us down and drag us home. Then he'd beat us up again to show how he'd missed us. Which you see, Pip, were a serious drawback to my learning. *(Mrs. Joe takes Pip's slate away.)*

MRS. JOE: Time for bed, boy. *(She gives him a slap for good measure.)*

JOE: Time for bed, Pip, old chap. *(Whispers.)* Your sister is much given to government, which I meantersay the government of you and myself. *(He hugs Pip. There is a distant boom of a cannon.)*

MRS. JOE: Hark, the guns.

JOE: Ay. It must be another conwict off, eh?

PIP: Off?

MRS. JOE: Escaped, escaped.

PIP: Please, Joe, where's the shooting come from?

MRS. JOE: Ask no questions, you'll be told no lies.

JOE: It comes from the Hulks, Pip, old chap.

PIP: Please, Joe, what's the Hulks?

MRS. JOE: This boy! Answer one question and he'll ask a dozen more!

JOE: Hulks is prison ships.

PIP: And please, Joe —

MRS. JOE: No more! Time for bed! Bed! Bed! Bed!

NARRATION: Conscience is a dreadful thing when it accuses a boy. Pip labored with the thought that he was to become a thief the next morning . . . which was Christmas Day.

(The cannon booms.)

Pip scarcely slept that night. When pale dawn came he crept into the forge where he stole a file, and thence into the pantry where he stole a loaf of bread, some brandy, and a beautiful, round firm pork pie. As he ran toward the marshes, the mist, the wind, the very cattle in the field seemed to accuse him. Stop thief! Stop that boy!

• • •

The churchyard. Pip runs toward the convict, whose back is to Pip. The man turns at Pip's whistle — but it is not the same man! Both gasp, then the man runs off. Pip empties his pockets, then Magwitch appears. He grabs the brandy.

MAGWITCH: What's in the bottle, boy?

PIP: Brandy. *(Magwitch stuffs the food into his mouth. He shivers as he eats.)* I think you've caught a chill, sir.

MAGWITCH: I'm much of your opinion, boy. *(He pauses, listens.)* You brought no one with you? *(Pip shakes his head.)* I believe you. You'd be a mean young hound if you could help hunt down a wretched warmint like me, eh? *(Pip watches him eat.)*

PIP: I'm glad you enjoy your food, sir.

MAGWITCH: Thankee, boy, I do.

PIP: But I'm afraid you haven't left much for him.

MAGWITCH: Who's him?

PIP: That young man you spoke of, who's with you.

MAGWITCH: Oh, *him*. *(He grins.)* He don't want no wittles.

PIP: He looked as if he did —

MAGWITCH: — Looked? When? *(He rises.)*

PIP: Just now.

MAGWITCH: Where?!

PIP: Right here, a few minutes ago. I thought it was you — he wore gray, like you, and he wore . . . he had the same reason for wanting a file. He ran away.

MAGWITCH: Did he have a scar on his face?

PIP: *(Nods.)* Here.

MAGWITCH: Give us that file, boy. *(Magwitch starts to file his leg irons.)* And then ye'd best go — they'll be missing you! *(Pip nods, then runs off.)*

NARRATION: As Pip ran home, he could still hear the file sawing away at the convict's fetters. He fully expected to find a constable waiting to arrest him when he got home. But there was only Mrs. Joe, readying the house for Christmas dinner.

• • •

The forge kitchen.

MRS. JOE: — And where the deuce ha'you been now? Company's expected!

PIP: I was . . . down to hear the carolers. *(She gives him a crack on the head.)*

JOE: Merry Christmas, Pip, old chap.

NARRATION: Dinner was set for half-past one. There was one guest . . .Mr. Pumblechook, wealthy seed-and-corn merchant in the nearby town. He was Joe's uncle, but he was Mrs. Joe's ally.

PUMBLECHOOK: Mrs. Joe, I have brought you a bottle of sherry wine, and I have brought you a bottle of port wine, in honor of the Day.

MRS. JOE: You was ever the soul of generosity, Uncle. *(They sit at table. She cuffs Pip.)* Stop fidgeting, boy — he wriggles as if he had a guilty conscience.

PUMBLECHOOK: Then he must indeed have one. Boys, Joseph — a bad lot!

MRS. JOE: Will you say the blessing, Uncle Pumblechook?

PUMBLECHOOK: For that which we are about to receive, may the Lord make us truly thankful.

ALL: Amen.

PUMBLECHOOK: D'you hear that, boy? Be ever thankful to them what has brought you up by hand.

PIP: Yes, sir.

PUMBLECHOOK: Joseph, why is it the young are never thankful? I declare, boys are naturally wicious!

MRS. JOE: Too true, Uncle Pumblechook.

JOE: Have some gravy, Pip? *(He ladles it onto Pip's plate.)*

PUMBLECHOOK: Not too much — the Lord invented the pig as an example of gluttony to the young. *(To Mrs. Joe.)* He's no end of trouble to you, is he, ma'am?

MRS. JOE: Trouble? You cannot know what trouble he's been.

JOE: More gravy, Pip old fellow, old chap, old friend?

PUMBLECHOOK: I suppose this boy will be apprenticed to you, soon, Joseph?

MRS. JOE: Not for another year. Till then he'll eat me out of house and home — but I'm forgetting! I've a delicious pork pie, yet! *(Pip drops his fork.)*

PUMBLECHOOK: Ah, pork pie! A morcel of pie would lay atop any dinner you might mention, and do no harm, eh?

MRS. JOE: I'll just go fetch it. *(She goes. Pip rises in terror, rushes to the front door to escape. Simultaneously, a sharp knock at the door, and a scream from Mrs. Joe. At the door, Pip is confronted by a pair of handcuffs, held by a soldier.)*

LIEUTENANT: Hello, young fellow — Does the blacksmith live here?

MRS. JOE: *(Off.)* Stop! Stop, thief, my pie — it's been stolen.

LIEUTENANT: Well?

PUMBLECHOOK: This is the blacksmith's, yes.

LIEUTENANT: Sorry to disturb your Christmas dinner —

PUMBLECHOOK: Think nothing of it, my good man.

LIEUTENANT: — But we've caught two convicts, and need these irons repaired. Can you do it?

PUMBLECHOOK: Not me, him. He's the smith. Certainly he can do it. *(Mrs. Joe enters, distraught.)*

MRS. JOE: My pork pie — it's gone —

LIEUTENANT: *(To Joe.)* By the way, is this your file?

JOE: *(Examines it.)* Which it are!

LIEUTENANT: It was found in the churchyard —

MRS. JOE: Thieves, thieves . . . *(Pumblechook is already pouring port wine down her throat.)*

• • •

NARRATION: Christmas dinner was over. When Pip arrived at the boat landing with Joe, he recognized *his* convict — and the other, with the scarred face. *(The convicts glare at each other. The Lieutenant takes the handcuffs from Joe, snaps them on Magwitch. The other man, Compeyson, lunges at Magwitch and is pulled off by soldiers.)*

MAGWITCH: I took 'im! I caught the villain! I turned 'im in, don't forget.

COMPEYSON: This man — this man has tried to murder me!

MAGWITCH: See what a villain he is — look at his eyes! Don't forget, I caught 'im for ye! *(Magwitch turns, notices Pip. Pip gives him a tiny shake of the head.)* I wish ter say something respectin' this escape. It may prevent some persons from lying under suspicion alonger me.

LIEUTENANT: You'll have plenty of chance later —

MAGWITCH: — But this is a separate matter. I stole some wittles up in the willage yonder. Likewise a file —

JOE: Halloa, Pip?

MAGWITCH: And some liquor. And a pie. *(To Joe.)* Sorry to say, I've eat your pie.

JOE: God knows you're welcome to it, as far as it was ever mine. We don't know what you have done, but we wouldn't have you starved to death for it, poor miserable fellow. Would us, Pip? *(Pip shakes his head. The Lieutenant calls out, "Ready! move!" The prisoners are marched off; Magwitch stops, turns back. He and Pip stare at each other for a moment, then he goes off. Darkness.)*

• • •

The forge kitchen.

NARRATION: It was not long after the incident on the marsh that Mrs. Joe returned home in the company of Mr. Pumblechook, in a state of rare excitement.

(Joe smoking his pipe in a chair, Pip on the floor beside him. Mrs. Joe and Pumblechook burst in.)

MRS. JOE: If this boy ain't grateful this night, he never will be! *(Pip tries to look grateful.)* It's only to be hoped she won't fill his head with silly ideas.

PUMBLECHOOK: I doubt it. She knows better.

JOE: Which someone mentioned a she?

MRS. JOE: Unless you call Miss Havisham a he —

JOE: Miss Havisham? That odd, solitary lady in the town?

MRS. JOE: She wants this boy to go play there. Of course he's going — and he'd better play, or I'll work him! *(She cracks Pip on the head.)*

JOE: Well, to be sure. I wonder how she come to know Pip?

MRS. JOE: Noodle — who says she knows him? *(She cracks Joe on the head.)* Couldn't she ask Uncle Pumblechook if he knew of a boy to go play there? Isn't it barely possible that Uncle Pumblechook may be a tenant of hers; and might he go there to pay his rent? And couldn't Uncle, out of the goodness of his heart, mention this boy here — to whom I have ever been a willing slave?

PUMBLECHOOK: Now, Joseph, you know the case.

MRS. JOE: No, Uncle, Joseph does not know the case. *(To Joe.)* For you do not know that Uncle, aware that this boy's fortune might be made by Miss Havisham, has offered to deliver Pip to her tomorrow, with his own hands! What do you say to that?

JOE: *(Mystified.)* Thankee kindly, Uncle Pumblechook.

PUMBLECHOOK: My duty, Joseph. *(To Pip.)* Boy, be ever grateful to those what brought you up by hand. *(He gives Pip a box on the ear.)*

NARRATION: Miss Havisham's house was of dismal bricks. Most of its windows were boarded up. There was a tall iron gate before which Mr. Pumblechook and Pip appeared at ten the next morning.

• • •

Miss Havisham's. The garden, then a room. Mr. Pumblechook rings the bell.

PUMBLECHOOK: Right on the dot of ten, boy.

PIP: No sir, I believe we're early. See, her big tower clock says twenty to nine.

PUMBLECHOOK: It must have stopped. My timepiece is always correct. *(Estella appears.)*

ESTELLA: What name?

PUMBLECHOOK: Pumblechook.

ESTELLA: Quite right. *(She unlocks the gate. Pumblechook pushes Pip through.)*

PUMBLECHOOK: This is Pip.

ESTELLA: This is Pip, is it? Come in, Pip. *(Pumblechook tries to follow.)* Do you wish to see Miss Havisham?

PUMBLECHOOK: I'm sure Miss Havisham wishes to see me.

ESTELLA: Ah, but you see, she don't. *(She shuts the gate in his face, leads Pip on.)* Don't loiter, boy.

NARRATION: Although she was about Pip's age, to him she seemed years older — being beautiful and self-possessed — and being a girl.

(She leads Pip upward, with a candle in her hand. She knocks. A voice says "Come in." Estella gestures Pip into the room, then leaves. It is dark. There is a banquet table with a huge cake. Miss Havisham is seated before it.)

HAVISHAM: Who is it?

PIP: Pip, ma'am.

HAVISHAM: Pip?

PIP: Mr. Pumblechook's boy, ma'am. Come to play.

HAVISHAM: Come nearer, let me look at you. Come closer.

NARRATION: Once Pip had been taken to see a waxwork at a fair. Once he had been taken to an old church to see a skeleton in the ashes of a rich robe, which had been dug out of a vault. Now waxwork and skeleton seemed to have dark eyes that moved, and looked at him.

HAVISHAM: Come closer. Ah, you are not afraid of a woman who has never seen the sun since you were born?

PIP: No.

HAVISHAM: You know what I touch here?

PIP: Your heart.

HAVISHAM: Broken. *(Pause.)* I am tired. I want diversion. Play. *(Pip does not move.)* I sometimes have sick fancies; and I have a sick fancy that I'd like to see someone play. Play. Play, play! *(Pip does not move.)* Are you so sullen and obstinate?

PIP: I'm very sorry, but I can't play just now. I would if I could, but it's all so new here . . . so strange and fine and . . . melancholy.

HAVISHAM: So new to him, so old to me; so strange to him, so familiar to me; so melancholy to us both. *(Estella enters.)* Let me see you play cards with this boy.

ESTELLA: With this boy!? Why, he's nothing but a common laboring boy!

HAVISHAM: *(Aside to Estella.)* Well? You can break his heart.

ESTELLA: What do you play, boy?

PIP: Only Beggar My Neighbor, miss. *(Estella brings out a deck of cards, deals. They play. Pip drops some cards.)*

ESTELLA: He's stupid and clumsy — look at his hands, so coarse! *(They play.)*

HAVISHAM: *(To Pip.)* You say nothing of her. What do you think of her, tell me in my ear.

PIP: *(Whispers.)* I think she is very proud.

HAVISHAM: Anything else?

PIP: I think she is very pretty.

HAVISHAM: Anything else?

PIP: I think she is very insulting and I'd like to go home.

HAVISHAM: You may go soon. Finish the game. *(They play.)*

NARRATION: The girl won. Her name was Estella. Pip was asked to return the next week. Estella took the candle and led him out.

ESTELLA: *(Going.)* You're crude. You're clumsy. Your boots are ugly!

NARRATION: The girl saw tears spring to Pip's eyes. Pip saw her quick delight at having been the cause of them. And for the first time, he was bitterly aware that life had been unjust to him. He quickly dried his eyes so she would not catch him weeping.

ESTELLA: Why don't you cry again, boy?

PIP: Because I don't want to.

ESTELLA: Yes you do. You cried before, and you'll cry again —

NARRATION: Pip headed for home with the shameful knowledge that his hands were coarse and his boots were ugly, and that he was much more ignorant than he had thought himself the night before.

• • •

The forge kitchen. Pumblechook, Mrs. Joe and Joe wait eagerly. Pip enters.

PUMBLECHOOK: Well, boy? How did you get on?

PIP: Pretty well, sir.

PUMBLECHOOK: "Pretty well?" Tell us what you mean by pretty well, boy.

PIP: I mean pretty well.

PUMBLECHOOK: And what is she like?

PIP: Very tall and fat.

MRS. JOE: Is she, Uncle? *(Pause. Pumblechook nods vaguely.)*

PUMBLECHOOK: Now, tell us what she was doing when you went in?

PIP: She was sitting in a big black velvet coach. *(His listeners are amazed. Pip smiles.)* Miss Estella handed her wine and cake, into the coach. We all had wine and cake — on golden plates!
(Astonished pause.)

PUMBLECHOOK: Was anyone else there?

PIP: Four black dogs.

PUMBLECHOOK: Large or small?

PIP: Immense!

PUMBLECHOOK: That's the truth of it, ma'am, I've seen it myself the times I've called on her. *(He bows, exits with Mrs. Joe. Pip whistles a tune to himself.)*

NARRATION: After Mr. Pumblechook departed, Pip — or his conscience — sought out Joe.

PIP: It was all lies, Joe.

JOE: Really? The black velvet coach was a lie?

PIP: Yes.

JOE: Even the golden plates?

PIP: I wish my boots weren't so thick, Joe, I wish — *(He throws his arms around Joe, buries his face in Joe's shoulder.)*

NARRATION: He told Joe how miserable he'd been made to feel, by Uncle Pumblechook and Mrs. Joe, and by the very beautiful young lady who had called him common.

JOE: One thing, Pip, lies is lies and you mustn't tell any more of 'em. That ain't the way to stop bein' common. As for that, in some ways you're most oncommon. You're oncommon small. You're an oncommon scholar.

PIP: I'm not, I'm ignorant and clumsy.

JOE: Pip? Even the four black dogs was lies?

• • •

NARRATION: Although Pip could not improve the quality of his boots, he set about to remedy the quality of his education by taking lessons from Mr. Pumblechook's great-aunt's grand-niece — Biddy — who lived in the neighborhood.

BIDDY: *(Holds up a slate to Pip.)* Six times four.

PIP: Twenty-four.

BIDDY: Seven times four?

PIP: Twenty-eight.

BIDDY: Eight times four? *(A pause. Pip isn't sure of the answer and, to tell the truth, neither is Biddy.)*

PIP: Thirty-four? *(She nods approval.)*

NARRATION: And a week later he returned to Miss Havisham's at the appointed hour.

• • •

Miss Havisham's. The garden, then a room.

ESTELLA: Follow me, boy. Well?

PIP: Well, miss?

ESTELLA: Am I pretty?

PIP: Very.

ESTELLA: Am I insulting?

PIP: Not so much as you were last time.

ESTELLA: No? *(She slaps his face.)* Coarse little monster, why don't you cry?

PIP: I'll never cry for you again. *(As they cross, they pass Mr. Jaggers coming from the other direction.)*

NARRATION: As Estella led him through the gloomy house, they encountered a singular-looking gentleman coming toward them.

JAGGERS: Well, well, what have we here?

ESTELLA: A boy.

JAGGERS: Boy of the neighborhood?

PIP: Yes, sir.

JAGGERS: How d'you come to be here?

ESTELLA: Miss Havisham sent for him, sir.

JAGGERS: Well, behave yourself. I've a pretty large experience of boys, and you're a bad set of fellows. Behave! *(He continues out. Estella and Pip enter Miss Havisham's room.)*

HAVISHAM: So, the days have worn away, have they? A week. Are you ready to play?

PIP: I don't think so, ma'am.

HAVISHAM: Are you willing to work, then? *(Pip nods. She takes his arm, leans against his shoulder.)* Help me to walk, boy. *(They circle the table.)* This is where I shall be laid when I am dead. *(She points with her stick.)* What do you think that is?

PIP: I cannot guess.

HAVISHAM: It's a great cake. A bride-cake. Mine.

PIP: There are mice in it, ma'am.

HAVISHAM: Yes. This cake and I have worn away together, and sharper teeth have gnawed at me.

NARRATION: Breathing the heavy air that brooded in the room, Pip suddenly had an alarming fancy that all was decaying — that even he and Estella might presently begin to decay.

HAVISHAM: Now you must play at cards. *(Estella gets the deck.)* Is she not pretty, Pip? *(Pip sighs, nods. Estella deals.)*

NARRATION: And so the visits ran, with little to distinguish one from another. Estella always won at cards. Once, some relations called upon Miss Havisham.

A POCKET:. How well you look, ma'am.

A POCKET: Happy birthday, cousin —

A POCKET: — And many happy returns of the day.

HAVISHAM: You see, Pip? The vultures have descended again, my Pocket relations. But the Pockets shall not have a penny of mine, never! You may go, Pip.

NARRATION: Pip was all too glad to take his leave. He was about to let himself out by the garden gate, when he was stopped by a pale young gentleman.

(Young Herbert appears, munching an apple.)

YOUNG HERBERT: Halloa, young fellow. Who let you in?

PIP: Miss Estella.

YOUNG HERBERT: *(Pleasantly.)* Do you want to fight? Come on. *(He tosses the apple over his shoulder, strips off his cap, jacket, and shirt.)* I ought to give you a reason for fighting. There — *(He claps his hands together under Pip's nose, gently pulls his hair. He dances around Pip, fists doubled.)* Standard rules, is that agreeable? *(Pip nods. Herbert dances around, throwing punches that miss Pip. Pip finally gets one off, and it levels Herbert. Estella peeps out to watch.)*

PIP: Oh dear, I'm sorry —

YOUNG HERBERT: Think nothing of it, young fellow! *(He jumps to his feet, squeezes a sponge of water over his head, dances around again. Pip lands another punch, Herbert falls.)*

PIP: Oh, look, I'm really so sorry, I —

YOUNG HERBERT: Perfectly all right. *(He gets up, picks up the sponge, throws it.)* See, I'm throwing in the sponge. That means you've won. *(He offers his hand. They shake.)*

PIP: Can I help you?

YOUNG HERBERT: No thankee, I'm fine. *(He picks up his jacket and cap. As he goes off, Estella passes him, sticks out her tongue. He shrugs, leaves. Pip stares after him. Estella comes to him.)*

ESTELLA: You may kiss me, if you like. *(He kisses her on the cheek, then, overwhelmed, he flees.)*

• • •

NARRATION: If Pip could have told Joe about his strange visits — If he could have unburdened himself about his love for Estella, or even about his fight with the pale young gentleman — But of course he could not, for Joe's hands were coarser and his boots thicker than Pip's own! So Pip confided in Biddy — it seemed natural to do so. He told her everything, and Biddy had a deep concern in everything he told her.

(Pip and Biddy are strolling, sharing a piece of toffee.)

PIP: Biddy, I want to be a gentleman.

BIDDY: Oh, I wouldn't if I was you, Pip.

PIP: I've my reasons for wanting it.

BIDDY: You know best, but wouldn't you be happier as you are?

PIP: I am not happy as I am! I am disgusted with my life.

BIDDY: That's a pity for you, isn't it?

PIP: I know. If I was half as fond of the forge as I was a year ago, life would be simpler. I could become Joe's partner someday. Who knows, perhaps

I'd even keep company with you. I'd be good enough for you, wouldn't I, Biddy?

BIDDY: Oh yes, I am not over-particular. *(Pause.)* Is it Estella?

PIP: It's because of her I wish to be a gentleman.

BIDDY: Do you wish to be a gentleman to spite her or to win her?

PIP: I don't know. Biddy, I wish you could put me right.

BIDDY: I wish I could . . .

• • •

NARRATION: But Biddy could not put Pip right. Things went on in the same way. His dreams and discontent remained. Time passed. Finally, one day Miss Havisham looked at him crossly —

HAVISHAM: You are growing too tall! What is the name of that blacksmith of yours?

PIP: Joe Gargery, ma'am.

HAVISHAM: I shan't need you to come play here anymore. So you'd better be apprenticed to Mr. Gargery at once.

PIP: But —

HAVISHAM: But what?

PIP: — I don't want to be a blacksmith! I'd rather come here!

HAVISHAM: It's all over, Pip. You're growing up. Estella is going abroad to school next week. Gargery is your master now. *(She glances at Estella, whispers to Pip.)* Does she grew prettier, Pip? Do you love her? Shall you miss her? *(Pip turns away, she crosses to Estella.)* Break their hearts, my pride and hope, break their hearts and have no mercy.

• • •

NARRATION: Pip was indentured as apprentice blacksmith to Joe Gargery the following week. Miss Haversham's parting gift of twenty-five pounds was cause for celebration in some quarters.

(Mr Pumblechook and Mrs. Joe toast.)

Pip did not celebrate. He had liked Joe's trade once, but once was not now. He was wretched.

(Sound of an anvil. Glow of a forge fire.)

Nonetheless, Pip labored. And Pip grew. Always he would gaze into the fire at the forge and see Estella's face. He heard her cruel laughter in the wind. He was haunted by the fear that she would come home, witness his debasement, and despise him. On the surface, however, Pip's life fell into a routine. Days he worked with Joe at the forge. Evenings he became his own teacher — for he had long outstripped Biddy in learning. Once a year, on his birthday, he visited Miss Havisham.

HAVISHAM: Pip, is it? Has your birthday come round again? Ah, you're looking around for her, I see. Still abroad, educating for a lady . . . far out of reach and prettier than ever. Do you feel you have lost her?

NARRATION: Time wrought other changes. Mrs. Joe Gargery fell gravely ill, and lingered in a kind of twilight, tended by Biddy, who was more sweet-tempered and wholesome than ever. Pip was now a young man, old enough to accompany Joe to the local public house of an evening. And so, in the fourth year of his apprenticeship, on a Saturday night at the Three Jolly Bargemen . . .

• • •

The pub. Pumblechook, Joe, and Pip at a table. Jaggers sits at a distance, in the shadows. Others are also drinking. A barmaid serves. Pumblechook is reading from a newspaper.

PUMBLECHOOK: "The wictim is said to have spoken the name of the accused before he died, according to a witness for the prosecution. And medical testimony brought out during the third day of the trial by the prosecution points to —"

JAGGERS: I suppose you've settled the case to your satisfaction? *(Pumblechook peers into the shadows.)*

PUMBLECHOOK: Sir, without having the honor of your acquaintance, I *have.* The werdict should be "guilty."

JAGGERS: I thought as much. *(He rises.)* But the trial is not over, is it? You do admit that English law supposes each man to be innocent until he is proved — *proved* — guilty?

PUMBLECHOOK: Certainly I admit it, sir.

JAGGERS: And are you aware, or are you not aware, that none of the witnesses mentioned in that questionable journal you read has yet been cross-examined by the defense?

PUMBLECHOOK: Yes, but —

JAGGERS: I rest my case. *(He peers around the room.)* From information I have received, I've reason to believe there's a blacksmith among you by the name of Joseph Gargery. Which is the man?

PUMBLECHOOK: There is the man. What have you done, Joseph?

JAGGERS: And you have an apprentice who is commonly known as Pip — is he here?

PUMBLECHOOK: Aha! I knew that boy would come to no good!

JAGGERS: I wish a conference with you two — a private conference. *(The others drift away, grumbling.)* My name is Jaggers, and I am a lawyer in London. I'm pretty well known there. I've some unusual business to transact with you. *(Pip and Joe glance at each other.)* Know first that I act as the confidential agent of a client. It is his orders I follow, not my own. Having said that: Joseph Gargery, I've come with an offer to relieve you of this apprentice of yours.

JOE: Pip?

JAGGERS: Would you be willing to cancel his indentures, for his own good? *(Joe thinks, nods.)* You'd ask no money for doing so?

JOE: Lord forbid I should want anything for not standing in Pip's way.

JAGGERS: Good. Don't try to change your mind later. *(With great formality.)* The communication I have come to make is . . . that this young man has great expectations. *(Pip rises. He and Joe gape.)* I'm instructed to inform him that he will come into a handsome fortune; that he is to be immediately removed from his present sphere of life and from this place, that he is to be brought up as a gentleman — in a word, as befits a young man of great expectations. *(Joe and Pip stare wordlessly for a moment.)*

PIP: Joe —

JAGGERS: — Later. First, understand that the person from whom I take my instruction requests that you always bear the name of Pip. You've no objection, I daresay? Good. Secondly, Mr. Pip, the name of your benefactor —

PIP: — Miss Havisham —

JAGGERS: — the name of your benefactor must remain a secret until that person chooses to reveal it. Do you accept this condition? Good. Good. I've already been given a sum of money for your education and maintenance. From now on, you will please consider me your guardian.

PIP: Thank you —

JAGGERS: — Don't bother to thank me, I am well paid for my services, or I shouldn't render them. Now then, education: You wish a proper tutor, no doubt? Good. Have you a preference?

PIP: Well . . . I only know Biddy, that's Mr. Pumblechook's great-aunt's grand-niece —

JAGGERS: — Never mind, there's a man in London who might suit well enough, a Mr. Matthew Pocket.

PIP: Pocket — is he a cousin of Miss Havisham?

JAGGERS: Ah, you know the name. He is. When do you wish to come to London?

PIP: Soon — directly!

JAGGERS: Good. You'll need proper clothes — here is twenty guineas. You'll take the hackney coach up to London — it's a five-hour trip. Shall I look for you a week from tomorrow? Good. Well, Joseph Gargery, you look dumbfounded.

JOE: Which I am.

JAGGERS: It was understood you wanted nothing for yourself.

JOE: It were understood and it are understood and ever will be.

JAGGERS: But what if I was instructed to make you a present, as compensation for the loss of his services —?

JOE: — Pip is that hearty welcome to go free with his services to honor and fortune, as no words can tell him. But if you think as money can compensate me for the loss of the little child what — what come to the forge and . . . and . . . ever the best of friends. *(He weeps.)*

PIP: Oh, Joe, don't . . . I'm going to be a gentleman! *(Darkness.)*

• • •

NARRATION: That night Pip sat alone in his little room at the forge, feeling sorrowful and strange that this first night of his bright fortune should be the loneliest he had ever known. The next morning, things looked brighter — only seven days until his departure. Seven long days. But there was much to do. First he visited a tailor.

PIP: *(Rings Bell.)* I beg your pardon . . .

TAILOR: *(Unimpressed.)* I beg yours.

PIP: I am going to London.

TAILOR: What of it?

PIP: I shall need a suit of fashionable clothes. *(Pip drops coins one by one into the hand of the tailor, who becomes obsequious. During the following Pip goes behind a screen and changes his clothes as.)*

TAILOR: I beg your pardon, my dear sir. Fashionable clothes, is it? For London! You've come to the right place, you shall be quite correct, I assure you, quite the thing! Indeed, one might call you the "glass of fashion."

We'll turn you out from top to toe as fine as any London gentleman could wish!

NARRATION: And thence, to Mr. Pumblechook's, to receive that great man's blessing.

PUMBLECHOOK: *(Raising a glass.)* Beloved friend, I give you joy in your good fortune. Well-deserved, well-deserved! And to think that I have been the humble instrument leading up to all this . . . is reward enough for me. So here's to you — I always knew you had it in you! And let us also drink thanks to Fortune — may she ever pick her favorites with equal judgment!

NARRATION: And thence to Miss Havisham's, with barely suppressed excitement . . . and gratitude.

(Pip emerges from behind the screen. His London suit is almost comical in its exaggeration of high fashion. It is de trop.*)*

HAVISHAM: This is a grand figure, Pip.

PIP: Oh, ma'am, I have come into such good fortune!

HAVISHAM: I've learned of it from Mr. Jaggers. So, you've been adopted by a rich person, have you?

PIP: Yes, Miss Havisham.

HAVISHAM: Not named?

PIP: Not named.

HAVISHAM: You've a promising career before you. Deserve it! You're always to keep the name of Pip, you know? *(He nods.)* Good-bye then, Pip. *(She puts out her hand, he kisses it clumsily.)*

NARRATION: Finally, the morning of his departure dawned.

• • •

The forge kitchen.

PIP: You may be sure, dear Joe, I shall never forget you.

JOE: Ay, old chap, I'm sure of that.

PIP: I always dreamed of being a gentleman.

JOE: Did you? Astonishing! Now me, I'm an awful dull fellow. I'm only master in my own trade, but . . . ever the best of friends — *(He flees in tears.)*

PIP: *(To Biddy.)* You will help Joe on, won't you?

BIDDY: How help him on?

PIP: Joe's a dear fellow, the dearest that ever lived, but he's backward in some things, Biddy . . . Like learning and manners.

BIDDY: Won't his manners do, then?

PIP: They do well enough here, but if I were to bring him to London when I come into my property —

BIDDY: — And don't you think he knows that? Pip, Pip . . .

PIP: Well?

BIDDY: Have you never considered his pride?

PIP: His pride? Whatever do you mean? You sound almost envious —

BIDDY: If you have the heart to think so! Can't you see, Joe is too proud and too wise to let anyone remove him from a place he fills with dignity — *(Joe enters, blowing his nose.)*

JOE: It's time for the coach, Pip.

PIP: Well then. *(He picks up his valise.)*

JOE: I'll come wisit you in London, old chap, and then — wot larks, eh? Wot larks we'll have!

PIP: Good-bye, Biddy. *(He kisses her cheek.)* Dear Joe — *(Joe grab Pip's hat, throws it up in the air, to hide his tears.)*

JOE: Hoorar! Hoorar! *(With waves and cheers, the "coach" departs for London.)*

• • •

NARRATION: When his coach finally left the village behind, Pip wept. Heaven knows we need never be ashamed of our tears, for they are the rain on the blinding dust of earth, overlaying our hard hearts. Pip felt better after he had cried — more aware of his own ingratitude, sorrier, gentler. But by now it was too late to turn back to Joe, so he traveled forward. The mists slowly rose and the world lay spread before him. And suddenly there was —

COACHMAN: London!

PIP: London! *(Pip climbs off the "coach," clutching his valise. He stares around him at the crowd.)*

NARRATION: Not far from the great dome of St. Paul's, in the very shadow of Newgate Prison, Pip alighted and stood before an ugly stone building.

• • •

Jaggers's office. Wemmick appears at Pip's knock. Jaggers is inside the room, washing his hands. He pours water from a pitcher into a basin, as:

PIP: Is Mr. Jaggers in?

(Wemmick pulls him inside.)

WEMMICK: Am I addressing Mr. Pip? He's been expecting you. I'm Wemmick, Mr. Jaggers' clerk. *(He leads Pip to Jaggers.)*

JAGGERS: Well, Mr. Pip, London, eh?

PIP: Yes, sir.

JAGGERS: I've made arrangements for you to stay at Barnard's Inn. You'll share young Mr. Pocket's apartments.

PIP: My tutor?

JAGGERS: His son. I've sent over some furniture for you. And here's a list of tradesmen where you may run up bills. And you will, you will — you'll drown in debt before the year is out, I'm sure, but that's no fault of mine, is it? Good. Wemmick, take him over to Barnard's Inn, will you? I must get back to court.

(He exits. Wemmick picks up Pip's valise, they stroll.)

WEMMICK: So, you've never been to London? I was new here, once, myself. But now I know the moves of it.

PIP: Is it a very wicked place?

WEMMICK: You may get cheated, robbed, and murdered in London. But there are plenty of people anywhere who'll do that for you. Here we are, "Mr. Pocket, Jr." *(He knocks.)* As I keep the cash, we shall likely be meeting often. *(They shake hands, Wemmick goes.)*

• • •

Barnard's Inn. Herbert comes to the door.

HERBERT: Mr. Pip?

PIP: Mr. Pocket? *(They shake hands.)*

HERBERT: Pray, come in. We're rather bare here, but I hope you'll make out tolerably well.

PIP: It seems very grand to me.

HERBERT: Look around. It's not splendid, because I don't earn very much at present, still I think . . . bless me, you're — you're the prowling boy in Miss Havisham's garden!

PIP: And you are the pale young gentleman!

HERBERT: The idea of its being you!

PIP: The idea of its being you! *(They laugh, both strike a boxing pose.)*

HERBERT: I do hope you've forgiven me for having knocked you about? *(They laugh, shake hands again.)*

NARRATION: Dinner was sent up from the coffeehouse in the next road and the young men sat down to get acquainted.

PIP: Mr. Pocket, I was brought up to be a blacksmith. I know little of polite manners. I'd take it as a kindness if you'd give me a hint whenever I go wrong.

HERBERT: With pleasure. And will you do me the kindness of calling me by my Christian name: Herbert?

PIP: With pleasure. My name is Philip.

HERBERT: Philip. Philip . . . no, I don't take to it. Sounds like a highly moral boy in a schoolbook. I know! We're so harmonious — and you have been a blacksmith . . . would you mind if I called you "Handel"?

PIP: Handel? Why?

HERBERT: There's a piece of music I like, *The Harmonious Blacksmith*, by Handel — *(He hums the tune.)*

PIP: I'd like it very much. So . . . we two go way back to Miss Havisham's garden! *(They eat.)*

HERBERT: Yes. She's a tartar, isn't she?

PIP: Miss Havisham?

HERBERT: I don't say no to that, but I meant Estella. You know the old lady raised her to wreak revenge on all the male sex?

PIP: No! Revenge for what?

HERBERT: Dear me, it's quite a story — which I'll begin, Handel, by mentioning that in London it's not the custom to put the knife in the mouth — scarcely worth mentioning, but . . . Also, the spoon is not generally used overhand, but under. This has two advantages: You get to your mouth more easily, but to your cravat less well. Now, as to Miss H. Her father was a country gentleman. There were two children, she and a half-brother named Arthur. Arthur grew up extravagant, undutiful — in a word, bad! So the father disinherited him — Have another glass of wine, and excuse my mentioning that society as a body does not expect one to be so strictly conscientious in emptying one's glass as to turn it upside down.

PIP: So sorry.

HERBERT: It's nothing. Upon her father's death, Miss H. became an heiress. She was considered a great match. There now appears on the scene — at the races, say, or at a ball — a man who courted the heiress. This is twenty-five years ago, remember. Also remember that your dinner napkin need not be stuffed into your glass. At any rate, her suitor professed love and devotion, and she fell passionately in love. She gave the man huge sums of money, against all advice — particularly against my father's — which is why she's never liked us since, and why I wasn't the boy chosen to come play with Estella — Where was I? Oh yes, the marriage day was fixed, the wedding dress bought, the guests invited, the bride-cake baked. The great day arrived — but the bridegroom failed to. Instead, he sent his regrets. That morning a letter arrived —

PIP: Which she received while she was dressing for her wedding? At exactly twenty minutes to nine?

HERBERT: Which is why she had all the clocks in the place stopped at that moment! It was later discovered that the man she loved had conspired with her brother to defraud her. They shared the profits of her sorrow.

PIP: Whatever became of them?

HERBERT: Fell into ruin and disappeared, both of 'em. Not many months after, Miss H. adopted Estella — she was a tiny child. And now, my dear Handel, you know everything I do about poor Miss H.

PIP: But I know nothing of you. If it's not rude to ask, what do you do for a living?

HERBERT: *(Dreamily.)* I'd like to go into business. I'd like to be an insurer of great ships that sail to distant ports.

PIP: I see.

HERBERT: I'm also considering the mining business . . . Africa.

PIP: I see.

HERBERT: Trading in the East Indies interests me.

PIP: I see. You'll need a lot of capital for all that.

HERBERT: True. Meanwhile, I'm looking about me. Temporarily employed in a countinghouse, but looking about me for the right opportunity

PIP: And then . . . what larks.

HERBERT: Pardon? *(Pip laughs, Herbert joins him.)*

• • •

NARRATION: Pip took up his studies with Herbert's father, Mr. Matthew Pocket. He was joined in his classes by another student, a haughty young man named —

DRUMMLE: — Bentley Drummle, seventh in line for a small baronetcy. And who, may I ask, are you?

NARRATION: Latin, French, history, mathematics in the mornings.
In the afternoons sports, of which the favorite was rowing on the river.

DRUMMLE: No, no, no, Mr. Pip. Starboard's there. This is port!

PIP: Thank you very much.

DRUMMLE: Now you dip the blade of the oar into the water — that's the wide part, Mr. Pip.

PIP: You're too kind. But I did grow up near the river.

DRUMMLE: Yes, I've heard about you. Your rowing lacks form, there's no style to it, is there? Still, you're strong. One might say you've got the arm of a blacksmith! *(Pip glares at him.)*

NARRATION: To his surprise, Pip enjoyed his studies with Mr. Pocket. He also enjoyed his tailor, his linen draper, his glove maker, his jeweler —

· · ·

Jaggers's office. Jaggers washes his hands. Wemmick watches.

JAGGERS: Well, how much do you need this time?

PIP: I'm not sure, Mr. Jaggers.

JAGGERS: Fifty pounds?

PIP: Oh, not that much, sir.

JAGGERS: Five pounds?

PIP: Well, more than that, perhaps.

JAGGERS: Twice five? Three times five? Wemmick, twenty pounds for Mr. Pip.

WEMMICK: Twenty pounds in portable property, yes, sir.

JAGGERS: And now excuse me, young man, I'm late to court. *(He goes. Pip stares after him.)*

PIP: I don't know what to make of that man!

WEMMICK: He don't mean you to know, either. He always acts like he's just baited a trap. He sits watching, and suddenly — snap! You're caught. By the way, if you've nothing better to do at the moment, perhaps you'd like to come home with me for supper. I live down in Walworth.

PIP: Why, that's very kind of you. Yes.

WEMMICK: You've no objection to an Aged Parent?

PIP: Certainly not. *(They stroll.)*

WEMMICK: Because I have one.

PIP: I look forward to meeting her —

WEMMICK: Him. Have you been to dine at Mr. Jaggers' yet?

PIP: Not yet.

WEMMICK: He'll give you an excellent meal. While you're there, do notice his housekeeper.

PIP: Shall I see something uncommon?

WEMMICK: You will see a wild beast tamed.

· · ·

Walworth. The garden, with drawbridge.

NARRATION: And so they arrived at Mr. Wemmick's cottage in Walworth. The place was odd, to say the least.

WEMMICK: Step over the drawbridge, if you will, Mr. Pip. *(Pip crosses over with Wemmick, who has grown very affable.)* I must warn you, our little cannon fires at nine o'clock every evening, Greenwich time, so you won't be alarmed.

PIP: It's wonderfully . . . original here. *(The Aged Parent enters, pulling a small cannon on wheels.)*

WEMMICK: Ah, here's the Aged. *(Very loud.)* Well, Aged Parent, how are you this evening?

AGED PARENT: All right, John, all right.

WEMMICK: Here's Mr. Pip, come to tea. *(To Pip.)* Nod at him, Mr. Pip, that's what he likes. He's deaf as a post, he is. *(Pip nods at the Aged, who nods back.)*

AGED PARENT: This is a fine place my son's got, sir. *(Pip nods. Aged nods.)*

WEMMICK: Proud as punch, ain't you, Aged? *(All three nod.)* There's a nod for you, and there's another for you. *(To Pip.)* Mr. Jaggers knows nothing of all this. Never even heard of the Aged. I'll be grateful if you don't mention it — the office is one thing, private life's another. I speak now in my Walworth capacity.

PIP: Not a word, upon my honor.

WEMMICK: When I go to the office, I leave the castle behind me, and vice versa. One minute to nine — gun-fire time. It's the Aged Parent's treat. Ready? Here we go! *(There is a big boom.)*

AGED PARENT: It's fired! I heard it! *(All three nod happily.)*

NARRATION: A few weeks later, Pip was invited, along with Herbert and Bentley Drummle, to dine at Mr. Jaggers' . . .

• • •

Jaggers's home. A dining table.

JAGGERS: *(Aside, to Pip.)* I like your friend Drummle, he reminds me of a spider.

PIP: He's not my friend, we merely study together. He's a poor scholar, and he is incredibly rude.

JAGGERS: Good. You keep clear of him, he's trouble. But I like such fellows. Yes, he's a real spider. *(Molly appears. Jaggers turns to her.)* Molly, Molly, Molly, Molly, may we sit down?

(She nods. He turns to the others.) Ah, dinner is served, gentlemen. *(They sit, she serves.)*

NARRATION: Pip studied her carefully. The night before, he had been to the theater to see *Macbeth.* The woman's face resembled those he had seen rise out of the witches' cauldron. She was humble and silent . . . but there was something about her . . .

JAGGERS: So, Mr. Drummle, in addition to conjugating the past conditional tense of French verbs, you gentlemen also go rowing for exercise?

DRUMMLE: We do. And your Mr. Pip's rowing is better than his French —

HERBERT: — I say, Drummle!

DRUMMLE: But I'm stronger with an oar than either of these fellows.

JAGGERS: Really? You talk of strength? I'll show you strength. Molly, show them your wrists.

MOLLY: *(Cringes.)* Master, don't —

JAGGERS: Show them, Molly! *(He grabs her arm, runs his finger up and down her wrist delicately.)* There's power, here. Few men have the sinews Molly has, see? Remarkable force, beautiful power. Beautiful. That'll do, Molly, you've been admired, now you may go. *(She goes.)* To your health, gentlemen. *(Darkness.)*

• • •

BIDDY: My dear Mr. Pip: I write at the request of Mr. Gargery, for to let you know he is coming up to London and would be glad to see you. He will call at Barnard's Hotel next Tuesday morning at nine. Your sister continues to linger. Your ever obedient servant, Biddy. P.S. He wishes me most particular to write "what larks!" He says you will understand. I hope you will see him, even though you are a gentleman now, for you had ever a good heart and he is so worthy. He asks me again to write "what larks!" Biddy.

NARRATION: With what feelings did Pip look forward to Joe's visit? With pleasure? No, with considerable disturbance and mortification. What would Bentley Drummle think of someone like Joe? And what would Joe think of Pip's expensive and rather aimless new life?

• • •

Barnard's Inn. A knock at the door. Joe enters, awkwardly dressed in a suit.

PIP: Joe! *(Joe holds his arms out to embrace Pip, Pip sticks out his right hand. They shake.)*

JOE: Pip, old chap.

PIP: I'm glad to see you, Joe. Come in, give me your hat! *(Joe remembers he has one, removes it from his head, but holds fast to it.)*

JOE: Which you have that grow'd and that swelled with the gentlefolk!

PIP: And you look wonderfully well, Joe. Shall I take your hat?
(Joe continues to clutch it.)

JOE: Your poor sister's no worse nor no better than she was. And Biddy is ever right and ready, that girl. *(Herbert enters from bedroom.)*

PIP: Here's my friend, Herbert Pocket. Joe. *(Herbert extends his hand, Joe drops his hat.)*

HERBERT: Your servant, sir.

JOE: Yours, yours. *(He picks up the hat.)*

HERBERT: Well. Have you seen anything of London, yet?

JOE: Why, yes, sir. Soon as I left the coach, I went straight off to look at the Blacking Factory warehouse.

HERBERT: Really? What did you think?

JOE: It don't come near to its likeness on the labels.

HERBERT: Is that so?

JOE: See, on the labels it is drawn too architectooralooral.
(Herbert nods. Pip covers his face in mortification. Joe drops his hat.)

HERBERT: You're quite right about that, Mr. Gargery — he is, Pip. Well, I must be off to work. It's good to have met you.
(He offers his hand. Joe reaches, drops his hat. Herbert goes out.)

JOE: We two being alone, sir —

PIP: — Joe, how can you call me "sir"?!

JOE: Us two being alone, Pip, and me having the intention to stay not many minutes more —

PIP: — Joe! —

JOE: I will now conclude — leastways begin — what led up to my having the present honor, sir. Miss Havisham has a message for you, Pip, sir. She says to tell you Miss Estella has come home from abroad and will be happy to see you.

PIP: Estella!

JOE: I tried to get Biddy to write the message to you, sir, but she says, "I know Pip will be glad to have that message by word of mouth." Which I have now concluded. *(He starts to go.)* And so, Pip, I wish you ever well and ever prospering to greater height, sir —

PIP: — You're not leaving?!

JOE: Which I am.

PIP: But surely you're coming back for dinner?

JOE: Pip, old chap, life is made of ever-so-many partings welded together, and one man's a blacksmith, and one's a white smith, and one's a goldsmith. Diwisions among such must be met as they come. You and me is not two figures to be seen together in London. I'm wrong in these clothes. I'm wrong out of the forge. You won't find half so much fault in me if you think of me in my forge clothes, with my hammer in my hand. And so, ever the best of friends, Pip. God bless you, dear old chap, God bless you, sir.

NARRATION: And he was gone. After the first guilty flow of repentance, Pip thought better of such feelings. He dried his eyes, and did not follow Joe into the street to bring him back. The next day Pip took the coach down from London. He did not bother to call in at the forge . . .

• • •

Miss Havisham's. Estella waits in the shadows. Pip enters.

HAVISHAM: So, you kiss my hand as if I were a queen?

PIP: I heard you wished to see me, so I came directly.

HAVISHAM: Well? *(Estella turns, smiles at him.)* Do you find her much changed?

PIP: I . . .

HAVISHAM: And is he changed, Estella?

ESTELLA: Very much.

HAVISHAM: Less coarse and common? *(Estella laughs.)* Go into the garden, you two, and give me some peace until tea time. *(Estella takes his arm, they wander out.)*

PIP: Look it's all still here.

ESTELLA: I must have been a singular little creature. I hid over there and watched you fight that strange boy. I enjoyed that battle very much.

PIP: You rewarded me very much . . .

ESTELLA: Did I? *(She picks up a clay pot of primroses, smells them, plucks one and puts it in Pip's buttonhole.)*

PIP: He and I are great friends, now. It was there you made me cry, that first day.

ESTELLA: Did I? I don't remember. *(She notices his hurt.)* You must understand, I have no heart. That may have something to do with my poor memory.

PIP: I know better, Estella.

ESTELLA: Oh, I've a heart to be stabbed in or shot at, no doubt. But I've no softness there, no . . . sympathy. If we're to be thrown together often — and it seems we shall be — you'd better believe that of me. What's wrong, is Pip scared? Will he cry? Come, come, tea's ready. You shall not shed tears for my cruelty today. Give me your arm, I must deliver you safely back to Miss Havisham. *(They return to Miss Havisham, who takes Estella's hand and kisses it with ravenous intensity. Estella goes out.)*

HAVISHAM: Is she not beautiful, Pip? Graceful? Do you admire her?

PIP: Everyone who sees her must.

HAVISHAM: Love her, love her, love her! If she favors you, love her! If she wounds you, love her! If she tears your heart to pieces, love her, love her, love her!

PIP: You make that word sound like a curse.

HAVISHAM: You know what love is? I do. It is blind devotion, unquestioning self-humiliation, utter submission. It is giving up your whole heart and soul to the one who smites you, as I did. That is love.
(Darkness.)

NARRATION: Love her! Love her! Love her! The words rang triumphantly in his ears all the way back to London. That Estella was destined for him, once a blacksmith's boy! And if she were not yet rapturously grateful for that destiny, he would somehow awaken her sleeping heart!

• • •

Barnard's Inn.

PIP: I've got something particular to tell you.

HERBERT: That's odd, I've something to tell you.

PIP: It concerns myself — and one other person.

HERBERT: That's odd, too.

PIP: Herbert, I love — I adore Estella!

HERBERT: Oh, I know that. My dear Handel, you brought your adoration along with your valise the day you came to London.

PIP: She's come home — I saw her yesterday. I do love her so!

HERBERT: What are the young lady's sentiments?

PIP: Alas, she is miles and miles away from me.

HERBERT: If that's so, can you not detach yourself from her? *(Pip turns away.)*

Think of her upbringing — think of Miss Havisham! Given all that, your love could lead to misery.

PIP: I know, but I cannot help myself. I cannot "detach."

HERBERT: Well. But perhaps it doesn't matter — perhaps your feelings are justified. After all, it would seem you've been chosen for her. Yes, I'm sure it will work out!

PIP: What a hopeful disposition you have.

HERBERT: I must have — I've not got much else. But since the subject's come up, I want you to know first — I'm engaged.

PIP: My dear Herbert! May I ask the bride's name?

HERBERT: Name of Clara. Clara Barley.

PIP: And does Clara Barley live in London?

HERBERT: She does. Oh Pip, if you could see her — so lovely!

PIP: Is she rich?

HERBERT: Poorer than me — and as sweet as she is poor. I'm going to marry her —

PIP: That's wonderful, Herbert. When? *(Herbert's face falls.)*

HERBERT: That's the trouble. A fellow can't marry while he's still looking about him, can he?

PIP: I don't suppose he can. But cheer up, it will all work out. Yes, I feel it . . . it *shall* work out!

• • •

ESTELLA: Dear Pip: I am coming to London the day after tomorrow, by midday coach. Miss Havisham insists that you are to meet me, and I write in obedience to her wishes. Yours, Estella.

NARRATION: And suddenly she was there, in London!

(Estella hands a valise and hatbox to Pip.)

PIP: I'm glad, so glad you've come.

ESTELLA: Yes. I'm to live here with a chaperone, at great — ridiculous expense, really. She is to take me about. She's to show people to me, and show me to people.

PIP: I wonder Miss Havisham could part with you.

ESTELLA: It's all part of her great plan. She wants me to write her constantly and report how I get on —

PIP: Get on? Get on? With what? With whom? *(Estella smiles.)*

ESTELLA: Poor Pip. Dear Pip.

BIDDY: Dear Pip: I am writing to inform you that your sister died at peace the night before last. Her funeral was held this morning. We discussed whether to wait until you could attend it, but decided that as you are busy in your life as a gentleman we should go forward with the affair as we are. Yours, Biddy. P.S. Joe sends his fond wishes and sympathy.

NARRATION: Pip got on, he became accustomed to the idea of his great expectations. He grew careless with his money, contracting a great quantity of debts. And Herbert's good nature combined with Pip's lavish spending, to lead them both into habits they could ill afford. They moved their lodgings from the spartan Barnard's Inn to more luxurious quarters in the Temple, on the banks of the Thames.

(Herbert and Pip enter, each holding sheaves of bills.)

PIP: My dear Herbert, we are getting on very badly.

HERBERT: My dear Handel, those very words were on my lips! We must reform.

PIP: We must indeed. *(They look at each other, toss the bills up in the air, watch them float down.)*

NARRATION: Their affairs went from bad to worse, so they began to look forward eagerly to Pip's twenty-first birthday — In the hope that Mr. Jaggers, by way of celebration, might give Pip some concrete evidence of his expectations.

• • •

Jaggers's office. Jaggers is washing his hands.

WEMMICK: Happy birthday, Mr. Pip. *(To Jaggers.)* He's here.

JAGGERS: Well, well, twenty-one today, is that not the case?

PIP: Guilty, sir. I confess to being twenty-one.

JAGGERS: Tell me, Pip, what are you living at the rate of?

PIP: I . . . don't know, sir.

JAGGERS: I thought as much. Now it's your turn to ask me a question.

PIP: Have — have I anything to receive today?

JAGGERS: I thought we'd come to that! Take this piece of paper in your hand. Now unfold it. What is it?

PIP: It's a banknote . . . for five hundred pounds!

JAGGERS: And a handsome sum of money, too, you agree?

PIP: How could I do otherwise?

JAGGERS: It is yours. And at the rate of five hundred per year, and no more, you are to live until your benefactor chooses to appear.

PIP: Is my benefactor to be made known to me today?

JAGGERS: As to when that person decides to be identified, why, that's nothing to do with me, I'm only the agent —

PIP: But she —

JAGGERS: — She?

PIP: — My patron —

JAGGERS: — Hah! You cannot trick me into giving evidence, young man. Now, excuse me, I'm off to court. *(He goes, followed by Wemmick. Pip stares at the banknote, holds it up, suddenly starts to smile.)*

NARRATION: The following Sunday Pip made a pilgrimage down to Walworth to see Mr. Wemmick. For he had an idea about how he would like to spend at least part of his money.

• • •

Walworth. Pip crosses over the little drawbridge. The Aged Parent greets him.

AGED PARENT: Ah, my son will be home at any moment young man. *(Pip nods.)* Make yourself at home. You made quaintance with my son at his office? *(Pip nods.)* I hear he's a wonderful hand at his business. *(Pip nods.)* Now to be precise, I don't actually hear it, mind, for I'm hard of hearing.

PIP: Not really!

AGED PARENT: Oh, but I am! Look, here comes John, and Miss Skiffins with him. All right, John?

WEMMICK: All right, Aged P. So sorry I wasn't here to greet you, Mr. Pip. May I present Miss Skiffins, who is a friend of mine, and a neighbor. The Aged and Miss Skiffins will prepare tea, while we chat —

PIP: I wish to ask you — you are in your Walworth frame of mind, I presume? *(Wemmick nods, the Aged nods, they all nod.)*

WEMMICK: I am. I shall speak in a private and personal capacity. *(Miss Skiffins leads the Aged away.)*

PIP: I wish to do something for my friend, Herbert Pocket. He has been the soul of kindness and I've ill-repaid him by encouraging him to spend more than he has. He'd have been better off if I'd never come along, poor fellow, but as I have, I want to help him. Tell me, how can I set him up in a small partnership somewhere?

WEMMICK: That's devilish good of you, Mr. Pip.

PIP: Only he must never know I had any part in it. You know the extent of my resources, Wemmick. Can you help me? *(Wemmick thinks for a moment.)*

WEMMICK: Perhaps . . . perhaps — yes! Yes, I like it. But it must be done by degrees. We'll go to work on it! *(Miss Skiffins appears.)*

SKIFFINS: Mr. Wemmick, dear, the Aged is toasting.

PIP: I beg your pardon, but what did she say?

WEMMICK: Tea is served. *(They go off)*

• • •

NARRATION: Before a week had passed, Wemmick found a worthy young shipping broker named Clarriker — who wanted intelligent help — and who also wanted some capital — and who might eventually want a partner. Between this young merchant and Pip secret papers were signed, and half of Pip's five hundred pounds disappeared. The whole business was so cleverly managed that Herbert hadn't the least suspicion that Pip's hand was in it.

(Herbert races in to find Pip reading.)

HERBERT: Handel, Handel, I've the most mighty piece of news! I've just come from an interview in the City — man name of Clarriker — I'm to have a position there and — oh, Handel, I start next week, and I might, in time —

PIP: I'm happy for you, Herbert, so happy —

NARRATION: Pip went quickly into his room and wept with joy at the thought that his expectations had at last done some good to somebody. But what of Estella? She rapidly became the belle of London, seen and admired by all. Pip never had an hour's happiness in her society — yet his mind, twenty-four hours a day, harped on the happiness of possessing her someday. On the occasion of Miss Havisham's birthday they were asked to come down from London together to visit.

• • •

Miss Havisham's. Pip bows. Estella kisses her cheek. Miss Havisham clutches Estella's hand.

HAVISHAM: How does she use you, Pip, how does she use you?

PIP: According to your designs, I fear.

NARRATION: And he suddenly saw his fate . . . In the cobwebs . . . In the decayed wedding cake . . . In the face of the clocks that had stopped . . . And his profound sadness communicated itself to Estella.

(Estella withdraws her hand from Miss Havisham.)

HAVISHAM: What, are you tired of me?

ESTELLA: Only a little tired of myself.

HAVISHAM: No, speak the truth, you're tired of me!

(Estella shivers, turns away.) You cold, cold heart.

ESTELLA: What? You reproach me for being cold? I am what you made me — take all the credit or blame.

HAVISHAM: Look at her, so thankless. I took you to my heart when it was still bleeding from its wounds.

ESTELLA: Yes, yes, what would you have of me?

HAVISHAM: Love.

ESTELLA: Mother-by-adoption, how can I return to you what you never gave me?

HAVISHAM: Did I never give her love? You are so proud, so proud!

ESTELLA: Who taught me to be proud? Who praised me when I learned my lesson?

HAVISHAM: So hard, so hard!

ESTELLA: Who taught me to be hard? —

HAVISHAM: But to be proud and hard to me — to me, Estella!

ESTELLA: I cannot think what makes you so unreasonable when Pip and I have ridden all the way down here for your birthday. I have never forgotten the wrongs done you. I've learned the lessons you taught me — God knows I wish I could unlearn them!

(Pause. Estella comes to her, kisses her.)

NARRATION: And as soon as the quarrel began, it was over, and never referred to again. *(Estella leads Miss Havisham off.)*

• • •

NARRATION: The following week, Herbert and Pip were dining at their club.

DRUMMLE: Gentlemen, raise your glasses. I give you Estella.

PIP: Estella who?

DRUMMLE: Estella of Havisham, a peerless beauty.

HERBERT: *(To Pip.)* Much he knows of beauty, the idiot.

PIP: I am acquainted with that lady you speak of. Why do you propose a toast to one of whom you know nothing?

DRUMMLE: Ah, but I do know her. I escorted her to the opera last night.

NARRATION: Now she was seen around the town with Drummle, at the theater, at a ball, at the races . . . But wasn't she destined for Pip? He took comfort in that thought, and in Herbert's happiness — for he had Clara Barley. And so, two years passed.

• • •

The Temple apartment. Night. Pip sits reading.

NARRATION: It was the night of Pip's twenty-third birthday. The weather was wretched, wet and stormy. St. Paul's had just chimed eleven when — Pip thought he heard a footstep on the stair.

PIP: Who's there? *(He puts down his book, takes up a candle.)* Answer! There's someone down there, is there not?

MAGWITCH: *(In shadows.)* Yes.

PIP: What floor do you want?

MAGWITCH: The top. Mr. Pip.

PIP: That is my name. Pray, state your business. *(Magwitch slowly emerges from the shadows, warmly dressed in seafaring clothes. He holds out his hands to Pip.)*

MAGWITCH: My business?

PIP: Who are you? Explain, please. *(Magwitch advances.)* I don't understand — keep away — !

MAGWITCH: It's disappointing to a man, arter having looked for'ard so distant and come so far, but you're not to blame for that. *(He gazes at Pip admiringly.)* You're a game 'un. I'm glad you grow'd up a game 'un. *(He takes off his cap. Pip freezes.)* You acted nobly out on that marsh, my dear boy, and I never forgot it! And now I've come back to you! I've come back to you, Pip, dear boy! *(And to Pip's horror, Magwitch throws his arms around him and embraces him. Darkness.)*

END OF ACT I

ACT II

The Temple. As it was at the end of Act I. Magwitch embraces the horrified Pip.

MAGWITCH: I've come back to you, Pip, dear boy!

PIP: I know you now, and if you're grateful for what I did on those marshes years ago, that's fine, but —

MAGWITCH: You look to have done well since then.

PIP: I have — please release me, I beg you. *(Magwitch lets go of Pip.)*

MAGWITCH: May I be so bold as to ask *how* you have done well since you and me was out on those shiverin' marshes?

PIP: How? I've been chosen to succeed to some property.

MAGWITCH: Might a warmint ask *what* property?

PIP: *(A long pause.)* I . . . don't know . . .

MAGWITCH: Might there be some kind of guardian in the picture, then; some lawyer, maybe? And the first letter of this lawyer's name, could it be . . . J? For Jaggers?

PIP: My God — no! No, it can't be . . . you!

MAGWITCH: Yes, Pip, dear boy, I've made a gentleman on you — it's me wot done it! I'm your second father, lad, and I've come back to you, to see my fine gentleman — *(He embraces Pip again.)* Didn't you never think it could be me? *(Pip disengages with a wail.)*

PIP: Never! Never, never, never!

HERBERT: *(Entering in his dressing gown.)* I say, Handel, you're making an awful racket — oh, I beg you pardon, I didn't know you had company . . . *(Magwitch takes a knife out.)*

PIP: Herbert, this is . . . a visitor of mine. *(Pip sees the knife. To Magwitch.)* He's got every right to be here — he *lives* here! He is my friend.

MAGWITCH: *(Puts away knife, takes out little Bible.)* Then it's all right, dear boy. Take the book in your hand, Pip's friend. Lord strike you dead if you ever split in any way sumever. Kiss the book. *(Herbert does so.)*

PIP: Herbert, this is my . . . benefactor. *(Herbert gapes.)*

HERBERT: Oh . . . I . . . how do you do, my name's Herbert Pocket. I hope you're quite well . . . ?

MAGWITCH: How do you do, Pip's companion. And never believe me if Pip shan't make a gentleman of you, too!

HERBERT: I'll look forward to it. Ah . . . Pip? *(Pip shrugs at him, bewildered.)*

PIP: Tell me, do you have a name? By what do I call you?

MAGWITCH: Name of Magwitch. Christened Abel.

HERBERT: Abel Magwitch, fancy . . .

MAGWITCH: I were born and raised to be a warmint, but now I'm Pip's second father, and he's my son. More to me than any son. Every since I was transported to Australia, I swore that each time I earned a guinea, that guinea should go to Pip. And I swore that when I speculated and got rich, it'd all be for Pip. I lived rough so that he should live smooth. *(He admires Pip benevolently.)* How good-looking he have grow'd. There's a pair of bright eyes somewhere wot you love, eh, Pip? Those eyes shall be yourn, dear boy, if money can buy 'em. *(He beams at Pip, yawns.)* Now, then, where shall I sleep tonight?

PIP: Pray, take my bedroom.

MAGWITCH: By your leave, I'll latch the door first. Caution is necessary. *(He does so.)*

HERBERT: Caution? How do you mean, caution?

MAGWITCH: *(Whispers.)* It's death.

HERBERT: *(Whispers.)* What's death?

MAGWITCH: If I'm caught. I was sent up for life, warn't I? It's death for me to come back to England; I'd be hang'd for it, if I was took.

PIP: *(An anguished explosion.)* Then why in God's name have you come?!!

MAGWITCH: To see my dear boy. To watch him be a fine gentleman. *(He nods, beams, exits into the bedroom. Pip buries his head in his hands.)*

PIP: Estella, Estella . . . I am lost!

HERBERT: Hold steady — he mustn't hear you.

PIP: The shame of it, Herbert! I always thought Miss Havisham — I thought Estella was intended for me. Fool. Foolish dreamer! And now I awaken to find I owe my fortune to this man, this wretched . . . criminal! . . . who has risked his life to be with me! It's a terrible joke, isn't it? And you know what's the funniest part? I scorned my most faithful friend for these "expectations"! Joe, Joe . . .

HERBERT: Take hold of yourself, Handel. There are practical questions to answer. How are we to keep him out of danger? Where will he live? *(Dreamily.)* There are disguises, I suppose . . . wigs, spectacles. Given his intimidating manner, we can hardly dress him up as a vicar but . . . I think some sort of prosperous farmer's disguise would be best. We shall cut his hair! *(He looks at the suffering Pip.)* Get some sleep, Handel. You'll need it when morning comes.

PIP: When morning comes, Mr. Jaggers had better have a good explanation!

• • •

Mr. Jaggers's office.

NARRATION: The moment Pip walked in, Mr. Jaggers could see from his face that the man had turned up.

Jaggers immediately immersed himself in soap and water.

JAGGERS: Now Pip, be careful! Don't *tell* me anything — I don't want to be told a thing! I am not curious.

PIP: I merely wish to be sure that what *I've* been told is true.

JAGGERS: Did you say *told* or *informed*? *Told* would imply verbal communication, face-to-face. You cannot have verbal communication with a man who's still in Australia, can you?

PIP: Lawyers' games!

JAGGERS: Games? The difference between the two verbs could mean a man's safety — his life!

PIP: I shall say "informed," Mr. Jaggers.

JAGGERS: Good.

PIP: I have been informed by a man named Abel Magwitch that he is my benefactor.

JAGGERS: That is the man. In New South Wales, Australia.

PIP: And only he?

JAGGERS: Only he.

PIP: I don't wish to make you responsible for my mistaken conclusions, but I always supposed it was Miss Havisham.

JAGGERS: As you say, Pip, that's not my fault. Not a particle of evidence to support that conclusion. *(Pip leaves.)* Never judge by appearances — irrefutable evidence, that's the rule. Evidence!

• • •

The Temple.

NARRATION: During the following days, Pip studied Magwitch as he napped in the chair, wondering what evils the man had committed, loading him with all the crimes in the calendar!

(As Magwitch dozes in the chair, Pip studies him. Herbert enters, lays a sympathetic hand on Pip's shoulder.)

HERBERT: Dear Pip, what's to be done?

PIP: I'm too stunned to think. I could run away for a soldier.

HERBERT: Of course you can't. He's strongly attached to you.

PIP: He disgusts me — his look, his manners!

HERBERT: But you've got to get him out of England, to safety. And you'll have to go with him or else he won't leave.

PIP: You're right, of course. He's risked his life on my account; it's up to me to keep him from throwing it away altogether.

HERBERT: Well said! We'll see the matter through together — *(Pip seizes his hand in gratitude. Magwitch wakes up, smiles.)*

MAGWITCH: Ah, dear boy, and Pip's companion: I was napping.

PIP: Magwitch, I must ask you something. Do you remember that day long ago, on the marshes?

MAGWITCH: I do, dear boy.

PIP: You were fighting with another convict when the soldiers caught you — you recall?

MAGWITCH: I should think so! What of it?

HERBERT: If we're to help you, we must know more about that day . . . and about you.

MAGWITCH: You're still on your oath?

HERBERT: Assuredly.

MAGWITCH: *(He takes out his pipe, the young men sit.)* Dear boy, and Pip's companion, I could tell you my life short and handy, if you like: in-jail and out-of-jail, in-jail and out-of-jail. I know'd my name to be Magwitch, christened Abel — but I've no notion of where I was born, or to who. I first came aware of myself down in Essex, stealing turnips for my food. Thereafter there warn't a soul that seed young Able Magwitch but wot took fright of him and drove him off. Or turned him in. I can see me, a pitiable ragged little creetur, who everyone called "hardened." "This boy's a terrible hardened one." "This one spends his life in prisons." Then they'd preach at me about the devil and let me go. But wot the devil's a boy to do with no home and an empty stomach? So I'd steal food again, and be turned in again. Somehow I managed to grow up . . . tramping, begging, thieving . . . a bit of a laborer, a bit of a poacher. And so I got to be a man. One day I was lounging about Epsom races, when I met a man. His name was Compeyson. And that's the man you saw me a-pounding in the marshes that day long ago.

PIP: Compeyson.

MAGWITCH: Ay. Smooth and good-looking was Compeyson. He had book-learning, so he set hisself up as a gentleman. He found me, as I say, at the races. "To judge from appearance, you're out of luck," he says. "I've never been in it," I answers him. "Luck changes," he says. "What can you do?" "Eat and drink," says I. So Compeyson took me on, to be his man and partner. And what was his business? Swindling, forgery, stolen bank-note passing; suchlike. He had no more heart than an iron file. — There was another man in the game with Compeyson — as was called Arthur. *(Pip and Herbert glance at each other.)* Mister Arthur. Poor fellow was in a sad state of decline. Him and Compeyson had been in some wicked business together — they'd made a pot of money off some rich lady a few years before. *(Herbert and Pip look at each other.)* But Compeyson had gambled it all away long since. Mr. Arthur had the look of a dying man when I first took up wi' them — from which I should have took warning. Soon after I came, Mr. Arthur took very ill and began crying, delirious-like, that he was haunted. "She's coming for me — I can't get rid of her. She's all dressed in white, wi' white flowers in her hair." And Compeyson says to poor Mr. Arthur, "She's alive, you fool. She's living in her wreck of a house in the country." And Mr. Arthur says, "No, she's here, in her white dress; and over her heart there are drops of blood— you broke her heart! And now she's coming to hang a shroud on me!" And so he died. Compeyson took it as good riddance. Next day him and me started work. I won't tell you what we did. I'll simply say the man got me into such nets and traps as made me his slave. He were smarter than me. He used his head and he used my legs to keep his own self out of trouble. He had no mercy! My missus — no, wait, I don't meanter bring my missus in — *(He looks about him, confused.)* No need to go into that. But Compeyson! When we two was finally caught and put on trial, I noticed what a gentleman he looked wi' his curly hair and his pocket handkerchief, and what a common wretch I looked. Judge and jury thought so too, and even the great Mr. Jaggers couldn't get me justice that day. For when it's time for sentencing, it's him wot gets seven years and me wot gets fourteen! Arter the trial, we was on the same prison ship — I paid him back — I smashed his face in. You seed the scar, dear boy. Then I found a way to escape, and I swam to shore, where I first saw you, in among those old graves.

HERBERT: What an astonishing tale!

MAGWITCH: And true. Little Pip gave me to understand that Compeyson had escaped too, and was out on them marshes. And I vowed then and there, whatever the cost to me, I would drag that scoundrel back to the prison ship. And I did, too. I did.

PIP: Is Compeyson dead?

MAGWITCH: He hopes I am, if he's still alive. Well, I've talked myself near to death. Good night, dear boy. Good night, Pip's companion. *(He exits into the bedroom. Pause.)*

HERBERT: Handel?

PIP: Yes, I know. Miss Havisham's brother was named Arthur.

HERBERT: Compeyson is the man who broke her heart.

PIP: Herbert, before I get Magwitch out of the country, I must try to speak with Estella. I must see her once more.

• • •

NARRATION: Pip set off by the early morning coach, and was into open country when the day came creeping on. The fields were hung about with mists. At length the coach stopped at the Blue Boar Inn, which was in the neighborhood of Miss Havisham's house. When Pip alighted, he was amazed to see a familiar figure lounging by the Inn door.

PIP: Bentley Drummle!

DRUMMLE: You've just come down? *(Pip nods.)* Beastly place. Your part of the country, I think?

PIP: I'm told it's very like your Shropshire.

DRUMMLE: Not in the least like it.

PIP: Have you been here long?

DRUMMLE: Long enough to be tired of it.

PIP: Do you stay here long?

DRUMMLE: Can't say. And you?

PIP: Can't say. *(Drummle gives a brief, unpleasant laugh.)* Are you amused, Mr. Drummle?

DRUMMLE: Not very. I'm about to go riding . . . to explore the marshes. Out-of-the-way villages, here, I'm told, quaint little public houses. Smithies, too. Boy! *(A stable boy appears.)*

BOY: Yes, sir.

DRUMMLE: Is my horse ready?

BOY: Waiting in the yard, sir.

DRUMMLE: The young lady won't ride today, the weather is too foul. And boy —

BOY: Yes, sir?

DRUMMLE: Tell the innkeeper I plan to dine at the young lady's this evening.

BOY: Quite so, sir. *(Drummle goes. The boy turns to Pip.)* May I help you, sir? *(Pip in a rage, shies his valise at him.)*

• • •

Miss Havisham's. Miss Havisham is in her bath chair. Estella sits a little apart, knitting.

NARRATION: Pip found the two women seated by the fire. Their faces were lit by the candles which burned on the wall.

HAVISHAM: And what wind brings you down here, Pip?

PIP: I wished to see Estella, and hearing that some wind had blown her here, I followed.

HAVISHAM: Pray, sit down.

PIP: What I have to say to Estella, Miss Havisham, I shall say before you. It won't displease you to learn that I am as unhappy as you can ever have meant me to be. *(Miss Havisham says nothing. Estella knits.)* I have found out who my patron is. It's not a pleasant discovery. It's not likely to enrich my reputation.

HAVISHAM: Well?

PIP: When you first brought me here, when I still belonged to that village yonder that I wish I had never left, I suppose I was picked at random, as a kind of servant, to gratify a whim of yours?

HAVISHAM: Ay, Pip.

PIP: And Mr. Jaggers —

HAVISHAM: — Mr. Jaggers had nothing to do with it. His being my lawyer and the lawyer of your patron is coincidence.

PIP: Then why did you lead me on? Was that kind?

HAVISHAM: *(Striking her stick upon the ground.)* Who am 1, for God's sake, that I should be kind?!

PIP: In encouraging my mistaken notion, you were also punishing some of your greedy relations?

HAVISHAM: Perhaps.

PIP: There is one branch of that family whom you deeply wrong. I speak of my former tutor, Mr. Matthew Pocket, and his son Herbert. If you think those two to be anything but generous, open and upright, you are in error.

HAVISHAM: You say so because Herbert Pocket is your friend.

PIP: He made himself my friend even when he thought I had taken his place in your affections.

HAVISHAM: Yes, well?

PIP: Miss Havisham, I speak frankly: if you could spare the money to do Herbert a lasting service in life — secretly — I could show you how.

HAVISHAM: Why secretly?

PIP: Because I began the service myself, two years ago, secretly, and I don't wish to be betrayed. Why I cannot complete it myself is . . . it is part of another person's secret. *(Havisham stares into the fire. Estella knits.)*

HAVISHAM: Well, well, well, what else have you to say?

PIP: Estella, you know I've loved you long and dearly. I'd have spoken sooner, but for my foolish hope that Miss Havisham intended us for one another. Whilst I believed you had no choice in the matter I refrained from speaking, but now . . . *(Estella shakes her head, knits on.)* I know, I know. I've no hope that I shall ever call you mine. *(Again, Estella shakes her head. She knits.)* If she'd have thought about it, she'd have seen how cruel it was to torture me with so vain a hope, but she couldn't see. Poor Miss Havisham: Enveloped in her own pain, she could not feel mine. *(Havisham clutches her heart.)*

ESTELLA: It seems there are fancies . . . sentiments — I don't know what to call them — which I cannot comprehend. When you say you love me, I hear your words but they touch nothing here. I did try to warn you.

PIP: Yes.

ESTELLA: But you wouldn't be warned. I am more honest with you than with other men — I can do no more than that.

PIP: Bentley Drummle is here, pursuing you? *(She nods.)* Is it true you encourage him? Ride with him? — Is it true he dines with you today?

ESTELLA: Quite true.

PIP: You cannot love him.

ESTELLA: What have I just told you? I cannot love!

PIP: You would never marry him?

ESTELLA: *(Pause.)* I am going to be married to him.

PIP: Dearest Estella, don't let Miss Havisham lead you into a fatal step. Forget me — you've already done so, I know — but for the love of God, bestow yourself on a man worthier than Bentley Drummle!

ESTELLA: Wedding preparations have already begun. It is my own act, not hers.

PIP: Your own act, to fling yourself away on a brute?!

ESTELLA: Don't be afraid of my being a blessing to him! *(A pause. Miss Havisham moans.)* As for you, Pip, I trust you'll get me out of your thoughts within a week.

PIP: Out of my thoughts! You have been in every prospect I've seen since I first met you — on the river, in the wind, on the city streets. To the last hour of my life you cannot choose but remain part of me. O, God bless you. God forgive you! *(Miss Havisham clutches at her heart again. Pip kisses Estella's hand, leaves.)*

NARRATION: All done, all gone!

Pip wandered through the lanes and bypaths around the house . . .
Then he turned and walked all the way back to London.

• • •

NARRATION: It was past midnight when he crossed London bridge, closer to
one when he approached his lodgings. He was stopped by the night porter.
PORTER: Urgent message for you, Mr. Pip. *(Pip tears open an envelope, reads, as.)*
WEMMICK: Dear Mr. Pip: Don't go home. Yours, J. Wemmick.
NARRATION: Pip turned hastily away. He spent the remainder of the night in
an hotel in Covent Garden. Footsore and weary as he was, he could not
sleep. And after an hour, those extraordinary voices with which silence
teems began to make themselves audible. The closet whispered. The fireplace sighed. The washstand ticked. And they all spoke as if with one voice:
Don't go home. Whatever night-fancies crowded in on him, they never
ceased to murmur: Don't go home. When at last he dozed in sheer exhaustion, it became a vast, shadowy verb he had to conjugate, impera-
tive mood, present tense: Do not thou go home. Let him or her not go
home . . . Let us not go home. Do not ye or you go home. Early the next
morning Pip went to Walworth to consult Wemmick. This was obviously
not a matter for the office.

• • •

Walworth. Pip crosses over the drawbridge.

WEMMICK: You got my note?
PIP: I did.
WEMMICK: I hope you destroyed it. It's never wise to leave documentary evi-
dence if you can help it. *(He hands Pip a sausage speared on a toasting fork.)*
Would you mind toasting a sausage for the Aged while we talk?
PIP: Delighted.
WEMMICK: You understand, we're in our private and personal capacities here?
(Pip nods.) I heard by accident yesterday that a certain person had recently
disappeared from Australia, a person possessed of vast portable property.
Yes? I also heard that your rooms were being watched, and might be
watched again. — All right, ain't you, Aged P? *(He takes the toasting fork
from Pip, puts the sausage on a plate for the Aged.)*
AGED PARENT: All right, John, all right, my boy! *(They all nod.)*
PIP: Tell me, the disappearance of this person from Australia and the watching of my rooms — are these two events connected?

WEMMICK: If they aren't yet, they will be. *(They all nod.)*

PIP: Mr. Wemmick, have you ever heard of a man of bad character whose name is Compeyson? *(Wemmick nods.)* Is he living? *(Wemmick and the Aged nod.)* Is he in London? *(All three nod.)*

WEMMICK: I see you've got the point. When I learned of it, I naturally came to your rooms, and not finding anyone at home — or answering the door, anyway — I went to Clarriker's office to see Mr. Herbert. And without mentioning any names I explained that if he was aware of any Tom, Dick, or Richard staying with you, he had better get him out of the way.

PIP: Herbert must have been mystified.

WEMMICK: Not for long. He conceived a plan. Seems he's courting a young lady who lives in Mill Pond Bank, right on the river. And that's where Mr. Herbert has lodged this person, this Tom, Dick, or Richard! It's a sound idea, because although you're being watched, Mr. Herbert isn't . . . And as he visits there often, he can act as go-between!

PIP: Good thinking.

WEMMICK: But there's an even better reason for the move. This house is by the river. You understand? *(Pip shakes his head.)* When the right moment comes, you can slip your man aboard a foreign packet-boat unnoticed. Here is the young lady's address in Mill Pond Bank — Miss Barley's the name, and a very odd name it is. You may go there this evening, but do it before you go home, so they won't follow you.

PIP: I don't know how to thank you —

WEMMICK: One last piece of advice. You must get hold of your man's portable property as soon as you can. For his sake as well as yours. It mustn't fall into the wrong hands, must it? Well, I'd better be off to the City. I suggest you stay here until dark — you look tired enough. Keep out of sight and spend a restful day with Aged. Ain't that right, Aged P?

AGED PARENT: All right, John.

WEMMICK: Good-bye then, Mr. Pip. *(He goes. Pip stares into the fire.)*

NARRATION: Pip soon fell asleep before the fire. He and the Aged Parent enjoyed each other's society by falling asleep before the fire throughout the whole day. When it was dark, Pip prepared to leave. The Aged was readying tea, and Pip inferred from the number of cups, three, that a visitor was expected. Could it be that odd lady with the green gloves . . . Miss Skiffins? Pip made his way to Mill Pond Bank. It was an old house with a curious bow window in front.

• • •

Mill Pond Bank.

HERBERT: All's well so far, Handel. But he's anxious to see you. *(Clara enters.)* Ah, here's Clara, here she comes.

CLARA: Pip, is it?

PIP: And you're Clara, at last! Herbert's words fail to do you justice. *(He kisses her hand.)*

CLARA: Mr. Magwitch wants to know if he may come down. Let me go fetch him. *(She goes out.)*

PIP: Herbert, she's so lovely.

HERBERT: Isn't she? I know where my good fortune lies, money or no — *(Magwitch enters.)*

MAGWITCH: I've brought you nothing but trouble, dear boy.

PIP: You're safe, that's all that matters. You know you'll have to go away?

MAGWITCH: But how — ?

HERBERT: Handel and I are both skilled oarsmen —

PIP: And I've just hired a rowboat — I keep it tied up at the Temple stairs, near our rooms.

HERBERT: When the time comes, we plan to row you down river ourselves, and smuggle you aboard a foreign packet.

PIP: Starting tomorrow I'll go rowing every day. If they see me out on the river often enough, it'll be taken as habit. If I'm out there twenty-five times, no one will blink an eye when I appear the twenty-sixth.

HERBERT: A bit of practice in the evenings won't hurt me, either. I've grown soft, cooped up in that office.

MAGWITCH: Hah. Hah! I like it — I like your plan, lads.

• • •

Throughout the following montage, Compeyson, carefully muffled, lurks here and there.

NARRATION: Pip and Herbert went rowing the next day. The young men, it appeared, felt a sudden urge to exercise . . . And after the first few days, no one seemed to notice. Pip often rowed alone, in cold, rain and sleet . . . But no one seemed to notice. At first he kept above Blackfriars Bridge, but as the hours of the tide changed, he rowed farther, past the tricky currents around old London Bridge. Once he and Herbert rowed past Mill Pond Bank. They could see the house with the curious bow window from the river. Magwitch was safe inside that house. There seemed no cause for alarm. But Pip knew there was cause for alarm. He could not get rid of the notion he was being watched. Meanwhile, Pip's financial affairs began to wear a gloomy appearance, for he had vowed not to accept any more money from Magwitch, given his uncertain feelings about the man. And as the days passed, Pip continued to think of Estella. The impression settled heavily upon him that she was married. But he could not bear to seek out the truth of it, and clung to the last little rag of his hope. *(Compeyson appears directly behind him.)* He was miserable. And still, he could not get rid of the notion he was being watched.

(Pip turns around, but bumps into Mr. Jaggers, who is walking down the road.)

JAGGERS: Mr. Pip, is it?

PIP: Mr. Jaggers.

JAGGERS: Where are you bound?

PIP: Home, I think.

JAGGERS: Don't you know?

PIP: I . . . hadn't made up my mind.

JAGGERS: You are going to dine, you don't mind admitting that?

PIP: I confess it, guilty of dining.

JAGGERS: And you're not engaged?

PIP: I'm quite free.

JAGGERS: Come dine with me. *(Jaggers takes his arm decisively.)* Wemmick will be joining us, too. *(Wemmick falls in with them.)*

• • •

Jaggers's house. Molly is serving soup from a tureen.

JAGGERS: By the way, Miss Havisham sent you a message. She'd like to see you, a little matter of business. Will you go down?

PIP: Certainly. *(The three men sit down. Molly stands behind Jaggers' chair, silently.)*

JAGGERS: When? *(Pip glances at Wemmick, who silently mouths the word "soon.")*

PIP: I . . . soon. At once. Tomorrow. *(Wemmick nods.)*

JAGGERS: Splendid. So, Pip, your good friend, the Spider — *(To Wemmick.)* I refer to one Bentley Drummle — appears to have played his cards well. He has won the pool, eh? *(To Wemmick.)* I refer to a young lady.

PIP: It would seem he has.

JAGGERS: Hah! He's a promising fellow in his own way, but he may not have it all his way. The stronger of the two will win in the end; but who is the stronger, he or she? *(He sips.)* What do you think, Wemmick?

WEMMICK: *(Shrugs.)* Here's to the Spider — what's his name?

JAGGERS: *(Lifts his glass.)* Bentley Drummle: and may the question of supremacy be settled to the lady's satisfaction. To the satisfaction of both of 'em, it never can be. *(He drinks.)* Ah, Molly, the soup is delicious this evening.

MOLLY: Thank you, master.

JAGGERS: Our Molly doesn't like company, she prefers to keep her skills for my palate alone. *(She turns her head to one side, fidgets with an apron-string. Pip suddenly stares at her. Jaggers notices.)* What's the matter, young man?

PIP: Nothing — we were speaking of a subject that's painful to me. *(Pip and Molly lock eyes for a moment. Wemmick and Jaggers attack their soup.)*

NARRATION: The action of her fingers was not unlike that of knitting. The look on her face was intent. Surely Pip had seen such hands, such eyes recently. They were fresh in his mind. He stared at Molly's hands, her eyes, her flowing hair, and compared them with hands, eyes, hair he knew too well. He thought what those dearer hands might be like after twenty years of a brutal, stormy life —

And suddenly he felt absolutely certain that this woman was Estella's mother. Pip managed to get through the rest of his meal as best he could. At last, he and Wemmick thanked their host and took to the street.

(Pip and Wemmick stroll. They pass Compeyson without noticing him.)

PIP: Mr. Wemmick, we were speaking of Miss Havisham's adopted daughter at dinner. Have you ever seen her?

WEMMICK: Can't say I have. Something troubling you, Mr. Pip?

PIP: The first time I dined at Jaggers', do you recall telling me to notice the housekeeper. A wild beast tamed, you called her.

WEMMICK: I daresay I did.

PIP: How did Mr. Jaggers tame her?

WEMMICK: We're in our private and personal capacities? *(Pip nods.)* About twenty years ago she was tried for murder at the Old Bailey, and was acquitted. Mr. Jaggers was her lawyer, of course, and I must say his defense was astonishing. The murdered person was another woman, older than Molly, and even stronger. It was a case of jealousy. Molly was married to some sort of tramping man, and he got too familiar with the other woman. She was found dead in a barn near Hounslow Heath, all bruised and scratched — choked to death. There was no other candidate to do the murder but our Molly. — You may be sure Mr. Jaggers never pointed out how strong Molly's wrists were then. He likes to, now.

PIP: Indeed he does. How did he get her off?

WEMMICK: Molly was also suspected of killing her own child by this man of hers, to revenge herself on him. Jaggers told the jury that they were really trying her for that crime; and since there was no child, no body, no trace of a child or a body, they had no proof. I tell you, he got the jury so confused that they capitulated and acquitted her of killing her rival. She's been in his service ever since.

PIP: Do you remember the sex of the child?

WEMMICK: Said to have been a little girl, around three.

PIP: Good night, Mr. Wemmick, we part here. *(They go off separately. Compeyson follows Pip.)*

· · ·

Havisham's.

NARRATION: The following morning Pip journeyed down to Miss Havisham. There hung about her an air of utter desolation, an expression, almost, of fear . . .

HAVISHAM: Thank you for coming. I want to show you I'm not all made of stone. What do you wish me to do for Herbert Pocket?

PIP: I had hoped to buy him a partnership in the firm of Clarriker and Company. He's worked successfully there for the past year or so.

HAVISHAM: How much money do you need?

PIP: Nine hundred pounds.

HAVISHAM: If I give it to you, will you keep my part in it as secret as your own?

PIP: Faithfully. It would ease my mind about that, at any rate.

HAVISHAM: Are you so unhappy?

PIP: I'm far from happy — but I've got other causes of disquiet than any you know.

HAVISHAM: Pip? Is my only service to you to be this favor for young Pocket? Can I do nothing for you yourself?

PIP: Nothing, Miss Havisham. *(She takes pen, paper, writes a note.)*

HAVISHAM: This is an authorization to Jaggers to pay Clarriker nine hundred pounds to advance your friend. *(He takes the paper.)*

PIP: I thank you with all my heart. *(She takes another paper, writes.)*

HAVISHAM: Pip, here is my name. If you can ever write "I forgive her" under it, even after my death, it would mean so much . . .

PIP: Oh, Miss Havisham, I can do that now. I want forgiveness myself too much to be bitter with you. *(He reaches for hand, but she drops suddenly to her knees, sobbing.)*

HAVISHAM: What have I done, what have I done?

PIP: I'd have loved her under any circumstances. Is she married?

HAVISHAM: She is. What have I done? What have I done?

PIP: I assure you, Miss Havisham, you may dismiss me from your conscience. Estella is a different case.

HAVISHAM: I meant to save her from a misery like my own! I stole her heart and put ice in its place.

PIP: Better to have left her a natural heart, even if it were to break.

HAVISHAM: What have I done, what have I done?

PIP: Whose child was she? *(She shakes her head.)* You don't know? But Mr. Jaggers brought her here?

HAVISHAM: I asked him to find me a little girl whom I could rear and love and save from my own fate. One night, a few months later, he brought her . . . she was fast asleep. I called her Estella. She was about three.

PIP: Good night, Miss Havisham. And thank you for your kindness to Herbert. *(He kisses her hand, goes.)*

NARRATION: Twilight was closing in. Pip went into the ruined garden, and roamed past the place where he and Herbert had had their fight . . . Past the spot where she had kissed him . . . Past the little pot of flowers whose fragrance she had once inhaled . . . He turned to look at the old house once more — When suddenly he saw a great, towering flame spring up by Miss Havisham's window, and he saw her running, shrieking, with a whirl of flame blazing all about her, soaring high above her head. *(Screams. Fire.)* Pip raced back into the house, tore off his greatcoat, and wrapped her in it, beating out the flames with his bare hands. *(Screams. Then they subside. Silence.)*

HAVISHAM: What have I done . . . what have I done . . . Pip, Pip . . . forgive me . . . please, God forgive me . . . *(Darkness.)*

• • •

The Temple. Pip lies on the sofa, Herbert is dressing his burnt hands.

HERBERT: Steady, Handel, dear boy.

PIP: You are the best of nurses.

HERBERT: The right hand's much better today. The left was pretty badly burned, it will take more time —

PIP: Time.

HERBERT: Steady on! I saw Magwitch last evening. He sends his love.

PIP: And how is Clara?

HERBERT: Taking good care of him. She calls him Abel — she'll miss him when he goes.

PIP: She's such a darling. You'll be marrying soon, won't you

HERBERT: *(Grins.)* How can I respectably care for her otherwise? Now, this bandage will have to come off gradually, so you won't feel it. *(He works on it.)* You know what, Handel? Old Magwitch has actually begun to grow on me.

PIP: Yes. I used to loathe him, but that's gone. Don't you think he's become more gentle? *(Herbert nods.)*

HERBERT: He told me the story of his "missus" the other night, and a wild, dark tale it is. Ah, the bandage is off most charmingly. Now for the clean, cool one.

PIP: Tell me about his woman.

HERBERT: She was a jealous one, vengeful to the last degree.

PIP: What last degree?

HERBERT: Murder — am I hurting you? *(Pip shakes his head.)* She was tried and acquitted. Jaggers defended her, that's how Magwitch first came to learn of him. — Is the bandage too tight?

PIP: It is impossible to be gentler. Pray, go on.

HERBERT: This woman had a child by Magwitch, on whom he doted. After she killed her rival, she told Magwitch she would also kill their child. There, the arm's nicely done up. You're sure you're all right? You look so pale.

PIP: Did she kill the child?

HERBERT: She did.

PIP: Magwitch thinks she did. Herbert, look at me.

HERBERT: I do look at you, dear boy.

PIP: Touch me — I've no fever? I'm not delirious?

HERBERT: You seem rather excited, but you're quite yourself.

PIP: I know I'm myself. And the man we have been hiding in Mill Pond Bank, Abel Magwitch, is Estella's father!

• • •

Jaggers's office.

NARRATION: Pip was seized with a feverish need to verify the truth of it. As soon as he was able to leave his bed, he visited Mr. Jaggers. *(Jaggers and Wemmick are busy with paperwork. Pip walks in, hands Jaggers a note.)*

JAGGERS: And the next item, Wemmick, will be — *(He sees Pip.)* What's this? *(Reads.)* An authorization signed by the late Miss Havisham . . . nine hundred pounds, payable to the firm of Clarriker and Company, Ltd., on behalf of . . . Herbert Pocket? This must be your doing, Pip. I'm sorry we do nothing for you.

PIP: She was kind enough to ask . . . I told her no.

JAGGERS: I shouldn't have told her that, but every man knows his own business.

WEMMICK: Every man's business is portable property.

PIP: I did ask her for information, however . . . regarding her adopted daughter. She obliged, and I now know more about Estella than she does herself. I know her mother.

JAGGERS: Her mother?

PIP: And so do you — she cooked your breakfast this morning.

JAGGERS: *(Unperturbed.)* Did she?

PIP: But I know more, perhaps, than even you do. I also know Estella's father. *(Jaggers looks up, surprised.)*

JAGGERS: You know her father?

PIP: His name is Magwitch. He . . . lives in Australia.

JAGGERS: On what evidence does he make this claim?

PIP: He doesn't make it at all — he doesn't even know his daughter is alive.

NARRATION: Then Pip told Jaggers all he knew, and how he knew it. For once the lawyer was at a loss for words.

JAGGERS: *(Pause.)* Hah! — Where were we, Wemmick?

PIP: You cannot get rid of me so easily. I must confirm the truth from you. Please. *(Jaggers doesn't respond.)* Wemmick, you are a man with a gentle heart. I've seen your pleasant home and your old father; I know your kind and playful ways. Please, on my behalf, beg him to be more open with me —

JAGGERS: What's this?! Pleasant home? Old father?!

WEMMICK: So long as I leave 'em at home, what's it to you, Sir?

JAGGERS: Playful ways?!! *(To Pip.)* This man must be the most cunning impostor in London.

WEMMICK: It don't interfere with business, does it? I shouldn't be surprised if, when you're finally tired of all this work, you plan a pleasant home of your own!

JAGGERS: Me?!

PIP: The truth, I beg you —

JAGGERS: Well, well, Pip, let me put a case to you. Mind, I admit nothing.

PIP: I understand.

JAGGERS: Put the case that a woman under such circumstances as you have named hid her child away, and only her lawyer knew where. Put the case that, at the same time, this lawyer held a trust to find a child for an eccentric, rich client, a lady, to adopt.

PIP: Yes, yes.

JAGGERS: Put the case that this lawyer lived in an atmosphere . . . of evil. He saw small children earmarked for destruction; he saw children whipped, imprisoned, transported, neglected, hounded, cast out — qualified in all ways for the hangman. And he saw them grow up and be hanged. And always, always, he was helpless to intervene. Put the case that here was one pretty little child out of the heap that he could save. Put the case that the child grew up and married for money. That the natural mother was still living. That the father and mother, unknown to each other, were living within so many miles, furlongs, yards, if you will, of one another. That the secret was still a secret . . . until one day you got hold of it. Now tell me, for whose sake would you reveal the secret? *(Pause. Pip shakes his head.)* Now, Wemmick, where were we when Mr. Pip came barging in?

• • •

The Temple.

NARRATION: The next evening, Herbert came home from the office bubbling with joy, for Clarriker had offered him —

HERBERT: *(Rushing in.)* — A partnership! Think of it! We're establishing a branch office in the East Indies and I — I am to go out and take charge of it! I'll be able to take Clara and — it's a miracle! Are you surprised? No, of course not, you've always had more faith in me than I had in myself. But my dear Handel, after your commitment to Magwitch is over, perhaps . . . have you given any thought to your own future?

PIP: I'm afraid to think further than our project.

HERBERT: You might think of a future with me — I mean with Clarriker's, for in the East Indies we'll need a —

PIP: — A clerk?

HERBERT: Yes, a clerk. But Handel, you could expand into a partnership soon enough — look at me! Clara and I have talked it over — she worries about you too, the darling. You're to live with us. We get along so well, Handel . . . *(Pip, deeply moved, hugs him.)*

PIP: Not yet. Not for a while. After we've seen our project through there are some other things I must settle.

HERBERT: When you are ready, then?

PIP: When I am ready. And thank you.

NARRATION: That same evening, Pip received a message.

WEMMICK: Burn this as soon as you read it. Be ready to move your cargo out on Wednesday morning. J. Wemmick.

HERBERT: Wednesday!

PIP: We can be ready. Will you warn Magwitch?

HERBERT: I'll visit Clara tonight. But your burns haven't healed yet — I can tell your arm still hurts.

PIP: I shall be ready.

• • •

NARRATION: Tuesday. One of those March mornings when the sun shines hot and the wind blows cold . . . Summer in the sun, winter in the shade. The plan:

(Pip and Herbert pore over a map.)

PIP: The tide turns at nine tomorrow morning — it's with us until three.

HERBERT: Just six hours.

PIP: We'll have to row into the night, anyway.

HERBERT: Where do we board the big ship?

PIP: Below Gravesend — here. See, the river's wide, there, and quite deserted. The packet ship to Hamburg passes at midnight.

HERBERT: Wemmick has booked two passages to Hamburg. The two passengers are expected to make an . . . unconventional boarding, to say the least. *(They smile at each other. Compeyson lurks on the sidelines.)*

NARRATION: Wednesday. The relief of putting the plan into action was enormous. The two young men set out in their boat as was their habit. Pip felt sure they went undetected. They soon passed old London Bridge, then Billingsgate Market, with its oyster-boats. The White Tower. Traitor's Gate. Now they were among the big steamers from Glasgow and Aberdeen. Here, at their moorings, were tomorrow's ships for Rotterdam and Le

Havre. And there stood the packet scheduled to leave for Hamburg later that evening. Pip and Herbert rowed past it with pounding hearts. Finally they touched the little dock at Mill Pond Bank, where a man dressed as a river pilot was waiting. He climbed into the boat.

MAGWITCH: Dear boy, faithful boy, thankee. And thankee, Pip's companion.

NARRATION: Herbert and Pip rowed their cargo back out on the river.

MAGWITCH: If you know'd, dear boy, what it is to sit alonger my boy in the open air, arter having been kept betwixt four walls . . .

PIP: I think I know the delights of freedom.

MAGWITCH: No, you'd have to have been under lock and key to know it equal to me.

PIP: If all goes well, you'll be free again within a few hours.

MAGWITCH: I hope so. But we can no more see to the bottom of the next few hours than we can to the bottom of this river. Nor yet can we hold back time's tide than I can hold this water . . . see how it runs through my fingers and is gone?

NARRATION: The air felt cold and damp. Pip's hands throbbed with pain. In mid-afternoon the tide began to run strong against them, but they rowed and rowed until the sun set. Night. They passed Gravesend at last, and pulled into a little cove. They waited. Magwitch smoked his pipe. They spoke very little. Once Pip thought he heard the lapping of oars upon the water, and the murmur of voices — but then there was nothing. He credited it to exhaustion and the pain in his hands. They continued to wait silently by the river bank. Then — they heard an engine! The packet for Hamburg was coming round the bend — even in the dark Pip thought he could see the smoke from her stacks!

PIP: Yes, here she comes!

HERBERT: She's slowing down — start rowing!

NARRATION: They eased out on the river again, and headed toward the packet steamer — When suddenly, a four-oared galley shot out from the bank, toward them — On board were four oarsmen and two other figures. One held the rudder lines, and seemed to be in charge — The other figure sat idle: He was cloaked and hidden. The galley began pulling up fast toward Pip's boat — While Pip and Herbert rowed furiously toward the packet.

VOICE FROM GALLEY: You have a returned convict there — that man in the pilot's coat. His name is Abel Magwitch. I call upon him to surrender, and you others to assist!

NARRATION: With a mighty thrust, the galley rammed Pip's small boat. *(Sound of wood on wood, cries, water.)* Magwitch stood in the boat and leaned across, yanking the cloak from the other man's face.

MAGWITCH: Compeyson!

COMPEYSON: Yes, it's Compeyson.

VOICE FROM GALLEY: Surrender!

MAGWITCH: You shan't get away with it, not again, not this time!

VOICE FROM GALLEY: To starboard, to starboard — look out —

COMPEYSON: Help, he's got hold of me — he's pulling me — overboard . . . help! —

VOICE FROM GALLEY: We're going to capsize — watch — *(Screaming. The packet sounds its horn, thrashing in water.)* My God, the steamer! The steamer's upon us! Help — the steamer — headed toward us — *(The packet horn blows with increasing insistence. Shouts, cries, screams, splintering wood.)*

PIP: Magwitch . . . ! *(Then silence. The lapping of water.)*

NARRATION: As the confusion abated, they saw Magwitch swimming ahead. He was hauled on board and manacled at the wrists and ankles. He had sustained severe injuries to the chest and head. There was no sign of Compeyson. Magwitch told his captors they had gone down together, locked in each other's arms. After a fierce underwater struggle, only Magwitch had found the strength to swim to the surface. Pip, shivering and wet, took his place beside the wounded, shackled creature.

MAGWITCH: Dear boy . . . I'm quite content. I've seen my boy. Now he can . . . be a gentleman without me . . .

PIP: I will never stir from your side. Please God, I will be as true to you as you have been to me.

NARRATION: Magwitch was removed to the prison hospital, but was too ill to be committed for immediate trial. Pip tried to think what peace of mind he could bring to the wounded man.

PIP: His money — his property —

JAGGERS: — It will all be forfeit to the crown, Pip. I'm sorry.

PIP: I don't care, for myself. But for mercy's sake, don't let him know it's lost. It would break his heart if he thought I weren't to have it.

JAGGERS: You let it slip through your fingers. Poor Pip.

WEMMICK: When I think of the sacrifice of so much portable property! Your creditors will be after you now, I fear.

JAGGERS: However, I'll say nothing to Magwitch. Poor Pip. I'm late to court.

NARRATION: *(Voices echo.)* Late to court. Late to court. Late to court.

• • •

The prison hospital. Magwitch lies on a mattress. Pip enters.

MAGWITCH: Dear boy, I thought you was late.

PIP: It's only just time. I waited by the gate.

MAGWITCH: Thankee, dear boy. You never desert me.

PIP: Are you in much pain today?

MAGWITCH: I don't complain of none.

PIP: You never do complain: *(A prison doctor looks at Magwitch, shakes his head.)* Magwitch, I must tell you now, at last — can you understand what I say? *(Magwitch nods.)* You had a child once, whom you loved and lost? *(Magwitch nods.)* She lived. She lives, and has powerful friends. She is a lady, and very beautiful. And I love her! *(Magwitch kisses Pip's hand. He dies.)*

PIP: Oh Lord, be merciful to him, a sinner. *(Darkness.)*

• • •

The Temple. Pip lies sleeping on a sofa.

NARRATION: Now Pip was all alone. Miss Havisham and Magwitch were dead. And Herbert had left for the Far East. Pip should have been alarmed by the state of his financial affairs, for he was heavily in debt —

But that he scarcely had the strength to notice. For he was ill, very ill with fever. He dreamed he was rowing, endlessly rowing. He dreamed that Miss Havisham called to him from inside a great furnace. *(Creditors begin carrying off the rug, a chair, etc. In the end there is only the sofa and one chair.)* He dreamed he was a brick in the wall — The steel beam of a vast engine.

He dreamed that the creditors had carried off all his furniture but a bed and a chair — And that Joe was seated in the chair. He dreamed he asked for a cooling drink, and that the beloved hand that gave it to him was Joe's. He dreamed he smelled Joe's pipe. And finally, one day he took courage and woke up.

PIP: Is it . . . Joe?

JOE: Which it are, old chap.

PIP: Oh, Joe, you break my heart.

JOE: Which, dear old Pip, you and me was ever the best of friends. And when you're better — wot larks! *(Pip covers his eyes for a moment.)*

PIP: How long, dear Joe?

JOE: Which you meantersay, how long have you been ill? It's the end of May.

PIP: And you've been here all this time?

JOE: Pretty nigh. For Biddy said, "Go to him, he needs you!" And I do what she tells me. Now rest, Pip. I must write a letter to Biddy, else she'll worry.

PIP: You can write?

JOE: Biddy taught me.

NARRATION: Pip was like a child in the hands of Joe, who cared for him so tenderly that Pip half-believed he *was* a child again, and that everything that had happened to him since he left the forge was a dream. Finally the fever was gone. But as Pip grew stronger, Joe seemed to grow less comfortable.

JOE: Dear old Pip, old chap, you're almost come round, sir.

PIP: Ay. We've had a time together I shall never forget. I know for a while I did forget the old days, but — .

JOE: Dear Pip . . . dear sir . . . what have been betwixt us — have been. You're better now.

PIP: Yes, Joe.

JOE: Then good night, Pip. *(He tiptoes out.)*

NARRATION: And when he awoke the next morning, Joe was gone. *(Pip finds a note on Joe's chair.)*

PIP: *(Reads.)* Sir: Not wishful to intrude, I have departed. For you are well again, dear Pip, and will do better without Joe P.S. Ever the best of friends.

NARRATION: Enclosed with the note was a receipt for Pip's outstanding debts. Joe had paid them. *(Pip puts on his jacket, takes his hat.)*

PIP: I'll go to him — to the forge. Biddy was right, he has such pride, such honor. And Biddy — Biddy is there too. Perhaps she'll find me worthier of her than I once was. Perhaps — *(He rushes off.)*

NARRATION: The first person he encountered when he climbed off the coach was his old mentor, Mr. Pumblechook.

PUMBLECHOOK: So, young man, I am sorry to see you brought so low. Look at you, skin and bones. But I knew it! You were ever pigheaded and ungrateful. I always knew it would end badly. Lo, how the mighty are fallen! How the mighty are —

NARRATION: — But Pip could not wait to hear the conclusion of the greeting. He headed down a country lane to the forge. The June weather was delicious. The sky was blue, and larks soared over the green corn. He felt like a pilgrim, toiling homeward from a distant land.

BIDDY: It's Pip! Dear Pip — Joe, Joe, Pip's come home! Look at you, so pale and thin.

PIP: Biddy, dear girl.

BIDDY: How did you know to come today?

PIP: Today?

BIDDY: It's our wedding day. Joe and I were married this morning! *(Pip's face falls for an instant, than he brightens. Joe appears.)*

PIP: Married. Married!

JOE: Which he warn't strong enough fur to be surprised, my dear.

BIDDY: I ought to have thought, but I was so happy —

PIP: — And so am I! It's the sweetest tonic of all. Biddy, you have the best husband in the world; and you, Joe, the best wife. She'll make you as happy as you deserve to be. *(He kisses her.)* And now, although I know you've already done it in your hearts, please tell me you forgive me.

JOE: Dear old Pip, God knows as I forgive you, if I have anything to forgive.

BIDDY: Amen. *(He embraces them both.)*

PIP: And now, I must be off, to catch the coach to London. *(Joe and Biddy watch him go. For a moment, they look after him, arms around each other.)*

• • •

WEMMICK: Mr. Pip? I know it's a trying time to turn your mind to other matters, but —

PIP: — What? Anything, Wemmick.

WEMMICK: Tomorrow is only Tuesday . . . still, I'm thinking of taking a holiday.

PIP: Are you? That's very nice . . . ?

WEMMICK: I'd like you to take a walk with me in the morning, if you don't object.

PIP: Of course not. Delighted.

NARRATION: The next morning early, after fortifying themselves with rum-and-milk and biscuits, they did take a walk, to Camberwell Green. Pip was puzzled.

WEMMICK: Halloa! Here's a nice little church. Let's go in.

NARRATION: And they went in.

WEMMICK: Halloa! Here's a couple of pairs of nice gloves. Let's put them on. *(They do so. The Aged Parent and Miss Skiffins [still in her green gloves] appear with a clergyman.)* Halloa! Here is Miss Skiffins. Let's have a wedding. All right, Aged P?

AGED PARENT: All right, John!

CLERGYMAN: Who giveth this woman to be married to this man? *(No response.)* Who giveth this woman to be married to this man?

WEMMICK: *(Shout.)* Now, Aged P. You know, "who giveth."

AGED PARENT: I do! I do! I do! All right, John?

NARRATION: And so Mr. Wemmick and Miss Skiffins were wed, with Pip as witness. *(All kiss the bride.)*

WEMMICK: *(To Pip.)* Altogether a Walworth sentiment, you understand?

PIP: I understand. Private and personal, not to be mentioned in the office.

WEMMICK: If Mr. Jaggers knew of this, he might think my brain was softening. *(The Aged nods. They all nod.)*

• • •

NARRATION: Within a month Pip had left England. Within two he was a clerk in the Far Eastern branch of Clarriker and Pocket. Three years later he was promoted to associate director of that branch. For many years Pip lived happily with Herbert and Clara Pocket. When at last he returned to England, he hurried to the little village and the forge.

• • •

The forge kitchen. Joe sits smoking. Biddy sews. There is a small boy with a slate on Pip's old stool. Pip gazes for a moment, then enters. They embrace him. He picks up the child

JOE: We giv' him the name of Pip for your sake, dear old boy, and hope he may grow a little like you.

PIP: You must lend him to me, once I get settled.

BIDDY: No, you must marry and get your own boy.

PIP: So Clara tells me, but I don't think so . . .

BIDDY: *(Pause.)* You haven't forgotten her.

PIP: I've forgotten nothing that ever meant anything to me. But that poor dream has all gone by, dear Biddy, all gone by.

• • •

Miss Havisham's garden.

NARRATION: The next evening Pip's steps led him to Miss Havisham's gate. There was no house left, only ruins and a garden overgrown by weeds. *(A figure moves from the shadows toward him.)*

PIP: Estella!

ESTELLA: I wonder you know me, Pip. I've changed.

PIP: How is —

ESTELLA: My husband is dead.

PIP: I'm sorry.

ESTELLA: Don't be. He used me with great cruelty. It is over.

PIP: How strange we should meet here, where we first met.

ESTELLA: *(Pause.)* You do well?

PIP: I work pretty hard, so I do well enough. I want so little.

ESTELLA: I have often thought of you. Once you said to me, "God bless you,
God forgive you." Suffering has taught me what your heart used to be —

PIP: God has forgiven you, my dear.

ESTELLA: Ay. I have been bent and broken but, I hope, into a better shape.
Tell me we are friends, Pip.

PIP: We are friends.

ESTELLA: And shall continue friends apart? *(He starts to speak, hesitates, nods.
He bends and kisses her hand.)*

PIP: God bless you, Estella. *(She leaves through the garden gate. Pip looks around
the old place. He sees the little pot of flowers, now broken and charred, but
with a few blooms still growing. He picks it up, smells them, picks one and
folds it into his breast pocket. He sits on the old garden bench. As he does,
voices of the past rise up. They begin slow, but speed up, overlapping.)*

NARRATION: Philip Pirrip, late of this parish, and then, Pip, wot larks! Stop,
thief, stop that boy! Be grateful, boy, for them what has brought you up
by hand Love her, love her, love her! Wot larks. Coarse little monster,
why don't you cry. Cry. Cry. This young man has . . . great expectations
Wouldn't you be happier as you are? Did you never think it could be me?
Portable property, my dear Handel. You've the arm of a blacksmith. Love
her, love her, love her! I cannot love. I've come back to you, Pip, dear
boy, a wild beast tamed, name of Magwitch. What have I done? What
have I done? Going to be a gentleman, great expectations.
(Pip rises.)
Great expectations.
(He strides out the garden door. Darkness.)

END OF PLAY

Playing with Fire

ADAPTED FROM THE NOVEL
FRANKENSTEIN BY MARY SHELLEY

To the memory of Garland Wright, whose vision inspired me
To Michael Lupu, a wonderful creative presence

Adam, the Creature played by John Carroll Lynch, and Victor, performed by Curzon Dobell, in the 1988 Guthrie Theater production of *Playing with Fire* by Barbara Field, adapted from the Mary Shelley novel, directed by Michael Maggio. Set design by John Arnone and costumes by Jack Edwards. Photo credit: Joe Giannetti.

CONTEXTUAL NOTES ON *PLAYING WITH FIRE*

Did I request thee, Maker, from my Clay
To mould me Man? Did I solicit thee
From darkness to promote me?

Adam, from John Milton's *Paradise Lost*

Garland Wright asked me to prepare an adaptation of Mary Shelley's *Franken-stein* for a national tour that would terminate with a run on the Guthrie's main stage. After rereading the novel, I was elated and dismayed: The ideas were challenging and important, yet the writing itself failed to move me. I wanted to back out, suggesting that there were a dozen conventional adaptations in existence that might serve. At that point Garland asked me, "What do *you* see?"

"I see two old men sitting on Regency chairs on an ice floe, having the conversation that never appeared in the novel."

To my amazement, Garland encouraged me to write a "response" to the novel. Generous and trusting of him, but I was aware that the national tour had already been sold, and that I would have to incorporate some part of the novel to satisfy ticket holders.

I started by asking the questions that I (as the Creature) wanted to ask my creator. "Why did you make me?" "Since you made me, why did you not love me?" "If you could not love me, why didn't you make practical use of me for the good of humanity?"

Mary Shelley had killed her mother — that is, Mary Wollestonecraft had died giving birth to her daughter. And Mary Shelley, herself, had suffered still-born babies, and she had had childbed fever as a teenager. From this pain and sorrow, she made a creative leap in a dream about creating a living being in a laboratory with no harm to the maker. Thus young Victor Frankenstein is given powerful reasons to do the same thing.

I arrived at a play with *two* man-made creatures, the older one simply called the Creature and the newborn incarnation named Adam. Likewise, there are two scientists: Frankenstein, the old man, and Victor, the student who creates Adam. Frankenstein has arrived at the top of the world and the end of his life; Victor is his remembered vision of himself at the beginning of his journey.

And what did this creature look like? Certainly not like Boris Karloff. In the end, I found the drawings of William Blake, with their faintly limned anatomical details to be apt. This is no monster, but a machine of some elegance. I still wonder if, in a future production the Creature and Frankenstein might bear a strong familial resemblance.

During the writing of the early drafts, I had the enviable help of Michael Lupu, a dramaturg of the European school, who was meticulous and challenging about every idea, every scene, every comma. As we worked on, particularly in rehearsals, he was far better able to articulate my ideas than I was. He became my white knight, defender of the text. No playwright should be without a dramaturg like Lupu!

One day, early on, Garland suggested that we pick a scenic designer who would be an active artistic voice throughout the process. We both agreed that John Arnone could best translate my vision onto the stage. And so he did. There was no fake snow on the stage in this universe. Instead it had the austerity of an operating room or lab, trapped inside a prismatic world of quartz crystal. Much later, the late Michael Maggio came on board as director.

The show toured for five months, and I was able to fly around the country to watch it with audiences — a luxury few theaters can afford to give writers. I made changes that were included when the play opened at the Guthrie in July 1988.

PLAYING WITH FIRE
Adapted for The Guthrie Theater by Barbara Field

Director . . . . Michael Maggio
Set Designer . . . . John Arnone
Costume Designer . . . . Jack Edwards
Lighting Designer . . . . Marcus Dilliard
Sound Designer . . . . John Calder
Dramaturg . . . . Michael Lupu
Stage Manager . . . . Russell Johnson
Casting Consultant for the Guthrie . . . . Jason LaPadura
Chicago Casting Consultants . . . . Doug Finlayson,
Dennis McCullough

CAST

FRANKENSTEIN . . . . Stephen Pelinski
THE CREATURE . . . . Peter Syvertsen
VICTOR . . . . Curzon Dobell
ADAM, THE CREATURE . . . . John Carroll Lynch
ELIZABETH . . . . Olivia Birkelund
PROFESSOR KREMPE . . . . Michael Tezla

PLACE
The North Pole, and various stops in a voyage of memory.

TIME
The summer solstice — the last day or the first day, depending on point of view.

Playing with Fire

ACT I

An oak tree. A blinding flash of lightning, then blackness. A light comes up on the Creature, standing above, his back to us. He is staring into the distance. Then slowly, a light comes up below on Frankenstein. He is looking at the Creature. Slowly he raises a pistol and aims it at him. A beat. He speaks.

FRANKENSTEIN: Do you dream?
  (The Creature starts, amazed.)
  Do you sleep?
  (The Creature turns, sees the pistol. He does not move.)
  Do you know the word *funicular*? One of those little railway cars that travels up the mountainside? We've got them in Switzerland.
  (He forgets the pistol, his arm drops.)
  We'd go on outings: Papa and Mama, Cousin Elizabeth and me. I was a child —
  Why am I talking to you?
  (He jerks the pistol up again. A beat.)
  The funny thing about funiculars . . . there are no stops along the way, no place where you can simply hop out in transit. You've got to hang on till the very top.
  (Again, the pistol is forgotten.)
  I was frightened, riding up the side of the mountain. Do you understand *frightened*?
  (Creature freezes. Finally.)
CREATURE: Yes. *(A pause.)* You have not spoken a word in years.
FRANKENSTEIN: Centuries.
CREATURE: When you finally speak, you speak of funiculars?
  (He starts down the stairs. He is curious but wary.)
FRANKENSTEIN: Yes. Death is creeping up my body, I'm rotting —
CREATURE: No.
FRANKENSTEIN: Which is hilarious when you stop to think —
CREATURE: NO!
  (A long pause.)
FRANKENSTEIN: Have I caught you yet?

CREATURE: Not yet. Tomorrow, perhaps.

FRANKENSTEIN: Damn our ritual!

(He sits suddenly, puts down his pack.)

CREATURE: What?

FRANKENSTEIN: This blood-hunt has eroded into mere formality. Like that tribe in Africa: the man enacts the ritual of birth, even the screams, while his wife slips behind a bush and bears the child in silence.

(Sound of a girl's voice singing a lullaby.)

CREATURE: There are no wives here.

FRANKENSTEIN: I was speaking of our ritual: revenge.

CREATURE: To me that is no ritual, but if you have changed your mind —

FRANKENSTEIN: No, I will kill you. Tonight. God knows I've tried long enough. And failed. *(A pause.)* Where are we?

CREATURE: At the top of the world.

(Frankenstein rises eagerly, grabs his stick.)

FRANKENSTEIN: The very top? *(He scrambles up the stairs, looking over the terrain. His gait is uneven, stomping, as if he were unsure of the ground beneath his feet, which is true, for his feet are numb.)* Have we been here before? *(He searches the landscape.)* If the earth were flat, we'd fall off the edge, now. *(He stumbles, steadies himself.)* Diagnosis: Ischaemia of the tissue, gangrene, necrosis . . . Blood poisoning. Prognosis: I'm dying.

CREATURE: DON'T DIE! *(Echoing his howl, a woman's scream.)* Don't . . .

(Frankenstein rips off his sunglasses, rubs his eyes.)

FRANKENSTEIN: The sun —

(He looks up, sees Elizabeth, who has entered with a lamp. She smiles, comes to him.)

FRANKENSTEIN: It makes my eyes burn. *(He touches her cheek, but speaks to the Creature.)* Do your eyes tear? Do you cry?

CREATURE: You achieved even that.

FRANKENSTEIN: Fascinating. I don't cry. *(He lies down.)* I'm tired now, I want to rest.

(The echo of a lullaby. Elizabeth kneels beside him, smooths his eyes shut, then leaves with her lamp. While this is happening, the Creature opens Frankenstein's pack. He pulls out a lens and studies it curiously.)

FRANKENSTEIN: Don't run away while I sleep because I won't know which way to follow — How silly of me. At the top of the world, all directions are the same: south. *(The sound of a pistol, distorted.)* Why is the damned sun still up? It shines in my eyes.

CREATURE: It hangs in the sky without moving. It will not set —

FRANKENSTEIN: The solstice! *(He scrambles down the stairs with his stick.)* The summer solstice! It won't get dark tonight —

CREATURE: I am glad! I hate the dark.

FRANKENSTEIN: Something atavistic built into you, no doubt, a primitive terror.

CREATURE: The first time I saw the moon rise, I was alone in a wood and afraid. When I saw it sail up into the sky, I yelled and flung myself on the ground in a frenzy of joy. As long as there was light in the sky, I was not alone. The worst thing is to be alone. *(Again, the woman's scream.)* You tremble.

FRANKENSTEIN: I'm on fire, burning, which is ironic, since I happen to be sitting on a pile of ice. Do you understand irony? How could you, you lack context. *(A beat.)* Something — what? — is different tonight.

CREATURE: The sun — like a mirror — ?

(He studies the sun in the lens.)

FRANKENSTEIN: A lens.

CREATURE: And you have broken silence. Why?

FRANKENSTEIN: Why? Because you've slowed down, you've come within earshot. You used to keep a safe distance.

CREATURE: So you would not sneak up and kill me in my sleep.

FRANKENSTEIN: I should kill you now.

CREATURE: Go ahead. Shoot. Is your pistol rusty?

FRANKENSTEIN: *(He shoots the pistol into the air.)* Kill you with my bare hands. If I could stand to touch you.

CREATURE: If you could catch me.

FRANKENSTEIN: Put that down, it's mine.

(The Creature puts the lens down.)

Well? Why have you let me come so close?

CREATURE: Why did you choose to speak, after all these years?

FRANKENSTEIN: What do you want?

CREATURE: Talk with me, man to man —

FRANKENSTEIN: Don't be insolent!

(He picks up the lens.)

CREATURE: It is my right.

(Frankenstein shines the lens in his eyes.)

FRANKENSTEIN: You have no rights, you homoplastic junkyard. You are a piece of junk — a found object.

CREATURE: Stop!

(Frankenstein puts the lens down.)

CREATURE: You think you have hunted me for years? No, I have led you on, farther and farther away from your world, for one reason. *(Pause.)* So what is one day more or less? One day: a truce. Tomorrow we can start again.

FRANKENSTEIN: So you're finally beginning to get tired! *(A beat.)* Do you get tired? *(A beat.)* A one-day truce? Look at that sun, see? Motionless. How will you know when one day ends and the next begins.

CREATURE: When all the questions have been answered, then it will be tomorrow. I have many questions —

FRANKENSTEIN: Let me refer you to a good library.

CREATURE: The answers I seek are not in books. I know, for I have spent time in the best library in the world!

FRANKENSTEIN: There's a joke — you in a library.

CREATURE: I can read.

FRANKENSTEIN: Can you?!

CREATURE: I have read *Paradise Lost,* the history of your race.

FRANKENSTEIN: That's myth, not history. How did you —

CREATURE: It is the truth —

FRANKENSTEIN: Wrong! History is fact — observed events. No one ever recorded Adam's fall.

CREATURE: Its truth lies here, in the spirit, in the essence.

FRANKENSTEIN: You're pointing to your thorax. *(He stomps away, sits.)* I'm at the top of the world, talking philosophy with a monster . . . paradise lost, indeed. *(A beat.)* How did you learn to read?

CREATURE: You agree then, to the truce?

FRANKENSTEIN: Who taught you? I need to know —
    (Sound of a gunshot.)

CREATURE: First I ask a question and you answer; then it is your turn.

FRANKENSTEIN: For how long must I endure this catechism?

CREATURE: Until I know.

FRANKENSTEIN: Know what?

CREATURE: Until the sky grows dark. At that moment I shall surrender. You may kill me.

FRANKENSTEIN: I will kill you, and after . . . . *(He takes a journal and writing implement out of his pack and waits, pen poised.)* Well? Go on, your first question?
    (A long pause.)

CREATURE: Why do you hate me?

FRANKENSTEIN: Because you're hideous. Now it's my turn: Why did you destroy my life?

CREATURE: Because you hate me.

FRANKENSTEIN: You see? We're mired in verbal quicksand already.

(He puts down his pen, turns away.)

CREATURE: Please. I shall make it worth your while.

FRANKENSTEIN: What can you give me?

CREATURE: The contents of my mind.

FRANKENSTEIN: How you prioritize data? How you make choices? How you dream? Damn my curiosity! *(He takes up his pen.)* All right, start again.

CREATURE: Why do you not look at me?

FRANKENSTEIN: Because you're ugly.

CREATURE: How do you know, if you will not look at me?

FRANKENSTEIN: I'm acquainted with your face, to my sorrow.

(Again, the woman's scream, off.)

CREATURE: You do not know the meaning of the word *sorrow.* Besides, if you do not look, how will you aim your pistol when the time comes? How?

(Young Victor is pacing, anxious and terrified.)

FRANKENSTEIN: With mirrors, I'll do it with mirrors.

(He picks up the fragment, catches the light. A scream, off. The boy covers his ears with his hands and increases the tempo of his pacing. He sings to himself, trying to drown out the screams.)

VICTOR: Glory now to thee be given,

On earth as in the highest heaven.

With lute and harp in sweetest tone —

(The scream. His hands go over his ears again. He intones rapidly.) I swear to surrender my will to God, I'll go to church every day, I'll submit to Papa, too, I'll do whatever he asks, if she'll only stop screaming, and I swear I'll never sink into sin only please don't let her scream, also I'll never again think of Cousin Elizabeth's body if the screaming will stop — *(The remorseless scream. He curls into a ball of woe, rocks on the floor.)* Ourfatherwhichartinheavenhallowedbethynamethykingdomcomethy willbedoneonearthasitisinheavengiveusthisdayourdailybreadandfor giveusthytrespasses —

(A final wrenching scream, then silence. Then the frail cry of a newborn infant. Victor uncurls his body and sits on the floor exhausted and forlorn.)

ELIZABETH: *(Off.)* Victor?

VICTOR: Mama? Is it you?

ELIZABETH: Victor, where are you?

VICTOR: Elizabeth?

(Elizabeth enters with a lamp, sees him on the floor. She is his age, and pretty.)

ELIZABETH: You have a little brother. She said if it was a boy we must call him

William, after your father. William's such a sober name for that tiny —
Victor, your mother — she's dead.

(He flinches, turns away.)

ELIZABETH: I'm sorry, I really am.

VICTOR: Why? It's not your fault.

ELIZABETH: I only meant . . .

VICTOR: I knew she was dead. I knew the moment you stepped into the room
instead of Papa. Poor Cousin Elizabeth, always stuck with the dirty-work.

ELIZABETH: I'm not.

VICTOR: If she had lived, Papa'd be in here crowing like a barnyard rooster,
wouldn't he?

ELIZABETH: Don't do that.

VICTOR: Did you watch it being born? Did you see my mother die?

*(Frankenstein eagerly starts up the stairs, but stops halfway up, listening like
a spy.)*

ELIZABETH: I stood outside the door till after. The doctor came out and left
it ajar. Uncle closed her eyes and folded her hands, then he tried to say
a prayer, only he forgot the words so he kept starting over again to get it
right, only he couldn't. Justine told him it didn't matter, she said the mistress would fly up to heaven whether or not the master knew the words
to his prayer. Then Uncle began to cry.

VICTOR: Did he?

ELIZABETH: It was awful, Victor: The baby crying, and Uncle, and — I've never
heard Justine speak to him that way, and he didn't even notice. *(She begins to cry.)* I'm sorry, I can't stop crying.

(He gives her his handkerchief, feels her wet cheek curiously.)

VICTOR: I don't understand tears — I mean, the mechanism — why those ducts
suddenly activate — no physiological stimulus — it's not in any of my
books —

ELIZABETH: You ought to go see her.

VICTOR: See her?

ELIZABETH: View her.

VICTOR: I've never actually seen a corpse.

ELIZABETH: Are you scared? I'll come with you.

VICTOR: I'd like it better if I could go alone. Is Justine with the baby?

(She nods.)

VICTOR: Good. You take Papa down to the parlor. That's it, he's got to make
arrangements. For the funeral, that will keep him busy —

ELIZABETH: Why must he be kept busy? She's his wife, isn't she?

VICTOR: Was.

ELIZABETH: Was. Why don't you cry? It's permitted, your father did.

VICTOR: I'm going to watch her now.

(He goes out, taking the lamp.)

ELIZABETH: Victor? *(She turns to Frankenstein, smiles.)* It will be all right, I promise. I'll make it all right . . . *(She goes.)*

(Frankenstein jolts himself away from her memory, turns to the Creature.)

FRANKENSTEIN: It's my turn. *(He studies the Creature speculatively.)* Do you know the word *riddle?* My next question's in the form of a riddle: "Brothers and sisters have I none, but that man's father is my father's son." Who is "that man"?

CREATURE: But you had a brother.

FRANKENSTEIN: Don't be so literal-minded! Come on, it's a kind of test. Try. "Brothers and sisters have I none, but that man's father is my father's son."

(Somewhere, the sound of a pistol shot.)

CREATURE: What you said before, about touching me —

FRANKENSTEIN: Don't change the subject.

CREATURE: I am the subject.

FRANKENSTEIN: No, you're the object. You are an object. You're a miscalculation — no, a disaster.

CREATURE: You try to use words as weapons, but I have endured worse wounds.

FRANKENSTEIN: *(He takes up his pen eagerly.)* Have you? When? Where? Tell me.

CREATURE: My introduction to the society of men: I wandered into a village. At the sight of me, the children screamed. A woman fainted. The men of the village set upon me with stones and cudgels. I escaped into open country, nursing my wounds as I ran. In the next village, it happened again. I learned to travel by night. *(He moves toward Frankenstein angrily.)* Why are you writing it down? *(He tries to grab the journal.)* Look at me! Touch me!

FRANKENSTEIN: Odious.

CREATURE: Once you touched every part of me.

FRANKENSTEIN: You were only an abstraction then. Now you're real. *(Sound of a pistol shot.)* I'm collecting data. *(He opens the journal again.)* I need to test your ability to reason.

CREATURE: I can think as well as the next man. Better!

(He stalks up the stairs.)

FRANKENSTEIN: Come back — there are things I must measure, intangible things like language, inductive and deductive logic —

CREATURE: Measure away, I can do it all: logic, mathematics, language. And I have other, more shadowy accomplishments.

(Victor appears, below.)

FRANKENSTEIN: Such as?

CREATURE: Anger, grief, lust . . . love.

(Victor pauses to write those words into Frankenstein's journal.)

FRANKENSTEIN: I have been successful beyond my wildest dreams!

(He and Victor glance at each other, Victor exits.)

CREATURE: Then you acknowledge me?

FRANKENSTEIN: As an equal? No, never. As the creation of a fabulist, yes, the ogre from a fairy tale — do you know "fairy tale"?

CREATURE: "Once upon a time"?

FRANKENSTEIN: Yes.

CREATURE: Tell me one.

FRANKENSTEIN: I'm not your nanny, for God's sake! I'm trying to study you, for the sake of my records.

(Victor appears above.)

FRANKENSTEIN: All right. Once upon a time there was a young prince . . .

(He looks up at Victor, hesitates.)

CREATURE: And?

FRANKENSTEIN: Who lived and labored in an enchanted tower, high above the earth.

CREATURE: Is there going to be a princess?

FRANKENSTEIN: No. No princess.

CREATURE: Did the prince have magical powers?

FRANKENSTEIN: No. *(He looks up at Victor, who nods.)* Yes.

CREATURE: What could he do?

FRANKENSTEIN: He could turn an equation into flesh.

(Victor turns and goes off.)

CREATURE: Why?

FRANKENSTEIN: He was a builder.

CREATURE: Why was he a builder?

FRANKENSTEIN: Why, why, you're just like my little brother — no, I must be mad, you are like nothing else in this world!

CREATURE: True. *(Impatiently.)* Once upon a time, there was a prince in a tower . . .

FRANKENSTEIN: With the vision of a poet and the heart of a philanthropist. Are you following me?

CREATURE: Yes.

FRANKENSTEIN: He built . . . *(A pause.)* An architectural frame of some 200 parts, bound together with flexible cables and supported by a series of levers, pulleys and cranes, which worked together to locomote the frame. Then he padded it with insulation and wrapped it in a thin protective skin.

CREATURE: Did the machine have a motor?

FRANKENSTEIN: Oh yes, an excellent motor lay at its core, fueled by a blend of sugar, iron, albumen, salt, fat —

CREATURE: Did it fly?

FRANKENSTEIN: What?

CREATURE: Did it fly?

FRANKENSTEIN: No.

CREATURE: What did the prince's machine do?

FRANKENSTEIN: Do? What do you mean, "What did it do?" Nothing.

CREATURE: It did nothing?

FRANKENSTEIN: It had a series of electrical impulses, which traveled from a kind of data bank, through a labyrinth of circuits, in order to transmit messages.

CREATURE: And? And?

FRANKENSTEIN: And that's all; it lived. *(Suddenly very bitter.)* They lived . . . happily ever after. Since I was kind enough to tell you a story, the least you can do is answer my riddle!

CREATURE: Brothers and sisters have I none, but that man's father is my father's son. "That man" is your son.

FRANKENSTEIN: Correct.

CREATURE: The prince . . . how long did it take him?

FRANKENSTEIN: Two years from the time he dreamed up the idea until the moment when he switched on his machine.

CREATURE: Two years! I cannot think why he bothered to build a machine with no function. Why? What was the point?

(Sound of a woman screaming, distorted and attenuated.)

FRANKENSTEIN: The point?! Nature's cruelty was the point.

CREATURE: What does that mean? Nature is never cruel. Men are.

FRANKENSTEIN: What about women?

CREATURE: Women are also cruel.

FRANKENSTEIN: No, I mean that nature is cruel to women. A woman must lug those bits around inside her for nine months — tedious, not to say risky. And after gestation, the poor creature's born helpless, dependent on others for years.

CREATURE: But it seems a very efficient process.

FRANKENSTEIN: Except for one thing: the cost to the vessel. She can be hurt, she may even die trying to accomplish what I did at no risk in my laboratory.

CREATURE: I am gratified that my birth was so easy —

FRANKENSTEIN: Clever machine — you've got irony, after all!

CREATURE: I learned it from you. Even as we speak you provide — what did you call it? — context. Yes, much context for bitter irony.

(Elizabeth enters.)

VICTOR: *(Off.)* Elizabeth . . .

(Elizabeth smiles at Frankenstein and puts her finger to her lips, shushing.)

CREATURE: I ought to thank you.

FRANKENSTEIN: I'm delighted that I can enrich your experience.

(He takes her hand as she passes, kisses it.)

CREATURE: That is the duty of a parent, is it not? Education.

VICTOR: *(He enters, above.)* Elizabeth . . . there you are.

CREATURE: One thing makes me sad: there was no princess in your story . . .

(Victor carries some books, his hat. He comes down to Elizabeth.)

VICTOR: I couldn't squeeze these into my trunk, after all. Here, coz, *The Sorrows of Young Werther* and some scientific texts.

(He places them into her arms.)

ELIZABETH: Won't you need them at University?

VICTOR: The texts are old, practically medieval. Maybe they'll remind you of me.

ELIZABETH: Why, Cousin, because they're dense and impenetrable?

(Their laughter is uncomfortable.)

VICTOR: Maybe you don't want to think of me.

ELIZABETH: Justine's packed you such a hamper, all your favorites, enough food for ten men, really —

VICTOR: In case I run into a famine on the road. Good old Justine, she anticipates every emergency.

ELIZABETH: It's hard for her to let you go.

VICTOR: It won't be so long, a couple of years, three at most.

ELIZABETH: Hardly an eternity. I'll be twenty.

VICTOR: Yes. Well. I've said good-bye to Papa and William. Coz —

(She fumbles in her apron pocket, pulls out a little packet.)

ELIZABETH: I'd better give you this before I forget.

VICTOR: Coz, you didn't buy —

ELIZABETH: And if you don't like it, please feel free to —

VICTOR: I didn't remember to get you anything.

ELIZABETH: That doesn't matter, only I'm afraid you'll think my gift is presumptuous, that it's —

VICTOR: What's presumptuous, what do you mean? *(It is a miniature portrait in a gold frame.)* It's Mother . . . a portrait in miniature.

ELIZABETH: I had it copied from the one Uncle wears. It's a good job, isn't it?

VICTOR: Excellent, a superior likeness. Why do you think I'd find this presumptuous?

ELIZABETH: Because on the other side, there is another portrait . . .

(He turns it over.)

VICTOR: Elizabeth —

ELIZABETH: I'm ashamed.

VICTOR: Why? It's beautiful.

ELIZABETH: Foisting myself on you . . . in miniature. You'd better go, you'll be late for the coach.

VICTOR: Wait — I'm not good at this. Grown-ups speak in a kind of code, even you, lately. I don't understand it, I only know that once upon a time . . .

ELIZABETH: Once upon a time we were the best of playmates, weren't we?

VICTOR: Yes, then something changed. What? *(He sighs, looks down at her portrait.)* Whoever painted this, he's caught you . . .

FRANKENSTEIN: Have I caught you yet?

CREATURE: Not yet.

VICTOR: I'm glad. It means I can take you with me, in my pocket. *(He turns it over to look at the other side.)* Ever since Mama died, I've been burning to get out of here.

ELIZABETH: I know.

VICTOR: You still don't understand why I've got to go, do you?

ELIZABETH: You think you've some kind of vocation. Like a priest.

VICTOR: I want to learn to help people. But not as priests do, saving souls. There's another kind of salvation, if I can learn the way. And I will, if you have faith in me, coz.

ELIZABETH: With all my heart.

(He flips the miniature, pensively.)

VICTOR: Elizabeth, Mama once told me . . . she wanted you for me.

ELIZABETH: I know.

VICTOR: When she told me, I was astonished! It had never occurred to me that you didn't belong to me. Did I take you too much for granted?

ELIZABETH: If her wish is in any way distasteful to you —

VICTOR: Distasteful! I was always an obedient son, eager to do what she asked — look at me, please.

CREATURE: Look at me.

(*Frankenstein stares at his miniature. Elizabeth raises her eyes to Victor's.*)

VICTOR: (*He kisses the miniature, pockets it.*) You may breathe, Cousin Elizabeth. We'll marry when I've finished University. It's decided. (*He starts to go.*) Well. I guess we've said it all.

ELIZABETH: Not quite all. I love you, Victor.

VICTOR: Then wait for me . . .

(*He goes.*)

ELIZABETH: I will. I'll make you happy.

FRANKENSTEIN: I remember . . .

CREATURE: What?

FRANKENSTEIN: "Make me happy, and I shall again be virtuous."

ELIZABETH: Only come back to me . . .

(*She goes.*)

FRANKENSTEIN: You said that to me once.

CREATURE: I was bargaining at the time.

FRANKENSTEIN: As if I had the capacity to bring happiness to anyone . . .

CREATURE: I asked little.

FRANKENSTEIN: I gave you all I could, I gave you life.

CREATURE: I never asked to be born.

FRANKENSTEIN: Made.

CREATURE: Made, made, as if changing one word could justify such cruelty! For it was cruelty, wrapped up in sanctimonious platitudes about the salvation of Mankind! Why did you make me?!

(*A thunder clap echoes in the distance.*)

FRANKENSTEIN: When I was a boy . . . I saw a bolt of lightning strike an oak tree in our garden. There was a stream of fire; then, in the next instant, what had been green and filled with the sap of life was only a blasted stump: quite, quite dead. Death impressed me. The next year, my mother died. I sat by her corpse for hours, watching, hoping to catch that moment when the fibrin would coagulate in her tissue, the exact instant when rigor mortis would set in. After three days she began to smile.

CREATURE: She must have been an amiable lady, to smile in death.

FRANKENSTEIN: That was decay. We had to bury her the next day.

CREATURE: In that old churchyard by the lake?

FRANKENSTEIN: It gives the dead a pretty prospect at sunrise. You know the place?

CREATURE: I watched the funeral of your bride —

FRANKENSTEIN: *(He struggles up, in a rage. The Creature eludes him.)* Let me kill him now, let me strike him down!

(He falls. The Creature stops, moves toward him.)

FRANKENSTEIN: She belonged to me — "What God hath joined together, let no man put asunder." Let no monster — My whole life, do you understand, she belonged to me even when I was a child . . .

(The Creature takes the pistol, hands it to Frankenstein, who raises it, aims it at the Creature.)

CREATURE: I have never been a child.

(Frankenstein slowly lowers the pistol. He turns away from the Creature.)

You have not answered my question yet.

FRANKENSTEIN: Oh God! Your legs function, why don't you just go away?

CREATURE: First, my question —

FRANKENSTEIN: Go and leave me to die in peace.

CREATURE: Answer!

(Krempe and Victor appear above. An examination is in progress, Victor stands before the blackboard.)

FRANKENSTEIN: This isn't an examination —

CREATURE: Why did you make me? *(A beat.)* Well, go on —

KREMPE: Well, go on — !

CREATURE: Answer me!

VICTOR: *(Writes.)* Y equals X tangent theta minus one-half GX square of the cosine of theta —

CREATURE: Well? Answer!

KREMPE: Go on, define —

VICTOR: Where X is the horizontal distance, Y is the vertical height, theta is the angle at which the projectile is fired above the horizon, and G is the acceleration of gravity —

KREMPE: Enough!

CREATURE: I shall leave. You will be stranded all alone, without food.

VICTOR: About thirty-two feet per second, per second —

CREATURE: Sooner or later dark will come, and you will be alone. You will die alone.

KREMPE: Enough! You know it, you know everything, so far. So far. But your humble professor wishes to find out what you *don't* know. If you'll kindly turn your attention to Newton's equation for gravity.

VICTOR: *(Writes as he speaks.)* The gravitational force between two bodies varies as one over the square of the distance between then: one over r squared —

(He waits for an interruption, but none comes. Krempe is regarding the equation with wonder, as does Frankenstein.)

FRANKENSTEIN: Beautiful . . .

KREMPE: How beautiful nature is, how harmonious, how exact. Newton must have had an elegant mind, to express Nature's law so simply.

VICTOR: Yes, Professor.

KREMPE: But it didn't stop him from a foolish search for the Philosopher's Stone, did it? Well, what about your mind, Frankenstein?

VICTOR: Professor?

KREMPE: Dip into your vast wealth of knowledge, if you will be so kind, and define the concept of Heat.

VICTOR: Heat is a fluid, which —

KREMPE: Wrong!

VICTOR: Which flows from —

KREMPE: Wrong!

VICTOR: But Professor Krempe

KREMPE: Wrong! Heat was a fluid. Last week. Not any more.

VICTOR: I don't understand, I read that —

KREMPE: I've caught you at last!

VICTOR: But the textbook says —

KREMPE: The textbook? Obsolete! *(He pulls a letter out of his pocket.)* I've just received a letter. Count Rumford has done a new experiment. The game's changed, especially that nonsense about heat as a fluid. Throw it out! Discard it! Heat is now energy, the kinetic energy of motion of the particles composing the matter — it's friction — ! I've suspected as much for some time, but the news came only yesterday.

VICTOR: Then how could I be expected to answer correctly? How could I know?

KREMPE: Oh dear, you look ill — I trust you won't be sick on my floor.

VICTOR: It was a trick question!

KREMPE: Do laugh, Frankenstein. Where's your sense of humor?

VICTOR: I was hoping to pass my examination.

KREMPE: Such a single-minded boy. Well, what lesson have you learned from my poor little joke?

VICTOR: To keep up with the latest experiments?

KREMPE: I'd state it more baldly: Read your professor's mail — as often as you can sneak a look — Oh dear, have I offended your belief in the purity of science? You are an innocent. *(He takes Victor by the arm.)* Listen well: A scientist's responsibility is to find out, to get at the truth by fair means or foul. Then he must publish it to the world; and in this endeavor he must be the first. You understand?

VICTOR: Yes, Professor.

KREMPE: The first. Right now, I want to be the first to find out . . . about you. Such a clever student, with a fine mind. Not as elegant as Newton's, perhaps, but . . . I wonder what you're looking for.

(Victor turns away.)

KREMPE: You're so reserved. Have you an Philosopher's Stone lurking in your dreams? I wonder. Don't be shy, whisper your dreams in my ear. I'll make it worth your while. No? Never mind, where were we?

VICTOR: One over r squared.

KREMPE: Ah, yes, the elegant equation of Isaac Newton —

VICTOR: *(Regards the blackboard again.)* The elegant equation of Henry Cavendish.

KREMPE: I beg your pardon?

VICTOR: Cavendish, Henry. Cambridge University.

KREMPE: Never heard of him. About Newton's equation —

VICTOR: Cavendish. It is the Law of Gravity, yes; it's that and more . . . for it's also the law governing electricity. *(He writes.)* One over r squared, where one equals either the mass, in the case of gravity, or the electrical charge in the case of repulsion of electrically charged spheres.

KREMPE: Is that true? How extraordinary.

VICTOR: Nature is "beautiful," "harmonious," "exact."

KREMPE: And it's the same equation? A disturbing coincidence.

VICTOR: I get letters, too.

KREMPE: The joke's turned on me, how clever of you.

VICTOR: Thank you, professor.

KREMPE: It frightens me, your Exquisite. Precise. Ubiquitous. Universal equation. It implies some great master plan.

VICTOR: You mean a God?

KREMPE: Perhaps. I'm suspicious when the laws of nature behave too harmoniously. It makes me think some ambitious fellow's been fudging the numbers. Do you believe in God?

VICTOR: As a child I did. Now I know what God is.

KREMPE: What?

VICTOR: That. *(He indicates the equation.)* Electricity's at the bottom of everything, of life itself. And I never fudge my numbers, professor, there's no honor in that.

KREMPE: The academic gossip has it that during the past two years, while I thought you were my exclusive property, you have strayed over into the so-called medical sciences. They say you've studied anatomy?

VICTOR: Yes, sir.

KREMPE: Physiology? Galvanism? And other cloudy courses of dubious scientific merit?

VICTOR: Yes.

KREMPE: And you've passed the examinations?

VICTOR: Yes, sir.

KREMPE: Congratulations. But why would a boy with your potential follow such diverse disciplines? If I may posit a theory: You're up to something. What?

VICTOR: I don't know . . . yet. I'm just . . . curious.

KREMPE: Curiosity is a prerequisite for a scientist.

(Victor doodles at the blackboard, the same little equation. He stares at it.)

VICTOR: You want access to my secret dreams? For what it's worth, I'm interested in Life and Death —

KREMPE: My dear boy!

VICTOR: Not the theology, the physics: that instant when an object quickens; and its corollary, the moment of death. Are the two mutually exclusive or are they, perhaps, the same thing? Is death reversible?

KREMPE: A modest agenda.

VICTOR: My canvas will be modest, I promise: a minute section of tissue. I hope to animate it. *(He nods at the equation.)* And that — electricity — will be my passport between Life and Death.

KREMPE: *(He laughs.)* How very interesting.

VICTOR: What about my examination, Professor?

KREMPE: Congratulations, my boy. Summa.

VICTOR: I'm gratified. Have I really passed?

(Krempe nods.)

VICTOR: Then if I may ask one final question —

KREMPE: Anything, my dear boy —

VICTOR: Why do you hate me?

KREMPE: Hate you!? It's not easy being buried alive in Ingolstadt! It's not Cambridge, after all, no one dreams here, no one dares. I've wasted so many years beating knowledge into the brains of imbeciles, that when one bright hope comes along, I don't know how to act! Of all my students you are my bright hope.

VICTOR: I shall always rely on your wisdom, sir.

(A light begins to grow on the creature.)

KREMPE: I hope you mean that. Well, congratulations again. By the way, what kind of tissue do you plan to animate, a piece of grilled sole? Or a cutlet? Or perhaps a Schnitzel!

(They go, with the blackboard.)

FRANKENSTEIN: My obsession with Life and Death was no new whim! Always, even as a child, I was a collector, a classifier . . . I saved all my milk teeth — they're probably still in that green box in my cupboard, next to my fossils and the butterfly collection. Inanimate — no, exanimate objects, all. You see, even before the lightning struck, I was in love with death.

(The light on the Creature is, by now, quite warm. He has been studying his hand, how it works.)

CREATURE: I thought you were in love with —

FRANKENSTEIN: I am trying to explain! Death was as voluptuous as Elizabeth . . . and a lot safer. *(A pause.)* So I fled to Ingolstadt and sought sanctuary in the University . . .

(Krempe appears, below.)

FRANKENSTEIN: I planned to solve life's mysteries there.

KREMPE: Summa. Congratulations.

FRANKENSTEIN: After I passed my examinations I began my real work —

KREMPE: Whisper your dreams in my ear.

FRANKENSTEIN: *(To Krempe.)* My work —

KREMPE: I'll make it worth your while. Don't be shy —

FRANKENSTEIN: *(To the Creature.)* I began by making a small metallic arc — layers of zinc and copper — which I attached to the specimen, a simple bullfrog. When I applied the current, its muscles contracted. A stronger dose: It jumped. A third . . . its flesh began to smoke and burn. *(To Krempe.)* But as I sparked that poor bedraggled scrap into glory, I knew I could not go back, I must carry the experiment to its logical conclusion: a self-sustained, self-propelled unit.

CREATURE: Me.

FRANKENSTEIN: The idea of you.

CREATURE: You still have not told me why. Did it never occur to you that you needed a reason?

FRANKENSTEIN: *(To Krempe.)* It would have been immoral not to pursue such an idea.

CREATURE: Why?

KREMPE: To find out. To be the first.

(He goes.)

FRANKENSTEIN: To be the first! *(A beat.)* Lead into gold — refuse into flesh.

CREATURE: Refuse?!

FRANKENSTEIN: I visited dissecting amphitheaters and never came home empty-handed. I'd search freshly dug graves each night, profaning them with eager hands —

CREATURE: And that is what I'm made of?! Filth! Decay? Death!

FRANKENSTEIN: What did you think I made you of, watch-springs? No, your origins are sordid.

CREATURE: Horrible! To rob the sleeping dead —

FRANKENSTEIN: They raised no objections. Indeed, their ghosts may thank me: I've won them a kind of immortality —

CREATURE: Robbed them of their eternal rest — you are the worst kind of thief!

FRANKENSTEIN: How quick you are to judge — have you never stolen anything?

(The Creature turns away.)

FRANKENSTEIN: Ha — I've struck a nerve! Poor moralistic machine, do you believe in sin? I don't. Where's the sin up here at the top of the world?

CREATURE: If I stole your meat tonight while you slept, would you believe in sin?

FRANKENSTEIN: No, I'd applaud your appetite, your enterprise, and your skill as a thief.

CREATURE: No, you would judge me. You have a morality, a map of good and evil, but I fail to understand what it can be. And I am no thief —
(From his cloak he pulls out a book stealthily, then slowly climbs to the above as.)

FRANKENSTEIN: You lie! You have stolen everything.
(Victor, with an ill-wrapped brown paper parcel under his arm, is helping himself to a small flask of mercury. Krempe is spying on him.)

KREMPE: Who's in there? Stop, thief!

VICTOR: *(Emerging.)* Professor Krempe? *(He drops the parcel.)*

KREMPE: What? Is it — Frankenstein?! I thought some stranger was making off with University property.

VICTOR: I was told I could borrow a bit of mercury —
(Krempe tries to discover the contents of Victor's package during the remainder of the scene.)

KREMPE: So you're back in Ingolstadt.

VICTOR: I'm still in Ingolstadt, Professor.

KREMPE: In your attic all that time? That is devotion to your muse. *(He starts to laugh, then peers into Victor's face.)* But you look dreadful! Have you been sick?

VICTOR: Overworked.

KREMPE: You've been pushing yourself too hard, foolish boy. Get a laboratory assistant, you can afford it.

VICTOR: I prefer to work alone.

KREMPE: Let me recall . . . you were working on some . . . wait, some tissue or other . . . ?

VICTOR: A cutlet, you called it.

KREMPE: And you never laughed at my joke! You Swiss, no sense of humor. Tell me, did your experiment turn out?

(Victor nods.)

KREMPE: My compliments to the chef — oh, forgive me, I am a foolish fellow. Tell me —

VICTOR: Professor, if an astonishing power were suddenly placed in your hands, what would you do with it?

KREMPE: Me? I'd probably drop it. *(He laughs.)* Seriously, how can I answer your question — it's too vague. You must be more specific . . .

(Victor smiles.)

KREMPE: Please, you can trust me; after all, I was your professor —

VICTOR: And ever will be, sir, world without end. Well, I must be on my way.

KREMPE: I'd rather be your friend. Once I invited you to whisper your dreams to me.

VICTOR: You laughed at them. My experiment worked, Professor Krempe. Now I'm constructing a more complex model.

KREMPE: What can this model be? Let us say a young man, wise in the laws of physics, combines that knowledge with the medical arts. What does it add up to? What indeed. Does this construction have a motor?

VICTOR: A kind of motor.

KREMPE: And its structure — ?

(Victor picks up his parcel, starts to go.)

KREMPE: Victor. Shouldn't someone, a trusted ally, verify your work? I offer myself as collaborator. I could bring a certain credibility to the experiment —

VICTOR: I see. And after you verified?

KREMPE: We'd publish.

VICTOR: Would we? I see. *(A beat.)* I don't think so. I am, as you say, a secretive man.

KREMPE: You're a boy, playing with fire, without a thought to the consequences of your experiment!

VICTOR: Either it will work or it won't.

KREMPE: You're talking about results, not consequences!

VICTOR: What's the difference?

KREMPE: Responsibility. Something I understand!

VICTOR: Oh yes, "responsibility." You used that word once before. "A scientist's first responsibility is to find out, by fair means or foul." *(He glances at one of Krempe's papers, hands it back to him.)* You were right! A true man of science must pursue nature to her hiding place to penetrate her secrets. If in the process he disturbs the natural order . . .

KREMPE: Damn the consequences? I recognize you now, you are the New Man, a true child of the Revolution — You do know what's going on in France? *(Victor shrugs.)*

KREMPE: Social experiment of a high order, very exciting. You see, not all experiments takes place in the laboratory. For example, that clever chemist, Lavoisier — you know him?

VICTOR: I've heard of him.

KREMPE: He's lost his head. He was guillotined in Paris, last month, for no reason except that he was born into the wrong class.

VICTOR: That's a great pity, but what does that have to do with me?

KREMPE: His colleagues — your colleagues — have seized on this social revolution to serve their own ends. I hear they take the decapitated heads of the nobility and apply static electricity to reanimate —

VICTOR: How very interesting.

KREMPE: None of them consider the consequences, either. But they will get burned — That mustn't happen to you — I can prevent it. *(A beat.)* My offer of help still stands. I promise not to betray your secrets. Though secrets have a way of getting out into the world — What's that you've got in the butcher's paper?

VICTOR: *(Glances at Frankenstein, who mouths the answer.)* A . . . leg of mutton.

KREMPE: Good. Cook it with rosemary. The fragrance will be heavenly.

(He goes off, Victor goes the other way. The Creature is miles away in his mind.)

FRANKENSTEIN: Resurrection men.

(The Creature turns to him, startled.)

FRANKENSTEIN: That's what they used to call them . . . grave robbers. I was a resurrection man. There's a well-turned irony for you . . . religious metaphor . . .

(The Creature moves toward him anxiously.)

CREATURE: Once, under cover of darkness, I entered a great vaulted church built all of stones. There was music. The air was filled with perfume. There were many people; they paid me no attention, for they were busy at something.

FRANKENSTEIN: Prayer.

CREATURE: Prayer is a kind of ecstacy, is it not? I longed to share their passion. I did not know how. I could feel nothing in that stone hall. The music was beautiful. Do you pray? *(The Creature starts down the stairs.)*

FRANKENSTEIN: No.

CREATURE: Can you explain their ecstacy?

FRANKENSTEIN: Once, in my laboratory — I raised your heart high above my head — "Introibo ad altare dei" Then I lowered it inside the cavity of your chest —

(The Creature draws close to him, fascinated.)

FRANKENSTEIN: Don't come any nearer!

CREATURE: Do I intrude into a forbidden place? Maybe I have secrets too, forbidden to you.

(A pause.)

FRANKENSTEIN: What secrets?

CREATURE: Aha! You have come back to me.

FRANKENSTEIN: You cheated.

CREATURE: I am afraid to be alone.

FRANKENSTEIN: Afraid of loneliness, afraid of the dark — any other phobias? *(Beat.)* Tell me the thoughts you have in the dark.

CREATURE: You must know — you made me.

FRANKENSTEIN: Your mind wasn't part of my original calculation — your imagination wasn't. I failed in that.

CREATURE: Your failures are countless. You built a man without memory, without data. You gave him life, then you abandoned him.

FRANKENSTEIN: Tell me your secrets.

CREATURE: Dissect my brain and pluck them out.

FRANKENSTEIN: If I thought I could access your mind by anatomizing your brain, I'd have done it long ago. Your brain was the trickiest part, so many tiny microscopic connections, so delicate — you say you had no memory?

CREATURE: None before that first awful moment. The slate had been wiped clean.

FRANKENSTEIN: Your brain was slippery and cool to the touch. As I labored on you, my own brain boiled in my skull. The rest of you was ready now, your body symmetrical and perfect —

CREATURE: Perfect?!

FRANKENSTEIN: I made you without blemish. And — this touch of whimsy will amuse you — I made you without a navel.

CREATURE: What's a navel? Do you have one?

FRANKENSTEIN: Everybody has one.

CREATURE: And I none?

FRANKENSTEIN: It's what you have in common with Adam.

CREATURE: You said there was no Adam!

FRANKENSTEIN: Listen to me! You lay there, complete at last, my masterpiece. And I — my heart was racing in a fever of excitement — I thought I would explode!

(The laboratory suddenly explodes into sight, above.)

FRANKENSTEIN: Two years of my life, alone in that cold attic, all for this next few moments. Soon I would know! I walked around the table, drinking you in, my mind racing back through a labyrinth of graphs, calculations, charts . . . to the very beginning.

(Victor stands over the table where Adam lies.)

VICTOR: It's done.

FRANKENSTEIN: My hands were shaking, I was so nervous.

VICTOR: The Voltaic towers are in position.

CREATURE: I wish to God you had never begun —

FRANKENSTEIN: Have you checked everything?

VICTOR: I've gone over the steps a dozen times.

FRANKENSTEIN: Watch out — the metallic arcs have slipped.

VICTOR: The arcs — reattached —

FRANKENSTEIN: I haven't forgotten anything.

CREATURE: Me, master. You have forgotten me.

(As Frankenstein becomes more and more involved in the creation, the Creature separates himself more and more. He is desolate.)

VICTOR: It's all there, ready, the frontier . . . .

CREATURE: Once you start, you cannot go back. Please —

VICTOR: It is God's will that I cross the line.

FRANKENSTEIN: Begin passage of the Galvanic fluid —

CREATURE: Look at me, master —

VICTOR: Ready —

CREATURE: NO!

FRANKENSTEIN: Apply the divine spark!

(He turns and looks directly at the Creature, as Victor animates the body on the table.)

VICTOR: NOW!

(There is a storm of electricity. Adam opens his eyes and extends his arms.)

END OF ACT I

ACT II

Above: Adam is crouched on the table, Victor stares at him, Frankenstein is on the stairs, gazing up, rapt (Adoration of the Magi). *The Creature stands apart. The pistol lies on the ground, next to the journal and mirror. There is silence, then:*

CREATURE: I remember my beginning. One moment darkness, the void. The next, chaos, a confusion of information. Silence-light, darkness-warmth, cold-noise.

(Frankenstein opens his journal and starts to write his notes.)

FRANKENSTEIN: Disorganized data.

CREATURE: I heard, smelled, saw, all at once.

FRANKENSTEIN: *(Writes.)* Simultaneous functioning of senses.

CREATURE: A strong light pressed against my eyes, so I shut them. Darkness. Fear overwhelmed me. I opened my eyes and light poured inside me again. Fear ebbed.

FRANKENSTEIN: Were you afraid of the dark even in that first moment?

CREATURE: Even then.

(Frankenstein writes.)

CREATURE: I did not know what I was.

But I did know there was an I.

(Adam looks up and sees Victor.)

CREATURE: Then I saw the Other. At first I thought this Other was myself, or an extension of myself. It declared its independence by moving its lips. Noise came out.

(Victor speaks, but his words are garbled.)

CREATURE: Sounds without content, gestures without meaning. I knew that we were separate beings, yet bound together.

FRANKENSTEIN: What do you mean, you "knew" — ?

CREATURE: Knew it here, in my heart!

FRANKENSTEIN: You're pointing to your stomach.

CREATURE: At the sight of you, a sweet longing stole through my body . . . it must be thus with infants. I held out my arms, without knowing why . . .

(Adam stretches out his arms to Victor. He utters a soft cry. Victor backs off in horror.)

VICTOR: Oh, horrible, horrible!

CREATURE: Your disgust was clear, even to one with no context. I felt shame.

FRANKENSTEIN: Yet you presumed to stretch out your arms again.

CREATURE: Love overwhelmed me!

VICTOR: Keep away! Oh my God, keep away! What went wrong? What went wrong?

CREATURE: Pain-fear-shame . . . your gifts to me on the day of my birth.

(Victor, hysterical, takes a rope and ties Adam to the table, sobbing as he binds him.)

FRANKENSTEIN: My mind was reeling from the horror — I couldn't think —

(Adam cries helplessly.)

CREATURE: Because you were so preoccupied with my creation that you gave no thought to the instant after creation —

FRANKENSTEIN: I didn't know what to do with you!

(Victor runs off in horror.)

CREATURE: So you imprisoned my body; just as you had imprisoned my soul in ugliness —

(The Creature takes up the mirror fragment and studies his reflection.)

FRANKENSTEIN: Can't you see, I was obsessed with the problem, not the aesthetics of the problem. I chose your parts for their durability!

CREATURE: O wonderful! You made me deformed, then sent me into the world helpless against the ridicule your race heaped on me.

(He sets down the mirror fragment.)

You should have killed me then.

FRANKENSTEIN: How could I kill you? You worked! Your heart pumped, your brain functioned perfectly! Don't you see? I created you so that I could bring hope to mankind — how could I kill you? *(A beat.)* Beside, I was half-dead myself — delirious with brain fever — I collapsed and knew nothing for weeks — kill you — !? Beside . . . I was proud of my accomplishment.

CREATURE: There is an illogic here. Perhaps I should be measuring you.

FRANKENSTEIN: It's a short step from irony to sarcasm.

CREATURE: I am trying to understand. Where were we? Oh yes, in a typically humane gesture, you left me tied to a table, and then you swooned into your own soft bed —

FRANKENSTEIN: I beg your pardon — !

CREATURE: Valetudinarian — hypochondriac — you get sick at a moment's notice, quite a convenient skill, one I would have cultivated if you had not made my parts so "durable."

FRANKENSTEIN: I think you have just called me a coward.

CREATURE: A moral coward.

FRANKENSTEIN: I admit I failed you — I failed my machine. There, does that soothe your sense of moral outrage?

(Adam begins to stir, on his table.)

CREATURE: I am not a machine! You left me alone in that attic. Darkness came. Fear. Then I felt a keener pang: hunger. Thirst. You had not bothered to feed me. Even a dog gets his bone! *(A beat.)* But you did not come back. Hours passed. I tore free of my bonds and made my way to your chamber, stealing your cloak to hide my nakedness.

(Adam goes off, above.)

CREATURE: I paused to study you, as you lay safely wrapped in your coma. I drank you in, every breath, every muttered sigh. Then you opened your eyes. Your scream pierced my heart. I ran . . . past the town gates, into the woods. *(A beat.)* Night. I wept in terror. Then came the gentle moon, sailing over the trees. It bathed me in its light and for the first time, I tasted joy.

(Frankenstein makes a pretense of trying to write notes in the journal. Victor appears, whispers into Frankenstein's ear, prompting him to ask the next question.)

FRANKENSTEIN: How . . . did you manage to stay alive?

CREATURE: Experiment — I am not your child for nothing.

(Victor laughs at the irony, goes off. Frankenstein turns away.)

CREATURE: Did I say something to make you angry?

FRANKENSTEIN: Not angry.

CREATURE: One cold day I came upon the remnant of a fire. Drawn to the warmth, I thrust my hand into the embers. Trial-error.

FRANKENSTEIN: *(Writes.)* Auto-didact, very clever.

(To the Creature.)

You claim to know how to read.

CREATURE: You need not . . . patronize me. I have read books in the library of the Sorbonne.

FRANKENSTEIN: No one threw stones at you there?

CREATURE: All Paris was a freak show . . . a carnival of horror. No one even noticed me, so I left as I had come, with my head.

FRANKENSTEIN: You're quite proprietary about your head — don't forget, it belonged to someone else first. *(He laughs.)* Laugh, it's a joke! Do you understand jokes?

CREATURE: Not your jokes.

FRANKENSTEIN: Once someone accused me of having no sense of humor. But up here at the top of the world, the strangest things seem hilarious to me — do you think it's my fever? *(A beat.)* Tell me a joke. Go on, I promise I'll laugh.

CREATURE: Once I joined up with a carnival . . . the kind of shabby little fair that travels from town to town. I was given work as a freak.

(Frankenstein smiles encouragingly, he is ready to laugh at the joke.)

CREATURE: I was put on display in the big tent, with all the other freaks.

(Frankenstein laughs, Creature signals to wait.)

CREATURE: I have not come to the joke yet. When the day's work was done, the rest of them removed their makeup, their freakness. They waited for me to do the same. There was nothing to remove. *(He waits.)* You may laugh now.

(Frankenstein's smile has faded. The Creature gives his own version of a laugh. Krempe appears.)

CREATURE: Don't you find it funny?

(Krempe laughs.)

CREATURE: Shall I explain the joke?

(Krempe goes.)

FRANKENSTEIN: There are more important things I need to measure before our time is up . . . before I kill you. Before I die.

CREATURE: You never stop probing, do you? Does your mind ever rest? Why not?

FRANKENSTEIN: Data is meat and drink to me, it restoreth my soul. How did you learn to read? Tell me.

CREATURE: Many weeks after you and I parted company —

FRANKENSTEIN: After you ran away —

CREATURE: After you abandoned me — *(A beat.)* A bitter, black night. Water poured from the sky. At the edge of a dark forest, I came upon a hovel, little more than a sty. Inside it was warm and dry! Light poured through a chink in the wall, for my hovel leaned against a cottage!

FRANKENSTEIN: Inhabited?

CREATURE: A family: old man, son, daughter. Each day I studied them through the hole in the wall. By night I hunted for food. Inside my hovel I was as still as a mouse, they did not know I existed. My teachers.

(Adam appears below.)

FRANKENSTEIN: And you learned language by spying on them?

(Frankenstein turns, notices Adam behind him.)

CREATURE: My tongue was thick, so I practiced in the woods at night. The owls grew used to me.

ADAM: *(Smiling, he demonstrates for Frankenstein. His voice is clumsy.)* Wa . . . ter. Bread. Warm. Fa-ther. Ho-o-ome . . .

(Frankenstein corrects Adam's pronunciation of the word home. *Then Adam goes.)*

CREATURE: My family were poor, exiled from Paris. But they were educated, they owned a book or two. They taught me more than language.

FRANKENSTEIN: Manners?

CREATURE: Affection! The children honored their father; he repaid them with gentleness. I marked that. I studied it. Each evening by firelight, the son read aloud, the history of your race, *Paradise Lost.*

FRANKENSTEIN: I told you, that's a fairy tale.

CREATURE: In time I learned all the words by heart. Then one day, when they were gone from the cottage, I slipped inside and took the book.

FRANKENSTEIN: So you are a thief — I knew it.

CREATURE: Within days I had decoded its tiny black marks. I could read!

FRANKENSTEIN: That's remarkable, truly remarkable.

(He writes furiously in his book. Adam crosses above, pauses to read.)

ADAM: "Did I request thee, Maker, from my clay

To mold me man? Did I solicit Thee

From darkness to promote me?"

(Frankenstein applauds silently, Adam goes out as.)

CREATURE: Adam to his father. He did not ask to be born either . . . .

FRANKENSTEIN: Made. I could never get through that damned poem myself. And I'm not your father. Did you ever meet them face-to-face?

CREATURE: Why have you carried this piece of glass all the way to the top of the world?

FRANKENSTEIN: You've just answered my question with a question. Is this another game? A game-within-a-game?

(The Creature silently holds up the lens.)

FRANKENSTEIN: All right. I use it for fire. For example: If I tumbled into a stream and everything I owned got wet, that glass could still focus the sun's rays well enough to cause combustion.

CREATURE: A pity there's nothing here to burn. *(He plays with the lens.)* If this were mine, I'd flash signals to some distant planet and wait for a friendly answer.

(He puts the mirror down carefully. A pause.)

FRANKENSTEIN: That family, did you ever meet them? Well? Go on.

CREATURE: Outside the cottage. The old man sits in the sunshine. His children have gone walking in the woods. His countenance is so meek, I take the risk and approach. Sir, have you lost a book?

CREATURE: He does not flinch! He answers civilly that his son misplaced a copy of *Paradise Lost*. I found it in the forest, sir. I place the book in his hands. Can you imagine the rapture of my first conversation? First he speaks a thought, then I respond, and then he responds to me — like music, like a dance. Then the girl and boy come back. Here's a woodsman, children. He has brought back our missing book. You might say he's found Paradise. You can guess the rest. But try this for irony: That meek old man, guess why he had been so civil? Because he could not see me. He was blind! Laugh! It is a good joke!

(Frankenstein closes his book.)

FRANKENSTEIN: Did they hurt you?

CREATURE: I was quick to run. And this time I had two weapons: language, which helped me to know that revulsion would always be my fate, and the second — I still wore your cloak! In the pocket was a letter from Geneva, with a return address. I could read it. I would find you now!

FRANKENSTEIN: In my father's house. I was waiting for you . . . .

CREATURE: Did your father love you?

FRANKENSTEIN: I suppose so.

CREATURE: And your mate?

FRANKENSTEIN: Don't profane her memory by speaking of her! Yes. I loved her. I did love her.

(Victor is lying on a blanket asleep, his head in Elizabeth's lap. There is a picnic basket. Victor is having a nightmare.)

VICTOR: No, no! The monster —

ELIZABETH: Victor, wake up, wake up —

VICTOR: The monster —

ELIZABETH: I'm here.

(He opens his eyes, looks around.)

ELIZABETH: It was a dream.

VICTOR: A nightmare. You're in it, in Ingolstadt. You walk down the street toward me. I'm surprised to see you, glad. You hold out your arms and I run to you. I kiss your lips. Your lips become livid with death, your face slowly turns into my dead mother's face, with its grin of corrupted flesh. Maggots crawl across your brow, they make a crunching noise. Then you begin to change again, into a . . . monster. *(He pulls away from her abruptly.)* I hate this . . . weakness.

ELIZABETH: You're getting stronger every day.

VICTOR: I thought here in the sunshine it wouldn't follow me, but . . . *(He grabs the hamper, opens it.)* I'm dying of thirst. *(He removes a bottle of wine.)* A picnic in the sunshine. Perfect. Paradise. Maybe this is the dream.

ELIZABETH: I doubt it. Because an uninvited guest has invaded Eden.

VICTOR: What?!

ELIZABETH: There's a spider crawling on your shirt.

(He opens the wine.)

VICTOR: Did Justine remember to pack glasses?

ELIZABETH: If anything's missing, blame me. I organized the hamper.

(She extracts two glasses, he pours.)

VICTOR: You organize the entire household. Without much thanks, I'll bet.

ELIZABETH: I like to be useful.

VICTOR: Useful — you're irreplaceable. You mother William, Papa is completely dependent on you —

ELIZABETH: And you?

VICTOR: I wouldn't be here without your nursing. *(He toasts.)* Yes indeed, Death's Door and Back Again.

ELIZABETH: It's not funny — we thought we'd lost you. When Uncle brought you back to Geneva, you were half-dead, and raving.

VICTOR: What did I rave about? Did I say anything interesting?

ELIZABETH: There was a monster then, too. You were terrified.

(Victor looks into the hamper.)

VICTOR: What else have we got — I'm starving. *(He pulls out a toy boat.)* Is this edible?

ELIZABETH: I'd try the chicken first.

VICTOR: William's toys are everywhere. But where is William? *(He calls out.)* William . . . Will-iam!

ELIZABETH: He's playing ball down by the water. I did neglect him while you were sick — it's turned him solitary.

VICTOR: Tomorrow I'll take complete charge of him, I'll take him sailing.

ELIZABETH: Sailing! You could hardly make it up the hill today, how can you think of taking a boat out on the lake?

VICTOR: Fishing, then, is that sedate enough for you?

ELIZABETH: Do as you like, I'm not your doctor.

VICTOR: You're not my mother either —

ELIZABETH: I do know that.

VICTOR: Sorry. I'm really much stronger.

ELIZABETH: You're home now, for good. It's been so long since you left us . . .

VICTOR: A lifetime.

ELIZABETH: Do you miss your work? You never talk about it. I'm sure it's very complicated, filled with theories and numbers and . . . I probably wouldn't understand it anyway . . .

VICTOR: In Ingolstadt I had a workshop. I built things there.

ELIZABETH: What things?

VICTOR: It doesn't matter, it's finished, my work gave me bad dreams.

(He puts his head back in her lap, closes his eyes.)

FRANKENSTEIN: Do you dream? Of things that happened before I made you? Of what?

CREATURE: My family in the woods. I dream I knock on the cottage door, they open it, and when they see me —

FRANKENSTEIN: What?

CREATURE: Their faces light up with welcome. They pull me inside and shut the door against the night. From the fireplace, warmth and light embrace me. My family push me down into a good chair, right next to the old man. They feed me. Then I wake up.

FRANKENSTEIN: That's always the hard part.

(Elizabeth and Victor, as before.)

ELIZABETH: In my dream, we're sailing on a vast sea. The waves swell and rock the ship, but very gently, so we're not afraid. Children play on the deck — one of them slips under the railing, about to tumble into the sea. But you grab him just in time and he looks up at you and laughs. The sea grows calm.

VICTOR: That's you. Calm seas.

ELIZABETH: Calm surface. I've never been to sea — I've hardly been out of Switzerland.

VICTOR: I'll take you —

ELIZABETH: To Ingolstadt?

VICTOR: Don't speak of that place.

ELIZABETH: But your work . . . when we're married, I'll help you. Victor? Since you've come home, there are times — you seem to look through me, as if you were searching for another face, listening for another footfall. Is someone waiting for you in Ingolstadt? I'll release you — anything, to make you happy.

VICTOR: Happy? There is no one else, Elizabeth.

FRANKENSTEIN: Listen, do you hear how I lied to her?

VICTOR: You have no rivals, I swear it.

ELIZABETH: Then why are you so distant?

VICTOR: I'm not.

FRANKENSTEIN: I gazed into those gentle eyes and I lied.

VICTOR: As for Ingolstadt, the thought of it makes me sick to the soul. I'll never go back!

FRANKENSTEIN: *(He grabs Victor desperately to him.)* Who'd ever think that grass could be so green? When you look down from the funicular, the green makes your eyes ache. Look down. As we climb higher and higher, the color intensifies. I wave as I ride past, but I'm powerless to stop the little car.

(Victor pulls away.)

VICTOR: *(To Elizabeth.)* Did you ever read that book I left you, *The Sorrows of Young Werther?*

(She nods.)

VICTOR: "Whatever makes man happy must later become the source of his misery."

ELIZABETH: Have I made you miserable?

VICTOR: This has nothing to do with you.

ELIZABETH: Perhaps that was the wrong question. Did I ever make you happy?

VICTOR: Don't be ridiculous! I love you! I will marry you!

ELIZABETH: Never mind.

VICTOR: You don't get angry, do you?

ELIZABETH: Oh Victor, I'm not as complaisant as I pretend to be. Inside, I'm on fire —

(They come together, but he senses the presence of someone else, and pulls away.)

VICTOR: Elizabeth, he watches me —

ELIZABETH: Who does?

VICTOR: Always — in my sleep —

ELIZABETH: Who?

VICTOR: Even here with you.

ELIZABETH: Who does? When William wakes up from a bad dream, I rock him in my arms. He presses his face into my shoulder, I can feel his tears on my neck —

(She kisses him, Victor responds, but his lovemaking turns violent. Adam watches them from above.)

ELIZABETH: Wait, please, Victor — please stop — please, Victor — Not this way!!

(The struggle stops abruptly. They stare at each other, horrified. Finally, Elizabeth rises, disheveled and confused.)

ELIZABETH: I . . . I'd better go find William.

VICTOR: He's . . . playing ball . . . by the water . . .

(She runs off. Victor buries his head in his arms, then raises his head and sees Adam. They stare at each other in silence. Elizabeth, off, screams.)

ELIZABETH: *(Off.)* Victor! Victor!!

(He rushes after her. Adam takes a child's ball out from under his cloak, studies it. Then he goes.)

FRANKENSTEIN: A Titan playing games with the planet.

CREATURE: No, a child with a toy.

FRANKENSTEIN: Killer — thou shalt not — ! He was innocent.

CREATURE: So was I. I approached the child as he played by the water. I held out my arms to him. The smile died on his lips. He began to scream. The scream frightened me. I put my hands around his neck to silence him. He grew still. I did not mean to.

FRANKENSTEIN: In any court, you would be found guilty.

CREATURE: You could have raised a band of men. But you chose silence. Why?

FRANKENSTEIN: If I had gone to the authorities with my story, they'd have locked me in a madhouse.

CREATURE: Then why didn't you follow me yourself?

FRANKENSTEIN: You were violent. You had just killed my brother.

CREATURE: You didn't even try to stop me.

FRANKENSTEIN: You'd have killed again.

CREATURE: I would have done anything you asked. It was not too late!

FRANKENSTEIN: Too late for my brother.

CREATURE: "Brothers and sisters have I none . . . "

FRANKENSTEIN: Beside . . . I couldn't bear to destroy you yet. I still hadn't collected all my data.

CREATURE: Pathetic!

(Adam enters above.)

CREATURE: Once upon a time there was a prince who manufactured a human being out of spare parts. But he could not love it. And he would not accept responsibility for it. He refused to share his discovery with his peers so they could make use of it. He was even unwilling to kill it. All he could do was run away —

FRANKENSTEIN: *(To Adam.)* Murderer!

CREATURE: So he decided to go hiking in the Alps!

(He storms off.)

FRANKENSTEIN: Don't make it sound like a holiday! I wanted to climb high enough to obliterate my grief. Come back!

(Victor enters, climbs to the above. After a moment he senses he is being watched. He turns, sees Adam's shadow, then sees Adam.)

ADAM: Maker.

VICTOR: You!

ADAM: Maker —

VICTOR: You dare approach me?

ADAM: I have followed you for days.

VICTOR: Murderer, I'll trample you into dust.

ADAM: An idle threat, maker, for I would always win; and life, though it is only an accumulation of pain, is still dear to me. Put aside your wrath, for you and I must speak, we must negotiate — Why do you look at me so, my progenitor?

VICTOR: Why have you followed me here?

ADAM: Frankenstein, why are you equitable to all the world but me, to whom you owe the greatest justice?

VICTOR: I owe you nothing, and as for negotiation —

ADAM: Heed my words, maker, lest I shall grow angry, very angry. Do your duty to me, and I shall do mine to you and to the rest of mankind —

VICTOR: Vengeance is my duty!

ADAM: I am thy creature. I ought to be thy Adam, but instead you treat me like that fallen angel, Satan.

VICTOR: You are Satan, and this is Hell —

ADAM: I was benevolent! I was not born with malice in me. Misery has made me evil. Fellowship and love — all around me I see this bliss, from which I am excluded. You are my maker, responsible for my happiness. I beg you, master, make me happy. Make me happy and I shall again be virtuous.

(Frankenstein inches closer to them.)

VICTOR: How, in God's name, can I make you happy?

FRANKENSTEIN: How . . .

ADAM: Love me.

VICTOR: Impossible.

ADAM: Love me!

VICTOR: Men do not love their mistakes.

ADAM: Then what can I expect from your fellow men, who owe me nothing? Everywhere I am met with derision and hatred. Like Adam, I am alone. But he was happier than I, for his god made him perfect.

VICTOR: I can't undo what's done.

ADAM: I am wretched, cast out of Eden with no Eve to share my sorrow.

VICTOR: I cannot love you.

ADAM: Then make me one who will —

VICTOR: What?

ADAM: A mate, a creature of another sex, but like me . . . one who will live in sympathy with me. I can no longer live alone.

VICTOR: You are mad! One such fiend is plague enough. Two — !

ADAM: Do it, and I'll be good, I'll be —

VICTOR: You killed my brother!

ADAM: If I am wicked, you made me so. You! Do this, or else I shall work at your destruction ceaselessly, until I desolate your heart! No, wait — I meant to be reasonable.

FRANKENSTEIN: "Make me happy, and I shall again be virtuous." It is a child, a child . . .

ADAM: If I had a mate, we would work the land and tell tales at night by the fire. We would banish ourselves to some desert place, and we would be enough for each other, I swear!

VICTOR: My God . . .

ADAM: Dare I hope?

VICTOR: If I do this, will you obey me?

FRANKENSTEIN: *(To Victor.)* Don't — !

ADAM: I am thy creature.

FRANKENSTEIN: *(To Victor.)* Don't make the mistake twice!

VICTOR: I shall return to my workshop.

ADAM: A mate, a mate! *(He dances in ecstasy.)*

VICTOR: Only you must swear yourselves to exile. Do you swear?

ADAM: By the sun and the moon and the blue sky of heaven! Grant this, and you will never behold me again.

VICTOR: That is my dearest wish!

ADAM: Farewell, master. I shall watch your progress anxiously, for all my happiness is in your hands.

(Victor comes down the stairs. Adam stares after him, then goes.)

FRANKENSTEIN: The funicular, hurtling down, out of control, at such a breakneck speed . . . When I was a child I'd hide my eyes all the way down, my stomach in my throat — *(Disoriented, he looks around for the Creature.)* Where did it go?

(Victor leaves. Frankenstein calls out.)

FRANKENSTEIN: Come back. Come back, damn you!

(The Creature appears behind Frankenstein, watches him silently.)

FRANKENSTEIN: Don't leave me! Please, don't leave me alone . . .

(The Creature presents himself.)

FRANKENSTEIN: There you are. How dare you leave me here to die alone! Have I caught you yet?

CREATURE: Master . . .

FRANKENSTEIN: Why are you looking at me like that? Is it time to kill you? *(He grabs for his pistol, frantically.)* Time to load the pistol? *(He fumbles with it, tries to clean it.)* WHAT — ?!

(The Creature holds out a battered cup. Frankenstein takes it.)

FRANKENSTEIN: What's this?

CREATURE: Water. I melted the ice with your lens.

(Frankenstein drinks greedily. Krempe enters, below. Victor appears above.)

FRANKENSTEIN: *(To the Creature.)* So you came back.

KREMPE: *(To Victor.)* So you came back.

FRANKENSTEIN: I thought you'd gone forever.

KREMPE: Thought I wouldn't be seeing you again.

FRANKENSTEIN: I was . . . afraid.

(The Creature nods.)

KREMPE: Well? Aren't you going to ask me up?

VICTOR: I'm not set up to receive visitors.

KREMPE: While you were gone, I tried to bribe your landlord into letting me search your attic.

VICTOR: Did you?

KREMPE: He said you had the only key.

VICTOR: When I'm finished, I'll have a copy of the key made for you.

KREMPE: By then there'll be nothing left to see. *(He turns to go, comes back. Slyly.)* Do you plan to publish?

VICTOR: What?

KREMPE: Your findings, your results —

VICTOR: Publish?! *(He laughs incredulously.)* No, Professor, I plan to pack up and go home to Geneva. I'm going to be married.

KREMPE: And abandon your work? How immoral, to stumble across something which might benefit the world of men, yet withhold it —

VICTOR: My work's of no value.

KREMPE: No value! Think of the uses, the applications — !

VICTOR: Professor Krempe, do you know what I've discovered? Well? You don't even dare name it.

KREMPE: Let me in — rash boy —

(He tries to struggle up the stairs, but Victor easily forces him down again.)

VICTOR: Stop, sir, where's your dignity?

(Krempe stops struggling.)

VICTOR: Why don't you go into your own laboratory and —

KREMPE: I'm old. I don't have ideas, any more.

VICTOR: You're an excellent teacher, Professor.

KREMPE: Teacher?! No one remembers my name . . .

VICTOR: How lucky. My name they will curse.

KREMPE: Better cursed than forgotten.

(Victor watches Krempe go, then comes to Frankenstein.)

VICTOR: He damns me for doing it, then damns me for not sharing the glory with him! And he calls me immoral!

(He climbs up the stairs.)

FRANKENSTEIN: The man was always a fool. "Responsibility!" Doesn't he see? If a man of science is forced to worry about "responsibility," he'll never be free. He'll never dare to cross the frontier! *(The laboratory appears, Adam's Bride is on table.)* He may dream, yes, but only if his dreams can be applied to someone else's greedy ends . . . yours, for instance.

CREATURE: My mate.

FRANKENSTEIN: *(To the Creature.)* My idea was pure — your perverse application sullied it!

CREATURE: My mate . . .

(The shadow of Adam, watching Victor at work. Sound of thunder clap.)

FRANKENSTEIN: My heart sickened at the obscene work of my hands, but one hope drove me: When I was done you would go away, so I could go home to claim my bride.

(Victor stops his work and turns from the table. Adam approaches him.)

ADAM: Do not stop working.

VICTOR: It's too dark, I can't see what I'm doing —

ADAM: My bride . . . do not stop —

(Victor stares down at the table, then moves away.)

VICTOR: I can't go on.

ADAM: Tomorrow —

VICTOR: No tomorrow. I can't — she might have a temperament a thousand times more malignant than yours. You have murdered —

CREATURE: I did it out of desperation.

VICTOR: She might murder for the sheer delight of it.

ADAM: I will take responsibility!

CREATURE: I am not you, after all.

ADAM: I have sworn to exile in some desert place —

VICTOR: You've sworn, but she has not.

ADAM: She would obey me . . . my bride.

VICTOR: There's something else, the delicate matter of . . . attraction.

ADAM: I do not understand.

VICTOR: She might loathe you, and reject you as the rest of the world has done. Then you'd kill again.

CREATURE: I am not evil at heart . . . I am no killer.

VICTOR: And if you two reproduced?! A race of devils would walk the earth — no —

(Victor suddenly starts to tear apart the mate.)

ADAM: Stop!

CREATURE: Stop!

FRANKENSTEIN: Never! Never!

(Bits of the Bride fly in all directions.)

ADAM: Please — for mercy's sake — stop!

(He stares at the carnage in dismay.)

CREATURE: You have destroyed her.

FRANKENSTEIN: Yes!

ADAM: My last hope is blasted.

(He takes the hand of his Bride and cradles it against his cheek.)

VICTOR: Never will I make another like you, equal in deformity and wickedness.

(Adam throws away the hand.)

ADAM: Shall each man have a wife for his bosom, and I none? Are you to be happy, while I sink in my wretchedness? Answer me, slave!

VICTOR: What did you call me?

CREATURE: Slave! I reasoned with you, but you would not hear.

ADAM: Slave. You are my creator, but I am your master, now! If there is a God in heaven, he will give me revenge!

VICTOR: Heaven . . . is my world, without you.

CREATURE: I will be with you —

ADAM: I will be with you on your wedding night!

(Victor goes.)

FRANKENSTEIN: "I will be with you on your wedding night."

ADAM: Revenge!

(He goes.)

CREATURE: Stop — please. I do not wish to go on.

FRANKENSTEIN: Stop what?

CREATURE: Our catechism.

FRANKENSTEIN: Not yet, it's not night.

CREATURE: Yes, look — a shadow —

FRANKENSTEIN: That's only a cloud sliding in front of the sun.

CREATURE: Master, I cannot endure —

FRANKENSTEIN: I warned you, there are no stops along the way. You're in now, till the end. Tomorrow . . . tomorrow I'll feed the worms. Are there worms in this part of the world? Where were we? Oh yes, "I will be with you on your wedding night." Strange — I mistook your words.

CREATURE: What did you think I meant?

FRANKENSTEIN: That you wanted to kill me. Failure to grasp the consequences, just what my professor always predicted. Don't you see? I went home to Geneva, expecting to be married and murdered in that order. And you — ?

CREATURE: I was going to a wedding. I was going to a wedding night.

(Elizabeth and Victor whirl on in a kind of dream, arms about each other.)

FRANKENSTEIN: She had waited for me so long. Poor Elizabeth, poor coz, my secret's dreadful beyond your wildest nightmare. Trust me a little longer. Soon enough you'll know all. "Trust me?!"

(Elizabeth puts her fingers on Victor's lips and gestures him away. Alone, she continues to whirl, removing her dressing gown. Adam moves in on her while her back is to him. He places his hands on her arms and kisses her bare shoulder. She leans back into his embrace, then slowly he turns her around. She stares at him, bewitched. He closes his hands around her throat and chokes her. He kisses her again, then lets her slide slowly to the floor. The sound, off, of a woman's scream.)

CREATURE: No, that's not right, she never screamed.

(Victor re-enters, picks up the body, carries it up the stairs, and sets it down.)

VICTOR: By the sacred earth which covers my shame, I swear. By my eternal grief, I swear. I shall hunt you across the planet. Now is the time for my revenge. Preserve my life till I have accomplished it!

(He pulls out a revolver, raises it, aims it at Adam, but cannot shoot. Adam laughs.)

ADAM: Follow me, my enemy, follow me . . .

(He goes off. Sound of thunder. Victor goes.)

CREATURE: Kill me now.

FRANKENSTEIN: No.

CREATURE: Execute me, master.

FRANKENSTEIN: You? Why?

CREATURE: For my crime . . .

FRANKENSTEIN: No, no, I confess. Guilty —

CREATURE: But I did it —

FRANKENSTEIN: No, I killed her. I did it with mirrors. You I acquit. You may go.

CREATURE: Master, where would I go?

FRANKENSTEIN: Don't call me master! What lessons did I teach my master-piece? Bitterness and pain, indifference to the pain of others, that was my tuition. Go where you like, you'll find your way.

CREATURE: Without you I have no destination, no value.

FRANKENSTEIN: Oh, yes! Your heart beats, your brain functions. But your moral-ity — that was no design of mine. How curious . . . you are more moral than your maker. It must be something built into you, I suspect. I won-der what organ controls morality? *(He laughs.)* My fever's gone. Feel — *(The Creature looks shocked. Frankenstein laughs, lets the Creature touch his head.)*

FRANKENSTEIN: I'm losing heat. Everything does in the end, even anger.

CREATURE: Does evil lose heat? I am evil, and still warm.

FRANKENSTEIN: There is no good and evil. Just you and I are left rattling around on this planet, all alone. A parody of God chasing a parody of the Ideal Man. There were times I forgot whom I was hunting —

CREATURE: Who was pursuing me, or why.

FRANKENSTEIN: It's getting dark. Prometheus puts out the lights.

CREATURE: You can't die — you must forgive me —

FRANKENSTEIN: Nothing to forgive. My bride has turned to dust.

CREATURE: Mine is past memory.

FRANKENSTEIN: Here's her portrait. She had it painted especially for me so I wouldn't forget her. You may hold it.

CREATURE: She was very beautiful. Master? What do you see?

FRANKENSTEIN: You. Me. I never noticed until now —

CREATURE: Then why am I ugly?!

FRANKENSTEIN: I don't know, I wish I did. I remember your beginning. You lie inert on a slab in a cold attic. I apply the spark of life — now. You —

CREATURE: I open my eyes —

FRANKENSTEIN: And in that instant you become a nightmare. I made you beau-tiful enough. Life made you hideous.

CREATURE: If you could go back to that moment, would you do it again?

FRANKENSTEIN: Of course. But this time I wouldn't — *(He smiles.)*

CREATURE: What?!

FRANKENSTEIN: *(Whispers.)* Tenebrae . . .

CREATURE: *Tenebra* . . . is the Latin word for darkness.

FRANKENSTEIN: It is . . . a service in the Church . . . just before Easter . . .

middle of the night. One-by-one all the candles are snuffed out, until there is total darkness.

CREATURE: I would be afraid. Master, don't leave me — !

FRANKENSTEIN: Then you sit in the dark and wait.

CREATURE: For what?

FRANKENSTEIN: For the first crack of dawn — No, I won't leave you behind again. *(He takes out his pistol.)*

CREATURE: Yes. Redeemed . . . I am . . . Will you do it now?

FRANKENSTEIN: Close your eyes. Do you dream? *(He aims the pistol.)*

CREATURE: Once I spied on you. You were with your mate. She pressed you to her heart. That is my dream.

FRANKENSTEIN: And mine. I'll take you home.

CREATURE: I am happy.

(Frankenstein's arm sinks. He is dead.)

CREATURE: Shoot, master. Master? Answer. Please —

(Frankenstein starts to fall, but the Creature catches him in his arms.)

CREATURE: Please, master, answer . . .

END OF PLAY